Guderian 1941

Guderian 1941

The Barbarossa Campaign

David R. Higgins

Pen & Sword
MILITARY

An imprint of
Pen & Sword Books Ltd
Yorkshire - Philadelphia

Pen & Sword
MILITARY

First published in Great Britain in 2023 by
PEN & SWORD MILITARY
An imprint of
Pen & Sword Books Ltd
Yorkshire – Philadelphia

Copyright © David R. Higgins, 2023

ISBN 978-152-676212-2

The right of David R. Higgins to be identified as Author of this work has been asserted by him in accordance with the Copyright, Designs and Patents Act 1988.

A CIP catalogue record for this book is available from the British Library

All rights reserved. No part of this book may be reproduced or transmitted in any form or by any means, electronic or mechanical including photocopying, recording or by any information storage and retrieval system, without permission from the Publisher in writing.

Typeset in Chennai, India
by Lapiz Digital Services.

Printed and bound by TJ International

Pen & Sword Books Ltd incorporates the imprints of Pen & Sword
Archaeology, Atlas, Aviation, Battleground, Discovery, Family History, History, Maritime, Military, Naval, Politics, Social History, Transport, True Crime, Claymore Press, Frontline Books, Praetorian Press, Seaforth Publishing and White Owl

For a complete list of Pen & Sword titles please contact

PEN & SWORD BOOKS LTD
47 Church Street, Barnsley, South Yorkshire, S70 2AS, England
E-mail: enquiries@pen-and-sword.co.uk
Website: www.pen-and-sword.co.uk

Or

PEN AND SWORD BOOKS
1950 Lawrence Rd, Havertown, PA 19083, USA
E-mail: Uspen-and-sword@casematepublishers.com
Website: www.penandswordbooks.com

Contents

Preface .... *vii*
Acknowledgements .... *viii*
Maps .... *ix*
Heinz Wilhelm Guderian .... *x*

Introduction *1*
Chapter 1.   *Barbarossatag*, 22 June 1941 .... *19*
Chapter 2.   Race to Minsk, 23–25 June 1941 .... *47*
Chapter 3.   Closing the Minsk Pocket, 26 June–1 July 1941 . *72*
Chapter 4.   Securing the River Dnepr, 2–9 July 1941 .... *95*
Chapter 5.   Mogilev and Smolensk, 10–20 July 1941 .... *114*
Chapter 6.   Roslavl', 21 July–7 August 1941 .... *134*
Chapter 7.   Turning from Moscow, 8–26 August 1941 .... *150*
Chapter 8.   Capping History's Largest Encirclement,
             27 August–23 September 1941 .... *163*
Chapter 9.   Orel, 24 September–31 October 1941 .... *183*
Chapter 10. Tula, 1 November–5 December 1941 .... *201*

Aftermath *218*
Appendix A Second Panzer Group, 22 June 1941 .... *221*
Notes *233*
Select Bibliography *259*
Index *263*

Preface

Although numerous books, articles, and papers have covered Operation Barbarossa either in whole or in part, I believe an opportunity exists to address the challenges of orchestrating an army-sized, armour-centric German spearhead during the 1941 campaign. Over the roughly five-month period where (full) General (*Generaloberst*) Heinz Guderian's Second Panzer Group/Army carved a seemingly inexorable swath across Soviet-annexed Poland, Belorussia and Ukraine (Soviet Socialist Republics), and Russia (Soviet Federative Socialist Republic) a myriad factors needed to be overcome to affect battlefield success. In covering active combat operations involving a fluctuating mix of mobile, foot, and horse-bound formations, numerous organic and temporarily attached units and integrated air support focusing on one of Barbarossa's four main armoured vanguards seemed an excellent vehicle through which to convey the overall complexity of Guderian's command, and by extension that of his peers in the wider war effort.

Instead of an omniscient view in which both Wehrmacht and Red Army forces are given equal coverage and level of detail, being from the German perspective any information about the enemy would often be clouded and incomplete to approximate the fog of war to the reader; with any elaboration relegated to the notes to avoid muddying the narrative. Aside from any outside direct or indirect influence related to Guderian's command, coverage is exclusively on Second Panzer Group/Army. Although translated German designations have been employed when appropriate, the widespread use and understanding of some seemed better left in their original form. Based largely on primary German and Soviet sources, the reader is presented with comprehensive coverage of not just the events and personalities, but the reasons behind decisions that were made, and their results and consequences. Set within what was arguably the Second World War's deciding theatre, the conflict's immense size and scope, not to mention its viciousness and barbarity reminiscent of the Thirty Years War (1618–48), made for a compelling subject from which valuable lessons can be extrapolated and applied to the modern political and military arena.

Acknowledgements

I would like to thank the following individuals for their kind support, without which, this book, and my other military history endeavours, might not have been possible. Joseph Miranda, Editor-in-Chief (*Strategy & Tactics* magazine); Colonel (ret.) Jerry D. Morelock, PhD, Editor-in-Chief (*Armchair General* magazine); Nick Reynolds, commissioning editor, Osprey Publishing; David Fletcher, former curator (Bovington Tank Museum); Charles Lemons, former curator (Patton Museum of Cavalry and Armor); Jari Saurio, curator (Parola Armour Museum); Mark Whitmore, former Director of Collections & Research (Imperial War Museum); Colonel (ret.) David M. Glantz; *Oberleutnant der Reserve* Otto Carius; Bogusław Winid, former Ambassador Extraordinary and Plenipotentiary, Permanent Representative of the Republic of Poland to the United Nations; Peter Williamson, co-founder, Breakthrough Entertainment; Thomas Jentz, for taking time out of his measuring to talk with me atop an Aberdeen Jagdpanther; The Rada of the Belarusian Democratic Republic; Rupert Harding, Lisa Hooson, and Tara Moran, Pen & Sword Books; Dr Craig Luther; G.G. Bysyuk (Г.Г. Бысюк), Director of the Memorial Complex 'Brest Hero Fortress'; Agata Kowalewska, Stawicka Institute of Meteorology and Water Management, National Research Institute (Warsaw, Poland); John Calvin (http://www.wwii-photos-maps.com); Neil Peart's enduring example; my wife, Diana; and Griffin, Lily, and Nimbus for their moral support. I would also like to thank my mother (*h*+) for fostering self-reliance, humour, risk tolerance, and a healthy scepticism of authority; as well as all those formative family vacations to historical sites and battlefields – even the ones where those people happened to prevail.

Any errors or omissions in this work were certainly unintended, and for which I alone bear responsibility.

Maps

While consideration was given to showing Soviet formations where German intelligence (frequently incorrectly) understood them to be, this made for unnecessary confusion, and instead they are depicted accurately based on the initial map/chapter date. To minimize visual clutter individual divisions are sometimes grouped into their parent corps or army, and each associated Red Army organizational write-up only includes formations whose symbols are visually presented. The fully-black German formation symbols indicate their generalized locations on the chapter/map's first day, with a lighter version representing their positions at the selected period's end. Movement arrows depict primary German advance routes, which overlap to indicate sequence. As representative of the numerous rivers/crossings Second Panzer Group needed to secure along its path to Moscow, Maps 3 and 4 show bridge locations along the main and secondary roads. In contrast to the earlier emphasis on showing low-lying wood and marshland, the hilly terrain around Tula necessitated its focus for Map 11 (and called for omitting Soviet location bubbles to minimize visual clutter). The foundations upon which the book's maps were created included Armee-Oberkommando 2, Ia. Anlage 8-14 zum KTB Russland and Der Feldzug gegen Sowjet-Russland: Band I. Operationen Sommer-Herbst 1941 vom 21. Juni–6. Dezember 1941, as well as Polish 1:100,000 Wojskowy Instytut Geograficzny, edition 1937–8 and USSR produced 1:100,000, General Staff of the Red Army, edition 1940.

Heinz Wilhelm Guderian

Although not intended as a biography considering this book's subject matter, and Heinz Guderian's prominent position in Germany's military pantheon, cursory coverage of his background is warranted. Born on 17 June 1888 in the picturesque town of Kulm, his ancestry extended far back into the Prussian territory between the rivers Vistula and Neman. Although familial military and professional backgrounds predominated through his paternal grandmother, Emma Guderian (née Hiller von Gaertringen), and included general officers who fought under Friedrich II, *genannt* 'the Great', and during the Revolutionary Wars against France, like many of the Junkers aristocracy who traced their lineage to the Teutonic Knights, Heinz's family lacked the wealth so often associated with them. Having shown the requisite aptitude at age 9 to be placed in a track towards university, after three years in Gymnasium a 12-year-old Heinz (and his younger brother, Fritz) were accepted to the Karlsruhe Cadet School in south-western Germany. In what was undoubtedly a jarring first step towards becoming an officer in the Kaiser's Army, the boys entered a world of discipline, hierarchy, hazing, ill-fitting uniforms, limited quantities of mediocre food, negligible privacy, physical activities, and a curriculum that included geometry, religion, history, French, drawing, and philosophy. Within two years Heinz was accepted to the prestigious Main Cadet School at Gross-Lichterfelde (Berlin) for secondary schooling, where top-notch instructors led courses on history, mathematics, languages, Latin, and especially military science. Illustrative of his having taken to the Prussian/German military philosophy, process, drill, and formality, and his growing reputation, his company commander wrote that 'Guderian has conducted himself excellently in every relationship and has given his younger comrades a good example through loyalty to duty, [and an] excellent attitude. His appearance as a superior is calm and secure.' Following graduation in 1907, Guderian served for six weeks in the Hanoverian Jäger Battalion No. 10 under his father, Friedrich, before attending the War Academy in Metz from April to December. Upon his graduation his Leaving Certificate read, 'an excellently qualified and equally aspiring young man, physically very skilled and [a] good rider, of solid character, amiable manners and [an] outstanding inclination for the profession'. On completing the instruction he received a lieutenant patent (commission) in January 1908.

After a very brief stint with 10th Engineer Battalion and a year-long assignment with 3rd Telegraph Battalion (5th Cavalry Division) Guderian married Margarethe Goerne after a two-year courtship in October 1913 before being accepted into the very selective War Academy for the General Staff. With a global conflict breaking out the following year, however, the classes attending the facility were subsequently mobilized, with Guderian serving with his former division as leader of 3rd Heavy Radio Station and later in a similar signals/intelligence position with Fourth Army. While wireless technology was in its infancy, applying it in close contact with combat-active staff commands provided valuable experience with untethered communications. As a captain serving in the Ypres and Verdun sectors, he was left with a deep disdain of static combat and attritional waste. Guderian commanded II./14th Infantry Regiment at Reims in September 1917 and starting the following month served in staff positions until the war's end.

Having opted to remain in the military post-war, Guderian served with the War Ministry's Central Border Defence-East, and other positions in the area towards preserving his country's eastern territorial integrity and maintaining a physical frontier with Soviet Russia, lest Entente-friendly nations re-establish Poland as a political entity and effectively surround Germany to its detriment. Given the chaotic years after the Armistice, he served as a company commander. Along with many within the German military he was an avowed monarchist, and although no proponent of the present weak, democratic Weimar government, he helped put down Spartacist forces that attempted to supplant it for a Communist one. As Inspector of Motor Transport Troops in eastern Germany, where only few trenchworks and defensive positions were available to maintain a defined front line, he gained considerable insight into the use of armoured cars and mobile forces to figuratively fight with a rapier instead of a cudgel. Guderian studied the works of contemporaries in the field, and wrote brief military journal articles about his take on motorized and cavalry operations during the First World War. In his 1934 book *Achtung! Panzer!*, Guderian neglected to mention many of his influences, in particular Austrian Lieutenant General (*General der Artillerie*) (ret.) Ludwig Eimannsberger, and the contributions of foreign and domestic military theorists, as well as those specialists and senior commanders working to put them into practice. As a proponent of applying concentrated, mixed-unit armoured and motorized forces, with close-air support, and maximum violence to breech an enemy's defences and range deep into their soft command and control, and logistics zone to bring about rapid victory Guderian was known to aggrandize himself by assuming the position of a maverick and outsider who was at odds with more conservative peers and members of the General Staff. In reality many of these new ideas about conducting a modern war of movement were widespread.

On assuming command of 3rd Prussian Motor Transport Battalion in 1930 he worked to put these theories and his past experience into practice by reorganizing its subordinate units into scout, antitank, and tank companies that communicated via radio; an application largely seen as a novelty at the time.

Considering the name Guderian had built for himself and the legally elected German Chancellor and self-appointed 'Führer' a year later in 1934, Adolf Hitler, desiring to showcase his nation's fledgling armoured force that had recently thrown off what had been promoted as the shackles of Versailles, in 1935 the former was made commander of the newly-minted 2nd Panzer Division. Given this plum position when he had only been made a colonel three years previously, Guderian was tasked with leading XVI Motorized Army Corps, which comprised Germany's first three panzer divisions and participated in the bloodless 1938 Austrian Anschluss. As a leading proponent of mixed unit, deep manoeuvre tactics and operations, without undue immediate concern for his flanks believing movement would bring security, later that year he was made Lieutenant General (*General der Panzertruppe*) and Chief of Mobile Troops in charge of recruiting, training, and doctrine for Germany's armoured and motorized forces. Achieving spectacular battlefield success in Northern and Central Poland, as commander of XIX Motorized Army Corps in 1939 and in France and the West the following year, Guderian was naturally chosen to lead one of Germany's four armoured and motorized vanguards slated for the invasion of the Soviet Union.

Introduction

During the early twentieth century what German-Slavic animosity that existed in North-Central and Eastern Europe extended back at least to the Wendish portion of the Second Crusade (1147–50), in which Christian forces fought to quell the pagan Balts and Slavic tribes east of the River Elbe, but also the end of the Mongol domination of the region a century later. Having devastated and depopulated much of their far western, occupied territories for some two decades, following their withdrawal from Europe in 1242 Slavic leadership moved to fill the resulting economic void by attracting enterprising, adventurous outsiders from the West. As part of this eastward expansion (*Ostsiedlung*), a steady flow of Germanic farmers, merchants, traders, and other incentivised parties relocated into the territory between the Baltic and Black Seas, including Ukrainian Volhynia and Bessarabia, and even the River Volga. Many of the participants viewed the migration as their cultural destiny, as Germanic, Dutch, Walloon, and Danish elements ascended into positions of power and influence. With Teutonic Knights having been brought from their anti-Islamic crusading in the Levant to put down Pagan Prussian tribes in the Baltic, during which the former carved out an independent state, not to mention the campaign to impose Christianity throughout the region, this aggravated what became lingering cultural and later national animosities.

As a framework from which the modern German military evolved the founding of the Kingdom of Prussia in 1701 provided a number of institutionalized practices intended to address that region's geopolitical situation, and limited population and resources. Due to Prussia's centralized location in Northern Europe, its lack of mountainous terrain or major rivers along its borders that could modify a defence and dissuade invasion, other options were necessary to provide national integrity and security. At the conclusion of the Thirty Years War in 1648 large swathes of Central Europe lay in ruins. While many of the numerous principalities that comprised the Holy Roman Empire escaped the marauding bands of brigands or more established mercenary forces due to luck or location, the Margrave of Brandenburg had been devastated. To help pre-empt, counter, or disincentivise future threats from larger, more powerful adversaries in the West (France), South (Austria), and East (Poland and Russia) effective diplomacy backed by a reliable, professional military were critical to providing operational flexibility, and thereby options, from which to secure a desired battlefield and, by extension, political outcome. Due to the kingdom's limited natural resources, and its core regions of Brandenburg, Magdeburg, and

Pomerania being predominantly rural, limited funding required that Prussian/ German leadership opt for quality over quantity. As such a force was suited to conducting rapid, brief campaigns to secure military and political goals, while minimizing casualties and avoiding drawn-out attritional conflicts in which it would eventually lose given sufficient time and pressure, emphasis was placed on developing a culture of fortitude, industriousness, loyalty, austerity, and discipline.

In an effort to provide for his domain's defence King Friedrich Wilhelm I (1620–88) created a Prussian standing army, which, unlike other militaries that relied heavily on mercenaries, was based on conscription. Such an undertaking helped solve several problems, including the temporal nature of using men-for-hire, who outside of payment for services rendered generally held no allegiance to those under whom they fought and were just as inclined to turn on their employer should such compensation dry up. As a teenager Friedrich Wilhelm had been sent away to Holland to avoid the worst of the Thirty Years War. There, he witnessed how the Dutch military fought the more powerful Habsburg Spain during the overlapping Eighty Years War (1568–1648), and later adopted much of what he learned, such as fiscal discipline, drilling, and how a comparatively small army of disciplined, motivated soldiers and effective leaders could operate under state control. Possessing such a force also permitted consistency in training and weapons standardization, which in turn encapsulated martial principles and insight that also drew from French, Swedish, and even Imperial sources into a written doctrine that could be distributed and assimilated throughout his own military. Although limited available funding initially meant a rather modest force could be created, Friedrich Wilhelm I applied its permanence and loyalty towards balancing the power of Prussia's wealthy, landowning Junkers. As part of his efforts to centralize his absolutist authority and establish the trappings of a modern state he pulled his officer corps from this caste believing they collectively possessed high morals, and would serve to integrate a major component into the political whole of the Hohenzollern possession.

Building upon the economic, military, infrastructure, and political works of his father and grandfather during the mid-eighteenth century, Friedrich II implemented perhaps his greatest reforms with Prussia's military. By adopting frequent firearms drills, stiff-legged (*Stechschritt*) marching to improve close-order movement, and other combat-oriented training, in which an officer's orders were absolute, the average Prussian soldier understood his role and generally performed as directed on the battlefield, and with the requisite elan, albeit with a healthy dose of fear. As part of this effort to promote professionalism and ease logistics, standardization was emphasized for weapons, equipment, and uniforms, as well as the size and composition of battalions. A transition to a recruitment system that pulled obligatory youths from their respective domestic cantons steadily reduced the need for using foreign soldiers and promoted what became a national army. Ultimately, Friedrich II's talents as military commander and planner, his institutionalization of knowledge management, discipline, and a host of other accomplishments produced battlefield and political success in the Silesian Wars, and also greatly increased the prestige and power of the Kingdom of Prussia.

However superior the Prussian Army was on the mid- to late-eighteenth-century battlefield, under Friedrich II's grandson, Friedrich Wilhelm III, and his decision for going it alone against a more populous, resource-rich France, his forces were soon found to be complacent and their tactics and Grand Strategy outdated or unsuited when confronted with Napoleon I during the War of the Fourth Coalition (1806–7). Unlike the Prussian military, with their aging officers, stifling command and control, and brutal discipline, Napoleon I's emphasis on rapid, operational manoeuvre, combined arms divisions, and massed cavalry and artillery provided much greater flexibility and mobility. By incorporating dedicated, motivated officers and men that were well versed in the system, an extensive information network, and multi-echelon staffs the resulting tactical flexibility and command and control response times outperformed that of his adversaries. By tailoring doctrine towards his corps they became the foundation upon which to advance separately, outmanoeuvre an opponent, and concentrate to defeat them. In giving subordinates the authority to act on their best judgment when circumstances warranted it rather than await official orders a faster battlefield tempo could be implemented and maintained. Although such a system seemingly called for a less centralized combat decision process Napoleon retained his position as sole authority over his army's planning, tactics, and operations, while his staff focused on supplemental support functions.

In response to Napoleon's decisive victory at Jena-Auerstedt in 1806 against what had become a dated, increasingly outclassed Prussian Army, leaders with foresight such as Major General (*Generalleutnant*) Gerhard von Scharnhorst initiated efforts towards modernization that helped contribute to the defeat of his nemesis, France, during the War of the Sixth Coalition (1813–14). Towards institutionalizing a permanent cadre of skilled senior staff officers that would exist regardless of the nation's leadership he established a military society that was open to military, royalty, and even learned civilians to debate and formulate the best ideas from a wide spectrum of input. Aided by the Junkers' reduced power under the French thumb meritocracy was to officially replace nobility as a determining factor for entry into the officer corps. Education was to be stressed, and in attempting to build a solid, moral foundation upon which to instil discipline he correspondingly rejected allowing non-commissioned officers to be chosen by their peers. Scharnhorst also established the General War School (War Academy after 1859), which incorporated experiences and insights from the likes of famed Prussian Brigadier (*Generalmajor*) Carl von Clausewitz to formulate the institute's central doctrine. Having to contend with resistance from many of his fellow officers who felt there was little to learn from French 'mob heaps', under Scharnhorst's authority a fledgling General Staff developed from his Military Reorganization Commission. Instead of formulating a narrow set of rules, such as those French (later Russian) *Generalleytenant* Antoine-Henri Jomini espoused, this Prussian institutionalized, dynamic entity endeavoured to encapsulate the tenets of warfare and provide a backstop for field commanders. Together with others, such as Gneisenau, Boyen, Bülow, and Grolman, the goal was to infuse a culture of innovation and change into the Prussian military, and mitigate the more detrimental aspects of absolute obedience, in which leadership decisions went unquestioned. To minimize what disruptive repercussions his changes were having throughout the Prussian officer corps Scharnhorst sided with the traditionalists when possible and worked to counter any French-inspired democratization of the Army.

The Prussian/German General Staff

Building on what martial knowledge the cadets had accumulated, the General War School stressed avoiding an educational environment in which learning was delivered exclusively by the various instructors, but rather promoted a back-and-forth process that encouraged independent thinking, confidence, and motivation towards further learning. Those desiring to enter the highly selective facility needed to have at least five years of service and pass an entrance examination that tested knowledge and understanding in several subjects rather than rote memory. Over the next three years military subjects included tactics, fortifications, communication, siege warfare, general staff duties, and military history, as well as law, hygiene, geography, surveying, physics, law, mathematics, and French or Russian. Applicant names and units were unknown to the graders, with only about one-hundred candidates accepted annually to the institution's first-year programme. Roughly thirty students who performed satisfactorily and passed a very difficult second examination were promoted to a second and then the third year which further whittled their numbers down. Visits to fortifications, arms factories, and exercises of the railway regiment provided variety to classroom learning, and during three-month summer breaks the students attended manoeuvres and were taken on tactical field exercises in which they commanded imaginary units. Fewer than 10 students completed the full programme, and were subsequently posted to fill vacancies in what was a 50 to 100-man General Staff. With just one or two permanent officers designated as 'of the General Staff' (*'des Generalstabs'*) the remainder retained their regimental commands as 'on the General Staff' (*'im Generalstab'*).

Considering the much larger populations and industrial capacities of late-nineteenth-century Europe's major nations their correspondingly bigger and more complex field armies were beyond the capabilities of a single, Napoleon-like commander to effectively orchestrate. For Prussia the answer lay in grooming select officers that had been rigorously trained in a common War Academy curriculum, who in practice would function as iterations of a great captain. Having been appointed as Chief of the General Staff in 1857, Helmuth von Moltke (the Elder) expanded and consolidated the existing staff system and promoted non-military fields of study towards broadening a candidate's martial frame of reference. Each year, he selected the best twelve graduates from the War Academy for his personal training towards their becoming General Staff officers, during which they attended theoretical studies, annual manoeuvres, map exercises, war games, and other activities intended to promote emulating the master's thoughts, understanding, and actions. During wartime Moltke could provide directives to these former students, who would by then be commanding higher formations, and allow staffs to turn intent into action based on established doctrine and intentions. In contrast, the Supreme Commands of Germany's opponents often became bogged down in a mountain of paperwork and trivial details as they tried to control the entire army from a single, overworked headquarters; a situation that rapidly became unmanageable given the massive size of modern armies and their supporting infrastructure. Even if another commander of Napoleon's calibre came along, as their individual abilities would get swamped in a modern combat zone Prussia/Germany opted for consistent training and doctrine and a group of skilled, creative, and experienced senior leaders to balance the workload, and help formulate what were collectively believed to be the best solutions to a range of issues. For all its tactical and operational successes the General Staff too often viewed military solutions in conventional terms, where process, planning, training, and discipline prevailed, and asymmetric or indirect options were ignored or dismissed.

As a commander issuing detailed, unchanging orders in a top-down system risked being out-of-date, inaccurate, or inappropriate at the time of implementation, Moltke (the Elder) integrated into the German Army a command philosophy fleshed out by Sigismund von Schlichting and quantified as Mission Tactic/Command (*Auftragstaktik*) from what had been applied loosely since the early nineteenth century.[1] Stemming in large part from Clausewitz's push to have commanders avoid writing detailed, constraining orders, such a framework relied on a culture of trust, professionalism, and a common understanding in which officers conveyed their intent to subordinates who had been brought up in the same martial environment and inherently understood exactly what had been expressed and expected. As orders were disseminated through the leadership hierarchy the ability for one to independently alter it (*Selbständichkeit*) provided subordinates with the power to make changes reflective of their respective proximity to the action, while keeping to the spirit of their superior's intent. Faster to implement within the combat environment, and producing better, more timely orders compared with contemporary structures, this rather decentralized concept encouraged, if not demanded, individual initiative and decisive action from lower leadership levels in the absence of communication or direction from above, and was shoehorned with self discipline, independent thinking, and what was considered a leader's primary quality, a willingness to accept responsibility (*Verantwortungsfreudigkeit*). As these aspects of a Prussian General Staff matured and coalesced they provided a system in which the best and brightest junior and mid-level officers received specialized military instruction from which they developed an aptitude and eagerness for independent actions and applied collective wisdom, experience, and insight from the army's best minds intent on formulating critical thought and doctrine towards waging war.

By the turn of the twentieth century the strategic scenario Germany had hoped to avoid had begun to take shape, as the nation's neighbours had steadily formed entangling, mutually-supportive alliances that threatened the Central European state, and its aspirations of being a world power. Imperialism, and the resulting national prestige and wealth generated by exploiting their respective colonial possessions, incentivised an arms race. With Prussia (and a post-1871 unified Germany) having fostered a culture of nationalism and militarism based on battlefield and political success, and a General Staff emphasizing offensive operations to achieve success, conflict seemed unavoidable given the nation's disruption of its European neighbours' power and influence status quo. Although contrary to conventional military tenants promoting concentration or convergence of effort to achieve battlefield success, numerous historical examples illustrate that bold leadership and optimizing internal lines could pay considerable dividends at the tactical (Lee and Jackson at Chancellorsville (1863)) and operational/strategic (Friedrich II (the Great) during the Seven Years War (1754–63)) levels. In practice such actions required temporarily weakening one threatened sector to provide overwhelming strength in another, and once defeated to redirect forces to the original sector to overcome it as well. Considering railroads had proven such a critical operational and strategic asset during 'the War' (1861–5) regarding transporting large numbers of men, weapons, and supplies to various theatres and combat zones, Prussia developed its own network to optimize its inherent interior lines. Such efforts proved a considerable benefit that helped the nation secure victory in the Franco-Prussian War (1870–1), which, in turn, facilitated Germany's unification under its Chancellor, Otto von Bismarck, and spurred a growth in domestic population and manufacturing that four decades later would surpass all other European nations.

Soon after Germany's new Kaiser, Wilhelm II, ousted Bismarck from office in 1890 the former reversed the policy on Russia to see the nation in more fearful, adversarial terms, such that when the First World War (1914–18) brought the two nations into conflict the legacy of *Ostsiedlung* persisted, in which the German government sought to carve out a colonial empire in Central and Eastern Europe. Both the Kaiser and his Chief of the General Staff, Helmuth von Moltke (the Younger), envisioned a European race war that the latter felt would ultimately become 'a struggle between Teuton and Slav'. When the 'February Revolution' in St Petersburg overthrew Russia's ruling Romanov dynasty on 8 March 1917 Lieutenant General (*General der Infanterie*) Erich Ludendorff contacted the Communist/Bolshevik revolutionary Vladimir Lenin, who was living in Switzerland, with a promise of transporting him into Russia towards seizing power and facilitating a separate peace with Germany. Along with Germany also providing the Bolsheviks with military advisers, weapons, and industrial experts the moves were intended to hinder Imperial Russia's continuing war with Germany. On 6 November, Lenin launched the 'October Revolution' during which the Communists seized power, and early the following year signed the Treaty of Brest-Litovsk that secured peace and freed the German military to transfer large forces to the West to defeat Britain and France before the arriving American forces could bring their considerable industrial and manpower resources to bear. As German Foreign Minister Admiral Paul von Hintze stated in July 1918, 'The Bolsheviks are the best weapon for keeping Russia in a state of chaos, thus allowing Germany to tear off as many provinces from the former Russian empire as she wishes . . .'. With a large portion of the German Army subsequently freed up, these troops were transported by rail to the stalled front lines in North-Western France. Even though the Germans initially accomplished what was envisioned to be a war-winning offensive their broad reliance on foot and horse-bound movement lacked the endurance to maintain momentum and by April 1918 the Western Front had reverted to a stagnant war of attrition against a multi-national force that included Great Britain, France, and eventually the United States. In concert with a naval blockade, lack of natural resources, and internal social unrest, the German military was steadily forced into an unsustainable position from which it ultimately succumbed.

Inter-war
Considering the war had been fought on foreign soil, and the civilian homeland population had been kept largely ignorant of Germany's battlefield setbacks, the seemingly sudden cessation of hostilities came as a considerable shock. German formations simply abandoned their wartime positions and went home, where they performed a final display of martial pride by marching through urbanized areas to cheering German crowds before disbanding. With the senior German military leadership having previously persuaded Kaiser Wilhelm II to abdicate before the November 1918 Armistice the manoeuvre shrewdly pushed responsibility for the humiliation onto the new democratic parliamentary republic (later Weimar Republic) that supplanted the long-standing federal constitutional monarchy; a sentiment German military leadership was only too pleased to trumpet.

A weakened Germany was vulnerable to a leftist-inspired revolution, food insecurity (although not to the level of widespread famine found in Poland, Belgium, and Belorussia), and former adversaries looking for their political and economic pound of flesh. Incentivised to sway public opinion to bolster their weakened position German politicians professed the Allied-imposed Treaty of Versailles (1920) as being overly punitive, while the French authorities, such as Marshal Ferdinand Foch, naturally expressed a contrary sentiment. Motivated to ensure Germany's national security, and in doing so restablish their positions of power and influence, during the post-war period the nation's military, political, and business leaders worked to externally project the illusion of adhering to the agreement that in many ways was reminiscent of the harsh 1808 Convention of Paris. Forced to relinquish all of its pre-war colonies, 80 per cent of its pre-war fleet, 48 per cent of iron production, and nearly 14 per cent of its pre-war territory, along with the civilians living there, hardship and resentment motivated the German people to regain what had been taken, including their national pride. Prohibited from the possessing major assets of a modern military, including tanks, armoured cars, submarines, and its vaunted War Academy and General Staff, such a penalty presented a potential silver lining in that the German military could reinvent itself largely from scratch, and instead of being complacent and maintaining the doctrine, training, and tactics that helped win the last war could focus on succeeding in the next.

Under the leadership of the final Prussian Minister of War, and subsequent head of the new Reichswehr's Army Command, Brigadier Walther Reinhardt advocated several reforms, including incorporating elected, civilian authority, something many of his peers considered radical. To quietly rectify the German military's disadvantageous situation in addition to expanding the Troop Office (*Truppenamt*) to accommodate a covertly re-established General Staff, Reinhardt's 1920 replacement Brigadier Johannes 'Hans' von Seeckt established 'Special Group R' (Russia) to quietly conduct mutually beneficial military undertakings with Soviet Russia. With France having led the post-war effort that re-formed Poland as an Allied-friendly, political entity and physical buffer against the destabilizing Bolshevik threat from the East, it was at the expense of large parts of German and Russian territory, industry, and population. Seeing an opportunity to mutually benefit Europe's pariah nations, Seeckt established secret relations with Russia through which German military personnel provided technical expertise in return for the use of distant aircraft, armour, poisonous gas, and other facilities to test and train on new weapons and tactics. With the Prussian/German military long a proponent of wargaming to disseminate doctrinal changes, playtest oppositional methods, and apply operational concepts in the field, under his leadership this preparation was broadened to include a host of planning, staff, and terrain exercises, staff rides, and sand-table discussions. As part of a shared command responsibility intended to promote optimal tactical and operational decision-making a commander's Ia (chief-of-operations (division), aka chief-of-staff (corps and above)), was responsible for his formation's operation, including training, organization, and leadership. The latter could also take unresolved disputes to the next command level, although such disagreements were typically settled before being officially escalated.

With hundreds of thousands of deeply resentful combat veterans having returned to an economically crippled homeland, high unemployment, and shortages of all kinds, many of them found employment among their comrades, as part of various 'Black Reichswehr' paramilitary groups created under 'Special Group R'. Unwilling to support a Weimar government that was seen as too liberal, prone to squabbling without a clear direction or intent, and unable to counter the spreading influence of Communist Russia, which had already thrust its tentacles into large portions of Germany, such armed units frequently served to fill the peace and stability-enforcement void. Unable to legally possess a standing military larger than 115,000 personnel, the fragile Weimar Republic's volunteer Reichswehr was superficially little more than a national security or police force. Leadership promotions in the German Army were based on the officer efficiency reporting system dating back to that established by Friedrich Wilhelm I in 1725, but were frustratingly slow. With officers and NCOs required respectively to serve twenty-five and twelve years the correspondingly low turnover was intended to constrain the creation of a large leadership pool. As no upper limit was placed on the latter, however, they comprised a disproportionately high percentage of the whole. Combined with every soldier trained to temporarily fulfil the role of an NCO, who was similarly to assume officer duties if needed, the result served as a useful loophole. For officers an annual report was created for each towards their classification, with the highest two considered suitable for High Command or General Staff service. General officers were arranged on lists submitted every three months to the Army Personnel Office, and were designated as 'Born Leaders', officers who would perform well in the next higher command and officers who should be placed temporarily in the next higher command to first prove their abilities. Imbued with a deep loyalty to the State, officially apolitical, and mentally focused on the role of a soldier, a conservative mindset predominated among the German officer corps. As part of the transition to the increasingly technocratic nature of modern warfare the Motor Transport Troops Inspectorate of the 1920s had already accumulated armoured theorists and pioneers, such as Oswald Lutz, Ernst Volckheim, and, to a lesser degree, Heinz Guderian.

With right-wing, para-military and National Socialist elements having beaten back leftist Communist revolutionaries and restored a degree of stability within Germany the rise of Adolf Hitler into the nation's political realm and increasing positions of power during the early 1930s held for many the promise of returning to the perceived stability and strength of a centralized, autocratic government. Within a month of becoming Chancellor in January 1933 he was meeting with wealthy domestic industrialists to hash out a quid pro quo of financing his campaign for favourable government reciprocity, and the need for him to have absolute control to defeat the domestic incursion of Communism. Considering his world view included seeing war as a predominantly racial struggle, such conflict was to provide the forge through which Germany and its people would be made stronger. As such it was unsurprising that his progressive consolidation of power involved targeted violence and intimidation, alongside a projected strength that seemed so lacking within the Weimar government to stand up to the Allied nations and regain Germany's former glory. Feeling sufficiently strong to openly repudiate the Treaty of Versailles in 1935, Hitler reintroduced conscription and a true armed force, and by the decade's end had reacquired lost territory along Germany's perimeter. As yet another step in his ascension to absolute control of the military and nation the Führer replaced the Ministry of War with the High Command of the Armed Forces (OKW) under his direct authority. With the proudly independent Army High Command (OKH) now subordinated to the new command construct and correspondingly weakened the change exacerbated existing personnel and organizational rivalries and overlapping spheres of authority to the detriment of Germany's ability to wage war.

Unable to reacquire Polish-occupied lands through diplomatic efforts in 1939, Hitler's press for a military solution placed considerable strain on domestic industry, which in turn promoted consumer goods and food shortages that risked undermining popular support. With Britain, France, the Soviet Union, and other likely adversaries in a new European war ramping up their own respective military programmes acting sooner seemed preferable to delay. By exploiting the general war-weariness and apathy of its neighbours and conducting rapid campaigns against Poland (1939), in which the Wehrmacht possessed just six weeks of munitions and no large manpower reserve, and the West (1940) that avoided a costly and time-consuming, attritional rehash of the First World War, German leadership hoped to soon be in a position in which to move beyond the operational level of conducting war to the strategic. At the French campaign's successful conclusion in June 1940 Hitler directed his attention towards continuing German momentum and invading England, which if successful would obviate the possibility of fighting a prolonged war on two fronts, and on 16 July he issued a directive for what was designated Operation *Seelöwe* (Sea lion). Faced with expending precious blood and treasure in what would be a major logistical and resource-intensive undertaking that would adversely impact the coming fight in the East, not to mention the seemingly irreconcilable differences between how the Army and Navy senior commands envisioned conducting the action, the Führer soon incorporated threats and what he espoused as 'reason' to bring about a cessation of hostilities in North-Western Europe. With Britain physically separated from the threat by the English Channel and able to rely on its formidable Royal Navy, the resources of the nation's Imperial assets and those of its American and other allies, thoughts of surrender were never entertained.

With a sustained Luftwaffe bombing campaign having failed to dissuade or sufficiently weaken Hitler's remaining, active enemy opted for economic isolation for which the Kriegsmarine's U-Boat force seemed tailor-made to accomplish. Instead, he turned his attention eastward where once its mutually wary Soviet ally had been defeated, or at least neutered and pushed behind the Ural Mountains, Germany would have sufficient land to colonize and exploit as part of the Führer's rather unformed idea of Living Space (*Lebensraum*), nullify any British naval blockade, and to provide resources to conduct an extended conflict.

As an example of Hitler's public-facing mindset he expressed in *Mein Kampf* that, 'nations of inferior quality succeed in getting hold of large spaces for colonization all over the globe' and that, 'Those who show the greatest courage and industry are the nearest to [nature's] heart and they will be granted the sovereign right of existence'.[2] Towards a cumulative normalization necessary to accomplish such a mandate expansive, frequently extreme Party views on public health and hygiene that began as beneficial, legitimate disinfection campaigns expanded ominously to include the removal or elimination of societal elements deemed weak or undesirable. Having been long ostracized, marginalized, and demonized within European society, its Jewish population served as convenient scapegoats for a host of ills and grievances those in power could leverage to their political advantage. Although these virulently anti-Semitic policies extended into the nations Germany defeated, often with the enthusiastic support of the vanquished, it was in the predominantly Slavic East where they were given free rein. With the Red Army in a rebuilding and expanding period that would position them to seriously threaten Germany within a year or two, and Britain yet undefeated and already receiving overt military assistance from the United States despite the nation's officially neutral stance, Hitler faced a similar problem to Schliefen in the lead-up to the First World War; the need to initiate a pre-emptive offensive to remove the danger and the possibility of a two-front war. To foment the requisite elan and motivation to do what was required, during training German soldiers were regularly reminded that they were the paragons of Germanic superiority and through strength, duty, and willpower were destined to defeat what was characterized as a primitive, unsophisticated Red Army and Slavic culture.

Unlike the fighting in the West, according to a speech Hitler made to the Reichstag on 20 March 1941, the campaign in the East was to be 'A clash of two ideologies' in which the Soviet Union, being presented as a Jewish-inspired and controlled political system intent on global domination, required destruction. To elucidate he emphasized, 'We must forget the concept of comradeship between soldiers. A Communist is no comrade before or after the battle. This is a war of annihilation.' To do any less was presented as risking a lingering, decades-long fight in the East and ultimately Germany's very survival.

Barbarossa Planning

With the Foreign Secretary of Great Britain, Lord Halifax, having rejected Hitler's calls for capitulation on 21 July 1940 the Führer laid out his criteria to defeat the Soviet Union to Field Marshal (*Generalfeldmarschall*) and Commander-in-Chief of the Army, Walther von Brauchitsch. The next day Brauchitsch asked his chief-of-staff, (full) General Franz Halder, to initiate planning for an invasion, who in turn brought Colonel Eberhard Kinzel into the fold. As head of the subordinate Foreign Armies East he was responsible for evaluating all military intelligence on the Soviet Union, including its military strength, reserves, industrial capabilities, and transportation and communication networks. Determining Leningrad, Moscow, and Ukraine would need to be taken to secure most of the Soviet Union's industry and population, and deprive a then weakened enemy from continuing, in his opinion an advance as far as Arkhangel'sk (1,000km north of Moscow), Gorki, and Rostov-on-Don was warranted.

What had been accumulated was on 1 August 1940 moved to Halder's Operations Department under *Generalmajor* Hans von Greiffenberg, and to *Generalmajor* Erich Marcks, temporarily assigned from his duties as Eighteenth Army's Chief-of-Staff. Being the Soviet political centre and command and control hub, Halder emphasized Moscow as a primary target, in spite of his staff's concerns about repeating Napoleon's ill-fated 1812, and rather obvious direct route. Marcks nevertheless set about working out his superior's operation's goals and how they could best be accomplished given German capabilities. As part of a four-phase invasion German forces would strike for Leningrad and Smolensk before converging on Moscow and points east to the River Volga. South of the Polesie (Pripyet) Marshes, Kyiv and the River Dnepr would be targeted, after which that prong would link up with friendly elements moving south from the Soviet capital. Accepting Kinzel's assessment that the Red Army fielded 151 infantry and 31 cavalry divisions, and 38 tank brigades, Marcks believed of these 92 infantry and 23 cavalry divisions, and 28 tank brigades were positioned to oppose the Germans.[3] For Marcks success would consist of one thrust towards Leningrad and another at Kyiv that would progressively defeat the enemy rather than surround them near the frontier in massive Cannae-style pincers. Based on what had been rapid, successful campaigns against Poland in 1939 and the West the following year, considering the limited endurance of German air and ground forces due to the nation having not been placed on a war footing, Hitler envisioned a repeat in the East with five months deemed sufficient to achieve victory. Once the initial plan had been worked out Halder forwarded it to Major General (*Generalleutnant*) Eugen Müller's Supply and Administration Department on 3 September; the same day he made Major General Friedrich Paulus Deputy Chief of the General Staff. In that quartermaster role the latter spent the next several weeks calculating Soviet road and rail network capabilities and facilities, and the necessary number of German personnel to bring about success. Ominously, his conclusions indicated that for the *Ostheer* to reach Moscow it would use up all of its reserves.

To further work out details among senior Luftwaffe commanders a planning game was held on 29 November and 2 December ('Eastern Study') that focused on the initial distribution of Soviet forces and fortifications, and subsequent operational options. On 3 December an 'Eastern Operations' focus covered border engagements up to a Lake Peipus (Estonia)–Minsk–Kyiv line, with potential follow-up missions covered four days later. Hitler, favouring offensives to the north and south, disagreed with Halder stressing capturing Moscow as the campaign's primary objective.[4] In spite of this troublesome lack of a unified direction, Halder presented a preliminary plan on 5 December 1940 that appealed to Hitler's Clausewitzian tenet of destroying the enemy army to achieve victory, which given the nearly unlimited space into which the enemy could withdraw if not cut off quickly and annihilated risked over-extending German logistic capabilities, dissipating their strength, and undercutting operational momentum and flexibility. As a final major planning stage Brigadier Eduard Wagner's General Quartermaster department addressed the logistics necessary to support the massive German invasion force, including estimated consumption and advance rates, transportation capabilities, and fuel, food, ammunition, clothing, and equipment.[5] Throughout the planning process old prejudices and the need for the facts to match the political narrative often conspired to produce an incomplete understanding of Soviet resolve and capabilities. After all, if the German Army had so quickly defeated the French Army, widely believed to be the best in the world, how could the Red Army compare given its recent poor performance in Poland and Finland? With the German military having long fostered a culture favouring offensive, aggressive operations to quickly out-manoeuvre and defeat their opponent, its officers naturally gravitated towards related leadership positions at the expense of less glamorous supply and intelligence roles. The latter personnel, unlike other contemporary nations, came under the signal communication organization, which worked closely with and provided finalized information to the Army General Staff, with often inconsistent results.[6]

Deployment and operational orders were presented to Hitler at a February 1941 conference, and he subsequently ordered preparations to begin for concentrating in the East. Although Halder had revised his estimate that 155 Russian divisions would oppose the Germans, the well-trained, led, and motivated *Ostheer* would compensate for any enemy numerical superiority to pre-emptively settle the campaign quickly and decisively. On 10 March 1941 the Germans began establishing positions along the Soviet Union's border and ratcheting up propaganda and disinformation directed at their upcoming enemy's leadership and intentions. Twenty days later a final plan was presented under the designation 'Barbarossa'. Ominously, on 4 April Foreign Armies East adjusted the expected number of opposing Soviet divisions from 155 to 207, while on 21 June, the day before the invasion was to commence, Halder added to his diary that the Soviets had likely fielded closer to 221 divisions, although he neither adapted the campaign's planning nor argued for additional military assets to better address the threat.[7] In the final tally 141 German and 20 Axis divisions were arrayed against an estimated 213 Red Army divisions.[8] Halder further assumed that the massed Soviet forces near the border would prove unable to withdraw into the depths of the Russian mainland, as they would have to defend the industrial sites and raw materials in the Baltic States and in Ukraine.[9] In anticipation of the Greek Campaign's imminent conclusion, Halder fixed *Barbarossatag* for 15 May 1941. With the Reich's south-eastern flank thus secured, and the vital oil of allied Romania better buffered from Soviet aerial attack, it was felt that the Germans could concentrate by 10 April for a campaign against the Soviet Union. When this proved impossible, as the fighting ended ten days after the deadline, and the River Bug and other waterways across the planned German advance axis remained swollen from spring run-off, 22 June 1941 was chosen to begin the offensive.[10]

The OKW felt that the German Army and Luftwaffe would successfully conclude the coming campaign within the estimated thirteen-week cut-off, after which effective supply would likely cease, largely due to the vast size of Soviet-controlled Eastern Europe and the need to considerably expand the Polish railway network via Operation 'Otto'.[11] This would facilitate a steady build-up of predominantly infantry divisions and supply depots near the Soviet frontier. Much as the Germans had organized their operational logistics during the First World War, since August 1939 the chief of the Army's Field Transport Service, Major General Rudolf Gercke, controlled railway transportation, while Wagner oversaw the movement of supplies from the railheads to the front line. To address the much larger battlezone compared with those of the last two years between the railheads and Army dumps a motorized regiment from the large transport area (*Grosstransportraum*) was allocated to each of Barbarossa's three army groups. These respectively provided a theoretical 20,000 tonnes of supplies daily, although in reality vehicle attrition quickly reduced this amount. Organic supply columns from division and subsequently battalion echelons then transported their allocated food, ammunition, fuel, and other necessities to their own collecting points where front-line personnel picked them up. The State Railway (*Reichsbahn*) and the National Socialist Transport Corps (*Nationalsozialistisches Kraftfahrkorps* (NSKK)) provided the vast number of lorries necessary for the coming war of movement. Railway engineer troops (*Eisenbahnpioniere*) would re-establish the railways in Soviet-occupied Eastern Poland with a double-track line that would support at least twenty-four train pairs per day (supplying roughly 32,000 tonnes of fuel, ammunition, and food/

fodder). A Supply District (*Versorgungsbezirk*) would be established at a depth of roughly 400km, which for Army Group Centre was to be at Minsk. This would, in turn, provide for another 400km lunge against Smolensk. When German planners asked the *Reichsbahn* liaison for information on Russian railways they were told that it possessed none, having never been told that the Soviet Union was a target. In line with the often shaky intelligence the Germans had on their adversary, many thought, 'The poor condition of the Soviet railroads . . . would make it impossible for the Red Army to manoeuvre and to receive reinforcements and supplies'.[12]

To ascertain the Soviet Air Force's formations with which the Luftwaffe and German ground elements would contend Major Rudolf Loytved-Hardegg was assigned to First Air Fleet as Chief-of-Intelligence in March 1941. The institutionalized Soviet reticence in revealing insight into or information on their side of the border meant German intelligence frequently struggled to gain an understanding of the locations of enemy command centres, dispositions, and strengths. To perform his critical task Loytved-Hardegg was given a seemingly miniscule team of three officers, and the use of two radio intercept sites, a Lufthansa (civilian) and Luftwaffe long-range photo reconnaissance squadron, and the use of Security Service of the *Reichsführer-SS* records of those emigrating from Soviet territory. To provide these duties special Junkers Ju-86 P2 aircraft were used, which being able to operate at 12,000m was believed to be over 1,000m higher than Soviet planes were thought capable of flying.[13] With limited resources, capabilities, and time in the years preceding Barbarossa, Germany's focus on conducting war at the operational level meant they lacked aircraft capable of overflying the Ural Mountains hundreds of kilometres east of Moscow, and the region's considerable, and largely unknown, industrial and manufacturing facilities. Such often wilful ignorance, especially when it contradicted the Party narrative, greatly hindered determining Soviet resources and their endurance to remain in the fight.[14] As one of the questions Loytved-Hardegg was to answer was how much of the Red Air Force comprised modern planes, when a Soviet interceptor downed one of the Ju-86 P2s over Eastern Poland in April 1941 the action understandably raised German concerns. When an ethnic German metallurgist that had provided his technical skills in a Soviet aircraft factory had been allowed to immigrate to Germany, as per the 1939 Non-Aggressions Pact, any lingering doubts that the Soviets indeed possessed the necessary skilled talent and capabilities seemed quashed. When Loytved-Hardegg offered his assessment to the Supreme Commander of the Luftwaffe that the Soviets possessed roughly 2,000 airbases and 350 modern aircraft, *Reichsmarschall* Hermann Göring refused to even forward it on to the OKW believing such a 'primitive' people were incapable of such accomplishments. With fewer planes available for *Barbarossatag* than at the beginning of the French Campaign due to losses incurred during the Battle of Britain, with the present requirement to cover roughly ten-times the area the Luftwaffe would need to be selective in settling for local air superiority.

As an indication of the special type of warfare to be conducted in the East, on 13 May 1941 Hitler and the Chief of the OKW, Field Marshal Wilhelm Keitel, passed a directive authorizing any Wehrmacht officer to have civilians accused of actions against the German military to be executed absent trial. Six days later 'guidelines' were created for *Ostheer* personnel that characterized their future Red Army opponent as 'inscrutable, unpredictable, underhanded, and callous', not to mention having no qualms about resorting to 'treacherous methods of fighting . . .'. Such decrees violating international law, including the 'Commissar Order' (*Kommissarbefehl*), which called for the summary execution of Soviet commissars on capture, considering they were a major promoter of Bolshevism throughout the military, exempted Wehrmacht personnel from prosecution. While such a directive ran counter to traditional German military conduct, considering the campaign was to be one of annihilation to ensure the Reich's longevity, special circumstances were promoted as necessary. To assuage resistance Hitler regularly emphasized that unlike Germany the Soviet Union had refrained from signing the 1929 Geneva Convention on Prisoners of War or ratifying the 1907 Hague Convention IV on the Rules of War, including quantifying a legitimate combatant as one wearing a uniform and fighting within a defined, commanded unit. Translating this to mean the Soviets would eliminate captured German soldiers out of hand a pre-emptive approach was thus warranted, as was the resulting mix of contempt, neglect, starvation, and execution of their Red Army adversary. Many German commanders well understood the psychological and morale repercussions such actions would have on their men, not to mention the moral implications and disincentivising the enemy's surrender. In agreement, Halder lobbied Brauchitsch to issue an order on discipline as a counterbalance, which was done on 24 May 1941, but circumventing the Führer's wishes proved difficult. To further tamp down dissention, maintain order, and provide a degree of absolution among German military personnel, and later civilians, an anti-sedition law codified as the 'Undermining of military morale' (*Wehrkraftzersetzung*) criminalized a number of actions, including conscientious objection, questioning military reports, and disparaging Party ideology. Within a cultural framework of a unified German identity that emphasized race, struggle, and the State (*Volksgemeinschaft*) soldiers and civilians were expected to work towards common State goals. With much of this ideology presenting issues in defined, good versus evil terms based on cherished German values the Landsers in the field were collectively bolstered in acclimating them for the mentally and emotionally difficult actions they would undertake, especially in the East.

In facilitating the all-important, rapid battlefield tempo intended to keep the enemy off balance, minimize casualties and attrition, and most efficiently win a war of movement the German Army was intended to operate on a 24-hour cycle. As illustrated during the 1940 campaign in the West, just as much activity occurred at night as during the day.

> The [panzer] division was never slowed by friction, over-planning, and debate in the staff. The Commander's will dominated the scene, not the bureaucratic, decisionless [*sic*] presence of the staff. If the division commander had even the casual inclination to advance, he and the division advanced. With so little inertia and friction in the command style and organization of the division, when the division commander moved, the division moved with him.[15]

Considering Prussia/Germany's long and storied martial history and cultural sense of loyalty, duty, and honour many newly-minted Landsers had a powerful, theoretically apolitical foundation from which to compete and excel. To help eliminate friction as politics increasingly infiltrated into the German Armed Forces and the decisions of its senior officers Hitler quietly provided those at field marshal and (full) general rank with monthly, tax-exempt salary supplements. With the senior German leadership having early aligned the military with Adolf Hitler to their mutual benefit and graduating soldiers having to pledge loyalty to his person rather than a constitution, the levers of exploitation were established.

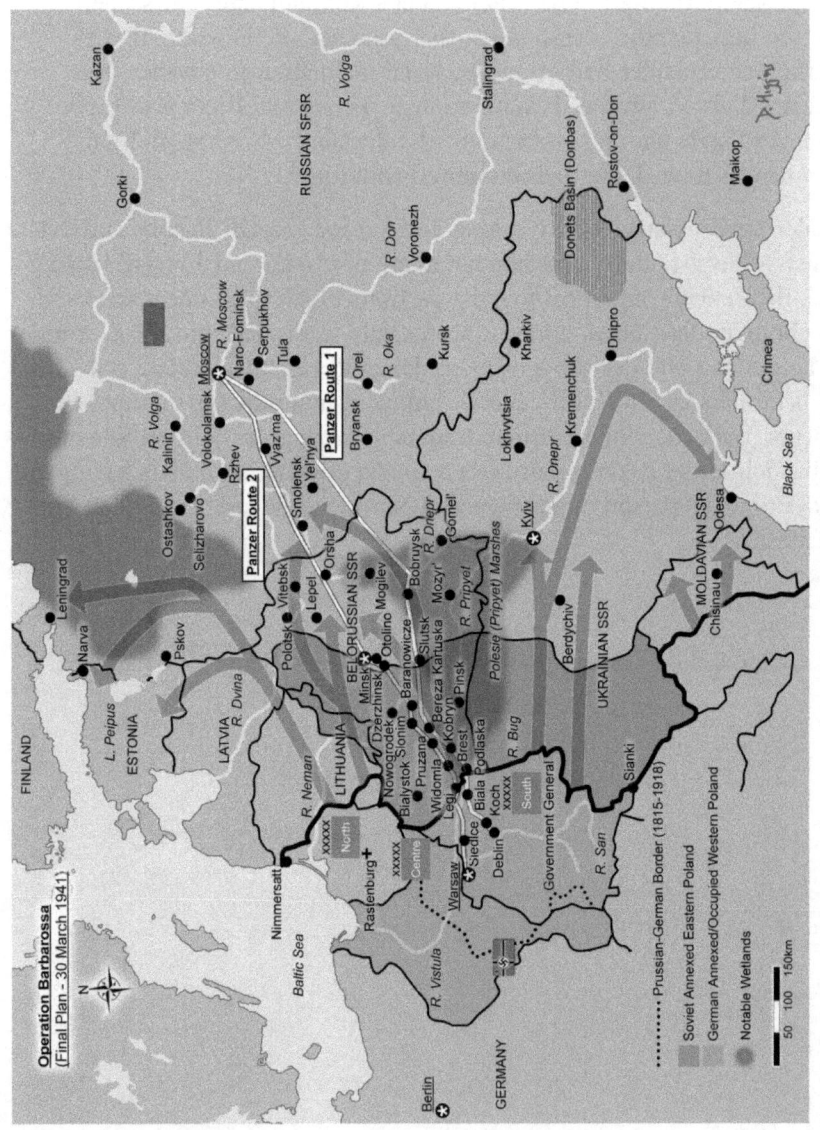

Map 1. As an extension and refinement of the 5 August 1940 'Marcks Plan' incorporating two army groups and a subsequent three-army group 'Preliminary Plan' four months later the 'Final Plan' map for Operation Barbarossa provides a general idea of the operational goals intended to rapidly cut off and destroy the bulk of the Red Army in 1941.

Chapter 1
Barbarossatag, 22 June 1941

'The objective is Moscow, every man must know this!'

Excerpt from Guderian's 22 June order of the day

With the shortest night of the year about to transition to dawn on 22 June 1941 a heavily armed contingent from the German 3./39th Motorized Engineer Battalion maintained an alert, hidden presence amid the canary grass and bulrush throughout the intervening 200m between the Polish village of Koden (Kodeń) and the timber trestle road bridge across the River Bug to Soviet-occupied Eastern Poland. Nearby, more engineers quietly manhandled their dark *Floßsack 34* pneumatic rafts to the floodplain and paddled through a sluggish current to a sandy ait (bar) that formed, as the annual spring flooding continued to recede. Being near the end of the moor-frog mating season a cacophony of watery croaking from the surrounding low-lying wetlands and meadows helped mask any unnatural or suspicious sounds that might alert Red Army sentries or patrols along the far shore. For all the weeks and months of quietly building up an invasion force, maintaining observational vigilance, and avoiding provocation no one wanted to give the show away at the last moment.

From the river's east bank the high, often precarious-looking wooden watchtowers the Germans had erected along their side of the post-1939 frontier remained shrouded in the same half darkness as their background. Reciprocally the tops of their Soviet equivalents that had been placed roughly every half-kilometre were just being silhouetted against a lightening eastern horizon. As the laden assault engineers settled into their very advanced positions they peered across the waterway through intermittent fog to the lowlands beyond for any indication that surprise had been compromised, but all seemed undisturbed. Although the river was only around 30m wide along this stretch and would only take a motivated team a minute or two to row across on a vector, the risk of putting German elements in such forward jump-off positions was seen as necessary to save precious time to best ensure securing the 24-tonne capacity bridge before the Soviets had the opportunity to blow it up. Completed in November 1931 to improve access to the village's St Anne's (Catholic) Church, should the crossing be lost the engineer's parent formation, 3rd Panzer Division, presently arrayed behind them along a 10km sector of the frontier between Kostomloty (Kostomłoty) to just south of Koden, would be unable to immediately unleash a steady stream of reconnaissance and supporting combat elements across to establish and expand a bridgehead. While the formation's amphibious *Tauchpanzern* in III./6th Panzer Regiment offered a backup option the added time allowed the enemy to concentrate against them, risked squandering the chance to unhinge their defences south of Brest, and placed additional pressure on neighbouring formations that lacked a fixed crossing.[1]

As one of the original three panzer divisions to be established following Hitler's 1935 open declaration of Germany's rearmament, 3rd Panzer Division's combat service record included campaigns in Poland (1939) and the West (1940), with many of its members even having served in the 'Condor Legion' during the Spanish Civil War (1936–9). Granted the honour of spearheading Guderian's right flank, the formation's veterans and vehicles now idled throughout the wooded areas west of the Bug and awaited the signal to attack. As German formations had done all along the front line, under Major General Walter Model's extensive, pre-Barbarossa training regimen meant the men of 3rd Panzer Division were well-versed in quickly organizing Kampfgruppen as circumstances dictated. Typically configured around a particular unit type and its commander, such groupings could be adjusted on-the-fly to best undertake battlefield roles and succeed amid changing combat situations. While the integration of different unit types to best ensure the strengths of one could compensate for another's weaknesses had long been an effective feature of martial forces, Seeckt added his emphasis on morale, character, and intelligence, and later his similarly gifted successor, Chief of the OKH General Ludwig Beck, progressively institutionalized the training and doctrine of such fluid, mission-oriented, and ad hoc battlefield groupings. As a key feature of propagating a rapid war of movement, as part of a Reichswehr such officers had helped mould the organization into a lean, motivated entity of leaders that eventually populated an expanded military to make it a tactically and operationally dominant entity.

As would be similar among the other *Ostheer* panzer divisions Model's Kampfgruppen included reconnaissance (3rd Motorcycle Battalion (Major Lothar von Corvin-Wiersbitzki)), armour (5th Panzer Brigade (Colonel Viktor Linnarz)), and one each centred on the division's motorized infantry (394th and 3rd Motorized Rifle Regiments respectively under Lieutenant Colonel Oskar Audörsch and Colonel Ulrich Kleemann). With several creeks and low-lying pastures bisecting much of the division's assembly areas the few narrow, compacted dirt roads were essential to not only support hundreds of tracked and wheeled combat vehicles, but what would be a steady stream of foot traffic and horse-drawn wagons. With Koden, Domaczewo, and the Terespol–Brest rail bridge the only intact crossings along Second Panzer Group's 110km sector their rapid capture was critical towards getting heavier German vehicles across in strength.[2]

Map 2. Western Front/Fourth Army (XXVIII RC (6, 42, 49, 75 RD), XIV MC (22 TD)). TsAMO, f.208, op.2511, d.206, l.1.

In contrast to Guderian's centre and right, Lieutenant General (*General der Panzertruppe*) Joachim Lemelsen's XXXXVII Motorized Army Corps on Second Panzer Group's left flank lacked any intact crossings over the River Bug within its Neple-Wieliczkowicze frontage. To quickly get critical armour across the barrier that was too deep to ford and avoid waiting for engineers to construct a bridge near Legi (Łęgi), which was to be part of Panzer Route 2, 18th Panzer Division had been given a tailor-made solution. Originally slated for the aborted, cross-Channel invasion of Great Britain the previous year, the formation possessed three of the four existing panzer battalions of amphibious tanks, which could navigate the waterway under their own power, entirely submerged if necessary. In deciding on a crossing site the village of Pratulin offered the best location within Brigadier Walther Nehring's limited attack sector, as it avoided the marshy terrain upriver where the Lesna fed into the Bug.

Over the preceding weeks, as the German build-up discretely unfolded the soldiers had familiarized themselves with their respective assembly positions west of the River Bug and monitored Soviet activities to glean what intelligence they could. Considering the high degree of planning and preparation that had gone into Barbarossa, such information would facilitate the expected rapid battlefield tempo and efficient movement and support for the vast number of German vehicles, horses, and men queued up in Western Poland. As the men of 3./39th Motorized Engineer Battalion continued to scan Soviet positions beyond the Bug's sandy riverbank they increasingly glanced at their watches as the minutes ticked down to 0310hrs.[3] In the intervening 5 minutes before H-hour (*X-Uhr*), and what promised to be a massive German preparatory bombardment along their key advance axes from Lithuania to Ukraine, engineers such as these were to rush forward with maximum violence to clear roadblocks and paths through minefields, bunkers, and other impediments to secure key assets and clear paths for follow-on forces.[4] Not far to 3./39th Motorized Engineer Battalion's rear several very improvised-looking Panzerjäger I Bs from 1./ and 3./521st Panzerjäger Battalion waited to provide over-watch fire support with their Czech-designed 47mm guns. As part of an effort to maintain the combat effectiveness of ageing, obsolete, and captured tank chassis their turrets were often replaced with gunshields affixed to the hulls to accommodate the greater weight and recoil of larger main guns, but at the cost of a very limited traverse.[5]

With only a few minutes remaining until the German barrage was to commence a seemingly miniscule number of bombers from II Air Corps (He-111Hs (53rd Bombardment Wing 'Legion Condor') and Ju-88As (3rd Bombardment Wing 'Blitz')) approached Guderian's sector of the Soviet frontier from the west at high altitude.[6] Sporting the widely used 'splinter' camouflage scheme of black-green and dark green, and an underside of light blue, the still dark sky made the aircraft difficult to see, even for those keeping watch for such an incursion. Due to the mission's specialized needs these 'Pathfinder' crews were hand-picked for their night-flying and blind-navigation experience gained primarily during the 1940 air campaign against Britain. Organized in roughly three-plane flights (*Ketten*), they respectively sought airfields that Loytved-Hardegg's team designated as having modern fighters, which needed to be eliminated to facilitate the Luftwaffe achieving and maintaining air superiority over the coming days. Such expertise was critical to the mission, as the strikes needed to occur just as Second Panzer Group's bombardment commenced to prevent the enemy airbases from being warned in sufficient time as to disperse or interdict. To ensure tight security commensurate with the mission's importance targeting packets had been given to each Luftwaffe group leader, who passed it down the appropriate command chain to the involved aircrews who received them no earlier than 21 June 1941. Although the Germans had conducted reconnaissance flights over Soviet airspace dozens of times during the last two months with little or no interference, there was no guarantee that the enemy would passively allow this newest incursion to proceed uncontested.[7]

Concerned that the bombers risked prematurely alerting the enemy, platoon leader Second Lieutenant Friedrich Möllhoff (3./39th Motorized Engineer Battalion) took the initiative and suddenly rushed forward. Two of his NCOs rose up in silent support and quickly followed their superior over the dirt road leading to the small frontier guardhouse and onto the timber trestle bridge, with its herringbone-pattern wooden deck. On approaching the far side Möllhoff unsuccessfully tried to lure out the Soviet guards with excited shouts requiring their assistance before firing his machine pistol at the handful of curious, shadowy figures. Nearby Landsers added their small arms fire that eliminated the small bridge contingent and ensured the crossing remained undamaged. While one NCO searched for explosives and associated detonating cords other engineers waded into the river holding floats to provide stability as they examined the structure from underneath. Just to the rear I./3rd Motorized Rifle Regiment was available for immediate support, while nearby a German forward artillery observer reported the successful action to his 143rd Artillery Commander (*Artillerie-Kommandeur* – Arko).[8] Over the next half-hour this information was passed to XXIV Motorized Army Corps' chief-of-operations, Lieutenant Colonel Otto-Hermann Brücker, who in turn telephoned the news to his Second Panzer Group equivalent, Lieutenant Colonel Fritz Bayerlein.[9]

With the passing Luftwaffe aircraft now several kilometres into what could now be safely assumed as enemy territory the bombers drastically decreased their altitude on approaching their targets. With the sun still below the horizon, and considering such an opportunity might not present itself again, payload accuracy was paramount to maximize destruction. With the targeted airbases coming into view each crew was undoubtedly pleased to see many of the dark-green Red Air Force planes parked in the open and lined up in neat, peacetime rows.[10] In the absence of resistance the German pilots could focus entirely on their immediate task and manoeuvred to achieve the most damaging results.[11] With bombay doors open, the Ju-88s swooped in at shallow attack angles before levelling off between 15 and 25m altitude to dispense SD-2s (demolition bomb (*Sprengbombe Dickwandig*)). As these 2kg submunitions fell a torsion spring opened their casings into 'wings' that imparted rotation to retard their descent, similar to the seeds of a Maple tree. Just over 2 seconds later they exploded in puffs of white-grey smoke to expel lethal fragments out to some 70m, which wrought havoc among their targeted soft-skinned aircraft and softer-skinned crews. As such, adequate spacing with any accompanying aircraft needed to be considered to avoid blue-on-blue damage or casualties. With each Ju-88 holding four vertical racks totalling 360 SD-2s several passes could be needed to adequately saturate a target-rich area.[12] For good measure bomber crewmen machine-gunned targets of opportunity during the passes before their mounts returned to base to refuel and rearm to join the day's conventional sorties.[13] As part of the much larger aerial armada to follow what amounted to thirty-one Soviet airfields and assorted infrastructure were only designated as targets once this pre-dawn strike concluded to best determine its effects and allocate resources.[14] With 2,770 combat aircraft in the East (nearly 70 per cent of the Luftwaffe's strength), due to the need to maintain an aerial presence in the West and Mediterranean, any advantage was to be taken to ensure that the much more numerous Soviet air assets were eliminated on the ground.

Assaulting the River Bug

At precisely 0315hrs red Very lights raced skyward from the German positions signalling the bombardment's commencement. Army Group Centre's artillery immediately opened up on known or suspected Soviet positions.[15] Because the Soviet Fourth Army's static border defences were mostly within 2km of the River Bug incoming gun and mortar rounds concentrated on this relatively shallow distribution of targets, particularly the Brest fortress with its bastions and ramparts.[16,17] German soldiers that witnessed the unleashing of Hell upon the enemy were suitably awed by the unique experience, including First World War veterans who had seen their share of such concentrated firepower. Much as various higher headquarters or organic engineer, bridging, and other units had been reallocated to directly support the assaulting formations, artillery for the three panzer and three infantry divisions nearest Brest was coordinated under a respective Arko, over whom Major General Erich Heinemann's 302nd Harko presided. Amid the din of exploding shells that quickly set the Bug's eastern shore ablaze and cumulatively turned the dark sky red, the rapid succession of 2,880 unguided rockets from 6th Rocket Launcher (*Nebelwerfer*) Battalion produced dramatic, concentrated destruction that was particularly effective against trenches and other relatively open areas between reinforced concrete casemates. Although only able to fire one round every minute, the accompanying 210mm

M18 cannons comprising the four heavy artillery battalions the commander of Army Group Centre, Field Marshal Fedor von Bock, had allocated to Second Panzer Group had a range of over 16km and could engage targets well behind the main Soviet defensive line, such as command and control assets, logistics, and assembly positions.[18] Perhaps the most impressive German firepower came from the lumbering, 600mm heavy mortars of 2./833rd Heavy Artillery Battalion positioned at the Terespol rail depot. As one-half of the battery, Mortar IV 'Thor' lobbed just three rounds before suffering a mechanical issue. Those 2,000kg shells that struck their target, however, produced stupefying explosions that brought down the fortress' 2m-thick walls, threw terrain and debris over 150m into the air, and produced craters upwards of 30m wide and 10m deep.

As the enemy positions through which they would soon advance were churned into smouldering ruins, Guderian's combat engineers and infantry from Wieliczkowicze to Wlodawa (Włodawa) paddled or motored their way across the River Bug. Contrary to expectations, resistance ranged from minor to non-existent in most sectors; something to which officers like Fourth Army Ic (Intelligence Officer) at Miedzyrzec (Międzyrzec), Major Erich Helmdach, could attest having been briefed on recent Army Group Centre listening reports (*Horchmeldungen*) from monitored enemy communications.[19] In addition to destroying physical structures the bombardment further disrupted the enemy's command and control, already contending with incomplete or undermanned defences, and eroded Soviet responses even had they emerged from their shelters physically and psychologically unscathed.[20] Considering the importance of facilitating XXXXVII Motorized Army Corps' rapid river crossing and eastward advance, 167th Infantry Division had been temporarily allocated to Lemelsen's control.[21] Having fought the previous year in France, the bulk of the veteran formation remained just to the rear where it could feed units forward as circumstances permitted on Guderian's extreme left. Being predominantly foot-bound and suited for holding ground, its role was to anchor the neighbouring 17th Panzer Division's outside flank and prevent Soviet interference along the River Bug and inland for a few kilometres.

In response to Hitler's desire to field additional panzer divisions for Barbarossa, and that optimal force ratios were still being worked out, one of the formation's two armoured regiments was to be removed and reallocated to build new formations. Since this left a single panzer regiment, with two or three panzer battalions each, the need for a panzer brigade construct was made unnecessary. While this reduced the number of tanks within each panzer division when comparing main guns the increasing availability of better, more powerful Panzer IIIs and IVs meant that with the addition of a second motorized infantry regiment the change actually improved the balance among component forces; a necessary change the British in North Africa and the Soviets were beginning to see given their respective tank-heavy armoured brigades and mechanized corps.

Just 10 minutes into the German bombardment assault groups from I./331st Infantry Regiment (167 ID) set off across the smoke-shrouded River Bug and soon reached the far bank, with its abundant willows and wetland flora. Although a few uncoordinated, squad-sized clusters of Soviet soldiers mounted a spirited volume of small-arms, machine-gun, and sniper fire, such as downstream near Nowosiolki (Nowosiółki), equally fierce and typically more powerful weapons returned the favour from the south bank to make short work of such defiance.[22] One of the many Soviet observation towers situated in a nearby grove of oak trees, with an excellent view of the enemy crossing, engaged with small-arms fire before German artillery blew up the structure. Wieliczkowicze and Kostary were just beyond, nestled into the hills that suddenly rose to 20m above the floodplain. Trying to ignore the occasional friendly artillery round that landed uncomfortably short, the Landsers organized for a reconnaissance-in-force. While such probing missions presented a considerable risk to the participants they better determined enemy strengths and locations to more accurately inform higher commands on how to optimally allocate follow-on forces into the expanding bridgehead. Depending on the sector, after some 20 to 30 minutes of sustained fire Second Panzer Group's artillery shifted trajectories to provide a moving, protective umbrella for German assault teams that could now go beyond the waterway. Although the barrage shook the ground and produced plumes of black smoke that obscured much of the low-lying terrain south of the River Muchawiec and the higher areas to the north, it soon became evident that the Brest fortress' thick walls had largely withstood the tremendous punishment.

By 0400hrs, as a waning crescent moon rose in east, lead elements of 17th and 18th Panzer Divisions respectively established a presence on the River Bug's opposite bank. Although subjected to enemy over-watch fire, NKVD guards manning their Outpost No. 7 near Nepli had the discipline to withhold using their small arms and machine guns until elements of the latter reached the half-way point of their crossing. Once through the minor inconvenience of a parallel line of barbed wire fencing that delineated Soviet territory more German forces were brought across. Using pneumatic rafts that had been lashed together and topped with sections of pontoon bridge decking, larger weapons and equipment, such as 37mm Pak 36, and MG-34 machine guns with sturdy tripod mounts were also shuttled across. Major General Hans-Jürgen von Arnim's 17th Panzer Division soon expanded beyond the far bank's slip-off slope and cleared an 8km stretch of enemy riverfront real estate, while the formation's 212 tank crews waited in anticipation of a 16-tonne pontoon bridge being constructed. To provide a defensive safeguard should an enemy assault arise some German engineers and riflemen dug shallow firing positions, while their comrades moved off into the surrounding rolling hills and over intervening tributaries. Soviet pickets provided harassing and sporadic small-arms fire, but most withdrew before an overwhelming enemy presence. Those that stubbornly fought on were bypassed and eliminated by follow-on German forces. Without enemy air or artillery hindering expanding the early morning gains engineers from 18th Panzer Division soon set about constructing their own 16-tonne pontoon bridge across the Bug.[23] By 0430hrs forward elements of 17th Panzer Division had progressed about 3km beyond the waterway and had cut the Ogrodniki–Wieliczkowicze road. To the right Nehring achieved a similar penetration through the marshy floodplain to reach higher terrain.[24] With XXXXVII Motorized Army Corps' spearheads making good progress, Brigadier Walter von Boltenstern's supporting 29th Motorized Infantry Division moved up from Siedlce to positions a few kilometres to Lemelsen's rear to cross at the earliest opportunity.[25]

Within 18th Panzer Division's frontage a 2km meander of the River Bug that protruded into enemy territory provided a favourable geographic feature from which Nehring carved out his bridgehead. Until 1939 a wooden bridge had run through this area to connect Legi with the north bank, but having since been destroyed only remnants remained. Lacking any established crossing in his sector, Nehring called on Major Manfred von Strachwitz whose I. Panzer Battalion (18th Panzer Regiment) possessed eighty amphibious Tauchpanzer IIIs and IVs that had been waterproofed with sealing compounds and tar commonly used to coat wiring or cabling applied to all apertures, joints, and openings. To keep water from other areas rubberized fabric was used over the cupola, mantlet, and bow machine gun. Although a bilge pump was included in each vehicle the threat of water penetration limited submerged operation to 20 minutes, during which time their drivers relied on a gyrocompass to maintain directional control. Considering the numerous, often broad rivers that crossed Army Group Centre's intended route across Eastern Poland, Belorussia, and Russia, the original 18m flexible air tube and surface buoy that were better suited for the deeper English Channel waters were no longer needed. Instead, a simple, rigid 3.5m tube was incorporated, which avoided drifting equipment becoming snagged or damaged on river debris. Considering the number of enemy-reinforced concrete casemates and built-up defences that might need to be quickly overcome, the division's Panzer II Ausf. F flamethrower tanks from 100th Panzer Battalion (Fl.) would provide critical, close support.

With the Luftwaffe's dawn attack having crippled or thrown into confusion most Red Air Force forward assets along Second Panzer Group's intended attack axis, the main German aerial offensive commenced at 0340hrs, as the opening bombardment waned. Amid the explosions, gunfire, and general mayhem Bf-109s from 51st Fighter Wing escorted the much slower Ju-87Bs from 77th Dive-bomber Wing over the Brest Fortress. Although a stubby Soviet I-153 biplane shot down one of the latter, the remaining German dive-bombers turned into their gut-wrenching, often vertical attack runs, to the accompaniment of their high-revving, wailing 'Jericho Trumpets' that continued to terrify, or at least unsettle those on the receiving end. A responsive plane to fly, its sturdy structure and drag-imposing features included fixed, 'pant' enclosed landing gear, high greenhouse canopy, and retracting dive brakes, as well as a system to automatically pull the plane from a dive lest the pilot black out from high G-forces. With direct aerial bombing of fixed, reinforced, or obscured enemy positions ensuring much greater accuracy than horizontal options or artillery, such assets continued to be employed to assist in not only crossing the Bug, but in facilitating the advance of ground forces. Although contrary to the doctrinal use for such aircraft, in which they were to operate in close, concentrated groups, in the Brest sector the dive-bombers loitered over the battlefield until called upon or targets presented themselves. As artillery rounds continued to arc through the airspace measures were taken to deconflict the area and ensure the relative safety of Luftwaffe planes and more importantly their veteran crews.

With their forward trench along the riverbank heavily damaged and no established defences in the immediate area the NKVD (People's Commissariat for Internal Affairs) border guards gravitated back to their Nepli outpost and attempted to maintain an all-around defence even though much of the area was now on fire. Having suffered several casualties in getting to the Bug's far bank, 18th Motorized Rifle Brigade's lead elements pushed ahead through weak resistance. To eliminate a particularly determined Soviet stand just north of the river around Czelejewo and an NKVD guard outpost some 150m to its east, parts of 18th Panzer Regiment and II./88th Motorized Artillery Regiment focused on eliminating it to broaden Nehring's expanding bridgehead.[26] In the immediate aftermath of 88mm guns being used to suppress resistance on the far bank at 0415hrs 120 infantrymen from 18th Motorcycle Battalion rushed across the Bug using light, wooden craft from 902nd Assault Boat Detachment. With their heavy outboard engines and lengthy, external driveshafts that provided vectored steering, the boats could move quickly with up to six passengers, including one typically up front with a machine gun, or to provide motor propulsion for configurations of pneumatic rafts to shuttle equipment, weapons, and light vehicles. With their motorcycles brought over to the bridgehead, they set off to scout ahead.[27,28] Half an hour later, just prior to the sun breaking the eastern horizon, I./18th Panzer Regiment Tauchpanzer IIIs and IVs were queued up along a sandy Bug floodplain and waited to cross what was a narrower, but more defined and deeper stretch of the river than near Koden.[29] Having recently trained in diving pools in Prague to work out any personnel or equipment kinks, the vehicles and crews were well prepared for their unique mission. Three minutes later Technical Sergeant Helmuth Wierschin's tank No. 1 drove into the meandering, 1-knot current.[30] To the wonder of many in attendance after a few minutes of mostly submerged operation the lead vehicle crawled up the far bank, which was covered with thickets, conifers, and deciduous trees.[31] One after the other the remaining *Tauchpanzern* followed suit, as the riverbed of sand, clay, and sediment provided sufficient ground adhesion for a crossing speed of around

3km/h. After several vehicles had successfully crossed and moved on to their assembly positions what had been a relatively stable riverbank successively degraded. Once safely on the far side the waterproofing seals were manually removed, with small charges respectively dislocating the rubber cover sheet and protective muzzle cap to make the vehicles combat ready.

Brest Fortress
Aside from the River Bug the Brest fortress presented a major physical impediment to Second Panzer Group's future supply lines. Initially built between 1833 and 1842, the complex comprised a central island and citadel and three surrounding artificial islands, each with their own fortifications: 'Kobryn' (northern), 'Terespol' (western), and 'Volyn' (southern). During the First World War the Germans had captured the structure in 1915 and again in 1939 during the Polish Campaign when Guderian's XIX Motorized Army Corps secured it before turning control over to the Soviets per their agreed partitioning of the conquered nation. Considering armour was unsuited to urban operations, let alone engaging an enemy-occupied citadel, Fourth Army's commander, Field Marshal Günter 'Hans' von Kluge, had temporarily loaned Guderian XII Army Corps, with its three infantry divisions and support elements. Based on incorrect information gathering, the Germans believed the Soviet 54th Tank Brigade occupied the opposite bank, with 141st and 150th Rifle Divisions respectively in support to the immediate north and south of the century-old complex.[32] Soon after contact, however, these forces were found to be 22nd Tank, and 6th and 42nd Rifle Divisions that comprised XXVIII Rifle Corps, but such operational-level intelligence shortcomings were of minimal, immediate consequence and given Guderian's irresistible offensive it was indicative of a broader failure that would soon present the Germans with a major problem at that of the strategic level. Kluge was an energetic and brave artillery commander who like many of his peers had staff experience extending back to the First World War, and possessed an operational mindset that gravitated towards proven, conventional battlefield solutions, which meant that more progressive, risk-tolerant leaders like Guderian saw him as old-fashioned and an impediment.[33] Known to his subordinates as 'Kluge Hans' ('Clever Hans'), Hitler had removed the then (full) general from the military in 1938 due to his questionable personal loyalty and disfavour with the Führer's overly aggressive policies that increasingly risked open warfare, but once this approached a reality Kluge was recalled to command Fourth Army throughout the Polish and Western, and now Eastern Campaigns.

Having travelled to 82nd Infantry Regiment's command post along 31st Infantry Division's right to witness the bombardment and initial combat operations, Kluge watched as the unit's assault teams crossed the River Bug to the ravaged, burning hellscape beyond.[34] XII Army Corps' subordinate formations had had experience with conducting combat river crossing during the previous year at the Rivers Aisne (34 ID and 45 ID) and Loire (31 ID). In a standard triangular attack configuration 7th Infantry Regiment conducted a similar assault on the division's left near Neple, while 12th Infantry Regiment served as a reserve to bolster any transition to a defensive posture or help exploit any success.[35] Although organic artillery and that provided by a higher headquarters offered critical support the tall foliage along the floodplain often blocked crew visibility at more forward positions.[36] To provide dedicated armoured support for the sector's exposed combat engineers and infantry as they advanced over rubble and cratered terrain, XII Army Corps had respectively allocated 3./ and 1./192nd Assault Gun (*Sturmgeschütz*) Battalion to I./ and III./82nd Infantry Regiment and 2nd Battery to assist the nearby 45th Infantry Division's assault on the Brest fortress. Comprising essentially turretless Panzer IIIs, these vehicles had a lower silhouette and 20mm more frontal armour, but without adversely impacting its power-to-weight, transmission, and suspension, and for comparatively less production complexity and cost. Although the vehicle's limited traverse, short-barrelled 75mm main gun had a low velocity, much to the gratitude of accompanying infantry, it could directly engage built-up positions, soft-skinned vehicles, and machine-gun nests out to around 4km using high-explosive rounds. Lighter Soviet tanks, such as BT-7s, which the Germans nicknamed 'Mickey Mouse' because of its pair of circular hatches that resembled ears, and T-26s, could be engaged to around 500m with armour-piercing projectiles.[37] With two fords having been detected near 3./192nd Assault Gun Battalion offering a feasible 1.5m crossing depth, the battery commander quickly initiated waterproofing modifications to seven of his vehicles, with their green skull/skeleton unit-identifying graphics.[38] Unlike the *Tauchpanzern* that were designed for limited submerged operation, this makeshift solution required the addition of compressors to pump out infiltrating water and help keep the assault guns from becoming waterlogged.

With 31st Infantry Division's advance elements moving east of the River Bug their combat engineers, like those in other formations, used short-range weapons, such as flamethrowers, explosives, grenades, and submachine guns, to clear areas of real or suspected threats. They were also proficient at placing and removing mines, demolitions, constructing bunkers and defensive positions, and other specialized services. As they subdued areas and moved on many of the Soviet rifle positions were simple one- or two-man holes that physically and psychologically isolated their occupants from their battlespace. As the Germans advanced they noticed many of the enemy shelters, communication trenches, and observation posts appeared unused, and the general absence of antipersonnel and antitank mines.[39] When Soviet forces were finally encountered those not resisting were often stunned and demoralized, and soon collected and directed to more securable areas.[40]

Along the Brest fortress' northern edge the Landsers of I./135th Infantry Regiment (45 ID) pushed past an irregular earthworks just to its north and an ammunition magazine and barracks near the riverbank. Nearby, its 3rd Infantry Company surprised the pair of Soviet guards who maintained a continual presence at the centre of the four-span, steel camelback truss and adjacent wooden rail bridges connecting Terespol and Brest and captured the structure at 0327hrs.[41] Assault teams from the division's 1./81st Engineer Battalion quickly followed. Having moved onto the rail line's 2m-high earthen embankment, the men passed maintenance and supply structures housing railway sleepers (ties) on their left, as well as a small, wooden pump house and supplying pond whose water served to regularly replenish the line's steam locomotives. En route the elevated structure provided a good vantage from which to see the destruction the German bombardment had wrought from Rzeczyca to the Brest fortress. Aside from negotiating the frontier's sandy grassland, friendly forces below continued to flood into Soviet-occupied Poland with relative ease. To contend with any enemy armour 3./31st Antitank Battalion (31 ID) was moved up to help secure the bridgehead with its towed 37mm guns, as was an 88mm gun, with its devastating, high-velocity firepower. Taking advantage of his neighbour's success, Captain Erich Hammon led his 1./192nd Assault Gun Battalion's half-dozen, squat assault guns sporting their red skull/skeleton unit insignia to the iron rail bridge and simply drove across at 0415hrs. Soon after reaching enemy territory, however, a fight flared up during which three of the vehicles were knocked out.

Near Terespol Second Panzer Group had armoured, wide-gauge trains Nos 27 and 28, onto which three captured French 35S tanks had been planted on cars, waiting to support the German advance ahead of the intended rail conversion work. As the Soviets had switched their system to a wide, 1,524mm gauge following their occupation of Eastern Poland in 1939, the Germans needed to change this to the 1,435mm standard used by the *Reichsbahn* and most of Europe.[42] In the months preceding Barbarossa Soviet and German rail shipments that crossed the mutual border per the 1939 and 1940 Commercial Agreements needed to undergo a cumbersome transsshipping process at the frontier before continuing to their destinations.

Just to the north-west an assault group from 31st Reconnaissance Battalion, which had been attached to 12th Infantry Regiment for the present operation, secured the fortified Kozlowicze (Kozłowicze) area, including Fort I; one of ten earth and brick defensive positions set 3–4km around the fortress perimeter and along the nearby ridge bisecting the River Bug's floodplain from that of the River Lesna (Leśna). With the front line expanding rapidly eastward, by 0530hrs III./82nd Infantry Regiment passed enemy slit trenches about a kilometre from the river running perpendicular astride the tracks before moving on Fort Count Berg. Constructed more than a half-century earlier due to the railway embankment obscuring visibility northward from the Brest fortress, the redoubt, with its irregular pentagon shape, thick, squat walls, earthen rampart, and comparatively high, double-arch main entrance, was ill suited to resist a modern military force and the range of weapons available to it. Although the Soviets managed to organize a post-bombardment defence, III./82nd Infantry Regiment overran the area following a brief fight against II./131st 'K.E. Voroshilov' Light Artillery Regiment. Just to the north I./82nd Infantry Regiment took Rzeczyca in a quick, two-pronged attack.

Further upriver, against minimal resistance the Landsers secured several small bunkers north of the main dirt road to Arkadja, while to the south they overcame a stretch of nearby border fence and Fort V. 31st and 34th Infantry Divisions respectively worked towards isolating the Brest fortress around its north and south. Between them 45th Infantry Division struck the fortifications head-on, using III./135th Infantry Regiment against the western complex where a tall, wooden tower had been used to observe their daily activities as far west as Terespol. I./130th Infantry Regiment was sent against the southern island and captured a stretch of what would be part of the extending Panzer Route 1 connecting Deblin (Dęblin) and Koch with Roslavl' and Moscow.[43] On the division's southern edge III./130th Infantry Regiment bypassed the fortress entirely and worked towards securing the nearest bridges over the River Muchawiec further to the east. If successful, this would sever critical escape routes for the fortress defenders and block or at least severely disrupt the Soviet 22nd Tank Division from extracting itself from its increasingly exposed position near the riverbank to the higher terrain around Gierszony and Fort IV.[44]

From 11./130th Infantry Regiment's attack sector across from the southern fortification Second Lieutenant Josef Kremers led a party of two rafts from 2./81st Engineer Battalion and seven from I./130th Infantry Regiment had just started on their mission when friendly artillery rounds suddenly struck their jump-off area. Having suffered several casualties and the loss of four transports, but not their resolve, the remaining soldiers continued with their mission.[45] After paddling across the Bug for a kilometre and heading up the Muchawiec, Soviet forces destroyed two more boats, but the determined group pressed on. Along with I./130th Infantry Regiment they secured the two westernmost bridges by 0355hrs, and just over 2 hours later the combined force captured the crossing north of Wolka (Wólka) where an enemy sniper killed Kremers. With all five structures over the Muchawiec in the Brest area soon in German hands they now prepared to hold their hard-won possessions until reinforcements arrived. At about 0600hrs four T-26s, two antitank guns and machine guns engaged 6./130th Infantry Regiment to which the German 2./98th Artillery Regiment responded with 105mm light field howitzer rounds that killed several Soviet soldiers and severed the tracks of their accompanying tanks.[46] With the force soon ejected from the area, the Germans moved into the targeted area to find that most of the enemy dead had succumbed to suffocation from the extreme changes in air pressure the explosions produced.⁴⁷ In addition to high-explosive rounds 105mm guns also lobbed ones filled with red and white propaganda leaflets to incentivise the enemy to give up.

In addition to covert forces already operating beyond the border assessing Soviet transportation and communication networks, force strengths, and locations, and similar items of insight, more recently inserted Abwehr (German military intelligence)-provided Brandenburger elements worked to exploit the confusion by cutting enemy communications, destroying bridges, and conducting other acts of sabotage to further degrade Red Army effectiveness.⁴⁸ To blend in and possess the necessary authority to perform their covert roles these commandos wore NKVD uniforms over their own and would discard the former at the appropriate time to avoid friendly fire and adhere to the established rules of war. While these well-trained personnel had typically been recruited in the regions in which they served to minimize anomalies with their personas, accents, and cultural background, wary Soviet personnel occasionally spotted a discrepancy, such as the faux uniforms being unusually new and stitched with a needle and thread.⁴⁹ A dangerous assignment given the near pathological Soviet need to maintain security and that actual NKVD personnel would have few qualms about subjecting the trespasser to a brutal interrogation and execution.⁵⁰

With the bombardment having damaged the area's roads advancing German combat and support units worked their way across or around shell holes and assorted debris. Following in their comrades' wake across the Bug and into the fortress, II./135th Infantry Regiment split into two prongs, each with reinforcement from 2./192nd Assault Gun Battalion, whose vehicles had a yellow skull/skeleton insignia. Further to the east a platoon of the vehicles entered the fortress to provide direct fire support for 1./ and 2./135th Infantry Regiment. Having penetrated into several parts of the central island's Citadel, at 0625hrs 45th Infantry Division optimistically reported that they would soon secure the area.⁵¹ Just over an hour later, however, opinions had faded, as the garrison defenders seemed intent on offering a determined, seemingly hopeless stand. With the tangled, confused nature of the present fighting amid tight quarters, ruined buildings, and churned-up terrain, German artillery was frequently forced to refrain from providing assistance to avoid risking friendly casualties.

Schweppenburg's Spearhead

Much as along Second Panzer Group's left and centre, Lieutenant General (*General der Panzertruppe*) Leo Reichsfreiherr Geyr von Schweppenburg's XXIV Motorized Army Corps made steady progress on Guderian's right in spite of very sandy, low-lying, heavily forested terrain over which it operated. With the Koden Bridge in German hands a 75mm infantry gun was brought forward to support the assault parties of Corvin-Wiersbitzki's 3rd Motorcycle Battalion, as they crossed the structure and along the lengthy causeway beyond before dispersing to scout ahead of 3rd Panzer Division. For Model the means, and seemingly the opportunity, existed to quickly strike eastward into what German intelligence (again wrongly) indicated were the Soviet 85th and 10th Rifle Divisions before they coordinated a response.[52] Know for his often brash, abrasive personality, Model's directness, disdain for protocol, and formality made him an acquired taste. Those few who knew him personally, however, revealed a good-humoured, devout, family man.[53] His service in the First World War, selection into the Reichswehr, and staff commands during the campaigns in Poland and in the West attested to his skilled, motivating leadership, but on his being given command of 3rd Panzer Division on 13 November 1940, as part of a spate of promotions and awards Hitler handed out to senior commanders following the Fall of France, many of the formation's veterans were given pause. Unlike many of the other panzer divisions that had been allocated captured, foreign armoured vehicles that made for a logistics and maintenance nightmare, in January 1941 3rd Panzer Division had been as uniformly outfitted with domestic weaponry and vehicles as resources allowed.

To maintain as fast a tempo as possible, and postpone having to await slower resupply vehicles, the attacking panzern typically carried extra fuel in externally mounted jerry cans or towed trailers. As the Germans advanced into what had recently been Eastern Poland they passed by homes of simple construction, with horizontal log beams that interlocked at the corners. These mostly windowless dwellings had entrances that faced away from the prevailing winds, while their hay-thatched, hip roofs helped retain heat from the centrally-located fireplaces, rightly prized by their owners as a necessity. Understandably, such structures burned easily when subjected to artillery fire or incendiary munitions and many civilians living in or near the targeted areas sought comparative safety in nearby fields and the area's many unoccupied concrete border guard outposts and bunkers.

With Second Panzer Group having established a firm hold along the Bug's eastern shore and its infantry, motorcycles, and other light forces having advanced eastward, construction troops (*Bautruppen*) began putting together their flat-bottom Bridge Equipment (*Brückengerät*) 'B' medium combat pontoon bridges, which comprised fixed approaches at either bank to provide a transition from land to the various interlocked roadbearers, chesses, and guardrails atop trestle sections and undecked steel pontoons. Due to their greater strength better suited to heavier vehicles, the 'K' variety was allocated to each panzer engineer equivalent.[54] In addition to these tactical structures that were suited for quick assembly required of assault crossings, higher headquarters possessed heavier, semi-permanent 'H' (heavy box girder on large decked pontoons) and 'S' (heavy railroad) varieties of bridge equipment. On Model's left 2./39th Motorized Engineer Battalion personnel began constructing a pontoon crossing downriver at Okczyn that once finished allowed 394th Motorized

Rifle Regiment to advance on the enemy-held village of Stradecz.[55] Later in the day, with the German advance progressing well, the pontoon bridge was disassembled and transported eastward to provide crossing capabilities closer to the quickly advancing front line.

Having recently moved into the area just south of the Brest fortress, a Soviet tank force in battalion strength approached the River Bug, with sixteen T-26s to help halt the German crossings that extended upriver to Koden. Along the unit's left motorized infantry and reconnaissance offered sporadic support.[56] Although the light Soviet tanks, with their uniform Protective Green paint schemes, possessed machine guns and capable 45mm cannons that fired armour-piercing and high-explosive rounds, German artillery from the opposite bank disgorged a withering fire that soon motivated the crews to withdraw. Inspired by the inter-war, British Vickers 6-tonne Type B the Soviet version was suited for the scale of mass production the Soviet Premier, Joseph Stalin, desired, but like the German Panzer II rapidly reached obsolescence as a front-line combat vehicle on a contemporary battlefield.[57]

With II./394th Motorized Rifle Regiment establishing a presence opposite Okczyn, 3rd Motorized Rifle Regiment followed up with a strike northward towards Stradecz where it engaged enemy infantry around the village train station.[58] Soviet artillery from nearby Gora Majakowa and Hill 153 brought down harassing fire on Model's command post, which drew counter-battery and Luftwaffe attention that soon silenced the threat.[59] With 3rd Panzer Division's lead elements making steady progress at 0400hrs Model relocated his forward headquarters to a stretch of high ground just north-west of the Koden Bridge to better conduct operations. Over the next hour elements of 3rd Motorized Rifle Regiment reported cutting the Wlodawa–Brest road and rail line running alongside. At roughly the same time two battalions of 394th Motorized Rifle Regiment crossed the Bug and pushed into the vegetated area north of Stradecz to overcome minor resistance from enemy concrete bunkers.

Save for a few stubborn, isolated Soviet pockets the formations along XXIV Motorized Army Corps' right encountered minimal resistance, as their infantry and engineers were ferried across the River Bug. In command of his fully supplied and fuelled 4th Panzer Division, Brigadier Willibald Baron (*Freiherr*) von Langermann und Erlencamp waited for 79th Motorized Engineer Battalion to construct a 16-tonne pontoon bridge across from Zbunin to get his heavier vehicles and weapons to the east bank, and near one of the many Soviet observation towers. Because such activity acted as a magnet for enemy fire 2./49th Panzerjäger Battalion positioned two platoons of 50mm Pak 38 (L/60) nearby to improve protective over-watch fire. On the division's right elements of 12th Motorized Rifle Regiment made for the single route extending north-east past Hill 149 and into the extensive woodland for Miedna. Until the crossing was completed and prime movers could be brought across Panje horses were used to drag towed weapon systems and wagons across the shifting, ankle-deep sand that conspired with the high temperatures later in the day to sap the Landsers' strength and hinder movement.

Considering the Polesie Marshes' tracts of swampy, primeval territory through which the same-named river flowed covered an area rivalling that of Britain, and would swallow up any conventional infantry (let alone armoured) division unwisely sent into it, Brigadier Kurt Feldt's 1st Cavalry Division was assigned to the sector along Guderian's southern flank. As a unique, and seemingly anachronistic, formation within the Wehrmacht its four horse regiments and motorized support units provided a good mix of signal, engineer, bicycle, and antitank capabilities, as well as sufficient firepower and manoeuvrability to deal with what threats could be expected in this fringe battlezone. Where the River Bug downstream from Zbunin was rather well defined, in the formation's flatter, marshier terrain upstream the river braided into several smaller paths distributed over a comparatively larger area. With the timber road bridge at Domaczewo having been secured after a short battle with Soviet border guards, 2nd Cavalry Regiment shot ahead for Rogozno (Rogoźno) along a wooded trail, while 1st Cavalry Regiment opted a for a more circuitous advance along Lake Biale's northern edge. Where knots of Red Army resistance that included two twin antiaircraft guns, mortars, and machine guns stymied the horsemen's efforts, 487th Infantry Regiment (267 ID) managed to skirt one of the outposts (No. 15) of '17th Red Banner' near Dubica and move into the marshy forests beyond. As part of their continuing support for the German crossing and advance, friendly artillery targeted a Soviet flag atop a tall pine pole where enemy infantry and field guns had been reported. Although resistance along the Bug had been sporadic, as the Germans converged on the Miedna area they encountered more organized enemy defences.[60]

Much as 167th Infantry Division acted as Second Panzer Group's left shoulder, on Guderian's far right 255th and 267th Infantry Divisions performed a similar function. With the latter organized into four Kampfgruppen, each respectively supported 1st Cavalry Division's northern and southern brigades; 487th Infantry Regiment adjacent to Domaczewo, and the nearly authorized strength 255th Infantry Division, which served as a reserve and provided a communication link with Bock's southern peer, Field Marshal Gerd von Rundstedt. To cover the 40km gap that initially separated Army Groups Centre and South, 286th Security Division (Fourth Army) had been positioned a few kilometres to the west. As a result of the greater area over which the River Bug flowed south of Zbunin its shallow depth allowed a thick covering of reeds and bulbrushes to protrude from the surface, and often enabled crossing by foot or horseback without undue difficulty.[61] Until 255th Infantry Division's engineers got their 16-tonne pontoon bridge up, as the German's had destroyed road and rail crossings during the 1939 fighting, artillery, vehicles, and equipment would need to be laboriously ferried across.

Due to the rather large gap between 1st Cavalry and 255th Infantry Divisions to the south the latter had detached its I./465th Infantry Regiment to fill the void where it would act as an independent formation attacking out of Dolhobrody (Dołhobrody) to clear the area of enemy forces. The rest of the division was organized into three Kampfgruppen, with the remainder of 465th Infantry Regiment striking for Przyborowo and beyond. Further south 475th and 455th Infantry Regiments respectively operated from near Wlodawa. With the German artillery barrage in 255th Infantry Division's sector having ended after just 20 minutes its forward elements crossed the Bug under the watchful eyes of friendly machine-gun crews on the left bank. German smoke rounds that had purposely landed upwind of their targets blinded many of the enemy positions, and although several of the Red Army soldiers manning them were dazed and demoralized, their comrades around Przyborowo remained defiant throughout the day.

After capturing 4km of the Wlodawa–Maloryta road 255th Infantry Division's forward elements were reorganized, while patrols moved passed Piszcza, where a lonely route extended to the south-east through marshland and irrigation canals. Encountering no resistance they continued on for Oltusz. As German forces advanced through enemy territory what maps that were available were largely inadequate and with aerial photography visually limited to open areas XXIV Motorized Army Corps personnel often relied on compasses to negotiate their way through the tall trees and largely uncultivated terrain, or in more urban environments tourist maps proved useful. Unlike the Germans, who had motorized mapping units at the division, corps, and army levels the Soviets lacked equivalent capabilities in the field and relied on what was produced in the rear, such as from Moscow. In such restricted environments, and with village names often having similar or identical spellings, it was critical that the Germans accurately determined and recorded their advance routes to avoid confusion, delays, and losses. Whether resistant to a repressive Soviet occupation or simply wanting to be accommodating to the victorious attacker who many viewed as liberators, civilians frequently provided intelligence, food, and directions. As part of an ongoing effort to maintain secrecy associated with Barbarossa the German press had been forbidden to publish maps depicting the Eastern Front, with the nation's Minister for Public Enlightenment and Propaganda, Joseph Goebbels, making the weak argument that 'Huge distances can scare the public.'[62]

Bypassing the Brest Fortress (South)

As the snaking columns of 3rd Panzer Division fanned out from their bridgehead at 0540hrs 'Kampfgruppe Audörsch' reported his motorized infantry capturing the small ridge at Gora Majakowa and what enemy artillery remained as being active. Having probed eastward along what was to be the division's primary advance route, 3rd Motorcycle Battalion soon discovered extensive marshland beyond Stradecz that threatened to preclude any large-scale movement. Just to the north the Soviet 22nd Tank Division forces near the Bug were steadily caught between Major General Hans Behlendorf's 34th Infantry Division skirting the Brest fortress' southern approaches and 'Kampfgruppe Audörsch' pouring forth from the Okczyn pontoon bridge and wisely began to pull out. Amid the chaos of fighting and roads clogged with panicked humanity what vehicles and heavier weapons that still worked were frequently abandoned. As the Germans held the Muchawiec bridges nearest Brest and that much of the area's soft terrain, with its carpeting mosses and broadleaf cattail, restricted movement what remained of 22nd Tank Division's forward elements gravitated northward to the crossing at Huznie. Many of the tankers, artillerymen, and others who lacked vehicle transport were soon cut off from Panzer Route 1 and needed to first walk eastward to near Franopol', where their 22nd Rifle Regiment was establishing a defensive position.[63]

At 0700hrs Linnarz led his armour-based Kampfgruppe over the Koden Bridge before turning north towards of Stradecz. Considering the very noticeable mass of Red Army men and vehicles attempting to withdraw from their forward positions, 30 minutes later Model was notified that between 0800 and 0900hrs Ju-87s were scheduled to attack a stretch of Panzer Route 1 east of Brest. In an attempt to prevent the enemy from relocating valuable rolling stock eastward other Luftwaffe assets were to target enemy rail centres, often well behind the lines, as part of their range of missions. At a broader perspective II Air Force Corps (*Fliegerkorps*) had carried out what it considered sufficient airstrikes within a 100km zone and was now doubling the distance.[64] With his bridgehead expanding eastward at 0845hrs Model's Command Post relocated once again, this time to the Stradecz train station. From there he went out beyond Gora Majakowa and the Miedna–Brest road to the front line near Faustynow (Faustynów) ordering one company of III./6th Panzer Regiment ahead as an advance section.

As Germany's tactical and operational success on the ground relied on the close coordination with the Luftwaffe under Field Marshal Albert Kesselring Second Air Force was assigned to support Army Group Centre's advance. Such services included achieving and maintaining air superiority, bombing enemy concentrations and potentially troublesome, built-up positions, as well as reconnaissance and resupply throughout its assigned battlespace. Nicknamed 'the Grim Reaper' ('*Der Sterber*'), due to his professed desire for a glorious, battlefield death, Bock held no affinity for the Party or civilians. Holding command of the most powerful of Barbarossa's three army groups, Second Air Force was commensurately the strongest such operational formation, and comprised VIII Air Corps to support Third Panzer Group and Ninth Army, while Second Panzer Group and Fourth Army received II Air Corps. To illustrate

Kesselring's mindset regarding his critical role he stressed that his commanders were to 'consider the wishes of the Army as my orders'.[65]

Along Model's right 4th Panzer Division had taken Durycze by 0515hrs and was crossing a 3km causeway that rose above extensive marshland that ran parallel to the River Bug and along a second road into north-western Miedna. To soften the next target in Langermann's path German long-range artillery fired on Maloryta ahead of his I./ and III./33rd Motorized Rifle Regiment, 12th Motorized Rifle Regiment, and a battalion of supporting heavy howitzers that subsequently attacked the village starting at about 0600hrs. After the two leading rifle companies had only progressed slowly, a third was brought up, as was an antitank company, which positioned itself ahead of 12th Motorized Rifle Regiment. From camouflaged positions in the surrounding woods Soviet small arms and machine-gun fire steadily increased. In support Soviet snipers that had tied themselves high in the trees proved particularly deadly. At 0900hrs 33rd Motorized Rifle Regiment (4 PD) captured Miedna and continued on through what to many Landsers was already feeling like an endless woodland expanse.[66]

Bypassing the Brest Fortress (North)
Soon after Strachwitz's amphibious armour began landing on the River Bug's right bank north-west of Brest his tanks knocked out several curious Soviet armoured cars and drove the remainder off. With a small bridgehead established Nehring crossed over in one of 18th Panzer Division's assault boats that were collectively ferrying his tactical headquarters vehicles across on rafts. Although every German tank possessed a radio receiver, and typically a transmitter, about thirty motorcycles were also brought over to facilitate communications and serve as mobile 'eyes' and messengers. Once a vanguard was organized Nehring, several of his staff, and Strachwitz joined the de-waterproofed *Tauchpanzern*, which set off to the north-east towards Pruzana (Prużana). As XXXXVII Motorized Army Corps contested with enemy strongpoints along the River Bug at Nowosiolki, Wieliczkowicze, Rudawiec (Rudavets), Motykaly (Motykały) Wielkie, and Nepli, much as along Guderian's right the low-lying terrain served to funnel German personnel through the more accessible stretches between the Rivers Lesna and Bug. The ridge just north of the waterway provided the foundation through which Panzer Route 2 would connect Warsaw with Minsk and Moscow.[67]

As 18th Panzer Division expanded its bridgehead, at about 0600hrs east of Czelejewo NKVD border guards scraped together a defence of their outpost (No. 5). Having little more than small arms and a few mortars, they tried to maximize their stand by holding fire until the Germans closed.[68] Unwilling to expend time on the impediment the attackers bypassed what became a 5-hour holdout for follow-on forces. A few kilometres to the south-east Guderian crossed the Bug at 0650hrs in an assault boat near Kolodno and what was left of the destroyed bridge at Legi. Maintaining its position off of 17th Panzer Division's right flank, Nehring's 6./18th Panzer Regiment struck out as a vanguard along the road running east through Motykaly Wielkie. As soon as Guderian's command car and two wireless vehicles had been ferried across at 0830hrs he set off after this force to gain firsthand knowledge of the formation's initial progress. Apparently attempting to take a shortcut, Guderian used a nearby trail to approach Motykaly Wielkie from the south before heading east along Panzer Route 2 to continue his search. On reaching Wistycze, without encountering the enemy or Nehring's armour, he stopped near the four low, and surprisingly intact, bridges over a stretch of the River Lesna where it briefly splits into rivulets. Seeing Second Panzer Group's command entourage arrive on the scene, and likely believing enemy combat forces were nearby, the small contingent of Soviet soldiers guarding the structure quickly abandoned their duties and disappeared.

Ordered to move beyond a wooded area about a kilometre north of Wieliczkowicze by 0600hrs I./331st Infantry Regiment (167 ID) crossed the Bug to a seemingly deserted far bank. Just to the north the rather wordy '17th Red Banner (Brest) Border Detachment of the Belorussian SSR NKVD' rushed from their outpost (No. 3) headquarters around Wolczyn (Wołczyn) to help stem the flow of German infantry.[69] At 0700hrs eighteen aging, twin-engine Soviet SB bombers made an unexpected appearance and targeted German armour crossing the Bug, and each was soon shot down; their unprotected, gravity-fed fuel tanks providing no favours. Although hundreds of these planes operated from Western Front's sector, inexperienced crews and poor communications necessitated their employing rigid flying formations that mimicked the leader's path. Once the shock of the Luftwaffe's early morning shellacking wore off the few Red Air Force fighter pilots that got airborne often performed better than the Germans had expected, even resorting to ramming enemy planes as a desperate last resort. With few Soviet reconnaissance aircraft over the frontier their fighters and attack aircraft needed to perform the role with expected results.[70] Back on the ground I./331st Infantry Regiment reported that Kostary and the area to its north were free of Soviet forces, although an indeterminate number remained at large along the southern edge of the forest near Wieliczkowicze. In its limited role covering 17th Panzer Division's left 167th Infantry Division made slow, but steady progress throughout the day to secure Nowosiolki and areas just to the east, and kept the nearby, largely inexperienced Soviet 49th Rifle Division (XXVII RC) at bay.

Brest Fortress

With Rzeczyca captured Brigadier Kurt Kalmukoff's 31st Infantry Division continued its predominantly walking advance through Brest's northern neighbourhoods. Soviet forces unable to escape the fortress' encroaching encirclement settled in for what was expected to be a brief siege, given that friendly forces would assuredly counterattack and drive the Germans back. Some 3km to the south 34th Infantry Division's forward elements worked their way across the flat, smoky farmland that bordered the River Muchawiec. 107th Infantry Regiment (34 ID) initially encountered negligible resistance until approaching the south-western edge of Gierszony. Its partner, 80th Infantry Regiment, received a similar reception, as its personnel captured Fort V, and moved on Arkadja and Fort IV. Just to the west nine Red Air Force bombers conducted a brief attack at 0750hrs, which briefly disrupted enemy ferry operations, but just over an hour later the German 31st and 34th Infantry Divisions had linked up to effectively surround the still very active Brest fortress. These two formations continued eastward to subdue the city proper, and the especially stubborn resistance around the railway station.

Having campaigned with Guderian's XIX Army Corps in 1939 over the very area in which they now operated, those veterans of 3rd Panzer Division were familiar with the challenges of the region's roads and terrain. As Model's armoured cars, motorcycles, and halftracks reconnoitred towards the northeast along their recently adjusted route to bypass Brest what appeared as viable routes and accessible terrain on the maps and aerial reconnaissance were in reality a sizeable tract of marshland running from Zbunin to near Brest. En route to meeting with Audörsch to investigate the problem Model's command vehicle got stuck. Presented with having to negotiate a way across several kilometres of soft ground, deep sand, and a tangle of criss-crossing dirt trails to reach Panzer Route 1 at 1430hrs Model received his XXIV Motorized Army Corps commander's approval to change 3rd Panzer Division's advance axis to the Stradecz–Brest and Gierszony–Huznie Roads closer to Brest, even though it meant negotiating what would be a chaotic mass of withdrawing civilian refugees and enemy soldiers.

To the south at 1000hrs, just as 12th Motorized Rifle Regiment (4 PD) had entered the large wooded area about a kilometre beyond the Bug, they encountered enemy resistance for the first time.[71] The Soviet defenders fought from bunkers and prepared positions backed by antitank guns, to which the Germans responded with mortar and artillery fire. By early afternoon 12th and 33rd Motorized Rifle Regiments respectively fought their way into Brodziatyn and Orlanka. With the confining woodland fighting occasionally degenerating into close-combat 4th Panzer Division continued to the Maloryta–Kobryn road in what had become something of a race with 3rd Panzer Division to reach Panzer Route 1 first and gain bragging rights for leading XXIV Motorized Army Corps into the heart of Belorussia.

Peliszcze Tank Battle

With what remained of the barrage-battered forward elements of the Soviet 22nd Tank Division having struggled to reach the River Muchawiec's north side and withdraw along Panzer Route 1, by 0800hrs they were arriving in the countryside around Zabinka (Żabinka) where the division's T-26s had conducted gunnery training the night before.[72] Nearby, the Soviet XXVIII Rifle Corps had similarly pulled back from its positions defending Brest, including portions of its 6th and 42nd Rifle Divisions that had avoided XII Army Corps cutting them off.[73] Within an hour some sixty of the light tanks had concentrated in the area, which although numerically inferior to the armoured onslaught moving against them, what vehicles, men, and weapons that were being thrown together could serve as a sacrificial rapier to hinder Lemelsen's advance and buy time for the Soviet Fourth Army to organize a counterattack.[74] Nearby, XIV Mechanized Corps fell back towards Kobryn and Zabinka.[75] Luftwaffe aircraft continued their seemingly constant strafing and bombing missions, as well as reconnaissance and artillery observation, and although much of the terrain was wooded and obscured air crew visibility, with most of the Red Army in some stage of pulling out this handicap was usually mitigated.

Near midday Second Panzer Group was using six pontoon bridges to cross the River Bug, in addition to the three permanent ones that had survived destruction. Considering the vast amount of combat resources queued up to use them the structures soon proved insufficient to maintain the desired flow to fill the expanding front. With ever increasing portions of 18th Panzer Division now moving through Czelejewo and over the River Lesna, Lemelsen and Nehring tagged along with the formation's vanguard to get firsthand accounts of the battlespace. Off of their left-rear 17th Panzer Division made for a bridge upriver at Rudawiec. Some 50km to the east and moving directly towards XXXXVII Motorized Army Corps a pair of Soviet tank columns and what towed artillery had received motorized transport hustled through Poddubno along the Pruzana–Widomla road.[76] Although some of the route was obscured by woodland German aircraft that had been called for exploited the more open areas to strafe and bomb the enemy from the rear. Even though its two, fixed MG-17 machine guns' 7.92mm ball rounds were unlikely to penetrate the tanks' 6mm engine deck armour the overall effect of such attacks sowed confusion, damage, and casualties. Reacting to the aerial threat several Red Army tankers set DT machine guns into their T-26 model 1939 turret bustle roof housings and according to Soviet sources managed to down one of the German aircraft. Having reportedly lost thirty tanks during the fight 30th Tank Division nevertheless continued its westward advance.[77] After passing into the hilly, thicket-covered terrain before Peliszcze the mixed Soviet force halted at 1230hrs and sent motorcycles ahead to look for the oncoming enemy. 18th Panzer Division's vanguard soon obliged and the riders hastily returned to the main force. Although outmatched in firepower, armour protection, crew size, and other combat attributes against the German Panzer IIIs and IVs, several T-26s assumed ambush positions and accompanying infantry dug trenches to provide a combat modifier.[78] Amid the generally open terrain, with its undulating hills of clover meadows and oat fields both sides respectively manoeuvred towards each other from wooded, slightly elevated positions. As they converged on a shallow valley just west of Peliszcze a large, pine crucifix that had been erected at the village's Catholic church presented a visual contrast to the unfolding combat.

Frantic, largely inaccurate firing from both sides commenced, but with the T-26s' comparatively thinner armour their heavier German counterparts could effectively engage in a stand-up fight. Soviet tanks were subsequently knocked out or immobilized, with many burning along with their crews. Greater Soviet tank numbers in this initial engagement, however, began to force the German vanguard back towards Widomla, but the timely arrival of Ju-87s reaped additional destruction between 1500 and 1600hrs against the more crowded enemy groupings. As the planes returned to their bases the second Soviet tank regiment appeared at Peliszcze to reinforce the counterattack. Looking to avoid a fight and seek a more advantageous position the German tanks withdrew, while a few crews turned their turrets around to continue firing rearward in what was more a waste of ammunition than effective tactic. By 1730hrs 18th Panzer Division recorded the destruction of three-dozen enemy tanks, of which the supporting Luftwaffe undoubtedly deserved some of the credit. Unwilling to offer pursuit and contend with the bulk of 18th Panzer Division the Soviet tankers also pulled back to reorganize.[79] Having remained with Nehring's command since late morning, at 1630hrs Guderian returned to Kolodno to check on XXXXVII Motorized Army Corps' progress crossing the Bug. He re-crossed the river 2 hours later and went to his forward command post at Bohukaly (Bohukały) to be briefed on Second Panzer Group's overall progress; his headquarters proper being located in nearby Biala Podlaska (Biała Podlaska). According to Guderian, 'The most dangerous opponent of a tank is an enemy tank.' and that, 'If it cannot be beaten, the breakthrough can be seen as a failure, as the infantry and artillery will also fail to get through.'[80]

Moving Eastward
In contrast to the inconsistent resistance German forces had encountered along the River Bug, 45th Infantry Division struggled to subdue a trapped, increasingly desperate enemy within the Brest fortress who knew little of the larger battle and held out hope of reinforcement or relief per a Soviet counterattack. Within the fortification's thick walls the Germans achieved limited gains for high casualties, especially among officers and NCOs, who as in any conflict were targeted to degrade command and control, and morale. In the early afternoon XII Army Corps' reserve, 133rd Infantry Regiment, was inserted into the

fight, while more infantry, antitank guns, and howitzers were brought up to provide direct support. To assist his efforts to take the central citadel the commander of 135th Infantry Regiment commandeered passing assault guns from 3./201st Assault Gun Battalion, which proved very useful in the kind of close, direct infantry support for which they were intended. During a noon visit to XII Army Corps' command post Bock determined that the effort to take Brest fortress via a *coup de main* had failed. An hour later 45th Infantry Division's commander, Brigadier Fritz Schlieper, concurred and correspondingly pulled back from the contested area once darkness had descended, and opted to instead pulverize the defenders using heavy artillery. That evening Kluge also went to XII Army Corps' command post to stress that with numerous bridges in the area secured and Panzer Route 1 generally open to German traffic the defenders would simply be contained and starved out.[81] Unlike a rapid war of movement in which a defender could be kept off guard and forced to react to an attacker's actions, within the built-up, rubble-strewn citadel success was measured in hard-fought metres. Soviet snipers abounded, especially from unexpected locations, such as piles of rubbish, while riflemen and machine-gun crews resisted from windows and open areas within the complex's numerous brick structures. Trapped and having been subjected to the politically-motivated rhetoric of Commissars that included the Germans would shoot any who surrendered, the defenders resigned themselves to a fatalistic fight.[82] By day's end 45th Infantry Division had lost as many men as it did during six weeks of fighting in the West the previous year. In the context of an anticipated brief campaign perhaps such casualties were seen as acceptable. In reality they were a harbinger of the lengthy, brutal war of attrition to follow.

By late evening on 22 June XXXXVII Motorized Army Corps had advanced several kilometres to the north-east, with two panzer battalions from 18th Panzer Division having reached as far as Poddubno at 1950hrs. With 167th Infantry Division being predominantly foot- and horse-bound and unable to maintain a comparable rate of advance, at 2035hrs Lemelsen returned the formation to LIII Army Corps (Second Army). To emphasize his appreciation for the vital assistance he also sent the division's commander, Major General Hans Schönhärl, a personal letter to the effect. To the south, with Model's redirected advance axis now running along the Tomaszowka–Brest road, a new advance detachment (*Vorausabteilung*) was created. III./6th Panzer Regiment, a company of motorcycle infantry, and elements of divisional engineers provided a sufficiently mixed force to deal with most situations expected in a rapid advance into what was largely an unknown enemy presence. Setting out from Stradecz at about 1630hrs the Kampfgruppe soon received heavy antitank fire from a village east of the Bug from Kostomloty and a lead group of Panzer IV *Tauchpanzern* from 12./6th Panzer Regiment moved off-road in a line to engage the threat from some 800m. Stopping to fire to impart the requisite accuracy, the tanks'

75mm cannons soon silenced the concealed enemy antitank guns.[83] While the accompanying motorcycle infantry pinned down Red Army elements in the woods and marshlands between the advance route and the river, III./6th Panzer Regiment quickly pushed on. By 1830hrs 'Kampfgruppe Corvin' had taken Franopol' and a large number of abandoned enemy artillery pieces, and was in a good position from which to send 3rd Motorcycle Battalion on to Kobryn.

At 2100hrs 3rd Panzer Division's vanguard arrived at the high, wooden bridge over the River Muchawiec at Huznie, with Model and his staff following close behind. With the all-weather, Brest–Minsk road intersection just a kilometre away III./6th Panzer Regiment was able to shoot up Soviet vehicles and T-26 tanks retreating to the east. Often, internally stowed ammunition was hit and transformed the obsolete armour into funeral pyres against the fading daylight. After doing what damage they could Model's vanguard finally drove onto Panzer Route 1 and made for Kobryn. Seemingly free of the fighting along the Bug, after just 16km the unit was forced to halt before a portion of the bridge near Bulkowo, which the Soviets had partially burned. With the infantry of 3rd Rifle Brigade well to the rear and enemy soldiers offering fragmented, harassing fire as they retreated through the area III./6th Panzer Regiment's commander, Captain Ferdinand Schneider-Kostalski, had his tanks leave the road and establish an outward facing perimeter in the darkness. With Model having been forced to take a rather circuitous route to Bulkowo, XII Army Corps' lead infantry elements had advanced nearly as far eastward to take Bratylowo (Bratyłowo) (I./82nd Infantry Regiment) and a stretch of high ground around Koszelewo (II./ and III./82nd Infantry Regiment).[84]

To add to Model's stress his supply trains had yet to even cross the River Bug, and without a steady flow of priority items like fuel, water, and ammunition his extended command would soon lose its combat effectiveness. Combined with operating in often surprisingly deep, sandy terrain that exacerbated traffic jams and dust, what little fuel efficiency most military vehicles possessed translated into much higher consumption rates than anticipated during the invasion's planning stage. Having arrived at Model's forward position, 1./39th Motorized Engineer Battalion personnel began constructing a 16-tonne bridge that was slated to be completed by the next morning. Although III. Panzer Battalion's armour could be re-waterproofed and technically capable of crossing the River Muchawiec, orchestrating the effort at night was out of the question. Besides, Schneider-Kostalski had found a suitable crossing until the bridge was back in operation.

To the south-west once the pontoon bridge was ready for vehicular traffic at 1630hrs 1./35th Panzer Regiment led the unit across the Bug.[85] At about dusk the regiment's commander, Colonel Heinrich Eberbach, around which a Kampfgruppe had been formed, sent 34th Motorcycle Battalion ahead to provide scouting and screening towards the north-east from Brodziatyn, with armoured vehicles following at about 2100hrs. After a cautious 5-hour drive along confined forest trails and in nearly total darkness the weary drivers and crewmen reached the all-weather Maloryta–Kobryn road without opposition. From this location 'Kampfgruppe Eberbach' manoeuvred behind the enemy 75th Rifle Division and threatened its lines of communication with its increasingly distant Fourth Army parent.

By the end of Barbarossa's gruelling first day the Luftwaffe could take great pride in having pulled off the greatest victory in aerial warfare history and set an auspicious start to the campaign, given that German sources indicated 1,811 enemy planes had been destroyed (322 airborne; 1,489 ground) along the entire front for the loss of just 78 aircraft.[86,87] In largely removing Red Army opposition the operational surprise Second Panzer Group, and that of the *Ostheer*, had achieved progressed with little aerial interference, and reciprocally benefited from additional Luftwaffe support. To discuss subsequent actions at 1830hrs Kluge went to Bohukaly where he argued that Soviet forces were conducting a planned withdrawal and intended to orchestrate a determined defence further east. Guderian, however, stressed that the enemy had been badly shaken and could only offer sporadic, localized resistance. Considering German intelligence had been unable to provide a complete picture of Soviet forces and intentions, such opinions were undoubtedly tinged with speculation based on the respective commanders' experiences, personalities, and motivations. As a demonstrated tactician, intellect, technician, theorist, and organizer Guderian's impetuousness, volatility, ambition, and self-serving nature worked to set him at odds with peers and superiors, and promoted myopia to events beyond his immediate control. Having already demonstrated a willingness to violate unity of command, as illustrated during his arguably reckless, but ultimately decisive thrust to the English Channel in 1940, Guderian was unlikely to conform given such validation.

Chapter 2

Race to Minsk, 23–25 June 1941

With XXXXVII and XXIV Motorized Army Corps' spearheads having pushed through the partially completed and manned Soviet border defences along the River Bug, on 23 June it was critical for the Germans to maintain operational momentum and keep the enemy off balance. Even though unexpectedly soft, often impassable terrain and a limited number of crossings served as traffic chokepoints that adversely impacted the potential gains on *Barbarossatag*, the largely under-trained Soviets were showing no signs of mounting a concerted defence outside of the Brest Fortress, and to lesser degrees around Zbunin, Domaczewo, and Przyborowo.[1] Already German motorcycle and motorized reconnaissance battalions had spearheaded their parent divisions deep into enemy territory. Typically operating up to a 40km frontage the latter's four- and eight-wheeled armoured cars and associated vehicles relied on speed and agility to accomplish their information-gathering missions. Observing and reporting meant enemy contact was to be avoided, although their crews were trained to fight using coordinated fire and movement tactics. Since a hidden enemy was inclined to return fire even if unseen, German forces would regularly shoot into woods or other terrain that obscured visibility on the chance a potential threat was flushed out, while still at distance. By facilitating the German advance sluggish enemy forward formations would be cut off from resupply and deprived of effective command and control, and would help ensure the many bridges en route to Minsk could be secured before they were blown up. With Guderian having instituted three priority levels for his forces those designated as '1' led the way to the east and north-east of Brest. Those with '2' and '3' respectively followed once the higher value formations had passed, including a vast amount food, fuel, ammunition, spare parts, and a host of other supplies that had queued up west of the River Bug followed suit as conditions allowed.[2] For Guderian's lead panzer divisions, secondary roads, however poor, were critical to alleviate traffic congestion that hindered logistics, increased fuel use, and upset carefully crafted timetables. As captured Soviet soldiers were a low priority for relocation away from the battlezone until activity subsided they remained at collection points east of the Bug.[3] For all of the combat experience, leadership, and elan embodied in the German Army of mid-1941 without a steady flow of supplies

47

even the best fighting force would soon lack the resources and endurance necessary to remain viable in the field.

Considering much of the terrain between the River Muchawiec and the Polesie Marshes comprised soft, sandy lowlands vehicles were generally relegated to what passed as roads, the better of which more often radiated from nearby Brest rather than along the German advance axis. On XXIV Motorized Army Corps' left 3rd Panzer Division's forward position presently terminated around Bulkowo, while 'Kampfgruppe Corvin' shot past Radwanicze for Panzer Route 1. As a result elements from the Soviet 22nd Tank and 6th Rifle Divisions still withdrawing eastward were forced away from the thoroughfare at a critical time. With Model looking to resume his advance as soon as possible at dawn on 23 June the men of 1./39th Motorized Engineer Battalion remained true to their word having repaired the crossing over the Muchawiec as estimated. Since badly needed German fuel transports had finally made it to the forward positions at 0430hrs, III./6th Panzer Regiment was soon replenished and set off once again along Panzer Route 1 for Kobryn, some 30km away. As the second of two routes expressly prioritized for Guderian's armoured traffic barring civilian refugees clogging these thoroughfares, enemy activity, or damage a rapid advance rate could be expected. Half an hour later 1st Motorized Reconnaissance Battalion set off in tow, and along secondary roads. Per doctrine the various scouting forces typically went out and returned by different routes to help maintain security and cover a wider area. 3rd Motorcycle Battalion followed, but after a short drive turned north to use the Muchawiec bridgehead 80th Infantry Regiment (34 ID) had just established at Zabinka.

At 0620hrs 'Kampfgruppe Corvin' reported enemy forces, including armour from 22nd Tank Division, continuing to retreat from southern Brest and onto the main road to Kobryn. 6th Panzer Regiment elements engaged such opposition, which at times reflected a shooting gallery against the gasoline-powered Soviet T-26s. With time a critical battlefield factor, however, Linnarz's 5th Panzer Brigade-based Kampfgruppe remained focused on helping clear the way ahead of XXIV Motorized Army Corps' advance towards Minsk, and leaving better suited motorized and foot-bound infantry to cover its extending flanks and plug gaps in the German line. At 0700hrs Model ordered 1st Motorized Reconnaissance and 3rd Motorcycle Battalion to work with III./6th Panzer Regiment to quickly blow through any defence of Kobryn.[4] Operating with 31st Infantry Division's advance detachment under III./17th Infantry Regiment's commander, Lieutenant Colonel Hans-Joachim von Stolzmann, the seven assault guns of 1./201st Assault Gun Battalion helped clear out troublesome enemy forces defending the town. Having entered Kobryn at about 0845hrs on 23 June the Germans managed to knock out several more Soviet T-26 tanks, and took one intact bridge over a section of the Muchawiec that recrossed Model's advance, although not before a second crossing was destroyed.

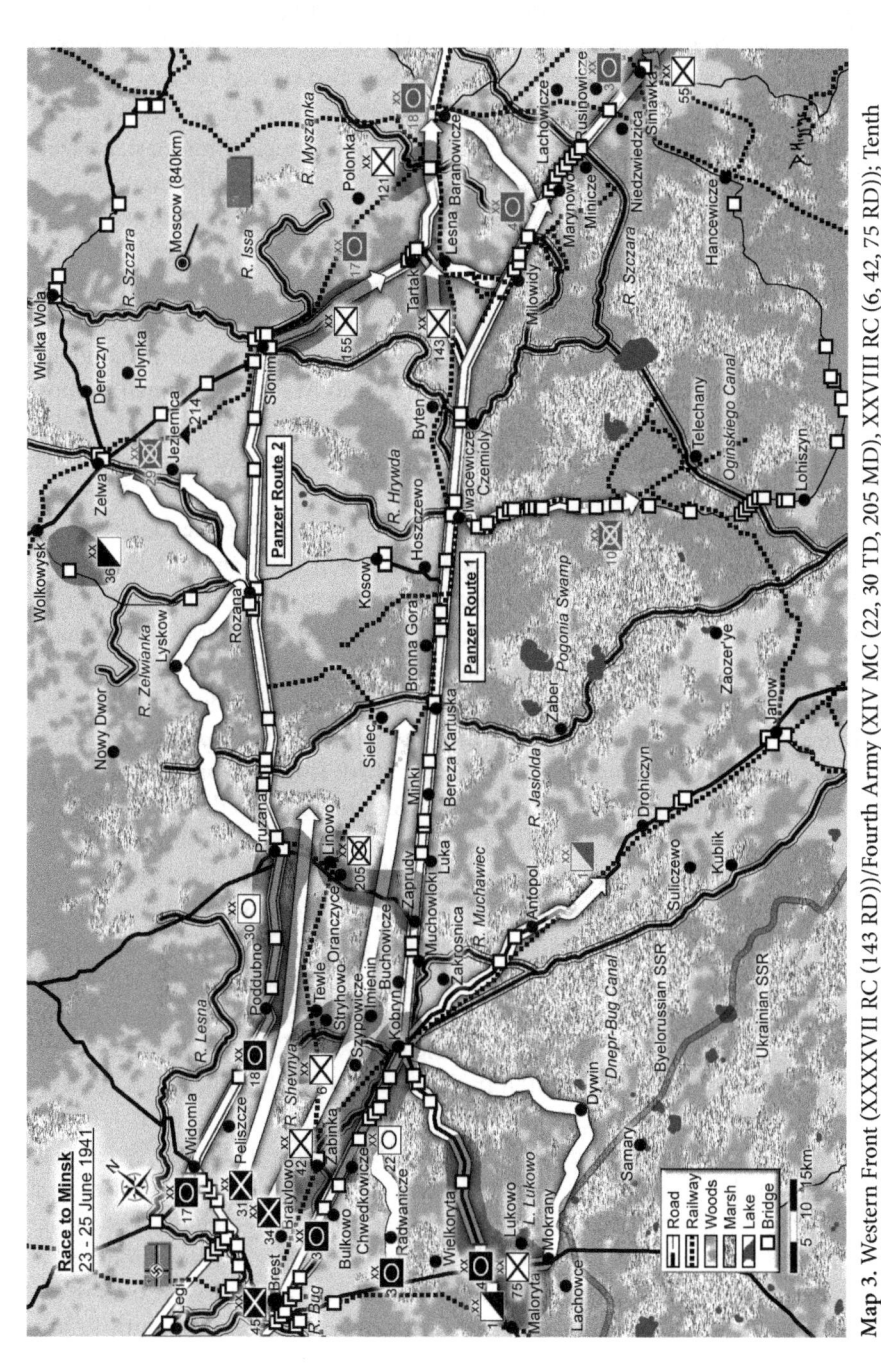

Map 3. Western Front (XXXXVII RC (143 RD))/Fourth Army (XIV MC (22, 30 TD, 205 MD), XXVIII RC (6, 42, 75 RD)); Tenth Army (155 RD), VI CC (36 CD); Thirteenth Army (55, 121 RD). TsAMO, f.208, op.2511, d.206, l.1. TsAMO, f.929, op.1, d.8, l.1.

Along Model's right rear the absence of proper roads continued to impede 4th Panzer Division's progress and its vital fuel, and other supply transports. Soon after arriving in the woods west of Miedna, Langermann's armoured vanguard, 'Kampfgruppe Eberbach' (35 PR), had also started for Kobryn from the south-west. Having served as an infantryman in the First World War until receiving a severe facial wound in 1915 that destroyed much of his nose, a hazel-eyed Second Lieutenant Eberbach had spent much of the conflict convalescing from his injuries and subsequent reconstructive surgery. As commander of 35th Panzer Regiment (4 PD) through the campaigns in Poland and the West during the morning he led it along the Maloryta–Kobryn road for Panzer Route 1, and passed where 34th Motorcycle Battalion had recently cleared the Wielkoryta area. While the Soviet 75th Rifle Division had been making good use of the brief summertime darkness to pull back onto Maloryta in small groups, where the light from a burning Brest could be seen to the north-west, with 4th Panzer Division pushing through the area exfiltration would be all the more difficult.[5]

As commander of XXIV Motorized Army Corps, Schweppenburg was an educated, cultivated personality, who spoke Russian, French, and English in addition to his native German. The Prussian aristocrat, whose title originated in the long-dissolved Holy Roman Empire, also possessed considerable experience leading a division and corps in combat. Should Soviet armour unexpectedly appear on his right at 0400hrs 267th Antitank Battalion established a blocking position south of Tomaszowka where sand had actually built up to form dunes, while the advance detachment from its parent 267th Infantry Division occupied a position amid the lakes to the east and astride the route leading to Maloryta. Along the same road 255th Infantry Division moved through Oltusz and over Hill 189, its 255th Reconnaissance Battalion being sent towards Mokrany to determine enemy dispositions. With extensive, often wooded marshland comprising much of the battlespace south and east of Brest thirsty Landsers drinking from these sources risked malaria, typhoid, dysentery, and other contaminated water-borne diseases, not to mention ever-present lice and swarms of biting mosquitoes. As most soldiers in the Red Army during this time lacked inoculations and medicine was often in short supply, such ailments could decimate a formation if not properly addressed.

For the first few days of the German invasion SS-Motorized Division 'Reich' personnel remained west of the Bug, as part of Guderian's reserve, XXXXVI Motorized Army Corps, where they were tasked with minor duties that included regulating traffic. While regular Army personnel often looked down on these politically-oriented soldiers as separate and inferior rivals for arms and glory the men in the few Waffen-SS (fka SS-Combat Support Troop (*Verfügungstruppe*) until 19 July 1940) combat-active formations had much to prove on the battlefields of Poland, the West, Yugoslavia, and Greece. Considering the difficult, realistic training programme that Major General (*SS-Gruppenführer*) Paul Hausser had instituted the fighters it produced were instilled with a deep sense of camaraderie, their special status in the nation's military and Party, and unquestioning loyalty to their leadership. Having served in staff roles during the First World War and later a member of the Reichswehr, his leadership produced a force whose handful of premier divisions rivalled the best of the regular Army. Promoted as an elite group the troopers' bravery and elan were as evident as their frequent recklessness that often incurred unnecessary casualties.

At 0740hrs, after just one day of operations, forward German formations began to report inadequate fuel shipments were hindering their respective operations. In addition to the region's poor road network and typically heavy traffic congestion that tasked engines and transmissions, German fuel transports proved especially vulnerable to the numerous bypassed clusters of enemy soldiers and snipers still in the fight. Such drags on what petrol, oil, and lubricant (POL) 'consumption rates' (*Verbrauchssatze*) that an asset was estimated to consume per 100km of operation often meant commanders had to prioritize frequently limited distribution. As foreign tanks and tracked chassis were commonly used to supplement those produced in Germany the dearth of domestically built lorries similarly complicated logistics, repairs, and replacements.

Pruzana Tank Battle

Having spent a few hours at his headquarters at 0400hrs on 23 June Guderian drove for Pruzana to ascertain 18th Panzer Division's situation and progress. Considering Second Panzer Group's exposed left flank was key to his successfully completing his role in containing and defeating what promised to be a sizeable portion of Red Army forces around Bialystok and Minsk, and hopefully contributing to a brief, victorious campaign, Guderian would largely command from XXXXVII Motorized Army Corps' sector for the foreseeable future. Although the Soviet XIV Mechanized Corps had been battered and depleted during 22nd Tank Division's fighting withdrawal from the Brest sector, and 30th Tank Division's scrap at Peliszcze the day before, the corps tried to put together a force for a counterattack.[6] At 0600hrs XIV Mechanized Corps, as well as XXVIII Rifle Corps, with what remnants of its 6th and 42nd Rifle Divisions that escaped encirclement in the city's fortress and 75th Rifle Division initiated respective attacks at several points along Second Panzer Group's frontage.[7] As the Germans pushed towards the River Jasiolda (Jasiołda) II./ and III./18th Panzer Regiment destroyed several enemy tanks for very few losses. With the latter unit having arrived at the waterway at 0730hrs without encountering serious opposition it soon established a small bridgehead, which expanded as follow-on forces arrived. Faced with a German torrent that bypassed stubborn points of resistance to flood into its rear area headquarters, artillery, and supply elements the Red Army defenders were soon sent reeling.[8] By maintaining a rapid tempo Second Panzer Group was able to avoid stagnating into an attritional fight that invited unnecessary casualties and materiel losses that would rob them of the necessary depth of resources and endurance to successfully conduct what promised to be a gruelling campaign.

Not known for remaining long at his more established headquarters to the rear, Guderian began the day being driven to its new location south of Widomla in his cabriolet Horch 901 Typ 40 staff car to meet with Lemelsen. As with other senior leadership vehicles its very visible command pennants almost seemed to beckon enemy snipers looking to take out the men with whom they were associated. Second Panzer Group's commander then continued on to 17th Panzer Division where the leader of its 17th Rifle Brigade, Brigadier Karl *Ritter* (Knight) von Weber, reported on his situation. At 0830hrs Guderian moved on to Nehring before returning to Lemelsen and finally to the front line at Pruzana. Even though Guderian's penchant to roam his forward areas risked hindering his staff's ability to contact him for critical, time-sensitive direction his chief-of-staff typically remained behind to function in the General's stead. Because the four panzer group spearheads in operation during Barbarossa needed to be as agile and responsive as possible each had an attached motorized panzer group headquarters, along with corps mapping, military police, and postal detachments. Commensurate with the size and importance of a panzer group a large, sophisticated motorized panzer group signals regiment allowed for immediate, cross-country communication down to regiment level, as well as to higher commands.

With XXXXVII Motorized Army Corps' forward elements largely clear of the enemy's immediate border fortifications and defensive positions, at 0900hrs Lemelsen's lead elements again engaged the Soviet 30th Tank Division employing dozens of T-26s and a regimental-sized force from 205th Motorized Rifle Division out of the Szypowicze area.[9] The bulk of the latter formation created what at the time probably seemed like wholly inadequate defensive positions south of Pruzana that loosely tied in with others extending to Zaprudy and along the River Muchawiec. Considering the River Jasiolda's broad, marshy floodplain Red Army infantry and corps engineers prepared positions at Bereza Kartuska, with its 48m-long rail bridge just east of the town. Unwilling to destroy crossings prematurely and trap friendly forces on the wrong bank the Soviets were often caught off guard by rapid, bold enemy advances and failed to do so. The Soviet tankers managed to rebuff a German tank battalion, but quickly ran into heavy German antitank and artillery fire into which Luftwaffe aircraft added its weight, as groups of panzern attacked from different directions and greater distances than the Soviets could effectively reply. With 17th Panzer Division having advanced north of Pruzana and threatened 30th Tank Division's open right flank by 0930hrs the Soviet counterattack had been checked and withdrew to the town's eastern outskirts.

Some 30km to the south-west 3rd Panzer and 31st Infantry Divisions gave 22nd Tank Division a drubbing that sent it back from Zabinka and along the Brest–Bereza Kartuska rail line onto a blocking position about 5km northwest of Kobryn. To hamper any enemy offensive the Soviets had previously ensured that rail lines from the River Bug eastwards were through-traffic, and devoid of marshalling yards and other such facilities.[10] Although supported with elements from 6th Rifle Division and possessing sufficient POL due to their recent acquisition from a Kobryn warehouse depot, 22nd Tank Division's sixty-seven light tanks remained short of ammunition and crewmen, as it tried unsuccessfully to fully disengage from Model and 31st Infantry Division.[11] Suffering heavy losses, especially from Luftwaffe attacks that Soviet sources indicated occasionally fell on their comrades on the ground, 22nd Tank Division was unable to defend Szypowicze. A minor counterattack with Soviet armour and an infantry detachment from 6th Rifle Division tried to hinder 3rd Panzer Division's progress north-west of Kobryn with predictably poor results.[12] With Lemelsen's command typically advancing faster than his Red Army adversaries could withdraw the latter was kept off balance and unable to offer more than brief, uncoordinated resistance.

At 0950hrs 18th Panzer Division's vanguard entered Pruzana. With Soviet forces having recently left the area, as several German soldiers moved in to fill the vacuum in the absence of resistance many dismounted and scavenged through the town. Food that the Soviets had confiscated was dolled out to the residents, while other items of value were divvied up among the Landsers.[13] During the late morning 30th Tank Division made another counterattack to recapture Pruzana, but in the early afternoon German elements struck near Zaprudy to unhinge Fourth Army's left flank and forced the defenders to retreat for Sielec along the River Jasiolda some 25km to the east.[14] XXVIII Rifle Corps moved into positions along the Rivers Shevnya and Muchawiec, and skirting Panzer Route 1 to near Muchowloki (Muchowłoki). While its 42nd Rifle Division defended positions north of Szypowicze 6th Rifle Division and 459th Rifle Regiment (45 RD) covered Kobryn.

With German military doctrine placing considerably more weight on conducting offensive actions, those of the defensive were viewed as occasionally necessary tactical or operational pauses. While several factors went into determining the penetration and effectiveness of main armaments and ammunition what mostly brought a tank success was its crew. With the Germans benefiting from several combat modifiers, including superior gun optics, and command and control, greater combat experience, and three-man turrets that allowed the gunner, loader, and commander to focus on their respective duties, they possessed paths to tactical, and eventually operational, victory that their adversary lacked. A large proportion of Red Army tank crews were new to their roles due to recent military expansions and reorganizations that frequently removed veterans of the recent fighting against Poland and Finland to help establish new formations. Amid what had largely become a confused, chaotic Soviet withdrawal, poor communications, outdated orders, and fear of displaying unsanctioned initiative further degraded their capabilities.

As had been expected, given the pressure the Soviet Third and Tenth Armies were under to avoid encirclement, at 1230hrs Second Panzer Group reported numerous enemy tanks gravitating on a prominent valley north of Pruzana. Within 5 hours 18th Panzer Division was moving through Poddubno en route to this potential threat. At about 1800hrs Lieutenant Colonel (Br. Eq. Wing Commander) Werner Mölders' 51st Fighter Wing (*Jagdgeschwader*), with their green mottling over grey aircraft and very identifiable yellow cowlings and tails, conducted ground attacks using their 20mm guns to knock out what they estimated to be twenty-five T-26s from 30th Tank Division. Even though few Soviet aircraft roamed the skies many of their tanks had a painted white triangle on their turrets as 'Identification Friend or Foe'. With XXIV Motorized Army Corps having pushed through enemy positions along the River Jasiolda continued resistance to Guderian fell to the XIV Mechanized and XXVIII Rifle Corps' increasingly improvised defence. Later, as the panzern passed near the wooded or otherwise concealing terrain around Pruzana, Soviet infantry resorted to jumping onto individual vehicles to fire small arms into unbuttoned hatches or lob Molotov cocktails onto the rear deck where the flaming gasoline would drip into engine grilles.[15] As such incendiaries typically comprised a bottled mix of phosphorus dissolved in oil and gasoline or a self-igniting phosphorus/sulphur, on impact its contents became exposed to oxygen and caused a fire that much like napalm was almost impossible to extinguish and produced horrific burns on contact with skin.

At 1915hrs Guderian was notified that Nehring had established a bridgehead over the Jasiolda and 5km of surrounding swampland north-east of Pruzana.[16] Although fuel shipments had yet to arrive, as late as 2100hrs Lemelsen hoped to secure a crossing over the River Szczara, still some 60km away, as soon as possible to help block any Soviet breakout through the Slonim area, with its sandy soil, and pine, black alder, and oak. With the German VIII Army Corps (Ninth Army) already turning southward and behind the Soviet Third Army, on Guderian's side of the forming pocket getting infantry forces to the sector was critical to help prevent a mass enemy escape to the south. Because the town was situated in the Szczara valley and offered a physical gap in the Belorussian Ridge that ran from near Bialystok to north of Minsk the opening drew an increasing number of Soviet formations looking to break out. Reciprocally, the area presented Lemelsen with a similar ingress route through which to make contact with Third Panzer Group. Over the last 2 days Second Panzer Group estimated to have destroyed 220 Soviet tanks out of some 1,000 within Western

Front's area of operations, of which 18th Panzer Division accounted for half.[17] At midnight on 23/24 June 5th Motorized Machine-Gun Battalion was activated from Bock's reserve and allocated to XXXXVII Motorized Army Corps to help bolster this threatened 'inner' (northern) flank until additional infantry moved up.

With the Luftwaffe possessing air superiority, if not outright supremacy in some sectors, Red Army forces were at a considerable disadvantage in knowing where Guderian's fast-moving spearheads were at any given time. Confusion and fear often translated into a rush to avoid German advances, whether real or imagined, and the abandonment of large amounts of Soviet weapons and equipment before they could be destroyed meant that with the Germans typically occupying the post-fight battlefield such materiel fell into their laps; some of it was factory fresh and unused. Whether in working order or requiring repair, captured assets typically had a short life given the lack of resupplied spare parts and ammunition. Immobilized vehicles or larger weapon systems were similarly left behind for wont of fuel transport. With the Soviet Fourth Army coalescing against the River Jasiolda, and the villages of Drohiczyn and south to Kublik along the shallow, 21m-wide Dnepr–Bug Canal, by 1900hrs 18th and 3rd Panzer Divisions had punched a 45km gap in Fourth Army's line between Pruzana and Bereza Kartuska.

Beyond the Frontier

While 45th Infantry Division and assorted support units continued their frustrating task to subdue the obstinate Soviet defenders within the seemingly anachronistic, but still viable Brest complex, XII Infantry Corps' remaining formations, 31st and 34th Infantry Division, continued to push eastward to clear lingering elements from the Soviet 42nd and 6th Rifle Divisions between Panzer Routes 2 and 1. Better suited than other unit types at holding ground German infantry were overwhelmingly foot- and horse-bound, due to the Wehrmacht fielding 154 divisions for Barbarossa alone (more than twice the number the United States created during the entire war), they were expected to cover dozens of kilometres each day. Unauthorized to use Panzer Routes 2 and 1, they were frequently relegated to a network of sandy roads that exhausted men and houses, and caused regular traffic jams, in what soon became a losing effort to keep pace with their armoured and motorized comrades and plug the intervening gaps. By 0600hrs on 23 June 34th Infantry Division was again moving through the area's beige-, green-, and maize-coloured farmland between Panzer Route 1 and the multi-track Brest–Minsk rail line running roughly parallel to the north-east.[18] Burdened with weapons, ammunition, and equipment the shifting terrain and high temperatures added to the men's discomfort, as they snaked along numerous wilderness trails. With movement and firepower naturally prioritized company field kitchens were soon far behind and the men relegated to temporarily supplementing that carried with locally procured food. By 0830hrs follow-on elements of its parent 34th Infantry Division reached Panzer Route 1, but were unable to use it due to 3rd Panzer Division's lengthy vehicle train extending from Kobryn back to the Bug, and beyond. Such congestion was unlikely to clear up soon, as XXIV Motorized Army Corps' operational reserve, 29th Motorized Infantry Division, was only now approaching the waterway's western shore intent on following Schweppenburg's armour along the same road.[19] As an option to facilitate the flow of traffic along his left Guderian authorized Boltenstern's men to use the Terespol Bridge per XII Army Corps' approval, and at 1530hrs ordered Nehring's fuel columns to move over 17th Panzer Division's assigned crossing to more quickly get the vital shipment to the front. Schweppenburg viewed Guderian as brave, ambitious, and genuine, and cared for the soldiers under his command, and that they in turn liked and trusted him. The (full) General, however, could be strict with officers and overly blunt, but proved to be a thorough, progressive instructor.

To avoid the queue of vehicles moving across the recently repaired Bulkowo Bridge at 1005hrs Model and a group of 3rd Panzer Division officers drove to nearby Zabinka before turning south along the loose surface, all-weather road to Chwedkowicze to regain Panzer Route 1. With 1st Motorized Reconnaissance and 3rd Motorcycle Battalions roving along his intended route and the surrounding dirt trails to gather intelligence, and provide a screen against enemy ground observation and early warning for the bulk of the division, at 1022hrs the latter secured the settlement of Zakrosnica (Zakrośnica). As evidence of the often confused state of combat operations 40 minutes later 5th Panzer Brigade headquarters received a report that the Soviets had used chemical weapons in its area, although this was soon proven false. As III./6th Panzer Regiment entered Kobryn what Soviet T-26 Model 1933 and 1939 single-turret tanks, and at least one twin-turret variety, that formed to resist were quickly shot up or abandoned along the town's well-worn cobblestone streets. Given the defender's maximum armour thickness of just 15mm even the 37mm guns on some of the older Panzer IIIs could achieve penetration out to a kilometre, given a stationary target and perhaps a few initial ranging rounds. To eliminate Soviet machine-gun fire from several of the surrounding buildings, with their pale-yellow, salmon, and green paint schemes, German tankers returned high-explosive rounds, which eliminated the resistance and assisted rather vulnerable motorcycle infantry in rushing through the town to secure the Dnepr–Bug Canal crossing. Although a few German vehicles were lost, III./6th Panzer Regiment was soon heading north-east of Kobryn past abandoned or destroyed enemy weapons, vehicles, and equipment littering the road and berms to Bereza Kartuska.

Much like Guderian, Model was constantly on the front line orchestrating his command. By noon 3rd Motorcycle Battalion had pushed to Buchowicze and while no enemy was encountered the formation captured a considerable amount of abandoned war materiel. With 3rd Panzer Division now beyond Kobryn at about 1500hrs 35th Panzer Regiment (4 PD) moved into the area and followed in Model's wake. Around a soon-to-be toppled statue of Lenin that had been erected after the Soviets occupied Eastern Poland in 1939 several T-26s remained abandoned or knocked out in the town's central Liberty Square. Along the way several captured Soviet-made Ford lorries and vehicle tyres were soon put into service.[20] Further to the rear captured Soviet personnel were being collected at Miedna, among other places, until Second Panzer Group completed its crossing of the River Bug and the prisoners could be sent to more secure locations well to the west.[21]

At 1400hrs advanced elements of 3rd Panzer Division reached Minki, some 70km from where they started the day at Bulkowo, while nearly 2 hours later I./6th Panzer Regiment suddenly encountered Soviet T-26s that emerged from a wooded area at Buchowicze. Having led the battalion since the Polish Campaign, Major Gustav-Albrecht Schmidt-Ott was undoubtedly familiar with his command and its role, as he immediately led it in an indirect attack that according to German sources resulted in thirty-six enemy tanks being knocked out. Of these First Lieutenant Ernst-Georg Buchterkirch's 2./6th Panzer Regiment was credited with defeating a dozen; a successful action added to others around this time that cumulatively earned him the oak leaves for his Knight's Cross. By 1600hrs 3rd Panzer Division's vanguard reached Bereza Kartuska on the railway line to Minsk where it eliminated resistance before its 6th Panzer Regiment closed up and in the process freed recently captured soldiers from 4th Panzer Division. By additionally securing the bridge over the River Jasiolda the Germans could continue using Panzer Route 1 through what was a lengthy woodland stretch suited for enemy ambushes and close fighting that negated the standoff strength of tanks. Unable to maintain their increasingly exposed positions, 22nd Tank Division and a detachment from 6th Rifle Division departed from north of Kobryn for Imienin, where Luftwaffe support of the German ground effort to capture its airfield resulted in several Soviet tanks being destroyed and numerous casualties.[22] Considering the speed of the German armoured advance, the Soviet Fourth Army commander's headquarters at Kobryn was captured soon after its abrupt abandonment and with it valuable documents and other, often time-sensitive intelligence, given changing battlefield conditions. 42nd Rifle Division followed suit having moved through Stryhowo, while some 30km to the south-west 75th Rifle Division, its 34th Infantry and 68th Artillery Regiments fighting to break from encirclement, finally began pulling out of the Maloryta area. While the use of Luftwaffe parachute and glider forces (*Fallschirmjäger*) provided a highly-trained and motivated asset in securing the many river crossings in the West, and seemed eminently suited to repeating their performance in the East, the high casualties suffered in capturing the island of Crete the previous month dissuaded their further use as an airborne spear tip.

Much as how the Polesie Marshes physically separated Army Group Centre and South, the sparsely populated Pogonia and adjacent swamps through which the River Jasiolda flowed largely kept XXIV Motorized Army Corps from its 1st Cavalry Division to the south as it moved through Dywin. Not far down Panzer Route 1 and the Kobryn–Pinsk road Red Army remnants again attempted to create blocking positions ahead of the German advance. Indicative of the difficulty of organizing such actions XIV Mechanized Corps' 20th Motorcycle Regiment near Antopol was reportedly unable to halt their retreating comrades and senior Soviet officers needed to settle for one further back at Drohiczyn. Other passing motor vehicles and artillery were redirected towards Bereza Kartuska's defence.[23]

Maintaining Model's rapid advance, Major Fritz Beigel's 39th Motorized Engineer and 3rd Motorcycle Battalions continued to scout ahead of the main body. What sporadic, and occasionally spirited Soviet resistance that sprang up was soon rebuffed, dispersed, or eliminated, as these German vanguards approached Byten (Byteń), some 105km north-east of Kobryn, and near where Panzer Route 1 deviated from the road to Baranowicze for Slutsk. Where their Western adversaries tended to surrender when confronted with an unwinnable position, Soviet soldiers often fought on; much to their adversary's consternation and anger that only added to the reciprocity of violence. Many Red Army soldiers that had become isolated, unable to continue the fight, or were simply looking to remove themselves from the conflict often melted into less accessible regions to become 'civilians'.

With 4th Panzer Division having pushed through frontier wilderness roads to reach Kobryn the formation's Ib (2nd General Staff Officer), being responsible for rear-area services and logistics matters, relocated to the town at 1900hrs to coordinate activities for the division, such as traffic prioritization and movement, casualty removal, and even antiaircraft defences. Much as 29th Motorized Infantry Division had moved up behind Lemelsen's armoured spearheads, 10th Motorized Infantry Division did the same for Schweppenburg's to provide critical, mobile infantry. Forced from the Kobryn area, what remained of the Soviet 6th Rifle Division that had escaped encirclement at the Brest fortress had been split into ad hoc groups respectively withdrawing along Panzer Route 1 towards Bereza Kartuska and due east for Pinsk.[24] On abandoning Kobryn, Soviet forces blew up much of their fuel depot to deny the valuable asset to the enemy. With German fuel lorries having struggled to provide replenishment to increasingly distant spearheads at about 2200hrs on 23 June 4th Panzer Division elements in Kobryn fortuitously found ample petrol supplies that the rapidly withdrawing enemy had failed to destroy.

Weakened and lacking sufficient cohesion to effectively defend its newest positions the Soviet Fourth Army wavered and continued its retreat. Prior to pulling out and heading towards Slonim (Słonim) its 30th Tank Division refuelled at the district warehouse at Oranczyce (Orańczyce) before blowing it up.²⁵ The Germans had been able to destroy an artillery dump at the Bronna Gora (Góra) train depot, which further reduced available ammunition for the Soviets. Cut off from communication with its Fourth Army parent and forced to pull back through various farm trails and paths the increasingly fragmented Soviet 75th Rifle Division fought on in isolation. Having left the Kobryn area, remnants of the Soviet XIV Mechanized Corps and 42nd Rifle Division dispersed into the area between the Pogonia Swamp and the Dnepr–Bug Canal. By establishing a presence extending between Zaber and Suliczewo (Sulíczewo) and just west of Drohiczyn, the surrounding marshland and Jasiolda tributaries all but precluded conventional combat and would force the Germans to funnel their advance along the region's few suitable roads.

Just after 1900hrs forward detachments from 3rd Panzer Division reached the River Jasiolda, where Master Sergeant (*Oberfeldwebel*) Albert Blaich led his 12./6th Panzer Regiment to capture its bridge. Second Panzer Group's headquarters, 22km to the west, was relocating to Pruzana; its third location of the day.²⁶ Roughly 3 hours later the lead platoon of 7./6th Panzer Regiment under Second Lieutenant Karl Rühl secured an undamaged crossing over the River Hrywda, a tributary to the nearby River Szczara. With Blaich then gaining a crossing over the Szczara, both men received the Iron Cross, as did Beigel, for facilitating Schweppenburg's advance against often heavy resistance. Because the Brest–Baranowicze road transitioned to several kilometres of alternating 7m-wide causeways and bridges across the broad Szczara floodplain should these be destroyed the German advance would need to use the much less suitable dirt-road network around nearby Byten; given the extensive marshland to the south this precluded the movement of large, conventional forces. Considering Schweppenburg's rapid advance to date the next day's otherwise ambitious objectives of capturing Slutsk and Baranowicze seemed entirely plausible.

With XXXXVII Motorized Army Corps' lengthy columns still crossing the River Bug the reserve XXXXVI Motorized Army Corps continued to wait for its turn. Lean of build and sporting a dark, toothbrush moustache, its commander, Lieutenant General (*General der Panzertruppe*) Heinrich von Vietinghoff *genannt* Scheel, had been slated to command one of Operation Sea Lion's three invasion armies the previous September. While the majority of German forces were funnelled onto the few crossings to head east, returning transports occasionally needed to move in the opposite direction, which kept military police busy conducting traffic with their red/white control sticks and added to the difficulty of prioritizing and facilitating movement. With the respective Bug bridge officers having notified the reserve 10th Panzer Division's commander, Major General Ferdinand Schaal, that 17th and 18th Panzer Divisions would likely not complete their respective crossings until 24 June he proactively had his own traffic-control officers (*Straßenkommandaten*) move to the Bug's eastern bank to explore potential egress routes and his 49th Motorized Engineer Battalion to bring up its own bridge carriage to construct an additional crossing. Even after getting his formation across the river, however, the area's terrible traffic congestion continued for the foreseeable future.

Farthest ahead of any of Guderian's forces III./6th Panzer Regiment and 3rd Motorcycle Battalion had taken the Szczara Bridge just south of Byten, and at the start of 24 June 3rd Panzer Division had advanced an impressive 170km in 48 hours. At 0330hrs the formation set off once again, with 'Kampfgruppe Kleemann' as vanguard and II./75th Motorized Artillery Regiment immediately behind to provide a dozen 150mm field howitzers if needed. To be available to clear obstructions or construct crossings along Panzer Route 1 at 0500hrs Beigel set his engineer-based Kampfgruppe to the task, and address likely threats and contingencies as they arose.[27] Considering the rather narrow road on which most of the division moved, bridge construction columns were also positioned up front to provide an on-the-spot remedy for any destroyed river crossings encountered.

Soviet forces near the railway crossing south-west of Byten contested the German advance and light scout vehicles moved up to engage the threat. Red Army artillery struck the road and with no other acceptable options the panzern and motorcycle riflemen continued along their original route. In its continuing effort to conduct a fighting withdrawal from, while avoiding being cut-off, 22nd Tank Division fell back on Rozana (Rózana). Apparently, the Germans believed 6th and 42nd Rifle Divisions had ceased to be combat effective, and that 54th Tank Brigade (actually 22nd and 30th Tank Divisions) was fought down and dispersed by 24 June. To keep tabs on XXXXVII Motorized Army Corps' efforts and directly intervene to clear traffic bottlenecks, allocate resources, and sort out a myriad other issues as only the senior commander could Guderian drove along Panzer Route 2 towards Slonim to ascertain 17th Panzer Division's progress. With the retreating Soviets having destroyed the three road and two rail bridges over the Szczara, which bisected the town into east and west sections, Arnim was presented with conducting yet another opposed river crossing. To the south Major General Friedrich-Wilhelm von Löper's 10th Motorized Infantry Division convinced the Soviet 205th Motorized Division to fall back on Sielec and cross Panzer Route 1 near Bereza Kartuska for the relative safety of the Polesie Marshes. With German forces having penetrated into the rear of XXVIII Rifle Corps' remnants along the River Jasiolda at 1800hrs the Red Army formation dissolved eastward yet again to renew the fight, and passing infantrymen were frequently pulled from marching to help extract vehicles and carts that got stuck.[28]

To ease traffic congestion along Panzer Route 2 at about 1000hrs as elements of 18th Panzer Division reached Rozana they deviated slightly to the south before turning for Baranowicze along a generally parallel advance to the north-east. As an occupational hazard to operating near the front lines when Guderian passed Rozana those accompanying him used the command vehicle's machine gun to clear a path through an enemy infantry contingent that had moved into the area. As the alternate dirt roads slowed the formation's advance Lemelsen granted I./ and III./18th Panzer Regiments movement priority as they remained on the main highway behind 17th Panzer Division. Soon after the reinforced 88th Motorized Reconnaissance Battalion (18 PD) entered a badly bombed Slonim and secured the still intact, 160m bridge over the River Issa, near where it fed the Szczara. Still possessing air superiority, the Luftwaffe was largely free to repeatedly bomb Minsk during the day using groups of between eight and fifty aircraft, which caused large portions of the city's buildings and infrastructure to collapse into burning, smoking ruins. Included in the destruction the Western Front and Red Air Force headquarters buildings suffered direct hits.[29]

Frustrated at not inducing the Brest fighters to surrender, and having suffered considerable casualties in the process, the Austrian infantry and engineers of 45th Infantry Division fought cat-and-mouse actions through the facility's rubble, tunnels, and courtyards. With numerous shell holes cratering the surrounding area German movement near the fortress was slowed, and vehicles and carts that got stuck passing infantrymen were pulled from their marching to help extract them. In yet another effort to bring the fighting to a conclusion at 1130hrs German artillery hammered the citadel for 15 minutes, after which a shock force from I./133rd Infantry Regiment immediately rushed from their jump-off positions in the western fortification and into the residual smoke and rubble of the recently targeted sector. By the afternoon on 24 June 135th Infantry Regiment and II./133rd Infantry Regiment cleared the northern complex during which it freed recently captured German soldiers and reported accepting the surrender of 1,200 enemy fighters.[30] Having finally got Mortar III 'Odin' into action the previous day, on 24 June both weapon systems from 2./833rd Heavy Artillery Battalion fired into the Brest fortress where expending nearly all of the battery's thirty-six rounds the unit was removed back to Germany.[31]

Bereza Kartuska
255th and 267th Infantry Divisions (removed from XXIV Motorized Army Corps (24 June))

As was a common reallocation of assets to best deal with unfolding battlefield circumstances at 0940hrs on 24 June a portion of 53rd Motorized Rocket Launcher Regiment and a pair of M18 cannons from 604th Motorized Heavy 210mm Howitzer Battalion were reassigned from supporting 'Kampfgruppe Linnarz' to 394th Motorized Rifle Regiment. At 1000hrs a two-man Hs-126 reconnaissance aircraft from 10th Luftwaffe-Army Cooperation Staff (*Gruppenfliegerstab*) that had been allocated to Schweppenburg's command reported enemy forces were approaching Slutsk and that all bridges across the adjacent River Sluch' were intact. At 1145hrs 'Kampfgruppe Beigel' broke through to the nearby heights when at about noon aging Soviet, twin-engine SB bombers attacked 3rd Panzer Division. Soon after turning from Baranowicze for Slutsk, several of Model's tanks engaged enemy ground forces that included artillery support at Milowidy (Miłowidy). With the nearby Rivers Myszanka and Szczara having produced large stretches of sandy, soft terrain, another sunny and hot day meant vehicles could operate off-road with few restrictions. Under Lieutenant Colonel Oskar Munzel a Kampfgruppe around his II./6th Panzer Regiment continued along Panzer Route 1, when aerial reconnaissance reported on the Soviet Fourth Army's withdrawal and dispositions in his path. At midday a few companies from 394th Motorized Rifle Regiment moved up to support 'Kampfgruppe Linnarz' whose ammunition supply was getting low due to the difficulty of hauling supplies to the front line. Advance Supply Points were at least being established east of the Bug to improve the situation. After overcoming the Soviet force Lieutenant Colonel Werner von Lewinski ordered I./6th Panzer Battalion forward. At 1330hrs the tankers had taken Marynowo and the adjacent 30m-high hill that given the flat surrounding terrain provided an excellent platform from which to observe nearby enemy movements.[32]

Much as Kobryn served as a hub from which Panzer Route 1 ran to Minsk and another major road east to Pinsk, 5km north of Iwacewicze a highway to Slutsk offered XXIV Motorized Army Corps an additional option eastward.[33] Considering Second Panzer Group's great reliance on its two panzer routes, Second Air Force's (*Luftflotte 2*) 11th Antiaircraft Regiment allocated assets at critical locations along the way to protect key bridges. With German rail gauge conversion progressing slowly compared with ground operations these roads not only gave Guderian the opportunity to maintain a high battlefield tempo, but helped reduce traffic congestion. While rail car bogies could be converted, those on a locomotive remained fixed, which meant their operation was considerably constrained under German management. With such a large expanse of territory and changing political and economic considerations over the last few decades low-capacity, narrow-gauge supplementary tracks often appeared haphazardly placed and lacked uniformity; something the new owners would quickly try to rectify.[34]

Although forward Red Air Force assets had been savaged over the last two days, aircraft from further afield made sporadic appearances against Guderian's command, and on more than a few occasions downed German aircraft. As part of their attacks Soviet bombers typically flew in unwavering, easy-to-target formations, often without fighter support, and suffered accordingly. Enemy aircraft similarly struck near Model's command post at Niedzwiedzica, which at 1445hrs relocated to the high ground at Smolicze. The afternoon was no less active for Soviet planes attempting to disrupt the German advance. At 1725hrs half a kilometre north-west of Luka (Łuka) 6./11th Antiaircraft Regiment engaged a trio of SB bombers at an altitude between 2,900m and 3,700m and forced the planes to emergency drop their payloads, during which two German ammunition lorries were damaged. Nearly 20 minutes later 7./11th Antiaircraft Regiment located 5km south-west of Kobryn engaged a single SB at 1,800m without visible success.[35]

Looking to cease its retreat, however uncertain the duration, the Soviet Tenth Army had engaged German tank units in the morning from the marshland at the confluence of the Rivers Szczara and Hrywda. During the early afternoon 6th Panzer Regiment's vanguard was forced to halt before the second crossing of the Szczara near Minicze, as the Soviets had blown it up. Although the river was no wider than 15m, it flowed through soft, heavily wooded terrain that would make establishing an alternative crossing difficult and time consuming. With vehicles and heavy weapons forced to halt before the gap in Panzer Route 1 follow-on traffic naturally backed up. To maintain optimal functioning during such lengthy periods of operations, considering the additional fatigue to which the tank drivers were subjected, when such pauses were called fellow crewmen typically covered his watch and tried to grant him as much rest as possible. At about 1500hrs Model and his operations officers met with Schweppenburg who ordered 'Kampfgruppe Linnarz' to secure a bridgehead over the River Szczara.[36] Some 30 minutes later the coarse, monocled Major General, who had been travelling with II./6th Panzer Regiment in a commandeered eight-wheeled radio scout car (*Funkspähwagen*) from 2./39th Motorized Signals Battalion, arrived at the section of high ground just before the trouble spot. Forced to halt due to the backed up traffic, soon after Model began to walk to his destination and an artillery round struck the vehicle and killed the crew, but left him unharmed.[37] Throughout the afternoon 1./394th Motorized Rifle Regiment and motorcycle infantry tried to cross the flood plain, but the soft ground and Red Army resistance from several pre-1939 Polish bunkers that had been built along the Belorussian border to counter a Soviet invasion now stymied German efforts. Several panzern that had moved up engaged individual structures to assist the more vulnerable infantry who needed to pass through flat, open terrain before re-entering the surrounding forests of tall Scotch pine trees.[38] Fighting had also broken out behind the German vanguard where scattered Soviet elements had taken positions in the wooded areas astride Panzer Route 1 to harass and ambush enemy targets of opportunity.

While German engineers worked to replace the Szczara Bridge's damaged centre span accompanying, dismounted infantry provided covering fire against an enemy force of regimental strength defending the far bank.[39] Such delays needed to be addressed quickly to keep the German advance moving and minimize remaining a stationary target; an often difficult task when predominantly relegated to a single road. Determining to settle the matter Buchterkirch led his 2./6th Panzer Regiment down the highway and halted at the western end of the still burning bridge. As his tanks engaged targets across the river he stepped out of his vehicle and gathered a few dozen riflemen to assault and cross the structure. Reinforcing success, a company of motorcycle infantry used pneumatic boats from the II./6th Panzer Regiment's engineer platoon to reach the far bank.

With the Germans having established a comparatively strong presence beyond the Szczara, some 6km to the east Soviet infantry and armoured elements counterattacked to dislodge the incursion in what devolved into a fierce fight astride Panzer Route 1 roughly between Rusinowicze and Niedzwiedzica.[40] A company of engineers, one of motorcycle infantry, an artillery battery, and an antiaircraft battery joined Munzel's II./6th Panzer Regiment to form a new advance detachment that pushed through the newest scattering of damaged, abandoned, and destroyed enemy vehicles and equipment. Having maintained a march discipline some 30km behind Model, 4th Panzer Division encountered rather minimal action and its ammunition supplies remained satisfactory. Due to the latter formation having seized a flour warehouse in Kobryn, once its fire was put out, its bakery company provided a welcome supply of fresh bread for its hard-marching Landsers.[41] Long a common sight for armies on the march, herds of cattle, and also sheep, goats, pigs, and chickens, followed to the rear as self-transporting food.

Still subordinated to Second Panzer Group, 255th Infantry Division continued to operate well to the west around Maloryta as it worked to constrict and eliminate 75th Rifle Division's frustrating defence. During 23 June its 475th Infantry Regiment and 465th Infantry Regiment (minus one battalion) respectively blocked the crossroads about 12km north-east of the woodland village, while 267th Infantry Division cleared the forests along the Rogozno–Miedna line. 467th Infantry Regiment reached the wooded area 4km kilometres southwest of Piszcza, with 497th Infantry Regiment having entered Tomaszowka. 1st Cavalry Division moved eastward towards Pinsk along a crushed rock chaussée (paved road), with occasional damaged sections that required minimal detours. Although its structural width was a consistent 8m, its paved areas varied between just over 2–5m, with sections near Kobryn topping out at 6m. All of the crossings were well-constructed and capable of withstanding heavy vehicle traffic. NKVD personnel manned protective trenches along the route and acted as bridge guards, often alongside the structures' keepers. With both 255th and 267th Infantry Divisions now well behind the front lines and no longer practically controlled they were subsequently removed from XXIV Motorized Army Corps.

Slonim Tank Battle

Having arrived west of Slonim, an unscathed Guderian met with Arnim and Lemelsen before heading out to get a firsthand understanding of the battlefield situation confronting XXXXVII Motorized Army Corps. After visiting the nearby town at about 1530hrs the (full) General set off in a Panzer IV to quickly cross an active sector to reach 18th Panzer Division to order Nehring to push on towards Baranowicze. Managing to avoid yet another encounter with enemy infantry gathering in the Slonim area, Guderian was next driven to his command post at 2015hrs where the day's intelligence and communications reports indicated the foot-bound XII Army Corps had managed a sufficiently rapid advance to maintain a tenuous connection with Second Panzer Group's armoured and motorized spearheads. With Hoth's Third Panzer Group conducting similar high-tempo combat operations to the north the enemy's Third and Tenth Armies were steadily flanked and encircled between Bialystok and Minsk. As the Red Army pressure for self preservation increased, so did their efforts to break out. Always an educated gamble to ensure an economy of force was maintained to prioritize resources and enable the creation of reserves, with Guderian's resolve to strike straight for Moscow unchanged, he continued to advance with the majority of his command, while keeping a portion on cordon duty to adhere to Hitler's desire to direct sizeable German forces inward to ensure the surrounded enemy's destruction before moving on. Having achieved dramatic success conducting headlong rushes during the 1939 Polish Campaign and his dash to the English Channel nearly a year later, deviation from this high-risk/high-reward mindset was to Second Panzer Group's commander an act that threatened to relinquish the operational momentum generated and give the enemy time to organize and strengthen their defences further east. Understanding that the all-arms, fast-moving panzer divisions' greatest strength was running roughshod through the enemy's rear areas, with their soft, but critical command, control, and communications assets OKH managed to convince the Führer to adhere to the original plan.

Only now beginning to cross the River Bug at noon on 24 June using the bridge that had been constructed just downstream from Brest, 29th Motorized Reconnaissance and Motorcycle Battalions had led their parent formation towards Czarnawczyce. At the Widomla crossroads it was necessary to give priority to 18th Panzer Division's rear elements and then allow Boltenstern's command to follow in order to prevent the respective columns from mingling on Panzer Route 2; although the option to insert units into any gaps was up to Nehring. At 1705hrs, 18th Panzer Division engaged in a fierce fight near Slonim that included Soviet armour. Taking into account the importance of plugging the gap between 17th Panzer Division and Kluge's lead infantry formations, and preventing a major Soviet breakout into Second Panzer Group's northern flank, brief consideration was given to redirecting 4th Panzer Division to the task.

With 29th Motorized Infantry Division finally moving beyond the Bug in strength and would soon be available for the task, sending Langermann across most of Second Panzer Group's advance axis was unnecessary. On reaching Pruzana 29th Reconnaissance Battalion deviated from Panzer Route 2 and onto secondary roads through the Jasiolda marshland to reach Lyskow (Łysków) at 2230hrs and develop a line to Nowy Dwor (Nowy Dwór) to prevent Soviet forces from breaking out behind XXXXVII Motorized Army Corps's armoured spearheads. During the night of 24/25 June a Soviet column that included women and children attempted to escape encirclement and ran into 18th Panzer Division's forward command post near Slonim. Like any German position that halted in the field for even brief periods, nearby foliage was cut down and placed on and around vehicles and equipment to supplement what was already affixed and camouflage-patterned tents and coverings. A harrowing, night-long fight ensued around the suddenly isolated division staff. Although Nehring was away with his reconnaissance elements, by morning the Germans had cleared up the trouble.[42]

With the last of 17th and 18th Panzer Divisions finally having moved off into enemy territory, at 1400hrs XXXXVI Motorized Army Corps commander, Vietinghoff, ordered Schaal to relocate his forward command post from Siedlce to Widomla in preparation for 10th Panzer Division's crossing. With a proper bridge capable of supporting heavy traffic flows at Legi nearly complete 17th Panzer Division dismantled its 16-tonne pontoon bridge for reuse in crossing the Szczara near Slonim. While motorized reconnaissance elements of XII Army Corps reached an area upriver at 2300hrs the sizeable number of Soviet Third and Tenth Army forces that had slipped to the east prompted Bock to have Hoth and Guderian extend their still forming pocket centered around Bialystok to encompass Minsk as well. By day's end XXXXVII Motorized Army Corps' vanguard occupied positions about 30km east of Slonim, while that of XXIV Motorized Army Corps had crossed Eastern Poland to stand before the pre-1939 border with Belorussian SSR (Soviet Socialist Republic). With ground-based POL shipments continuing to have difficulty providing regular resupply supplementing Luftwaffe Ju-52/3m ('tri-motor') transports were used to fly them ahead, such as to the grass airfield just north of Pruzana between 25 and 28 June 1941.

Approaching Slutsk

During the morning of 25 June 3rd Panzer Division's forward elements continued their advance into Belorussia. At 0700hrs Schweppenburg, a cultivated, but shrewd commander, ordered Model to momentarily cease his attack towards Slutsk, as the situation to his north remained unclear. Having penetrated the enemy line between Lyadno and Gulevichi, just an hour later the Soviet 30th Motorized Rifle Regiment (30 TD) sacrificially threw itself into blocking

Panzer Route 1 for the next 7 hours. With only 18th Panzer Division moving on Baranowicze, where four Soviet rifle divisions had been identified, assistance was needed.[43] While Model's forward combat elements used the time to refuel and rearm a portion of 3rd Panzer Division was redirected northward to assist in removing the threat by rolling up its left flank near Lesna.[44] With what promised to be another long, hot day of marching and fighting 1st Motorized Reconnaissance Battalion (3PD) was soon sent north to reconnoitre Model's open left flank. With 31st Infantry Division having marched and fought for 100km through Tewle and Linowo to reach the River Jasiolda on 25 June its motorized units continued to press ahead. To assist Model's reconnaissance elements a German antitank platoon from Stolzmann's vanguard III./17th Infantry Regiment (31 ID) reported an absence of enemy forces, save for around the Lesna rail depot; a location pre-war German intelligence determined was the headquarters of the Soviet Western District.

4th Panzer Division, having earlier pushed through Kobryn, encountered a comparably light resistance, aside from regular harassment from Soviet aircraft. Out ahead of its parent formation by 0700hrs 35th Panzer Regiment (4 PD) was crossing the River Szczara near Iwacewicze, while 3./49th Panzerjäger Battalion had been tasked with assisting the division's motorcycle personnel defending Kosow. During the late afternoon fighting against what included Red Army armour and infantry a cluster of these soldiers attempted to outflank the German gunners; even going so far as to feign surrender under a white flag. A battalion detachment that included Schwarz's antitank platoon arrived just in time to halt the enemy attack. Further German assistance arrived north of Hoszczewo, and the Soviets soon vacated the area. Eager to get into the fight for now the young Bavarians had to be content with continuing behind Model; an easy trail to follow given the sights and smells of dead horses and enemy personnel, and charred, wrecked, and abandoned vehicles, arms, and equipment. Having been caught behind the fast-moving front line, clusters of Soviet soldiers that had abandoned heavier weapons continued to harass the German advance, as did swarms of biting gnats and mosquitoes. All that remained of many of the homes the retreating Red Army had burned to deny their use to the enemy, or were destroyed during fighting or bombings, were blackened chimneys. Their ethnic Belorussian owners, having suffered as an Orthodox minority subjected to 'Polonization' in the 1920s and 1930s, and later under Stalin's authority, during which his NKVD murdered tens of thousands of its clergy, intelligencia, and others, were now homeless or worse. For the passing Landsers subjected to Party propaganda designed to exploit often legitimate historic wrongs, and caricature and dehumanize the Eastern populations as an inoculation to conducting their war of annihilation feelings towards these frequently malnourished, bedraggled groups ranged from shock and pity to disgust and contempt.[45]

With German engineers having brought up a pair of 'K' variant, steel bridge spans and positioned them atop timber pilings and against the abutments of the damaged Szczara crossing, at 1100hrs the full force of Model's advance began anew. Nearby Filippovichi was in flames, and with the Soviet 55th Rifle Division elements active near Siniawka, 30th Motorized Rifle Regiment forced a brief delay against 3rd Panzer Division between Lyadno and Malyshevichi. To drive off at least one assault the towed 37mm PaK 35/36 flat trajectory guns from 1./543rd Panzerjäger Battalion were used to support I./394th Motorized Rifle Regiment. By 1500hrs German artillery, air support, and armour cleared Model's way forward, although his 1st Motorized Reconnaissance Battalion remained at the airfield just south-east of Baranowicze to secure it for Luftwaffe aircraft that would soon be relocating closer to the front. Such leapfrogging improved response times to assist situations on the ground and increased sorties. With his forward commands still operating relatively close to one another, earlier in the day Guderian made physical appearances at the headquarters of XII Army, XXIV Motorized Army Corps, and 4th Panzer Division before returning to his own that afternoon.[46] At 1900hrs the formation radioed for reinforcement from its parent formation, which then got XII Army Corps' approval to use Stolzmann's command. 17th Panzer Division was approaching the Baranowicze area along Panzer Route 2 and would soon be in position to bolster the German attack. Unable to coordinate an effective defence the Soviet 55th Rifle Division fell back a few kilometres to Semezhevo, while leaving a sprinkling of harassing forces along the enemy's advance, including snipers affixed high up in the trees.

At 0515hrs on 25 June a column of Organization Todt reported to 10th Panzer Division for the repair of the bridge paths at Legi. Under the Reich Minister for Armaments and Munitions, Doctor of Engineering Fritz Todt's civil/military engineering entity was known for constructing large-scale projects like the Autobahn and the West Wall. Possessing considerable resources and experience building combat and logistics related assets they were well suited for improving roads, railways, airfields, fortifications, and bridges beyond the remit or ability of the Army engineers.

Fight for Slonim

At 0315hrs on 25 June XXXXVII Motorized Army Corps ordered 29th Motorized Infantry Division to counter a broad, determined Soviet force looking to breakout along a Wolkowysk (Wołkowysk)–Slonim axis. 29th Reconnaissance and 29th Motorcycle Battalions subsequently skirted the River Zelwianka's right bank for Jeziernica and the high ground around Hill 214 and blocking the Zelwa–Slonim road. The bulk of the division soon moved through Rozana to take up observation and blocking positions west of the waterway. Due to the intervening floodplain's marshy terrain should a Soviet advance prove unstoppable Boltenstern's men could destroy the Zelwa Bridge and considerably hinder their breakout into XXXXVII Motorized Army Corps' vulnerable left flank. While Red Army infantry could directly cross the Zelwianka with some difficulty artillery, equipment, and vehicles would need to be abandoned or moved alternative routes several kilometres up and down river.[47] With Hoth's leading formations having reached the River Neman just 20km north-west of Wielka Wola, 29th Motorized Reconnaissance Battalion sent patrols to establish contact with Third Panzer Group. At 0645hrs 29th Motorized Infantry Division's Air Support Officer (*Fliegerverbindungsoffizier*; aka *Flivo*) reported to Second Panzer Group that reconnaissance aircraft from 31st Luftwaffe-Army Cooperation Staff reconnaissance had spotted enemy forces that had already moved into the area, as well as south-east of Slonim. Just over an hour later Guderian's Ia was notified that Ninth Army was hard pressed in combat and would temporarily assume a defensive posture while it consolidated its gains.[48] Given the possibility of containing and defeating the Soviet Third and Tenth Armies, and removing what was optimistically thought to be the primary impediment between Army Group Centre and Moscow, Bock determined to make every effort to defend the Slonim area.[49]

To provide the necessary command and control between air and ground entities Air Support Commanders (*Koluft*) were assigned to Army/Panzer Group and Army Group echelons to advise the respective headquarters on Luftwaffe issues and capabilities. For Second Panzer Group, Colonel Karl von Gerlach had held the position for the last three months and had authority over all Luftwaffe assets that had been attached to Guderian, including anti-aircraft, signal, and short-range reconnaissance. Reflecting the tactical and operational flexibility of their Army comrades, Luftwaffe higher commands dictated the goals of a mission, while lower echelons down to squadron and even flight level typically decided on what tactics, weapons, and formation sizes and compositions they would employ to best ensure success. Liaison Air Support Officers used specially trained Ground Control or Signal Liaison Officers at corps or division level who operated in an armoured vehicle near the targeted location.[50] As Second Panzer Group swept across Eastern Europe when a ground commander needed air support, the liaison officer passed the request to Second Air Force with the location and type of target, estimate of force required, and any expected opposition, while the initiating headquarters monitored the communications network.[51] Using code words across common radio frequencies to provide timely, direct air-ground communication and mission updates accuracy and awareness of fast-moving panzern was improved; an important benefit considering air recognition devices such as coloured panels, lights, flares, smoke, and small vehicle flags were often insufficient in friend/foe identification.[52] Communications (*Kurier*) Squadrons were also available to move messages and photographs around the combat zone, using radio, vehicles, and aircraft.[53]

At 1215hrs XXXXVII Motorized Army Corps headquarters telephoned that of its parent command that the enemy presence in its sector had been expelled and that Panzer Route 2 was again cleared and useable at least through the Slonim area. As the full weight of Second Panzer Group was now on the move its large size and rapid advance regularly overburdened Guderian's telephone and radio network. With upwards of 80 per cent of radio traffic focused on administrative matters messages could remain in the queue for up to 4 hours.[54] 18th Panzer Division sent its 101st Motorized Rifle Regiment through Slonim in preparation for an attack on Baranowicze, while to the west 29th Motorized Infantry Division captured Jeziernica at 1450hrs.

With the German Fourth and Ninth Armies having advanced sufficiently eastward to pinch off the Bialystok Pocket west of Minsk, Guderian focused on bagging another large haul of enemy men and materiel that encompassed the Belorussian capital, in accordance with Bock's order. At 1645hrs the general directed 18th and 3rd Panzer Divisions to respectively make for Baranowicze and Slutsk. Although this had the effect of dispersing forces the region's rudimentary road network would never support a greater concentration of Second Panzer Group even if its commander wanted it. At 1900hrs a Soviet attack in brigade strength, with supporting armour, crashed into a German Motorized battalion and knocked out five panzern at Kosow. Upset with what were instances of increasing violence during 25 June, Lemelsen protested to his officers about the 'senseless shootings of both prisoners-of-war and civilians'.[55] As with other armies German small-unit cohesion (*kleine Kampfgemeinschaft*) and mutual reliance on comrades provided an effective support mechanism; a dynamic critical to mentally and emotionally adjusting to the greater level of violence and vitriol than what was encountered in previous campaigns. Recruitment from defined military areas (*Wehrkreise*) throughout the Reich reinforced this bond by giving soldiers from the same formation a shared cultural framework. With the soldiers on the ground possessing limited battlefield visibility knowing what units operated on the flanks or in support could affect morale and resolve.

Continuing to provide protection along key points of the two vital panzer routes, elements of 11th Antiaircraft Regiment had mixed results against Soviet aircraft entering their respective sectors. At Czemioly (Czemioły), for example, just before 0900hrs on 25 June 6th Antiaircraft Company failed to hit any of the six enemy SB bombers (2,500m altitude), while at Bereza Kartuska, just north of where 34th Infantry Division had established a presence, 8th Antiaircraft Company similarly had no luck in hitting these Soviet planes that had subsequently ascended to 2,950m. 9th Antiaircraft Company 2 hours later also unsuccessfully engaged SB bombers (1,800m) over the Szczara near Minicze, but 6th Antiaircraft Company finally brought down a lone SB at 2,700m.[56]

While the Iwacewicze–Telechany road remained in its original sandy state Soviet forces that had occupied the area in 1939 improved the remaining stretch to Pinsk into a more stable dirt alternative that was suitable for heavy, year-round vehicular traffic. With 10th Motorized Infantry and 1st Cavalry Divisions respectively advancing from the north and west into the soft, low-lying country along the Polesie Marshes' periphery, what remained of the Soviet 6th and 42nd Rifle Divisions continued to withdraw; the former for the Oginskiego Canal, Lohiszyn, and Pinsk and the latter, the Zaozer'ye area. Seemingly anachronistic in a modern battlefield considering the previous world war had shown the virtual criminality of committing horse formations in a direct combat role, the light, mobile German horsemen were well suited to the uncultivated wilderness in which they now operated.

With German leadership still widely believing that the majority of Soviet forces were relatively close to their western frontier it was considered wise to first seal and eliminate the Minsk Pocket and prevent the escape of enemy men and resources that could continue the fight before renewing a unified eastern advance axis. During the latter phase XXXXVII Motorized Army Corps was to then strike eastward to the River Dnepr to secure the chalk and phosphorite mines at nearby Mogilev and Orsha, while along the formation's left flank Hoth's Third Panzer Group would advance on Polatsk and Vitebsk, some 200km north-east of Minsk, to maintain contact with Ninth Army and prepare for its next, and hopefully last, great encirclement around Smolensk. With the German effort to re-gauge Soviet rail lines still far to the rear and road- and air-supplied logistics slow, inconsistent, and hard on vehicles and fuel, time was also spent stockpiling the necessary ammunition, replacement parts, food, and other resources necessary to renew a sustained offensive. Considering the new and growing threat of Soviet forces moving from the east, the resulting pause was to be as brief as possible to avoid relinquishing operational momentum, which had a collective way of correcting localized battlefield setbacks.[57]

Chapter 3

Closing the Minsk Pocket, 26 June–1 July 1941

XII Army Corps (31st, 34th, and 45th Infantry Divisions) (Removed from Second Panzer Group (26 June))

With Second Panzer Group's lead armoured elements having advanced nearly 300km into Soviet-annexed Eastern Poland over the last four days early on 26 June Model's 3rd Panzer Division was just shy of the pre-1939 Belorussian border. At 0300hrs elements of its 5th Panzer Brigade reported engaging in a fierce fight along Panzer Route 1 just across the border where the River Moroch' split into several channels to the north. To keep the offensive moving his vanguard pushed through the encounter and within 2 hours rolled into Lyadno. To assist in protecting the more important bridges, as German formations moved across they were to respectively deploy a portion of their antitank assets for overwatch. Although Panzer Route 1 provided the area's optimal Rollbahn, which on the approach to Slutsk comprised easily traversed, compacted gravel, the necessity to use less desirable alternative roads as detours to mitigate traffic congestion or outmanoeuvre enemy forces reciprocally risked relinquishing what hard-won momentum had been achieved. As part of their fighting withdrawal Soviet forces were only too happy to exploit such enemy delays to orchestrate counterattacks and strengthen their successive fallback positions. With tens of thousands of Red Army having been cut off or otherwise forced from their conventional combat roles due to the enemy advance those desiring to avoid the risks or shame of surrender often gravitated to the less acessible woodland and swamps throughout German-controlled rear areas.[1]

To ascertain the Soviet XXXXVII Rifle Corps' strength along his 90km left flank Model ordered 1st Motorized Reconnaissance Battalion to work with a company from 543rd Panzerjäger Battalion to scout and hold the loose surface route through nearby Kleck up to around Nieswiez (Nieśwież). Given the underdeveloped border area, these two towns provided important road hubs near the Baranowicze–Slutsk rail line that would soon be integrated into the German logistics and communications network once the front moved through. With dirt trails extending from Nieswiez north to the Baranowicze–Minsk highway and east to what became an improved, loose surface road to Osipovichi they offered 3rd Panzer Division, and subsequent formations, additional lines of communication, movement, and resupply. Before dawn on 26 June elements of 4th Panzer Division performed similar, mixed-group scouting, with a company from each of I./35th Panzer Regiment, and 34th Motorcycle and 49th Antitank Battalions deviating from Panzer Route 1 at Milowidy for Lesna. En route the Kampfgruppe encountered 1./201st Assault Gun Battalion and motorcyclists from Stolzmann's advance detachment that recently moved into the area just south of the targeted village. Just after 0800hrs the small force moved beyond Tartak towards the onrushing 18th Panzer Division to seal off enemy forces lingering to the south-west. During the late afternoon II./35th Panzer Regiment moved north to help clear the area around the Baranowicze airfield.[2] Ahead of the seemingly inexorable German advance Red Army rear area personnel and civilians increasingly succumbed to panic and rumour based on ignorance of the actual status and proximity of combat operations. Indicative of collective fear, as the Germans approached the border village of Filippovichi, Soviet government and military personnel essentially abandoned Bobruysk and most of the town's food warehouses, even though the city was more than 150km to the east.[3]

At 0635hrs a battery from I./53rd Motorized Rocket Launcher Regiment was subordinated to 'Kampfgruppe Linnarz' to operate with I./394th Motorized Rifle Regiment. Although the six, tube-launched weapon systems lacked the accuracy of traditional artillery the physical and psychological effect on those receiving a concentrated barrage of up to three-dozen, 150mm high-explosive rockets was considerable. With their 2.5kg (TNT) warheads located at their rear the rocket's oxygen robbing blast occurred above ground to maximize damage, while leaving a comparatively shallow crater. As Model's vanguard approached Slutsk at 0850hrs on 26 June it reported sighting twenty Soviet tanks and several artillery pieces already in firing positions, as well as enemy motorized columns moving north from the town and slower horse-drawn carts heading in the opposite direction.[4] As German infantry and light-skinned vehicles passed along the flat, mostly open terrain between the 1939 Polish border and Slutsk bypassed Red Army snipers caused casualties and sufficient dread to make the oncoming enemy Landsers feel as if the war extended well back of the front line.

While most Landsers viewed enemy tactics that included fighting on after feigning surrender or injury, mutilating and killing captured German soldiers, and blending with the civilian population with considerable disdain as something unsportsmanlike, the resulting uncertainty, fatigue, and fear was a historical constant for a conventional force. Frustrated on the battlefield and caught between the onrushing German Army and their own Commissars and NKVD personnel who were all too eager to motivate with a bullet, or at least its threat, Soviet soldiers were frequently placed in situations where they felt it necessary to fight beyond any hope of success. Red Army officers were often similarly set

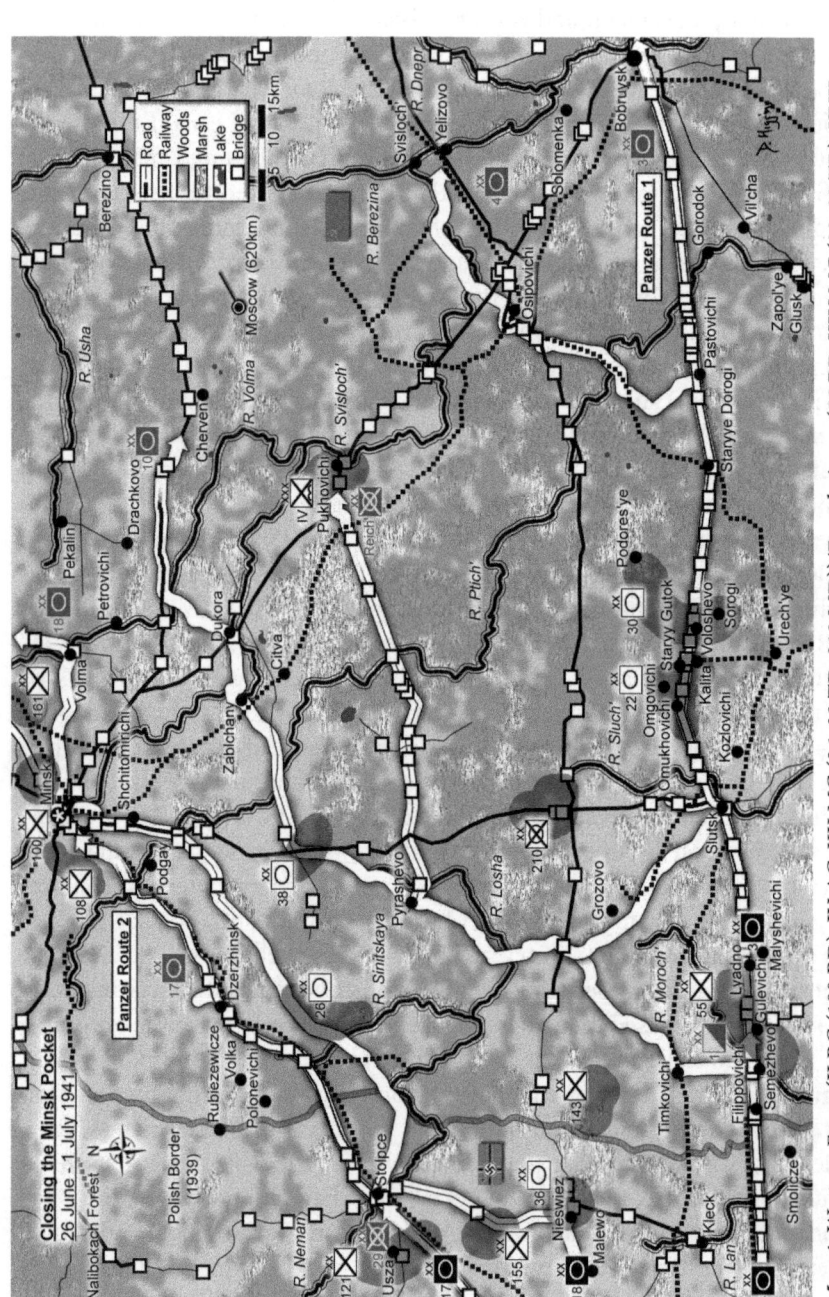

Map 4. Western Front (II RC (100 RD), IV AC, XX MC (26, 38 TD, 210 MD)/Fourth Army (55 RD, XIV MC (22, 30 TD), XVII MC (36 TD), XXXXVII RC (143 RD)); Tenth Army (155 RD); Thirteenth Army (121 RD, XXI RC (161 RD), XXXXIV RC (108 RD)). TsAMO, f.361, op.6079, d.26.

up for failure given the lack of sufficient tactical and operational communications, under-trained personnel, and a military system based on rigid, centralized control hierarchy that stifled on-the-spot initiative. Apprehension, confusion, mortal fear, and fatigue took a physical, emotional, mental, and spiritual toll and promoted an escalating cycle of reciprocity that was difficult to control or contain once unleashed.

As 3rd Panzer Division approached Slutsk they encountered reinforced concrete gun, antitank, and machine-gun casemates; observation posts, caponiers, and related fortifications that delineated this stretch of the pre-1939 Soviet Russian border.[5] Organized into independent clusters intended to block important thoroughfares, rather than along a shallow, linear string, many of the structures possessed side-facing firing points that allowed mutually supporting crossfire. Although several were occupied, many were in a neglected state, missing heavier weapons, and overgrown with vegetation. Continuing with their fighting withdrawal across Eastern Poland the fragmenting XXVIII Rifle Corps (6 RD, 42 RD) gravitated towards helping form a defensive line along the River Sluch'. To the south XIV Mechanized Corps approached the end of its combat effectiveness on approaching the southern approaches to Slutsk beyond Kozlovichi.[6] Elements of 30th Tank Division occupied second echelon positions around Podores'ye, Voloshevo, and Sorogi, while part of 55th Rifle Division organized at Urech'ye. Four more companies from XIV Mechanized Corps, including elements from 22nd Tank Division, filled in the line between Omukhovichi and Kalita. Between 0900 and 1030hrs 'Kampfgruppe Linnarz' fought 30th Motorized Rifle Regiment (30 TD), which because of its parent's depleted state had been subordinated to 55th Rifle Division.[7]

As part of his ongoing effort to reconnoitre the areas through which 3rd Panzer Division operated a reinforced platoon from 3rd Motorcycle Battalion had travelled over a myriad dirt farm and village paths beyond Timkovichi to check the left flank, but found no enemy. Returning from their excursion near Baranowicze, parts of 1st Motorized Reconnaissance Battalion similarly found no threats along the River Lan near Kleck, although at 1345hrs the unit reported capturing about 400 prisoners and sighting a Soviet armoured car scouting along the road from Nieswiez towards Malewo. As Model's third march column, 'Kampfgruppe Kleemann', approached the metre-deep River Szczara at 1535hrs Soviet aircraft twice attacked near the crossing. Considering what few aerial assets the Red Air Force could commit to the combat zone in the immediate aftermath of *Barbarossatag*, such actions were infrequent and typically caused minimal damage. With the Luftwaffe operating with near impunity its bombers frequently flew sorties unaccosted from the air, which freed fighters from accompanying their slower, more vulnerable comrades to concentrate on other tasks, such as supporting ground operations. As the Germans advanced ever eastward and had to contend with progressively strained logistics, battlefield attrition, and a Reich that had yet to transition to a war footing or prepare for a potentially lengthy fight, any advantage was welcomed.[8] During the afternoon one of the many German aerial reconnaissance flights over XXIV Motorized Army Corps' sector reported the bridges along Panzer Route 1 east of Slutsk appeared to be intact, although Soviet tanks had been sighted south of Milowidy, well to Model's rear.

At 1800hrs Schweppenburg met with Model to discuss forthcoming military operations, including that 3rd Panzer Division needed to operate in tighter combat formations and lingering enemy forces between Siniawka and Slutsk needed to be cleaned up. At 1830hrs Guderian ordered that in addition to Bobruysk, 3rd Panzer Division was to capture Rogachev to ensure at least two major Dnepr crossing sites would be available for XXIV Motorized Army Corps. Until 79th Motorized Engineer Battalion (4 PD) erected a crossing over the Szczara sometime the next morning, at 1850hrs on 26 June 3rd Rifle Brigade detoured onto secondary trails to ford the waterway and negotiate the surrounding marshland. In an apparent effort to facilitate the advance rate of its march columns 4th Panzer Division refrained from leaving the left side of Panzer Route 1 clear for supply transports.[9]

Unwilling to dally in the Slonim sector where frequently desperate Soviet efforts to force a breakout continued, and instead leave such blocking actions to follow-on infantry, at 0750hrs Guderian went to 17th Panzer Division to order Arnim to move directly on Stolpce (Stołpce).[10] After wirelessly contacting XXIV Motorized Army Corps to check on the progress of his left wing before Baranowicze at 0900hrs he went to 18th Panzer Division's headquarters at Lesna (Leśna) where he found Lemelsen and Nehring in attendance. The latter formation's forward elements had been subjected to heavy enemy artillery and encountered well-developed defensive positions on approaching the Iwacewicze–Baranowicze road. During the late afternoon 18th Panzer Regiment was allocated to eliminate the resistance, which included fighting in the forested area around Tartak, and open the main route to Minsk, but Soviet antitank guns knocked out eight panzern from I./18th Panzer Regiment and momentarily forced the unit back.[11] Unable to stand up to 101st Rifle Regiment's push west of Baranowicze and Lemelsen's forces from the south the Red Army defenders began disengaging to fall back to the north-east. 52nd Rifle Regiment awaited relief from its security duties near Slonim, and served as part of Lemelsen's cordon, while much of the remainder of 18th Panzer Division deviated from Panzer Route 2 to take secondary roads leading to Nieswiez and west of Kleck.

After pushing through Baranowicze 17th Panzer Division fought to gain Stolpce during which its distinguished, aristocratic leader was badly wounded. While Arnim officially remained division head, Brigadier Johannes Streich was brought in as his temporary replacement. A skilled armour commander in his own right the latter had been in OKH Leaders Reserve (*Führerreserve*) since

May 1941 after the commander of the recently activated Africa Corps, Major General Erwin Rommel, had replaced him for what he believed was an overly cautious effort that failed to capture the important Libyan port of Tobruk. Now, with Hoth just 29km north of Minsk, at 1430hrs Bock ordered Guderian to direct XXXXVII Motorized Army Corps inward and towards the city to ensure the pocket's southern edge was sufficiently strong to contain as many of the trapped enemy forces as possible. Although the field marshal espoused expanding his encirclement even further to include Smolensk, OKH was loathe to accept the unnecessary gamble given the risk of overextending Army Group Centre's resources. Although Bock also briefly considered redirecting Hoth further north for Polotsk, the move would disperse his panzer groups to continue their respective fights independently.[12] Hedging his bets on the matter, in far-off Berlin Goebbels strenuously tried to prevent speculated campaign end dates to better trumpet success when it appeared imminent.

29th Motorized Infantry Division (removed from XXXXVII Motorized Army Corps (27 June))

During the night of 26/27 June the Germans attacked XXVIII Rifle Corps' positions and by sunrise had taken the northern part of Slutsk. Throughout the morning XIV Mechanized Corps defended its sector along the Sluch' using an advanced detachment, a few rifle companies, five guns, and two armoured cars providing a degree of resistance from Panzer Route 1 to the Slutsk–Urech'ye rail line.[13] At 1300hrs on 27 June 'Kampfgruppe Linnarz' had its I./6th Panzer Regiment push through a recently secured Slutsk, much of whose centre had been turned into smouldering ruins after repeated Luftwaffe bombing since the conflict's beginning. With Soviet authorities having commandeered what working vehicles remained in the town during their exits, as was a common sight in wartime the exodus of civilian residents vacated the area largely on foot. To ensure the smooth flow of follow-on German forces I./394th Motorized Rifle Regiment was tasked with clearing the area of any lingering enemy forces. On their way out the Soviets blew up both of the town's bridges over the River Sluch', which being little more than 10m wide would present minimal difficulty for engineers to construct a replacement. To support Model's advance through the urban environment I./75th Motorized Artillery Regiment moved with his lead elements, while II. Artillery Battalion remained near Slutsk.

Having stubbornly defended its positions around Maloryta for the last five days and unlikely to be reinforced or resupplied, 75th Rifle Division's position had finally become untenable, as the German 267th and 255th Infantry Divisions had effectively surrounded the battered irritant. Low on ammunition for the few artillery pieces they still possessed and down to some 3,000 soldiers capable of further resistance, the command split into 3 groups to find viable extraction routes through the extensive swampland. One set off to the south-east and the Wlodawa–Kobryn road just south of Maloryta, while another moved for Mokrany.[14] The third group made for Lukowo (Łukowo) where it encountered entrenched German forces, with mortar support, although the rounds often sank into the area's soft, sandy terrain that degraded their blast effectiveness. Fighting through what degenerated into close combat, this final Soviet contingent forced a gap. The left-hand grouping similarly created an opening enabling the two forces to eventually merge outside of the snare. With much of the region unsuited for what Red Army vehicles still had fuel larger, towed weapon systems and equipment needed to be abandoned; after being disabled if circumstances permitted. Considering strong German forces blocking the road to Kobryn, the remnants of 75th Rifle Division turned eastward to cross the nearby Ukrainian SSR border and over extensive swampland to reach Samary, and their first supply of food and ammunition since hostilities began. Off to the north-east the German 10th Motorized Infantry and 1st Cavalry Divisions were manoeuvring to trap elements of 205th Motorized, and 6th and 42nd Rifle Divisions as they fell back on Pinsk.[15]

Since XXXXVII and XXIV Motorized Army Corps' spearheads were now well east of not only Fourth Army's infantry formations, but also a large number of bypassed Soviet forces, gaps in the front line, between German formations, and even their respective march columns allowed Red Army forces to slip encirclement to continue the fight, though usually without more than small arms. To commanders like Kluge, such instances served to reinforce their stance that containing and defeating the tens of thousands of increasingly trapped enemy personnel and capturing the mountains of materiel from Western Front were paramount and a prerequisite for easing any subsequent drive to and beyond the River Dnepr. For Guderian, as well as Halder and Hoth, the push for Moscow remained the primary focus and any inability to completely eliminate these enemy formations was offset by the damage and confusion armoured and motorized divisions would cause roaming through the enemy's operational rear areas. Although Luftwaffe aircraft and German infantry exacted heavy casualties along Second Panzer Group's advance axis, it also incentivised many Soviet soldiers into less accessible forested areas. To help root them out before they could reorganize 31st and 34th Infantry Divisions continued their exhausting advance that had already moved north-east of Bereza Kartuska.[16] With Guderian's command soon to pass east of the confining Polesie Marshes he began moving his XXXXVI Motorized Army Corps reserve across the Bug towards eventual insertion between XXXXVII and XXIV Motorized Army Corps, as they approached the River Berezina in strength. The formation's inclusion would not only fill out his expanding, and correspondingly thinning frontage, and help clear isolated enemy groups, but would assist in securing rear area rail and road networks towards facilitating the flow of logistics and communication.[17]

Plugging the Slonim Gap

As 17th Panzer Division pushed beyond Slonim, in its rush to reach Minsk and affect a linkup with Hoth a 70km gap opened along the formation's left-rear flank. Given Guderian's reluctance to peel off any of his own command for such actions, Kluge took control of 29th Motorized Infantry Division (XXXXVII MAC), which was moving into the vacuum. Surprised by the sudden decision, Guderian naturally began to vigorously lobby for the formation's rapid return. Given that Fourth Army was only now arriving in the Wielka Wola sector to plug the still open gap, the transfer, and that of 5th Machine-Gun Battalion, better aligned with Kluge's advance axis. At 0310hrs 29th Motorcycle Battalion radioed that Soviet BT-7 tanks were probing the sector between Holynka (Hołynka) and Dereczyn. It would take another 5 hours before 71st Motorized Infantry Regiment (29 MID) arrived to add weight to the forming German blocking position. Near the motorcyclists, 29th Reconnaissance Battalion similarly screened the threatened zone, while at about 0600hrs other elements from Boltenstern's command relieved a roughed up 52nd Rifle Regiment (18 PD) just west of Slonim.[18] As was an unfortunate but all too common an event during the chaos of combat at 0800hrs, 15th Motorized Infantry Regiment (29 MID) reported that friendly aircraft attacked the Zelwa Bridge causing German casualties.

On 27 June XXXXVII Motorized Army Corps' Ic received captured paperwork on a new, heavy enemy 'KV' tank of the type the Soviets had employed in prototype form during the 'Winter War' with Finland the previous year. Although troubling intelligence, the sudden appearance of the lighter T-34 on *Barbarossatag* had come as a considerable shock to those German forces engaging them. Half an hour after receiving the report 29th Motorcycle Battalion reported encountering such a vehicle, which being twice the weight of a Panzer III or IV and possessing thicker armour and a 76mm cannon, presented a potentially major problem. South-west of Jeziernica and along the River Zelwianka at 0915hrs 5th Motorized Machine-Gun Battalion had taken heavy losses contesting enemy infantry and requested heavy weapons be brought forward. While training could help acclimate the soldiers to the rigours of combat, in practice very stressful kill-or-be-killed actions triggered a rush of adrenaline, norepinephrine, and cortisol. As a result of a fight-or-flight response the sympathetic nervous system diverted energy from non-essential bodily processes to those involved in survival. Participants experienced a host of physical and physiological effects, including tunnel hearing and vision, muscle tremors, stress diarrhoea, vasoconstriction of minor blood vessels, decreased fine and complex motor skills, and increased respiration and blood flow to larger muscle groups. Following combat the soldiers' became utterly exhausted, as the body attempted to regain its homeostasis, making them vulnerable to counterattack.[19]

Within the hour the Germans captured Zelwa, which with the sector's defence increasingly solidified Soviet forces looking to escape were forced to move further east towards what was a fast-shrinking gap. As if keeping the masses of desperate enemy infantry and cavalry in check lacked sufficient difficulty 29th Motorized Infantry Division's 37mm and 50mm antitank gunners were commonly unable to knock out accompanying T-34s and KVs, beyond about half a kilometre.[20] Powerful German artillery, however, served to separate any accompanying infantry and supporting assets that the left often green Soviet tank crews 'blind' and vulnerable to direct-firing 105mm artillery and devastating 88mm fire. Coupled with similarly under-trained and equipped artillery support, and a dearth of radios that necessitated simple, set-piece tactical goals from which they were to avoid deviating, German combat engineers were frequently used to place demolition charges or bundled grenades under tracks, turret overhangs, and engine covers to finish the job. At 1815hrs the formation's 71st Motorized Infantry Regiment reported that the enemy snipers in the surrounding villages, wheat, flax, and rapeseed fields, and woods had been eliminated.[21] Fourth Army infantry would only arrive to relieve the exhausted 29th Motorized Infantry Division on 1 July. As XXXXVII Motorized Infantry Corps approached Minsk and the former Polish-Belorussian border they encountered a portion of the same partially manned and outfitted defensive lines 3rd Panzer Division was presently moving through near Slutsk.[22] Within this 'death strip' bridges, rail lines and depots, telephone lines, tunnels, water storage tanks, and electric power stations were found to have been rigged with explosives to deny them to the Germans.[23]

With XII Army Corps having assisted Guderian's spearheads in getting across the River Bug and beyond the frontier at 0130hrs on 27 June Second Panzer Group received the codeword 'Derfflinger' indicating that it, and its attached units such as 201st Assault Gun Battalion, were now removed from Kluge's subordination to that of Army Group Centre.[24] With Hoth having approached Minsk's northern outskirts the previous day the southern pincer had yet to close the yawning gap between Baranowicze and the Belorussian capital. Soon after a brief preparatory bombardment at 0400hrs on 27 June 18th Panzer Division assaulted the former, with its gridlike downtown, cobblestone streets, and low, wooden buildings, only to discover the enemy had vacated their positions during the night and relocated to the north-east. With Langermann in attendance, Eberbach led his armoured Kampfgruppe into Baranowicze at about 0600hrs, where just beyond Soviet resistance briefly flared up.

Four hours later and 120km to the east Model worked to exploit his successful crossing of the Sluch' and secure a bridgehead over the Berezina on what promised to be another sunny, hot day. To alleviate congestion along Panzer Route 1 and provide additional tactical options, 394th Motorized Rifle Regiment was sent along a dirt road that ran roughly parallel with the Slutsk–Urech'ye rail line, and from there through the wooded swampland to the River Ptich' and Vil'cha. At 1050hrs a Luftwaffe reconnaissance plane sent a motivating report on the absence of enemy military or civilian traffic along Panzer Route 1 all the way to Bobruysk and that all intervening bridges remained intact. Aside from III./6th Panzer Regiment engaging Soviet tanks and strong infantry forces south of Omukhovichi, XIV Mechanized Corps began pulling out of its shaky defence from the Sluch' south to the Slutsk–Urech'ye rail line. A much weakened 22nd Tank Division, 15km east of Slutsk, failed to hold its Omgovichi–Kalita–Staryy Gutok position, as did 30th Tank Division between Podores'ye and Sorogi. By 1600hrs I./6th Panzer Regiment had assumed the role of armoured vanguard and was soon moving through these still smouldering battlezones, its tanks maintaining 100m from the vehicle ahead and behind to avoid presenting a concentrated target. Adding insight to recent positive German intelligence gleaned from wired and wireless communication, and prisoner statements, a recently downed and captured Soviet DB bomber crewman revealed that Red Army morale was poor as they withdrew into the Bobruysk area before Schweppenburg.

In securing the area around Slutsk the Germans captured numerous Soviet-built Ford lorries and several fuel dumps, with at least one having been prepared for demolition. Given the large numbers of light T-26 and early model BT-7 tanks being fielded possessed petrol engines their German counterparts also made use of the bounty. Always intent on finding airfields close to the ever-extending front line during the afternoon of 27 June Mölders arrived near II./35th Panzer Regiment to determine the suitability of the Baranowicze facility. As what happened with other formations, as 4th Panzer Division advanced along Panzer Route 1 behind Model locals gathered to welcome them with flowers, and traditional offers of bread and salt; although such shows of greeting and appreciation often masked an ambivalence or suspicion. Having been subjected to nearly two years of oppressive Soviet occupation that included Stalin's NKVD perpetrating mass murder, torture, kidnapping, and forced deportations that only escalated following *Barbarossatag*, after the Red Army's expulsion anger, hatred, and resentment remained in their wake.[25] For the often sizeable Jewish populations throughout Stalin's western conquests the Soviet stranglehold on information, especially regarding its new German ally's policies and extra-legal excesses in Poland and elsewhere, following the signing of the Molotov-Ribbentrop pact in August 1939, few were aware of the mortal threat that would soon crash over them from the West.[26]

During its advance for Nieswiez, 18th Panzer Division slogged through intermittent heavy rainfall that soaked men and saturated the roads that vehicles quickly churned into a slurry. During the night Nehring captured the town and destroyed a handful of nearby enemy tanks.[27] Remaining on Panzer Route 2, 17th Panzer Division shot ahead to Minsk's south-western outskirts and established contact with Hoth's Third Panzer Group. Although what on Bock's situational maps perhaps showed a nearly complete encirclement of the Soviet Third and Tenth Armies, several openings in the cordon remained. While the majority of Guderian's command continued towards its originally targeted Smolensk–Yel'nya–Roslavl' sector, that once secured would serve as a springboard from which to conduct the final push on Moscow, Kluge's hard-marching infantry had moved up as far as Nowy Dwor, Rozana, and the lower Szczara. As part of XXXXVI Motorized Army Corps' activation at 0900hrs 10th Panzer Division finally began crossing the newly completed *'Generaloberst* Guderian Bridge' at Legi and began the long march along Panzer Route 2. Due to a radio silence gag, Schaal, like many of his peers, was unable to know the progress or location of many of his component units.[28] For Guderian the quick destruction of the enemy Tenth and Third Armies was certainly desirable to free up badly needed forces to secure bridgeheads over the River Dnepr in strength before Soviet strategic reserves arrived. In what was a worrying statement for such Moscow-first commanders on 27 June Hitler reiterated that 'it does not matter if we hit the enemy capital, but rather the enemy's forces'.[29]

To the River Berezina
Second Panzer Group (Fourth Army to Army Group Centre (28 June))

Having pushed his command with little rest for the last six days at midnight on 27/28 June Model's 'Kampfgruppe Linnarz' was forced to halt at the River Ptich', before what was the first of five destroyed bridges along the remaining stretch of Panzer Route 1 before Bobruysk. Although resistance at the waterway was light the group's commander was soon wounded. During the subsequent three hour delay badly needed fuel transports arrived and in the pre-dawn darkness 3rd Panzer Division's armoured vanguard renewed its advance via a time-eating, sandy detour through nearby Gorodok. Reinforcing the view Model's men held that they faced a battered, disorganized Soviet Fourth Army German intelligence intercepted an enemy telephone conversation that included, 'enemy [German] armoured breakthrough to be expected around Bobruysk. Put the entire air force into action at Bobruysk.' Whether this communication was coded or not, with so few radios and trained personnel, Red Army cryptography at tactical levels tended to be simple, such as word substitutions, and was frequently cracked. As part of the enemy's defence along the Berezina's far bank opposite Bobruysk they had blown up the town's two road bridges and its steel truss rail crossing.[30] With I./6th Panzer Regiment having moved around to the northern part of Bobruysk, and German artillery hammering its western approaches, elements of II./394th Motorized Rifle Regiment were soon sent across on pneumatic rafts and established a small bridgehead. Mölders and German artillery fire helped keep Soviet ground attacks at bay.[31] Having advanced as far as Lyadno, 4th Panzer Division continued to press ahead and looked to get out from under Model's increasingly large shadow. Now that 18th Panzer Division had arrived in strength a relieved 35th Panzer Regiment turned south from its Baranowicze excursion to rejoin the effort to secure crossings over the Berezina.[32]

On Guderian's left rain and secondary roads caused 18th Panzer Division lead elements to momentarily lose their way during the night of 27/28 June and it had yet to move beyond Nieswiez. With Luftwaffe aircraft having reported about seventy enemy BT-7s and T-26s and strong infantry and supporting forces having burst through the Stolpce area 30km to the north the general reiterated his urgent desire to have 29th Motorized Infantry Division returned to his control, as well as 5th Motorized Machine-Gun Battalion to stabilize the sector.[33] Although XII Army Corps was similarly no longer under his authority, 45th Infantry Division's struggle against the Brest fortress continued to adversely influence Second Panzer Group's advance. For nearly a week the weakening, but intransigent Soviet defenders had forced German logistics, reinforcements, and prisoner and casualty evacuation to detour around the obstruction. Although about one-third of 45th Infantry Division had already left the area to fight alongside 1st Cavalry Division, the remainder worked to finally settle the matter. To get the besieged enemy into a more malleable frame of mind between 1740 and 1800hrs seven Ju-88As from 3rd Bombardment Wing appeared high overhead. Six dropped a pair of SC-500 (kg) bombs each, while the seventh disgorged a single SC-1800 (kg) high-explosive variety. Tagged with the menacing nickname 'Satan', it had been delivered to the unit's airfield outside Deblin, specifically for this purpose.[34] With 45th Infantry Division personnel having been pulled back from the eastern fort's targeted area many gathered to watch the 4m-long ordnance disengage from its host, plummet to its target, and explode with a frightening blast and sheets of flame that motivated some 400 Red Army soldiers to surrender. Nearly all of the remaining 7,000 defenders gave up the following day.[35]

By the afternoon I./394th Motorized Rifle Regiment had cleared Bobruysk and at 1615hrs Corvin-Wiersbitzki's reconnaissance-based Kampfgruppe was ordered to secure the newest forward airfield just south of the town for Mölders' Staff/51st Fighter Wing. 4./53rd Fighter Wing was also set up for a brief stay at the Bobruysk airfield, with 91st Light Antiaircraft Battalion located nearby to protect the location and its prized Bf-109 F-1 and F-2 'Friedrich' models whose rounded, more aerodynamic cowlings and more powerful engines provided an improvement over the previous 'E' ('Emil') variants. As Model moved through Bobruysk most of the Soviet prisoners taken in the area were kept in the town's fortress until they could be properly relocated to the rear. Completed in 1820, the earthen and brick citadel sat atop a bluff along the Berezina, and like the one at Brest had historically helped secure Russia's Western border. Whether due to the retreating Red Army burning and destroying buildings and facilities to deny them to the enemy or from German bombs and artillery civilians either sought shelter in place and waited for the front line to pass through or set off eastward on foot in sad columns with what belongings they could carry to further clog the area's roads.

Having recently moved into the Slonim area to shore up the German cordon south-west of Minsk, with the pocket shrinking and less area to cover, 10th Panzer Division was redirected through Tartak and Lesna to Panzer Route 1. With Vietinghoff having ordered the formation to force a river crossing between Citva and Dukora and 'Reich' having finally started to cross the Bug at Koden on 26 June, a Kampfgruppe from the latter that included elements of its motorcycle, reconnaissance, antiaircraft, and engineer units was tasked with advancing east for Slutsk.[36]

With his XXXXVII Motorized Army Corps the most threatened of his three corps commands due to its proximity to the Minsk Pocket, Guderian maintained close contact with Lemelsen, whom he met 10km north of Milowidy to gain a forward impression of the situation.[37] As was common with senior German officers, Lemelsen had served in combat during the First World War and afterward was accepted into the Reichswehr. His command of 29th Motorized Infantry Division, a regular infantry division in Poland, and briefly a panzer division during the Dunkirk and Rouen fighting in 1940 under Hoth provided valuable insight and experience with orchestrating armoured and motorized formations prior to being given command of XXXXVII Motorized Army Corps later in the year. To his peers and superiors Lemelsen was a sophisticated, energetic leader who could clearly assess a battlefield situation, although he could succumb to indecision during times of difficulty. As part of its reconnaissance duties Luftwaffe aircraft scouted the high ground between Nowogrodek (Nowogródek) and Minsk along Panzer Route 2 to ascertain Soviet strengths and intentions.

1st Cavalry Division (removed from XXIV Motorized Army Corps (29 June))

In alliance with the opinion of those serving with Second Panzer Group the commander of 1st Motorized Reconnaissance Battalion (3 PD), Major Manfred Gusovius, once remarked that, '[Guderian] was always on the front lines, he could show up anywhere, and for that he was respected'.[38] True to form Guderian spent 29 June shuttling among his left-wing formations to more directly coordinate their coalescing cordon between Slonim and the Belorussian capital. Although ordered to focus on helping eliminate the Minsk Pocket, the general maintained what hard-earned eastward momentum Second Panzer Group had garnered over the last week. With Hoth's 20th Panzer Division penetrating the Belorussian capital at about noon on 29 June, and 17th and part of 18th Panzer Divisions, and 5th Machine-Gun Battalion extending the line roughly parallel with Panzer Route 2, the remainder of Nehring's forces pushed beyond Nieswiez along a secondary road to what was a heavily bombed, and still smoking, Stolpce. At 1800hrs 52nd Motorized Rifle Regiment (18 PD) began to cross the River Neman near the town. With traffic congestion and enemy attacks continuing to disrupt regular resupply 2 hours later I./52nd and elements of 101st Motorized Rifle Regiments engaged in a fierce meeting engagement along Poland's former eastern border with Belorussia to capture the road and rail bridges over the River Sinitskaya. About 3km south-west of Polonevichi I./40th Motorized Rifle Regiment (17 PD) also became engaged in heavy fighting against a trapped enemy whose fate was nearly sealed.[39]

Buttressing against Lemelsen's south-western flank, at 0412hrs 29th Reconnaissance Battalion moved into Holynka and just over 30 minutes later established contact with 15th Motorized Infantry Regiment (also 29 MID) in Dereczyn. After determining another alarm that the Soviets had used gas was proven false a reinforced 1./29th Reconnaissance Battalion probed northward for 15km to Wielka Wola and its destroyed wooden road bridge over the River Szczara. With masses of Soviet tanks seen moving with intent towards the still solidifying German perimeter south-west of Minsk an alarm was quickly issued to counter the threat. At about 1100hrs Soviet infantry and cavalry approached Slonim from the woods just east of the Szczara. In support a KV-1 Model 1939 and two T-34s entered the town where they destroyed a German tank and fired on an enemy headquarters and some field police. In the town centre a German antitank gun returned the favour and set one of the T-34s alight, while the KV-1 found its demise when it broke through a herringbone-decked timber bridge over the Szczara.[40]

With 17th Panzer Division moving into Dzerzhinsk it ran into determined resistance blocking Panzer Route 2.[41] At 1900hrs 10th Panzer Division's advance detachment was south of Lachowicze, while 'Reich's' vanguard marched on the town further behind. With several formations moving along Panzer Route 1 coordinating the flow of traffic continued to be a thankless, but critical service.[42] During the day Army Group Centre reported to OKW that, 'The enemy is fighting with the utmost stamina and courage.' Although not under Guderian's control, LIII Army Corps' fight deep on his right flank finally dislodged the remnants of the Soviet 75th Rifle Division from the Maloryta area.

Best used to deliver loads in one shot, with rail transport at least three-times more fuel efficient than lorries, as the front line continued to distance itself from the 1939 frontier converting the existing gauge to that of the *Reichsbahn* was paramount, given Germany's limited access to petroleum. By 29 June German rail battalions had laid re-gauged rail lines as far as Oranczyce, and two days later reached Baranowicze.[43] To best ensure a rapid conversion dedicated railwaymen provided a high level of rail-based transportation services than military surrogates, who by comparison often struggled with the myriad functions necessary to build, maintain, and expand not only the underlying infrastructure, but to efficiently move cargo. While military personnel could be instructed to perform these functions, in practice results typically fell short and were subject to abuses, delays, and confusion, such as when those in authority used rolling stock and sidings as mobile warehouses and offices, or altered timetables or commandeered trains to suit their own purposes. As part of their effort to deny as many assets to the onrushing Germans as possible People's Commissariat of Railways (NKPS) personnel and various railway brigades blew up bridges, depots, engineering equipment, water storage, and other facilities and infrastructure. Until such facilities could be made operational considerable stretches of track would be unavailable to German locomotives.

With steam locomotives operating along their specific section of track a rail line's capacity indicated the number of engines at each depot. To raise capacity additional locomotives needed to be added at each depot along the line, which commensurately meant increasing the respective depot's facilities. As Soviet locomotives were larger than those in the West and could transport more supplies than their German equivalents water and coaling stations were located at less frequent intervals, which meant additional support structures often needed to be constructed between the existing ones. Compared with Soviet trains, which averaged 120 axles in length and could transport 650 tonnes of cargo, German military equivalents usually had 90 axles that moved a maximum 450-tonne load. This translated into needing seventy and ninety trains respectively to move an infantry and panzer division. Unlike the modern rail network throughout the German Reich, where freight trains could operate upwards of 50km/h, what existed across most of Eastern Poland, Belorussia, and Russia was comparatively inferior having a much more rudimentary signalling and communications infrastructure that forced greatly reduced operating speeds.

For the last few days German forces had been noticing an increased desperation among the trapped Soviets, as evidenced by dense groupings of Red Army infantry often being repeatedly sent forward against a targeted sector of the German defences to shouts of 'Hurrah!' to bolster their resolve and hopefully weaken that of the enemy. Typically born from Commissar pressure and less experienced Soviet commanders frustrated at not finding success in more conventional breakthrough efforts they were unsurprisingly mowed down in large numbers. Although the Soviets sometimes penetrated as far as Panzer Route 2, the German 5th Motorized Machine-Gun Battalion, in particular, provided devastating, criss-crossing fire south of Baranowicze. In the aftermath of what were often harrowing engagements, when the Landsers moved across the battlefield they found many enemy dead with what appeared to be self-inflicted wounds; presumably under the not-always-wrong belief that worse awaited them should they surrender to the Germans.

With 1st Cavalry Division having pushed along the Dnepr–Bug Canal as far as Janow against declining resistance, being well to Guderian's rear on 29 June Kluge brought it under his slower Fourth Army. Always looking to acquire and retain as many formations under his authority as he could, and perhaps snub Kluge in the process, at 0900hrs on 29 June Guderian radioed Bock to press for the formation's return, as the horsemen relocated from the Pinsk sector, up through Hancewicze, to south-west of Slutsk. Receiving approval a little over 2 hours later via a teleprinter, at 1145hrs Guderian followed up by asking for 29th Motorized Infantry Division as well.[44] An hour later Kluge chimed in to insist it was presently impossible to pull Boltenstern's command from its present position given its need to keep an estimated two enemy cavalry and at least a pair of tank divisions contained around Wolkowysk.[45] Equally concerned about a major Soviet breakout in the sector, Bock concurred feeling that the formation, along with 5th Motorized Machine-Gun Battalion and parts of 10th Panzer Division, should remain part of Fourth Army barring an explicit emergency requiring their transition to Second Panzer Group. Guderian naturally continued to press to regain control of what had been recently lost, especially as the previously unaccounted for Soviet strategic reserves were being rushed to defend the River Dnepr. As the final geographic obstacle of consequence before Moscow, little time remained for Second Panzer Group to beat the enemy to the punch in strength and secure crossings.

As 18th Panzer Division approached south-western Minsk, Nehring's tankers engaged in brief fights around Podgay and Shchitomirichi just beyond.[46] Between Usza and the River Myszanka, Großdeutschland made its Barbarossa combat debut, having left its traffic-control duties west of the Bug and moved through Slonim to Polonka, to assume a north-west-facing blocking position. Per Lemelsen's evening order on 29 June to strike out alone for Borisov and secure its River Berezina crossing, Nehring readied to continue to the north-east early the next morning. With Hoth's 20th and 7th Panzer Divisions respectively in Minsk and along Panzer Route 2 to the east, however, XXXXVII Motorized Corps' vanguard needed to skirt the city's southern edge before striking for Borisov. The two-lane Minsk–Moscow Highway was alternately asphalt or gravel making it an arguably modern, albeit essentially unique Russian route, with the remaining 200km from around Vyaz'ma to the Soviet capital entirely paved.

Along Guderian's south flank at 0900hrs on 29 June 394th Motorized Rifle Regiment reported that prisoner interrogation indicated that Soviet forces along the Berezina were withdrawing. With 3rd Panzer Division patrols already operating out of their Bobruysk bridgehead the formation was ready to exploit the enemy's newest retreat. I./11th Antiaircraft Regiment secured the surrounding airspace, with particular emphasis on protecting the [remaining] bridge at Bobruysk. At 1010hrs 79th Motorized Engineer Battalion (4 PD) made its bridge 'B' available to 45th Motorized Engineer Battalion (XXIV MAC), which being near Slutsk was given priority and rushed ahead to the Berezina. In operation around Vil'cha, 1st Motorized Reconnaissance Battalion sent patrols south-west to Glusk and at 1700hrs another was ordered to investigate 394th Motorized Rifle Regiment's bridgehead at Bobruysk, prior to advancing for Titovka, and if the situation allowed, Liskovskaya.

At 1830hrs Soviet snipers targeted 394th Motorized Rifle Regiment's forward elements before Titovka, but resistance was otherwise unexpectedly light. When Soviet armour was engaged within an hour north-east of the village ground-to-air radio brought in Mölders' aircraft to engage the enemy with small bombs and armour-piercing ammunition, and prevent any Red Air Force bombers from striking the bridge.[47] At 2100hrs the German defence repulsed the enemy, which withdrew into a night-time fog before disappearing into distant defensive holes, from which they offered well-targeted rifle and machine-gun fire. Numerous killed and wounded lay scattered on both sides of the forest and in the forest 3km south-east of Bobruysk. 75th Motorized Artillery Regiment (3 PD) provided harassing fire into Soviet positions around Titovka, just beyond the Berezina's floodplain. In contrast to that of the Germans, Red Army counter-battery fire was isolated and seemingly without observation or coordination.[48] Soviet attacks continued into the night under the pale, flickering glow of starshells, but eventually subsided. Having been scattered along Guderian's right flank the depleted, fragmented Soviet XXVIII Rifle Corps continued to cross the River Berezina during the night of 29/30 June 1941, as the Germans moved up to fill the void. With combat reconnaissance and artillery preparation having sufficiently softened the Soviet defenders Model decided on an early morning attack to finish off remaining resistance.[49]

As the advance detachment of 'Reich' moved into the woodland around Grozovo and the River Losha it dispersed loosely organized enemy forces and individual tanks. Because it and 10th Panzer Division moved through the same 30km stretch between the former and Pyrashevo 16./SS-Infantry Regiment 'Deutschland' was placed at the latter location to provide traffic control.[50] Bringing up Vietinghoff's rear, 10th Motorized Infantry Division allocated its 20th Motorized Infantry Regiment and 40th Motorcycle Battalion to defend bridges in the Byten area against energetic enemy attacks from the woods to the north-west.[51] As 4th Panzer Division moved through Slutsk elements of 34th Motorcycle Battalion again swung north to scout and screen XXIV Motorized Army Corps' left flank. To keep close to Model 1./34th Motorcycle Battalion and 12th Motorized Rifle Regiment continued east along Panzer Route 1 as far as Staryye Dorogi, followed by 35th Panzer Regiment and the remainder of the division. On reaching Pastovichi at 1930hrs a I./12th Motorized Rifle Regiment deviated north to secure the road and rail bridges respectively at Svisloch' and Yelizovo. So tasked two small Kampfgruppen were formed; each including an infantry company, a reinforced engineer squad, and two antitank guns from 49th Panzerjäger Battalion.⁵²

1st Cavalry Division (to XXIV Motorized Army Corps (30 June))

On 30 June Guderian was flown to Third Panzer Group to meet with his northern counterpart, Hoth, to discuss final efforts in eliminating the Minsk Pocket, and more importantly how best to continue their eastward advance. The former also wanted to gain personal insight into the allegedly heavily enemy-occupied Nalibokach Forest, from which Kluge and Bock expected the Soviets to attempt a breakout to the south-east. During the afternoon Guderian reported not seeing a large enemy presence, but considering his desire to continue moving east of Minsk with all speed, such an observation could be viewed with some scepticism. As if to put the general's mind at ease that day OKH notified Bock of its desire for Army Group Centre to continue for Smolensk, even though Hitler was averse to sending Bock eastward to secure bridgeheads across the Dnepr before the Minsk Pocket was at least sealed if not eliminated. In such potentially grey circumstances Halder hoped likeminded commanders, such as Guderian and Hoth, would remain committed to maintaining their forward momentum and ask for forgiveness once success was achieved rather than request permission to unnecessarily deviate from the shortest path to Moscow. Although the German military had historically operated with a defined separation from the political arena with Hitler having assumed personal responsibility for the war's conduct, such efforts were seen to undermine and obstruct his usurped authority.

As the first sliver of dawn stretched across the horizon 'Kampfgruppe Moll' (3./12th Motorized Rifle Regiment) overcame difficult roads and terrain to arrive at an elevated position along the River Berezina at Svisloch'. On sighting three enemy vehicles Moll immediately crossed the rail bridge with the intent of holding the eastern bank and felling trees and piling other obstructions across the tracks to make them temporarily unusable. Almost immediately a Soviet armoured train pulled up from the east to engage the German railhead and drive 4th Panzer Division's vanguard back to the waterway's western bank. While Moll awaited follow-on reinforcements to negotiate the backwater trail leading back to Osipovichi Red Army forces from the train twice attempted to take the structure to place explosives. Fighting flared up 3km to the north as the bulk of I./12th Motorized Rifle Regiment moved into the Svisloch' area and its road crossing over the Berezina. A second Soviet armoured train approached slowly from the west near the town's depot to cut the German battalion's line of communications. A German antitank gun fired four rounds into the eastbound enemy train from 400m, which stopped the behemoth with a loud hiss of steam. With I./12th Motorized Rifle Regiment now contending with enemy infantry to its north and heavy fire from across the Berezina, the westbound train's dozen or so flatcar-mounted 76.2mm antiaircraft guns that had been affixed over the axles for stability as well as a similar number of smaller calibre, quad weapons and numerous machine guns behind protective plating presented a worrisome threat. Within 20 minutes of the battle opening two Soviet companies struck into the area south-west of the rail bridge, and although Moll's men beat it back at 0430hrs, enemy pressure grew in determination.

At 0415hrs 39th Motorized Engineer Battalion reported that the bridge over the Berezina would be ready at 0600hrs, although a second crossing at a nearby tributary was estimated to be finished between 1400 and 1500hrs that afternoon. At 0630hrs 1st Motorized Reconnaissance Battalion encountered Soviet horse patrols that soon withdrew, as did some enemy tanks moving up from the south. At X-Time (0915hrs) German artillery commenced, with 'Kampfgruppe Kleemann' and 75th Motorized Artillery Regiment setting off 15 minutes later. A grouping that included 1st Motorized Reconnaissance Battalion, a company from 3rd Motorcycle Battalion, and a pair of field ambulances were used to secure the Drut' bridges near Chechevichi and Mogilev. Four Panzer III command vehicle variants (model 'E1', fka 'B'), with their rear radio antenna cages, dummy guns, and fixed turrets that stemmed from removing internal components to provide additional space for map tables, were also included. Should the action prove unsuccessful the effort would reorient on Glybokovichi to the south. In addition to regular Red Army forces defending Mogilev thousands of factory workers had been organized into militias to help construct defences and hinder enemy progress.[53] 'Extermination battalions' had also been established to maintain order in the city and eliminate suspected German saboteurs and spies. At 0900hrs the Germans took Titovka and an hour later Model's Ia informed Schweppenburg's that 515th Motorized Engineer Regiment Staff's Colonel Hermann Bacher reported that the second bridge was unlikely to be finished until 2 July, and that 3rd Panzer Division's advance would be delayed until the structure's completion.

The attack began at 1015hrs on what was the second day of dry weather that marginally improved terrain and dirt roads. Still struggling to regain their balance and defend the Berezina 15 minutes later a Soviet troop attacked a security detachment from 3rd Motorcycle Battalion north of Solomenka. 3rd Panzer Division reconnaissance sighted individual Soviet vehicles moving into and out of the Bobruysk area, while further ahead a Luftwaffe aircraft reported that all bridges between the town and Rogachev remained intact. At 1130hrs 4th Panzer Division took the railway and road bridges near Svisloch'. Elements of 12th Motorized Rifle Regiment captured a Soviet train carrying military equipment near Svisloch' on the River Berezina.

During the pitch-black night of 29/30 June additional forces from 4th Panzer Division pushed through heavy rain and mud to reach Osipovichi. At 1730hrs 3rd Panzer Division expanded from its bridgehead at Bobruysk and engaged enemy armour before capturing Titovka. During the action at 1745hrs II./6th Panzer Regiment radioed that German artillery fire was striking their own front line. With a Soviet tank platoon having briefly approached the Bobruysk railway bridge at about 1800hrs half an hour later Schweppenburg telephoned that an 'Enemy armoured breakthrough [had occurred] at Bobruysk. [and for] all [available] Luftwaffe to deploy on Bobruysk'. With the support of effective artillery fire 3rd Motorized Rifle Regiment and II./394th Motorized Rifle Regiment inflicted heavy losses against yet another Soviet assault from established positions and rebuffed it. During the afternoon Soviet bombers harassed 3rd Panzer Division's advance, but German antiaircraft guns reportedly downed over twenty planes; seemingly in stark contrast to 11th Antiaircraft Regiment's recent efforts.[54] Having arrived the previous day 604th Motorized Heavy 210mm Howitzer Battalion (3 PD) used its long-range, 210mm M18 guns against enemy forces across the River Berezina. At 1900hrs Schweppenburg visited 3rd Panzer Division to express his appreciation for the formation's efforts and achievements, with Guderian later doing the same.

As 18th Panzer Division snaked its way around south-eastern Minsk during the morning of 30 June its leading motorcycle reconnaissance and some supporting armour ran up against what was believed to be the Soviet 121st Rifle Division defending the River Volma in strength across from its namesake town's bridge. At 1100hrs the Germans made a concerted effort to cross the waterway at the town, but what turned out to be 355th Rifle Regiment (100 RD) along the far bank blew the bridge up. With Soviet artillery rounds soon landing in the area the attackers turned back. A couple of hours later German engineers moved up and began disassembling nearby buildings to provide a makeshift crossing at a narrow portion of the waterway, but artillery stopped this effort as well. Until additional German forces could be brought up further efforts to cross the Volma were unsuccessful.[55] With the Soviet Tenth and Third Army's fate secured, the similarly battered Fourth and Thirteenth Armies continued to conduct a fighting withdrawal outside the pocket.

Lemelsen, like many German commanders, had been distressed that 'still more shootings of prisoners-of-war and deserters have been observed, [and] conducted in an irresponsible, senseless and criminal manner'. As he saw it, 'The German Army is waging a war against Bolshevism, not against the Russian people.' While Lemelsen held no such qualms about the summary execution of commissars and partisans, as their actions were seen as outside the bounds of acceptable military behaviour, and through it the liberation of the Russian people from 'the oppression of a Jewish and criminal group'.[56] While Guderian largely professed ignorance in the matter many of his subordinate commanders actively forbade it being carried out or allowed their men's conscience to guide them.[57] At the same time mobile, paramilitary action groups (*Einsatzgruppen*) worked with police, locals, and military personnel to carry out the murder of Jewish and Slavic elements of the population in the wake of the advancing front line.[58] Considering front-line formations already contended with stretched logistics and resources, such efforts only exacerbated the problem and turned what in many instances were large parts of the Soviet-occupied populations willing to fight Stalin against German interests.

Before dawn on 1 July I./52nd Motorized Rifle Regiment (18 PD) crossed the Volma at Petrovichi and dug in, while some forty accompanying tanks attempted to provide support before Red Army artillery forced the crews to disengage. With 100th Rifle Division depleted from recent fighting around Minsk and having begun to withdraw to the east its 331st Rifle Regiment proved unable to dislodge the small German bridgehead. To finally push through the opposition and move on Borisov, early in the morning Nehring had a Kampfgruppe formed under II./18th Panzer Regiment's commander, Major Wilhelm 'Willi' Teege. As an adjutant to the last German head of the covernamed 'Kama' armour training facility in 1933, he went on to acquire a reputation as an effective, respected armour commander.[59] To provide the necessary force mix to address likely contingencies I./52nd Motorized Rifle Regiment, and two companies from 18th Motorcycle Battalion accompanied Teege's tanks. To provide immediate infantry support many risked exposure and rode along, while a battery of four 105mm howitzers from I./88th Motorized Rifle Regiment was towed along.[60] By 0900hrs 'Kampfgruppe Teege' cleared the heavily wooded area east of Minsk to return to Panzer Route 2 and the relatively open terrain between Smolevichi and Borisov; an area the Luftwaffe had been bombing since 24 June 1941 to disrupt recent enemy support into the nearby Belorussian capital. Moving up behind elements of 101st Motorized Rifle Regiment and 88th Motorized Reconnaissance Battalion the group forged ahead through Drachkovo, over the Usha at Pekalin, and on to Smolevichi. Except for an enemy armoured train that harried the German vanguard from near the latter town to Zhodino, where the tracks ran closer to the road, little resistance was encountered.[61] In what made the Red Army appear to have an unlimited supply of men and armour Luftwaffe reconnaissance spotted about 100 enemy tanks approaching that sector of the River Berezina at 1400hrs.

As 'Kampfgruppe Teege' approached its goal two columns of up to twenty Soviet tanks lined the road to Borisov, but for all their dash without support each soon fell to the better armed, armoured, and crewed panzern.[62] The Germans fought through heavy casualties, especially I./52nd Motorized Rifle Regiment, which engaged in close combat to remove the Soviets from their unofficially named 'Stalin Line' fortifications. Passing burning enemy wrecks, 3./18th Motorcycle Battalion and I./52nd Motorized Rifle Regiment advanced along Panzer Route 2's right and left, respectively. Before nightfall II./18th Panzer Regiment pushed past the trenchworks, gun emplacements, and a 7km tank ditch (*Panzergraben*) the cadets from the nearby Borisov

Automobile and Tractor School helped create in the town's western portion. Seeing that the large, concrete Berezina Bridge still stood, the tankers shot ahead through enemy artillery fire and resistance that included the cadets to reach the structure. With the vehicle tracks apparently cutting the demolition wires, the Germans established a small bridgehead at 2150hrs against 175th Motorized Rifle Regiment (1 MMRD) from 1st Moscow Motorized Rifle Division.[63] Into the night of 1/2 July Teege's command continued to suffer enemy artillery fire, but held its hard-won position against heavy enemy attacks before counterattacking to expand their bridgehead during 2 July. With Hoth's 7th Panzer Division nearing Studenka what had been a rather isolated, forward position for 18th Panzer Division now received support on its northern flank.

Considering wireless was frequently the only means to maintain contact between the headquarters of Second Panzer Group and XXIV Motorized Army Corps, and that the threat to Guderian's left had diminished as the Minsk Pocket neared its end, on 1 July he flew to meet with Schweppenburg for a more lengthy discussion on the battlefield situation and future operations. Schweppenburg stated that his command was in an excellent position in which to continue its eastward advance against a largely fragmented and disorganized enemy. With a 200km stretch of Soviet rail gauge having been converted from Brest to Baranowicze, XXIV Motorized Army Corps had stockpiled ammunition and fuel for its push beyond the Dnepr; although the construction of additional supply depots and infrastructure was often neglected. German aerial reconnaissance had been encountering a build-up of fresh Soviet forces in the Smolensk– Mogilev–Orsha area. To capture crossings over the River Dnepr before these formations could reinforce the obstacle the Germans would once again need to move quickly and not wait days for foot-bound infantry to move up to hold the captured ground and prevent breakouts. In any case to remain stationary was anathema to a war of movement, in large part as remaining active helped mask its strength and location to the enemy.

On 1 July 10th Panzer Division approached the River Svisloch' where its I./86th Motorized Rifle Regiment provided close support for the vanguard, 90th Motorized Reconnaissance Battalion which fortuitously secured the still intact bridge near Zablchany. Soon found only to support 8 tonnes, during the morning the structure was damaged. To maintain at least some forward momentum while engineers repaired and reinforced the crossing German forces detoured to a second bridge 3km upstream. Once the division's 10th Motorcycle Battalion reached the river's east bank it continued on for Cherven, which it expected to reach that evening. En route, the motorcyclists became entangled in bitter forest fighting and only reached the location the next day with the assistance of I./86th Motorized Rifle Regiment that had rushed to assist.[64] Further south SS-Reconnaissance Battalion 'Reich' had rapidly moved up to the Svisloch' at Pukhovichi.

In the seemingly never-ending search for intact bridges, at 0800hrs Luftwaffe reconnaissance reported enemy motorized forces moving from Bobruysk to Mogilev over an intact crossing over the Drut'. Just south of Chechevichi one was seen burning at both ends, although the one over the River Dobysna at Liskovskaya had been listed as still standing. At 1115hrs another aerial report stated Soviet rail traffic along the Zhlobin–Rogachev line to the south, but nothing along the stretch between Bobruysk and Zhlobin where bridges respectively still stood. Just after noon 3rd Rifle Brigade reached Leytichi and encountered a gap where another crossing had recently existed. With air and artillery helping to subdue enemy resistance the unit bypassed the holdup during the late afternoon to reach the flat, open terrain beyond by 1800hrs. As a continued thrust with Model's advance detachment reached Liskovskaya near dark, however, they found the crossing had been destroyed. While a portion of 6th Panzer Regiment provided protection for 39th Motorized Engineer Battalion as it constructed a replacement bridge back at Bobruysk an hour before midnight a contingent from 1st Motorized Reconnaissance Battalion reached Kolbovo.[65] As a German patrol approached the nearby River Drut' at Chechevichi the Soviets blew up that crossing as well. 'Kampfgruppe Eberbach' set off for Chuch'ya to find a crossing over the Berezina.

To address the threat to his momentum at 1510hrs Guderian telexed a request for Bock to release a bridge column and motorized engineers to construct additional crossings over the Rivers Berezina and Dnepr, as well as more assault gun and antitank battalions. When high-velocity 88mm guns were unavailable, 47mm and 50mm varieties firing standard, antitank ammunition were found to be capable of penetrating the initial T-34 model (1940) at common engagement ranges of 400–600m. Longer distances typically needed more specialized, but rarer rounds like the tungsten-tipped Pzgr40. With a heavy rain grounding Luftwaffe support during the afternoon, as the latter pushed through what seemed an enemy-free zone around Glybokovichi the constricted, woodland road limited traffic to one direction. Strong Soviet forces, however, continued to resist near Leytichi and along the Ola, and from forested areas along Panzer Route 1.

Chapter 4

Securing the River Dnepr, 2–9 July 1941

29th Motorized Infantry Division (to XXXXVII Motorized Army Corps (2 July))

By the beginning of July 1941, Army Group Centre's rapid advance, like that of the *Ostheer* overall, had inflicted what to them seemed like a catastrophic defeat of Red Army forces between the frontier and the River Dnepr, and all that remained to achieve outright victory was to eliminate the numerous enemy remnants that had evaded encirclement and destruction and those formations deployed further east that had yet to be engaged.[1] Having sealed the Minsk Pocket, like many German formations that advanced ever deeper into the seemingly endless East, Second Panzer Group's initially narrow, breakthrough frontage had roughly doubled. To ensure a suitable density of front-line forces XXXXVI Motorized Army Corps was already crossing the River Bug and moving up to fill the sector between Guderian's armoured flanks. Considering the need to fight, manoeuvre, and receive a steady flow of supplies and reinforcements rested on controlling the region's generally poor road network, the Germans frequently needed to siphon personnel from other duties to hold critical assets, such as bridges, communications hubs, and counter bypassed enemy forces. Industry was unprepared to produce sufficient weapons, vehicles, and other assets in quantities necessary to weather a drawn-out, attritional war, and reserves were insufficient to keep up with the high casualties that soon dwarfed what had been suffered during the 1939 and 1940 campaigns. As their units were fought down many German commanders opted to husband their assets rather than engage in every fight that presented itself.

To maintain the fast pace of armoured operations German motorized infantry were typically mounted on lorries or more optimally armoured personnel carriers, which were always in short supply. As something of a compromise the vehicles incorporated a forward wheeled configuration that allowed it to be driven much like a civilian automobile, while rear-positioned tracks provided improved cross-country maneouvrability. Designed to carry a standard ten-man squad (Sd.Kfz 251/1) or a four-man half-squad (Sd.Kfz 250/1), in addition to a driver and co-driver, these 'rifle' (*Schützen*) or 'infantry' personnel (depending if they respectively served with a panzer or motorized infantry division) would dismount near the combat zone and fight on foot. As these lightly skinned, SPW (*Schützenpanzerwagen*) halftracks provided armour protection against little more than standard bullets and shrapnel they would remain nearby to offer support, such as from their shield-mounted, MG-34 machine guns.

By 2 July Second Panzer Group had advanced across much of the Central Berezina Plain between the Polesie Marshes and the Minsk Hills on which the Belorussian capital was located, and now occupied a forward line that extended south from around Borisov and along the River Berezina to Bobruysk. As was to be expected throughout the less developed regions German columns frequently encountered harassing sniper fire and fought off skirmishes that slowed, but never seriously halted their advance. Since most of the roads in the East lacked drainage ditches that promoted mud and muck the abundance of woodland allowed for the liberal laying of corduroy reinforcement sufficient to accept traffic, although most vehicles smartly continued to carry fascines for their own immediate use. Unwilling to idle, Model continued to push 3rd Panzer Division ahead of its Second Panzer Group peers to reach Rogachev and the River Dnepr, just ten days after crossing the Bug. With Bock having seemingly assuaged Hitler's worries that the shrinking enemy pocket extending from Minsk to Navahrudak, some 50km north of Baranowicze, needed to be thoroughly eliminated as a prerequisite for continuing the eastward advance, the Führer approved OKW's two-day-old order to advance on Smolensk. As was typical Guderian spent much of 2 July travelling among his forward formations, visiting 5th Motorized Machine-Gun Battalion, situated along 29th Motorized Infantry Division's left, to ascertain the strength and intentions of the encircled and increasingly desperate Soviet Third and Tenth Armies. Apparently satisfied, he was then driven to Lemelsen to discuss how best to contain any enemy breakout attempt closer to the Belorussian capital.

On the meeting's conclusion Guderian went to 17th Panzer Division's headquarters at Dzerzhinsk to listen to Streich report that all enemy efforts to escape through the formation's sector had been rebuffed. When the general subsequently returned to his command post, which had yet again relocated closer to the front he learned that only half of 17th Panzer Division had received Kluge's order to remain in place as pocket containment, while the remainder had disengaged for Borisov. Guderian apparently tried to inform Kluge of the miscommunication and the correspondingly weakened perimeter, but it was too late and he was summoned to his superior's presence for an 0800hrs, face-to-face meeting for the next day, 3 July.[2]

Retaining its contested bridgehead at Borisov anchoring Guderian's northern flank, with additional elements of 18th Panzer Division having closed up to the town Nehring continued with his eastward advance in strength. With some of the German tanks having to briefly leave Panzer Route 2 to gain some tactical flexibility many Soviet soldiers took advantage of the extensive woodland west

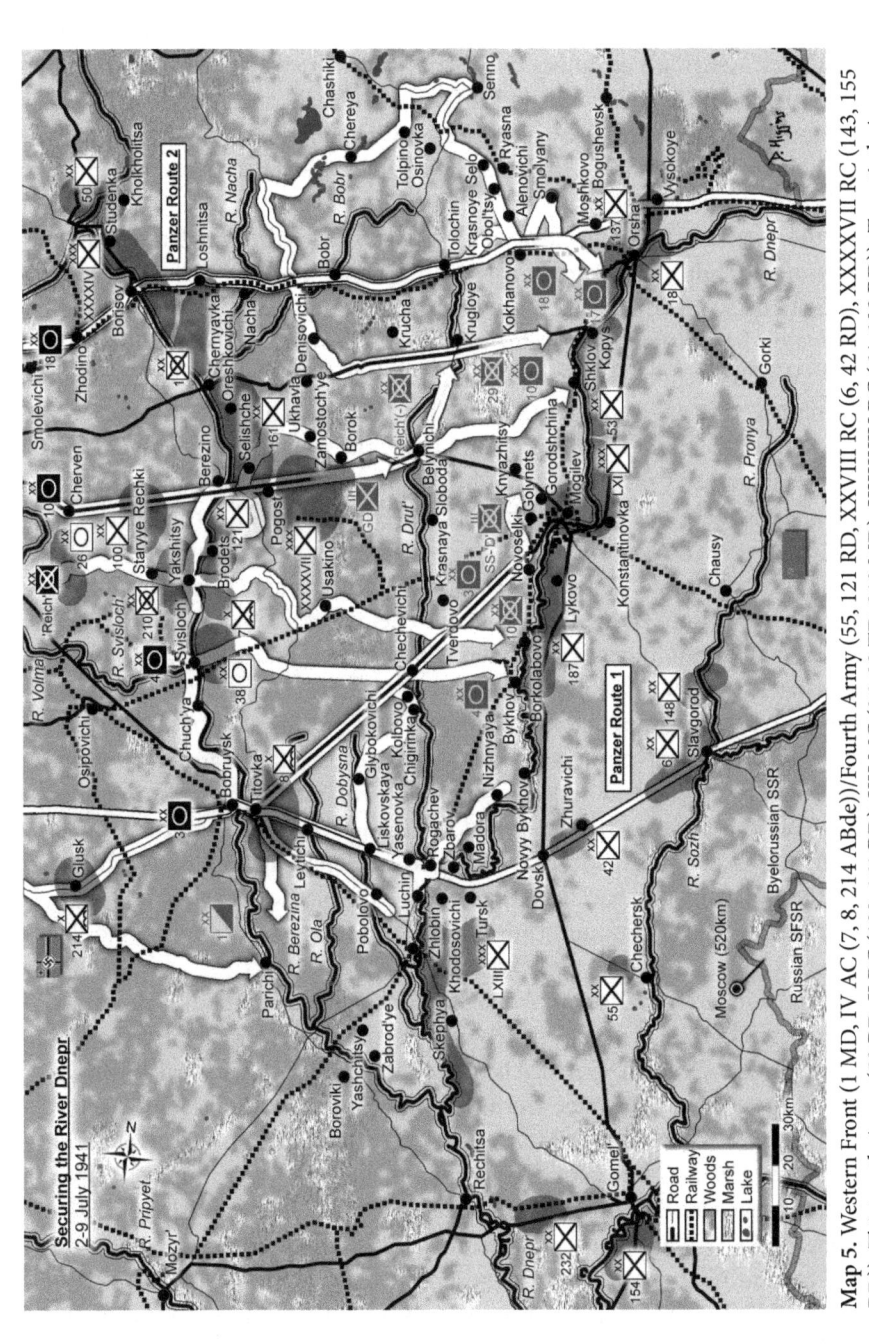

Map 5. Western Front (1 MD, IV AC (7, 8, 214 ABde))/Fourth Army (55, 121 RD, XXVIII RC (6, 42 RD), XXXXVII RC (143, 155 RD)); Thirteenth Army (50 RD, II RC (100, 161 RD), XX MC (26, 38 TD, 210 MD), XXXXIV RC (64, 108 RD); Twentieth Army (18, 53, 137 RD, LXI RC (110, 172 RD); Twenty-First Army (154 RD, XLIV RC (187, 232 RD), LXIII RC (61, 117, 148, 167 RD)). TsAMO, f.208, op.2511, d.49, l.9.

of Loshnitsa to hurl Molotov cocktails that according to the throwers engulfed and destroyed fifteen panzern. Once additional division forces arrived on scene the enemy tanks, seemingly lacking armour-piercing rounds, were unable to further hinder Nehring's advance. Possessing considerable freedom in the air, Luftwaffe pilots and crews could focus on their targets and cause numerous Red Army and civilian ground casualties and armour losses that eventually forced a halt to 1st Moscow Motorized Rifle Division's skilfully executed, but outnumbered counterattack.[3]

With the German bridgehead over the River Ola having held throughout the night of 1/2 July, 1st Motorized Reconnaissance Battalion moved on for Chechevichi to scout 3rd Panzer Division's left. At 0545hrs, heavy rainfall had prevented Model from bypassing the River Dobysna, some 30km east of Bobruysk. With no reported enemy activity 8./6th Panzer Regiment (minus one platoon) managed to cross just north of the bridge, which had recently suffered artillery damage to all but its western 15m. Once the panzer company manoeuvred to the structure's far end at 0730hrs engineers set about repairing it in relative safety, which took most of the day. Kleemann sent II./6th Panzer and I./3rd Motorized Rifle Regiments, along with a company of Panzerjäger I Bs and an antiaircraft battery to help clear the way to Rogachev. Just over an hour later Luftwaffe reconnaissance reported no enemy activity sighted along the Bobruysk–Zhlobin rail line or for a dozen kilometres around Chigirinka. Intent on capturing Rogachev with intact bridges, at 1010hrs. Munzel rushed ahead with two panzer companies and one of engineers to secure that over the Drut' an hour later. Reaching the heights of Yasenovka just after midday, the bulk of 'Kampfgruppe Kleemann' was crossing the prize, although the Soviets had just destroyed the one over the Dnepr a few kilometres to the east. Back under Guderian, 1st Cavalry Division briefly advanced along Panzer Route 1 before deviating at Gulevichi and back into the Polesie Marshes' less accessible fringes. To maintain a degree of communications with Schweppenburg's right Feldt led his horsemen along a secondary road to Urech'ye and Glusk.

As part of Guderian's effort to reach the Dnepr in strength, 1st Motorized Reconnaissance Battalion moved for Bykhov in the day-old wake of retreating Red Army forces. While the German scouts approached the Chechevichi Bridge over the Drut', Soviet resistance from nearby field fortifications forced a halt in woods west of Kolbovo. At 1800hrs the commander of II./3rd Motorized Rifle Regiment, Major Hermann Zimmermann, crossed the still intact railway bridge at Rogachev against minimal resistance in what was a promising push for a bridgehead. At 1940hrs Luftwaffe reconnaissance reported seeing no enemy presence around Glybokovichi or the predominantly coniferous woodlands to its east.[4] At 2225hrs 1st Motorized Reconnaissance Battalion reported taking Chigirinka and the surrounding field fortifications.[5] As the battered Soviet 42nd Rifle Division retreated to the Zhuravichi area on 2 July it received

1,000 reinforcements, but no longer possessed artillery. During the night of 2/3 July Kluge, with Fourth Army's staff, assumed command of Second and Third Panzer Groups during the critical closing and elimination of the Minsk Pocket. Collectively labelled Fourth Panzer Army, Second Army correspondingly assumed control of Fourth Army's remaining infantry corps. Although a bristling Guderian had recently threatened to resign should such a reorganization occur, the move enabled the field marshal to better orchestrate logistics, coordinate his armoured, motorized, and infantry formations, and perhaps control his often wayward commanders against the short-term risk of unnecessarily constraining operational momentum and flexibility.

Overcoming forest roads, marshy terrain, and an occasional destroyed bridge over one of the area's many creeks, as 'Reich' approached Staryy Rechki at 0915hrs it bumped into an enemy in battalion strength moving from Cherven to Yakshitsy. III./SS-'Deutschland' proved unable to quickly eject the Soviet forces, who established defences within the surrounding woods. SS motorized elements, however, pushed on to reach the River Berezina at Yakshitsy, where an enemy column of infantry and motor vehicles was sighted immediately to the south. Rushing to cross the village's 150m-long timber trestle bridge at 1710hrs on 2 July three SS assault guns set off to engage. While SS-'Deutschland' cleared its stretch of the west bank, as one of the squat German vehicles cautiously moved over the structure the Soviets detonated explosives affixed to two piers that brought that part of the 15m-high bridge down in a tangled heap of structural supports and decking, along with the assault gun; the crewmen survived with relatively minor injuries.[6] Temporarily halted along the waterway, SS-'Deutschland' organized for continuing operations, which came once the unit established a bridgehead during the night of 3/4 July.[7]

With sleep as much a necessary quanta for combat effectiveness as food, fuel, and ammunition during high-tempo combat operations a solid 6 to 8 hours per night was impossible. Combined with regular exposure to mortal threats, seemingly endless marching and riding in vehicles, and long hours on duty promoted a host of health issues from fatigue and irritability to impaired judgment and a suppressed immune system. As a short-term solution Pervitin tablets produced a surge of energy, significantly increased concentration, wakefulness, and motor activity, and decreased feelings of fear, hunger and thirst. One tablet of methamphetamine was commonly taken during the day and two more at night to stave off drowsiness. For what benefits the drug provided in the short term and promoted as less detrimental than coffee, in practice soldiers became addicted and suffered from dependence and ever-lengthening withdrawal times. In addition to declining concentration regular Pervitin use produced nervous disorders and occasionally death. In an effort to obviate associated moral responsibility for medical personnel the Führer emphasized that, 'Possible complications (from the use of drugs) and even losses should not bother the conscience of doctors. The situation at the front requires us to be fully committed . . .' To provide a more user-friendly ingestion method Pervitin-infused chocolate bars (*Panzerschokolade*) were made widely available. Only after a direct correlation between users and an increasing number of crimes, aggression, and suicides became evident was the product removed at the end of 1941, and even banned by the Reich Ministry of Health. For the Soviets vodka was the drug of choice, with soldiers drinking their ration to raise morale before combat, mask pain, and alleviate stress. Its use was so prevalent the Red Army even began producing the spirit in August 1941. Considering what soldiers in the field have endured throughout history, including exposure to the elements, disease, infection, lack of sleep, inconsistent, often poor food, and infestation, as well as a host of psychological maladies and stressors, discipline naturally suffered the longer one remained in the conflict zone. While training, camaraderie, culture, and other factors could mitigate issues of morale and motivation the average soldier was typically at their peak fighting ability for up to around twenty-five consecutive days at the front before the cumulative effects of the high-stress fighting within a 24-hour combat cycle promoted physical and emotional exhaustion.[8]

Second Panzer Group (Army Group Centre to Fourth Panzer Army (3 July))

By 3 July Army Group Centre had thrown up a strong cordon that progressively shrank the area in which the trapped Third and Tenth Armies could operate. While many German formations had been clearing areas of remaining resistance shortly after dawn a large Soviet force attempted to breakout to the southeast, only to have 15th Motorized Infantry Regiment (29 MID) and the attached 5th Motorized Machine-Gun Battalion block the effort. Later that morning 4./40th Motorized Rifle Regiment (17 PD) reported a 2km column of enemy infantry, artillery, and cavalry moving in a similar direction through the open barley and rye farmland between Rubiezewicze (Rubieżewicze), just inside of what had until recently been Poland's eastern border, and Volka. By 0730hrs, however, this escape was also beaten back. With the Minsk fighting seemingly approaching its conclusion, Guderian felt comfortable in openly focusing on securing River Dnepr crossings.[9] Given the pre-Barbarossa assumption that the majority of Soviet forces were located between the 1939 border and the River Dnepr it was perhaps unsurprising that Halder wrote in his journal that 'it is no exaggeration to say that the campaign against Russia has been won'. In a radio broadcast that day, Stalin urged the population to form guerilla units in the areas occupied by the enemy; something that pleased Hitler, as the call provided additional cover for the many excesses under the war of annihilation umbrella.

Having pulled out of Borisov ahead of the onrushing 18th Panzer Division, the Soviet cadets and what soldiers that had been quickly organized as they withdrew through the area continued to resist from the extensive woodland west of Loshnitsa. Scores of light BT-7M tanks from 12th Tank Regiment (1 MMRD) interspaced with T-34s and heavy KV-1s in the lead made an imposing arrival. Although the T-34 had already made an appearance against Hoth, and elsewhere along the German front, it was a new, often frightening experience for Nehring's men.[10] Under the watchful eye of Luftwaffe reconnaissance 18th Panzer Division's strong bridgehead east of Borisov was warned of the approaching threat, and several of its armour and antitank guns were arrayed 8km further east of the main German positions. As the Soviet tanks drove along Panzer Route 2 in platoon and company-sized groupings, the well-trained German gun crews, with their weapons' superior optics soon dispatched several BT-7s. The heavier armoured vehicles, however, presented more resilient targets and managed to briefly penetrate the German defences. While a T-34 knocked out at least one Panzer III, other panzern concentrated their fire on individual enemy vehicles to shoot off a track, jam a turret, or achieve a penetration given a favourable range, calibre, or angle. The Red Army's lack of vehicle-mounted, wireless radios (except perhaps in the group leader's tank) and a rigid command structure discouraged individual initiative.[11] With large portions of the Red Army lacking the training and experience to organize into competitive, task-oriented groupings like their opponents, Soviet commanders were typically forced to adopt simplistic, inflexible tactics and easily controlled formations that too often failed to adapt to changing battlefield conditions.

At 0800hrs on 3 July Kluge gave Guderian an expected dressing down about the previous day's apparent miscommunication in which part of 17th Panzer Division left its position along the Minsk cordon for the Dnepr. The field marshal even considered sacking both his senior panzer group commanders for actions that to him smacked of insubordination if not conspiracy. Guderian, however, seemingly assuaged his superior's concerns, and after the meeting drove to XXXXVII Motorized Army Corps' headquarters at Smolevichi. Not finding it he went to 18th Panzer Division's headquarters at Borisov to ascertain the situation that included an advance detachment having been sent ahead towards Tolochin. On his way back Guderian now found Lemelsen at Smolevichi and discussed XXXXVII Motorized Army Corps' situation being strung out along Panzer Route 2 from Stolpce to the Berezina. In addition to now coordinating an advance directly alongside Hoth, Second Panzer Group had an opportunity to secure the Dnepr, and cut off and destroy remnants of several Soviet formations that had been unable to withdraw faster than the Germans advanced, or had just escaped the Minsk encirclement.

Checked at Rogachev

As 3rd Panzer Division approached Rogachev during the morning of 3 July reconnaissance probed for crossings over the Dnepr, but found the town's road bridge on fire. Additional scouting along the road connecting the town with Novyy Bykhov found its bridge destroyed, but the apparent lack of enemy activity in the area implied a pontoon bridge could be assembled in relative safety. With enemy artillery trying to disrupt II./3rd Motorized Rifle Regiment's approach advance into Rogachev's western outskirts, Ju-87 support was requested from XXIV Motorized Army Corps to silence the threat. As much of Model's command spread out before the town at about noon his command post relocated to within a few kilometres of the Dnepr. Corps artillery and I./394th Motorized Rifle Regiment, however, remained held up near Bobruysk due to Lemelsen ordering Eberbach to have priority passage over the pontoon bridge just south of the town between 1000 and 1700hrs. With the colonel's offensive freedom of movement restored 35th Panzer Regiment now headed straight for Mogilev, while 3rd Panzer Division continued along Panzer Route 1 towards Rogachev. As Eberbach approached the River Drut', however, his command halted before a wooden timber bridge just north of Kolbovo that was sufficiently damaged to prevent its immediate use. With other 4th Panzer Division elements arriving from Svisloch' throughout the evening work commenced on finding a ford, although results were mixed due to the swampy, wooded terrain so common along the region's waterways.[12]

With I. and III./6th Panzer Regiment directed north-east of Yasenovka, after crossing a quiet River Drut' to enter Rogachev's north-western edge and I./394th and I./3rd Motorized Rifle Regiments began to add their weight against the town's defence, fighting on the ground heated up at about 1730hrs.[13] In spite of Soviet artillery fire from the Khodosovichi area and bombers adding to the Soviet stand, German infantrymen fought through to the Dnepr within 3 hours, in spite of the inability to establish communication with nearby armour to coordinate their firepower. Probing ahead of Model's right 3rd Motorcycle Battalion pushed into Pobolovo against weak resistance, and none south-east along the Dobysna.

At 0500hrs on 4 July Model received suggestions from the commanders of 3rd Rifle Brigade, 143 Arko, and 39th Motorized Engineer Battalion on how best to get across the Dnepr, while laying the foundation upon which a successful thrust beyond would be conducted. Later that morning Luftwaffe reconnaissance indicated little activity along the Rogachev–Slavgorod road, but that several bridges in the area had been destroyed, and the stretch best avoided. As part of the Soviet artillery fire intended to break up what was undoubtedly an imminent German amphibious assault from the Rogachev area, at 1130hrs word spread among those on the receiving end that what they called 'Yellow Cross', a blistering agent of the mustard-gas variety, had been used against them in addition to conventional ammunition. Landsers scrambled to don protective masks and quickly mix their white Losantin tablets with water and apply the liquid, often zealously, onto bare skin at risk of contamination. Soon deemed a false alarm, another round of such misinformation circulated that night, with the same conclusion.

With Model determining X-uhr for 1800hrs I./394th Motorized Rifle Regiment moved off to the north of Rogachev for use in an eastward thrust prior to effecting a Dnepr crossing or one that pivoted south, depending on circumstances. With the main strike occurring on his left, I./3rd Motorized Rifle Regiment was directed towards Luchin. At 1530hrs, 143rd Arko coordinated a heavy German battery with a loitering Fw-189A 'Eagle Owl' from 9.(Pz)/2nd Instruction Wing that provided observation and assistance with adjusting round trajectories onto enemy positions around Zhlobin. As a replacement for the Hs-126 the more modern twin-engine/twin-boom plane, like its Luftwaffe peers, used radios, but also dropped messages, using a smoke cartridge to assist in finding the time-sensitive message. Later that afternoon a nearby Soviet armoured train with an antiaircraft gun brought the aircraft down.[14] In what had become a common occurrence Ju-87s struck observed and assumed enemy artillery and infantry positions east of Rogachev along a stretch of the rain-swollen Dnepr. Judging by the unabated, heavy Soviet cannon fire, only the latter were seemingly effected. During the final hour before 3rd Panzer Division's slated attack time, Schweppenburg visited Model to enlighten his subordinate about XXIV Motorized Army Corps' broader status, including 4th Panzer Division having reached Bykhov, where a 16-tonne pontoon bridge was to be constructed.

At 1800hrs on 4 July 3rd Panzer Division began its attack to secure Dnepr crossings from which to strike eastward the following day. Having ordered 6th Panzer Regiment (minus its III. Panzer Battalion), and 1st Motorized Reconnaissance and 3rd Motorcycle Battalions to Novyy Bykhov where an 8-tonne pontoon bridge would be assembled across the 40–80m-wide waterway to allow infantry and light vehicles to carve out a modest bridgehead, he now had his artillery engage targets along the far bank downriver to Zhlobin, with 1st Observation Battalion's help to tamp down resistance and keep the enemy from redirecting reinforcements to the fresh fighting.[15] Ju-87s added their customary support against targets requiring greater accuracy to eliminate. At 2000hrs the Germans estimated there was one enemy battery of 150mm guns and a second comprising 220mm south-east of Khodosovichi, while smaller calibre Soviet artillery was more common north of Rogachev. Later in the day the commander of 143rd Arko, Colonel Kurt Forster, reported two enemy batteries had been put out of action with a single fire strike, although two to three more remained. Upwards of six more were detected south-east of Rogachev, with some long-range Soviet artillery in the Zhlobin area.

With Schweppenburg's Ia, Lieutenant Colonel Brücker, concerned for Guderian's open southern flank 3rd Panzer Division extended its right flank in that direction and downriver to the Dobysna's mouth, 3rd Motorcycle Battalion and a subordinated company from 543rd Panzerjäger Battalion were moved into the Pobolovo–Luchin area. Toward finding additional, preferably unlikely and therefore unexpected, Dnepr crossing sites Model sent a small, hopefully little noticed Kampfgruppe formed around a platoon of armoured reconnaissance cars and another of tanks, as well as motor transport for 3./39th Motorized Engineer Battalion to Novyy Bykhov. While II./394th Motorized Rifle Regiment made good progress in getting over the Dnepr to take Zbarov from the east at 0510hrs, it was Model's only bridgehead of the morning. To reinforce success at 0700hrs I./394th Motorized Rifle Regiment, which had recently been designated a reserve, was ordered to follow suit along a similar attack axis that skirted Madora and halted just beyond Nizhnyaya.

To facilitate 3rd Panzer Division's crossing west of Zbarov early in the morning a trio of Panzer III *Tauchpanzern* from 12./6th Panzer Regiment waded into the 50m-wide Dnepr.[16] After briefly submerging in the nearly 4m-deep water and emerging on the east bank Soviet fire destroyed one of the vehicles, but the others provided enough firepower to allow a Kampfgruppe of II./394th Motorized Rifle Regiment, elements of 6th Panzer Regiment, and some antitank guns to cross to the low-lying swampland awaiting them on the far bank.[17] A robust Soviet defence repleat with antitank guns, artillery, and machine guns served to stimy III./6th Panzer Regiment's efforts to cross closer to Rogachev. South of the town, in spite of I./3rd Motorized Rifle Regiment holding nearby Luchin, enemy forces in regimental strength on the opposite bank rebuffed II. Battalion's crossing attempt. As a result Kleemann suggested redirecting 3rd Motorized Rifle Regiment north to expand the bridgehead around Zbarov, but Model demurred. With 'Patrol Gusovius' (1st Reconnaissance Battalion) having just found Novyy Bykhov enemy-free, even though its bridge had been destroyed, 3rd Panzer Division's commander ordered the village held and 3rd Motorized Rifle Regiment to establish defences along the Dnepr's right bank. When Luftwaffe reconnaissance detected new Soviet artillery fire from the Tursk area the volume of surrounding antiaircraft ground fire prompted a request for German bombers to silence the threat. With Luftwaffe artillery observation directing German fire against upwards of five enemy batteries near Khodosovichi at 1040hrs 6th Panzer Regiment was ordered to the crossing at Bykhov, although without its I. Panzer Battalion, II./42nd Artillery Regiment (143 Arko), and 635th Engineer Battalion, with a bridge 'B' were allocated to 10th Motorized Infantry Division heading in the opposite direction for Zhlobin. By the early afternoon, even though additional 3rd Panzer Division forces moved into the area and were available to bolster the struggling Dnepr crossing, Model questioned whether the costs of continuing with a command that had been through two straight weeks of often heavy combat and lengthy driving remained warranted. Soon after, 3rd Rifle Brigade reported Soviet artillery had eased, but the Soviets seemed to have penetrated into the north-eastern edge of Zbarov. In response a German long-range combat group (*Fernkampfgruppe*, aka *Feka*), which organized the division's towed field guns and howitzers for missions such as counterbattery fire, concentrated on the area.[18]

Having set off along the Titovka–Mogilev road, on 4 July Langermann ordered 4th Panzer Division's spearhead to turn from the well-defended city for a crossing site over the Dnepr at Bykhov. Continuing on, a platoon of Panzer IIIs from I./35th Panzer Regiment crossed the box-girder road bridge over the Dnepr only to have awaiting Red Army artillery drop part of a span into the water behind them. In the ensuing fight on the east bank Soviet antitank and antiaircraft guns quickly knocked four of the panzern, but the German tankmen and what other forces that had moved into the small bridgehead held on until a 16-tonne pontoon bridge was constructed a few kilometres downstream to bring II./35th Regiment across.[19]

With Schweppenburg having reached the Dnepr at Rogachev and Bykhov, and XXXXVI and XXXXVII Motorized Infantry Corps pushing across the Berezina, Soviet forces facing Guderian largely fell back on Mogilev and Orsha.[20] Freed from its cordon duties west of Minsk, 17th Panzer Division renewed its eastward advance along Panzer Route 2 as a complete formation. Passing through a largely destroyed Minsk, with its lingering, post-bombing pall of black smoke, tangles of concrete, charred wood, bricks, and shattered glass littering the streets, along with destroyed vehicles, and dead soldiers, civilians, and horses assaulted the eyes and noses. Having left the area during the period of heaviest Luftwaffe attacks, many of the city's 240,000 residents milled about or returned with their salvaged belongings to an uncertain future. Lacking dedicated facilities to help hold the seemingly innumerable number of Red Army prisoners an area just outside the city had been turned into an open-air prison camp.[21] With such a large labour force potentially able to assist the war effort later that July, Todt asked Kluge for 10,000 Soviet prisoners, but believing the campaign in the East would be brief the field marshal refused. Guderian was then driven to XXXXVI Motorized Army Corps' sector where he visited Schaal at his 10th Panzer Division headquarters and later 'Reich's' commander, Paul Hausser, at Staryye Rechki. At the latter location the *SS-Gruppenführer* reported that 2./SS-Engineer Battalion 'Reich' had constructed a pontoon bridge just north of the damaged Yakshitsy crossing, and that since the morning I./SS-'Deutschland' and SS-Motorcycle Battalion 'Reich' had carved out a bridgehead beyond the Berezina around Brodets. Prisoners indicated a mix of Red Army cavalry and an infantry regiment in the area, but the river's marshy floodplain required corduroy roads did more to hinder 'Reich's' progress towards the River Drut' than enemy resistance. Seemingly illustrating an enemy shortage of brass, Soviet artillery cartridge cases were found to be made of iron.[22]

Having been unable to eliminate the Borisov bridgehead and their position increasingly untenable, by 4 July 1st Moscow Motor Rifle Division had pulled back to positions behind the River Nacha.²³ With this newest delaying effort along Panzer Route 2 soon failing the incremental Soviet withdrawal towards Orsha continued.²⁴ Some 30km to the south at 1500hrs the remnants of 100th Rifle Division proved unable to keep German mobile elements from crossing the Berezina near Chernyavka. To provide something of a strike force the formation organized a motorized rifle detachment that moved into the Pogost area to support 155th Rifle Division. Within 2 hours, however, a German regimental-sized Kampfgruppe, with armour and artillery, struck the latter formation and forced it to withdrawal to the north. Although 100th Rifle Division managed to retake Selishche, it was soon forced onto the defensive; much as 50th Rifle Division along a swampy stretch between Kholkholitsa and Studenka. During the night of 4/5 July 100th Rifle Division crossed to the Berezina's eastern bank where the river significantly narrowed and onto the nearby high ground at Oreshkovichi. From there the formation wormed its way through the surrounding forests and swampland to establish positions north-east of Berezino where it sent out reconnaissance forces to ascertain German strengths and intentions. Arrayed up to 3km along the northern edge of the Cherven–Belynichi road, the wooded terrain around the River Berezina provided an advantageous area from which to strike 10th Motorized Infantry Division's left flank as it pushed for Belynichi along the Drut'.

With the destruction of the Soviet Third and Tenth Armies behind him Hoth exploited the comparative absence of organized enemy resistance by striking out towards Vitebsk, while on his right Lemelsen focused on Orsha, where the Dnepr bent away to the eastern horizon. By 5 July the German Ninth and Fourth Armies had cleared what remained of the Minsk Pocket, while Third and Second Panzer Groups readied to conduct the next great offensive directed at Smolensk and points east. Although a gap of some 160–230km existed between these infantry formations and the armoured and motorized forces coalescing along the Dnepr, Brauchitsch authorized Guderian's plan to secure crossings over the major waterway, without objection from Bock or Kluge. Having marched for upwards of 50km every day into the seemingly vast enemy spaces, demoralized more than a few Landsers welcomed a firefight to break up the monotony and tried to take comfort in the belief that the war in the East would be over soon. Assuming the Soviets would prioritize its forces on defending the more obvious crossings at Orsha, Mogilev, and Rogachev, Guderian chose Bykhov as one, being in relatively marshy, wooded terrain that offered surprise to more quickly secure a strong bridgehead before an effective response could be sent against it.

In preparation the Germans cleared the Western Dnepr from Bykhov south to Zhlobin, while being careful to avoid bunching up around the potential crossing sites to maintain secrecy as long as possible. As part of their ongoing work to facilitate the German advance by helping to build bridges and improve roads and rail lines, Organization Todt supplemented its personnel with prisoner labour; a questionable practice, although not uncommon during wartime. During the evening of 5 July the Soviet XXXXIV Rifle Corps repeatedly struck in the direction of Borisov towards recrossing the Berezina, but by 2200hrs Lemelsen halted the effort short of its goal. As part of his increasing strength east of the Berezina a Kampfgruppe was formed around Colonel Rudolf-Eduard Licht's 40th Motorized Rifle Regiment to serve as a 17th Panzer Division's vanguard. To maintain contact with Hoth and alleviate the strain on Panzer Route 2, on reaching the River Bobr, Arnim left Panzer Route 2 to move along several dirt trails that led to Chereya. Although much of the area around Senno was subjected to heavy afternoon thunderstorms on 5 July that undermined the area's deep, sandy roads that held vehicles fast and strung out the march columns, 'Kampfgruppe Licht' had by chance avoided such weather and advanced to Osinovka along routes yet to be doused. At Senno strong enemy resistance with artillery was encountered, which prompted deploying for an attack to eliminate the threat.

As Germany's three army groups advanced eastward, the size of the battle-zone increased proportionately to the difficulty their respective commanders had in managing not only their front lines, but sizeable rear areas, and each had an assigned corps-sized formation to control the latter. Under Bock, the Commander of Army Group Centre's Rear Area, Lieutenant General (*General der Infanterie*) Max Schenckendorff's control of three security divisions, and assorted security and signals units, helped perpetrate Hitler's war of annihilation over broad swathes of recently bypassed or overrun enemy territory. Whether looking to settle old scores, sharing a political bent, or simply trying to survive by ingratiating themselves with the victors, Poles, Ukrainians, Lithuanians, and other ethnic groups in these areas often participated in the resulting pogrom and extralegal killings to varying degrees.[25] Others joined the fledgling Soviet partisan cause, which would soon blossom into a major combat, sabotage, and harassment element along German logistics lines and sap the strength of an *Ostheer*, as it conducted a largely conventional conflict to its front.

Orsha Counteroffensive

With Western Front having brought strategic reserves to bolster their positions west of Orsha–Vitebsk they were able to stymie much of Bock's momentum in the area. Along Panzer Route 2, 1st Moscow Motor Rifle Division and elements of the Soviet XXXXIV Rifle Corps that had pulled back from Bobr and its namesake river the previous day, on 6 July they struck back at 18th Panzer Division, as it approached Tolochin. Employing a converging attack from the north and south to capture the village and then Slaveni, by 1000hrs the counterattack had expanded out towards Ryasna, Obol'tsy, and Krasnoye Selo. During spates of heavy rain that turned low-lying sections of road into a viscous mess, Guderian met with Lemelsen to discuss the unfolding threat.[26] Lacking sufficient reconnaissance ahead of the latter's masses of armour, what began as a meeting engagement near Senno expanded, as more of the Soviet V Mechanized Corps pushed into the area towards Chashiki only to run into prepared German antitank defences.[27] With the Soviet 18th Tank Division (VII MC) striking westward out of the Bogushevsk area, and 17th and 13th Tank Divisions (V MC) moving up from the south-east, 27th Motorized Reconnaissance Battalion (17 PD) and accompanying German motorized infantry, engineers, and antiaircraft were sudden engaged in a firefight around Senno.[28] Unable to stand up to the pressure Weber's advance element withdrew during the evening and back across saturated terrain that frustrated on- and off-road movement.[29] As was, perhaps, typical with mobile operations of both sides, 109th Motorized Division followed behind V Mechanized Corps' armoured formations to help hold captured territory and provide immediate reinforcement. What had at first blush appeared as formidable Soviet armour and motorized force had by day's end showed signs of faltering.[30]

Weathering the previous day's fight, during what was a warm and sunny 7 July Nehring's tankers pushed back against 1st Moscow Motor Rifle Division beyond Moshkovo.[31] Having been flown in a Fiesler-Storch to Tolpino to get a firsthand idea of 17th Panzer Division's struggles against masses of predominantly T-26 and BT-7 tanks that Ninth Army's aerial reconnaissance had picked up two days earlier, Lemelsen called in Ju-87 support. While the plane's wing-mounted 50kg bombs could destroy lighter Soviet tanks with direct hits only the single 250kg could do the same to the heavier tanks.[32] With dozens of Soviet tanks having broken down or run out of fuel along their advance routes what vehicles still in action were subjected to antitank fire, aerial attacks, and for the comparatively few T-34s and KV-1s, German engineers, that took increasingly unsustainable losses.[33] With his left flank stabilized Lemelsen reallocated Streich from his temporary stint as commander for Weber, before returning to XXXXVII Motorized Army Corps' command post at Nacha.[34] Considering the seemingly newfound zeal, it was perhaps unsurprising that wireless intercepts picked up a new Soviet army headquarters near Orsha, which added to Guderian's suspicions that the enemy was working to bolster a defence line along the River Dnepr.[35]

In what was Guderian's centre the Soviet XX Mechanized Corps fell back onto the Mogilev area, with its depleted 210th Motorized Rifle Division near Novoselki, and the even worse off 26th and 38th Tank Divisions only now disengaging from the Drut' between Krasnaya Sloboda and Tverdovo. With SS-'Deutschland' engineers having constructed a bridge over the Berezina during the night of 3/4 July 'Reich' was able to resume its advance to the Dnepr, while preventing the enemy from doing so. Initially, a Kampfgruppe under SS-'Deutschland's' commander, *SS-Oberführer* (roughly equivalent to Brigadier) Wilhelm Bittrich, that included SS-Reconnaissance Battalion 'Reich' and engineers was sent ahead for Usakino to determine whether the terrain to the east could support the entire division.[36] With heavy rainfall soon undermining the already poor, potholed woodland roads, across which engineers needed to constantly lay corduroy support and repair crossings, Hausser had the remainder of the division move across 10th Panzer Division's wake to Selishche, Zamostoch'ye, and Borok. Largely willing its way forward through adverse weather and saturated terrain, 'Kampfgruppe Bittrich' was temporarily given I./103rd Motorized Artillery Regiment, while its remaining two artillery battalions occupied a wooded area to the north.[37]

Mirroring the fighting along Guderian's left flank, on his right strong Soviet forces crossed the Dnepr at Zhlobin and struck westward, with the apparent intent of striking Schweppenburg's rear areas.[38] Hitting a surprised 10th Reconnaissance Company, which served as 10th Motorized Infantry Division's spearhead, at Pobolovo at about 0230hrs on 6 July in little over an hour the German spearhead had pulled back. Unsure of the unfolding counterattack's strength and direction, Model kept I./ and II./6th Panzer Regiment in the area to intervene if necessary. With Luftwaffe reconnaissance indicating additional enemy forces advancing from the Orel–Bryansk area towards Gomel' if the Germans acted quickly they could eliminate the immediate Soviet threat south of Rogachev before it could be reinforced. Already Soviet strength in the Mogilev and Zhlobin sectors was greater than had been assumed and had countered Schweppenburg's efforts at affecting crossings. 41st Motorized Rifle Regiment (10 MID) soon moved up to surround Soviet forces at Pobolovo and halt what began as a reconnaissance-in-force.

Throughout the afternoon the addition of the division's III./20th Motorized Rifle Regiment, supporting elements, and two-thirds of 6th Panzer Regiment helped push the Soviets back across the Dnepr. During the fighting I./6th Panzer Regiment suffered particularly heavy looses, especially from T-34s firing from ambush positions that contributed to knocking out a reported twenty-two of the panzer battalion's tanks.[39] Although field repairs, cannibalization, or for seriously damaged vehicles being sent to an Army ordnance supply office and then to the manufacturer would put many back in action, given the steady decrease in available armour helped convince Guderian to refrain from pressing for establishing a bridgehead at Rogachev as being too obvious and well defended. With the retreating Soviet infantry blowing up Zhlobin's road bridge and the rail crossing just downriver at 1630hrs, Schweppenburg ordered 3rd Panzer Division to begin pulling out of its positions between Novyy Bykhov and Mogilev, as well as its hard-won bridgehead at Zbarov to reposition to the north and along 4th Panzer Division's left.

At 0100hrs on 7 July 1st Cavalry Division arrived at Bobruysk, where it rested in preparation for Second Panzer Group's push beyond the Dnepr.

Having fought Soviet forces across 400km of sparsely populated forests and marshland, the formation would now perform security and clean-up actions (*Säuberungsaktionen*) along the Berezina. To maintain combat effectiveness the horsemen were vigilant in mitigating cases of rabies, glanders, and other bovine ailments, and avoided contact with civilian and Red Army horses. To further isolate and protect the formation's principal assets, especially their Prussian Trakehner mounts, which were know for their endurance and athleticism, local stables and equipment were left unused and stray or unauthorized dogs were killed.

The next day the Soviet Twentieth Army continued its thrust into the border separating Hoth's sphere of influence from Guderian's. Continuing to withdraw eastward following its recent scrap with 18th Panzer Division, the Soviet 100th Rifle Division now engaged in fierce fighting a few kilometres south of Krucha against 'Reich', during which Red Army reporting indicated having destroyed several enemy tanks at Belynichi. By advancing over the flat farmland, woods, and dispersed hamlets south-east of Pogost the SS troopers attempted to turn the enemy's left flank. With 29th Motorized Infantry Division having deviated to the south-east for Denisovichi and the Chernyavka–Kopys road, during the night of 8/9 July 11th SS-Infantry Regiment pushed enemy elements back to around nearby Ukhavla in disorder.[40] To the north 17th Panzer Division similarly hit the Soviet V Mechanized Corps from around Senno before striking south into the Soviet 17th Tank Division's right flank to cut its supply route back along the Orsha–Lepel road. To anchor the area between Hoth and Guderian, while they each renewed their eastward drives, Lemelsen established a Blocking Group (*Sperrverband*) under Streich, incorporating 5th Motorized Machine-Gun Battalion, 611th Panzerjäger Battalion, and small complements of artillery, engineers, and reconnaissance.[41] Finally arriving from its hard-fought cordon duties west of Minsk, 15th Motorized Infantry Regiment (29 MID) secured the area near Bobr and sent out strong reconnaissance elements along a forest trail to Krucha and on to Krugloye.[42]

During what had been a grinding three-day battle, the Germans savaged the two Red Army mechanized corps sent against them.[43] With Hoth having pinned the enemy against Vitebsk, 17th Panzer Division worked its way southward to rejoin XXXXVII Motorized Army Corps around Panzer Route 2. Unlike Schweppenburg, whose command lined the Dnepr from Bykhov to Zhlobin and was ready to initiate crossings in force, Lemelsen, and XXXXVI Motorized Army Corps were still arriving along the waterway north of Mogilev to Soviet-held Orsha. During 8 July, while elements of 10th Panzer Division moved up to the Shklov area to drive a wedge between enemy's II Rifle Corps to the north and XX Mechanized Corps to the south, the bulk of 'Reich' crossed the River Drut' at Belynichi. To the south SS-'Deutschland' reached Gorodshchina en route to its comrades. Intent on maintaining security and concealing its build-up at selected Dnepr crossing sites, Second Panzer Group made maximum use of night-time movement. Typically gathering in wooded areas to hinder enemy observation, track marks and other signs of vehicular movement were obscured and netting and freshly cut foliage used to further blend into the background. In what had become a distressing pattern of divining the enemy's strength and intentions during the day's meeting at Hitler's Rastenburg headquarters (aka the 'Wolf's Lair' (*Wolfsschanze*)), set deep in the forests of East Prussia to help mask the site from observation, German intelligence reported that the new commander of the Soviet Western Front, Marshal Semyon Timoshenko, possessed eleven divisions; a figure that was soon found to be grossly underestimated.

Clearing the Dnepr

With the Soviets having fallen back onto Dnepr bridgeheads at Orsha, Mogilev, and Bykhov, Guderian switched to offensive actions on his far flanks to focus on the build-up required not only to achieve crossings, but provide the necessary forces and resources to then form a southern pincer for the encirclement of Smolensk. Looking for suitable alternative crossings Guderian spoke with Schweppenburg who would make an attempt at Bykhov on 10 July. Still needing to move up to the Dnepr in strength XXXXVI and XXXXVII Motorized Army Corps would respectively conduct their own efforts at Shklov and Kopys the next day. Having waited until the Germans approached, in order to get as many of their comrades to the eastern bank as possible, Soviet engineers blew up the latter's bridge on 8 July.[44] With Second Panzer Group's efforts during the Bialystok–Minsk Pocket having accounted for 151,176 of the 332,111 total enemy prisoners and 1,233 captured tanks out of 3,188 taken it came at a cost in hard-to-replace men and materiel.[45] With the German momentum continuously moving eastward their possession of numerous battlefields following their conclusions meant they typically captured massive amounts of enemy materiel, but also were in a position to recover much of their own damaged or destroyed assets.

As part of their counterattack south of Rogachev at 1000hrs Soviet soldiers attempted to cross the Dnepr near Zhlobin using individual inner tubes around their abdomens that allowed them to fire their small arms, but German forces rebuffed the effort.[46] At noon on 8 July 1st Motorized Reconnaissance Battalion (3 PD) reported strong enemy activity south-east of Zhlobin around Skephya. Well to the rear Reconnaissance Lehr Battalion (1 CD) scouted the swampy woodland between Parichi and Boroviki, but found no enemy; much as around Yashchitsy and Zabrod'ye. Aerial observation at 2000hrs added that the Gomel'–Rechitsa–Boroviki road was similarly free of Soviet forces, as was the Zhlobin–Gomel' rail line. Although Kluge had expressed his intention to attack on 9 or 10 July, 10th Motorized Infantry Division (with 143rd Arko) was still completing its quiet relocation from Zhlobin to north of 4th Panzer Division.

Having three days previously increased Barbarossa's end goal of advancing to an overly optimistic line between Arkhangel'sk and Astrakhan (where the Volga emptied into the Caspian Sea) to the absurdly unrealistic Ural Mountains, in laying out German operations east of the Dnepr, Hitler met with Brauchitsch and Halder to discuss how Bock was to destroy the bulk of Red Army forces in the Smolensk–Vitebsk–Orsha area to open the direct route to Moscow. With Kinzel reporting that 89 of the identified 164 Soviet rifle divisions had been rendered combat ineffective or destroyed, with similar losses in enemy tank divisions, and only 11 reserve divisions detected, the Red Army appeared to be weakening.[47] With Brauchitsch presenting such a rosy assessment to Hitler, the Führer envisioned that once Second and Third Panzer Groups completed the encirclement of Smolensk and the destruction of enemy forces contained within the subsequent pocket to clear the direct route to the Soviet capital Hoth would then reorient northward to assist Field Marshal Wilhelm Ritter von Leeb's offensive against Leningrad, or if unnecessary to advance to the northeast towards an eventual northern envelopment of Moscow. Guderian would commensurately advance into Eastern Ukraine to coordinate with Rundstedt. During the eventual fight for Leningrad and Moscow, German armour was to be withheld to preserve the valuable asset and the Luftwaffe brought in to flatten both cities, and target enemy manufacturing facilities out to the River Volga. Hitler also ordered the construction of winter quarters, although new tanks coming off the factory lines were to be kept in Germany and not sent to the front. In the wake of the Führer's increasing say in military matters that were too often based on inaccurate intelligence, wishful thinking, or personal insecurities that led him to dismiss information contradictory to his beliefs, or berate those providing it, the result often undercut the traditional role of the German General Staff in exercising extensive operational autonomy and responsibility.

Having gone to Second Panzer Group's headquarters early on 9 July to discuss the next stage of combat operations Kluge initially stressed allowing additional infantry forces to move up, but Guderian's arguments to the contrary, and his backing by Bock and the OKH, ultimately held sway. Getting Kluge's grudging approval after the meeting, Guderian went to XXXXVII Motorized Army Corps' headquarters where Lemelsen was unsure that 18th Panzer Division could push beyond Alenovichi to take Kokhanovo as a prerequisite to moving up to the Dnepr. Subsequently meeting with Nehring, who was optimistic about continuing the attack before the enemy could strengthen its side of the river, Guderian then spoke with Boltenstern who was of a similar mind.[48]

To cover Western Front's extended frontage all available Soviet formations needed to occupy positions well forward and without sizeable reserves, while emplacing combat modifying mines and obstructions as they became available.[49] At 1300hrs 1st Motorized Reconnaissance Battalion reported that the area around Yakshitsy, and south to the River Berezina was free of enemy forces, which combined with other similar reconnaissance reports along Second Panzer Group's right seemed odd given the Soviet incursion targeting Bobruysk. An hour later Luftwaffe reconnaissance provided information on Soviet fire from batteries east of Tursk, with additional flights along the Dnepr from Rogachev to near Novyy Bykhov. Again, no enemy preparations were apparent. At 1530hrs Feldt, the division Ia, the commander of 1st Horse Artillery Regiment, and that of 3rd Motorized Rifle Regiment met with Model to discuss 1st^t Cavalry Division's increasing responsibility in covering Guderian's far southern flank.

By the evening of 9 July even though Schweppenburg had been unable to secure Dnepr crossings on-the-bounce due to unexpectedly tough enemy resistance, XXIV Motorized Army Corps was largely in place and ready to undertake its next great encirclement. North of Mogilev 10th Panzer Division and 'Kampfgruppe Bittrich' ('Reich') had arrived before the waterway respectively north-west and south-west of Knyazhitsy and close to Shklov. To further sell to the enemy that Hausser intended to cross the Dnepr at Mogilev columns of empty lorries were to move into the area during the daytime and return the way they had come at night. 'Reich's' assault guns were to similarly move up to the Mogilev sector so that their engine noise could be heard across the Dnepr to imply the movement of a larger armoured force, prior to the vehicles being sent north for their actual crossing site. Given the lack of forward infantry formations, on the eve of Second Panzer Group's offensive Bock held reservations about the undertaking's success and repeatedly urged Kluge to reinforce Hoth's success further north at Senno and Vitebsk. Remaining of the same mind, the latter refrained from interceding at this late stage given the area's poor roads would unduly hinder the movement of these formations, the majority of whom had yet to cross the Berezina, and would give the enemy time to further strengthen their Dnepr defences. In the process Army Group Centre would secure the strip of largely open land between the Rivers Dnepr and Dvina, known as the 'Smolensk Gate', which led directly to Moscow. Of comparable importance, while the distance from the Reich border to Orsha equalled the 500km limit within which German planners estimated their logistics could adequately provide support, absent re-gauging the rail lines, for Second Panzer Group the distance was still only halfway to Guderian's ultimate goal.[50]

Chapter 5

Mogilev and Smolensk, 10–20 July 1941

On 10 July Guderian once again stood in strength before a major river, with the intent of conducting contested crossings, only this time against an enemy alerted to the threat. Under Twenty-First Army out of Gomel' the Soviet LXIII and LXVI Rifle Corps had been well positioned to strike Bock's right flank as Army Group Centre began to move east of the Polesie Marshes.[1] As Soviet ground forces were moved into the Smolensk battlezone, what dominance the Luftwaffe had achieved at the campaign's start was being steadily threatened, as the front moved eastward and Red Air Force supply lines lessened and replacement aircraft were reorganized and brought forward. To provide unified support for Guderian's efforts along the Dnepr, Fighter Wing 'Mölders' had been slated to aid XXIV Motorized Army Corps, while VIII and II Air Corps respectively supported XXXXVII and XXXXVI Motorized Army Corps.[2] With much of Schweppenburg's command having been directed to the area between a well-defended Rogachev and Mogilev 1st Cavalry Division was largely on its own holding his rather open right flank until LIII Army Corps arrived from the Berezina. Given that large Soviet forces from the Gomel' area under Twenty-First Army represented a major threat, Guderian felt confident that any temporary weakening of the sector was acceptable.

Along with its fellow armoured and Motorized formations 4th Panzer Division's logistics personnel struggled to maintain a consistent flow of vital supplies to an ever-distant front line, and acquire the additional manpower to guard the lengthy transportation network. To date some 480km of track had been regauged to provide a railhead from Brest to beyond Minsk using a simple technique of interspacing new rails with the old to avoid unnecessarily damaging the underlying foundation. Although Army Group Centre required an estimated thirty-four trains each day, no more than eighteen in a 24-hour period had yet been achieved. Combined with the occasional improper prioritization of supplies, damaged infrastructure, mechanical breakdowns, and increasing distances from rail heads, Landsers frequently relied on improvisation and finding alternatives to remain as combat effective as possible. They knew firsthand what OKH had emphasized, that, 'Every man must know that failed vehicles can not be replaced!' While regauged rail lines permitted the stockpiling of supplies between Borisov and Orsha, land and air assets would need to travel over 100km to transport them to XXIV Motorized Army Corps, such as 4th Panzer Division's Ammunition Distribution Point (*Munitionsausgabestelle*) No. 6 north-west of Bykhov.[3]

Having foregone the customary large build-up to ensure Second Panzer Group had the strength and endurance to cross and advance beyond the Dnepr, Guderian instead opted for surprise and speed to exploit the enemy's largely disorganized state. Even though this translated into some confusion to get as many forces to their slated crossing locations as possible and reorganize them to best effect, at 0500hrs on 10 July German artillery and rocket fire suddenly erupted near Bykhov, arced over the River Dnepr, and pummelled the far bank. A few kilometres to the north 604th Motorized Heavy 210mm Howitzer Battalion added its weight to more distant targets. Once the customary preparatory bombardment had concluded Ju-87s and other Luftwaffe support targeted any surviving Red Army forces of note. Although no resistance was initially encountered, at 0615hrs assault engineers from 4th Panzer Division rushed to two locations north of the village to get their pneumatic rafts and assault boats into the water and onto the eastern bank. During this time Luftwaffe reconnaissance reported several light smoke plumes 8km north of Zhlobin that implied Soviet campfires, and enemy rail traffic out of Gomel', but nothing to indicate surprise had been compromised. As an initial part of Model's repositioning a II./6th Panzer Regiment-based Kampfgruppe from Kleeman's larger command arrived at a forested area south-west of Chechevichi, having recently fought at Zhlobin. Although Luftwaffe reconnaissance continued to find a lack of enemy activity in the Novyy Bykhov area by midday, Soviet aircraft were becoming active and causing concern lest they interdict Second Panzer Group's crossings. At 1445hrs 1./39th Motorized Engineer Battalion was employed to facilitate Model's vanguard II./6th Panzer Regiment getting to the Dnepr's far bank. Having successfully taken the Koden Bridge during *Barbarossatag*, 3./39th Motorized Engineer Battalion had just completed repairs to the River Ola crossing at Leytichi and the one over the Dobysna. Following a morning of artillery and Luftwaffe strikes around Lykovo, 4th Panzer and 10th Motorized Divisions began transitioning to the Dnepr's far side respectively just south of Bykhov and near Borkolabovo. Once through the rather thinly spread enemy defence along the waterway the Germans pushed for Slavgorod and the River Sozh against uncoordinated, often surprised Soviet second echelon elements from XXXXV Rifle Corps and Fourth Army.

With the Germans having repaired the destroyed bridge over the River Lakhva at 1525hrs 4th Panzer Division reported it had secured the road on the eastern bank against opposition. To determine the extent of enemy defences south-west of Mogilev Major Ernst Wellmann's Kampfgruppe organized around his I./3rd Motorized Rifle Regiment and advanced along the Dnepr's western bank. Moving to within a dozen kilometres of the city's centre, at about 1830hrs

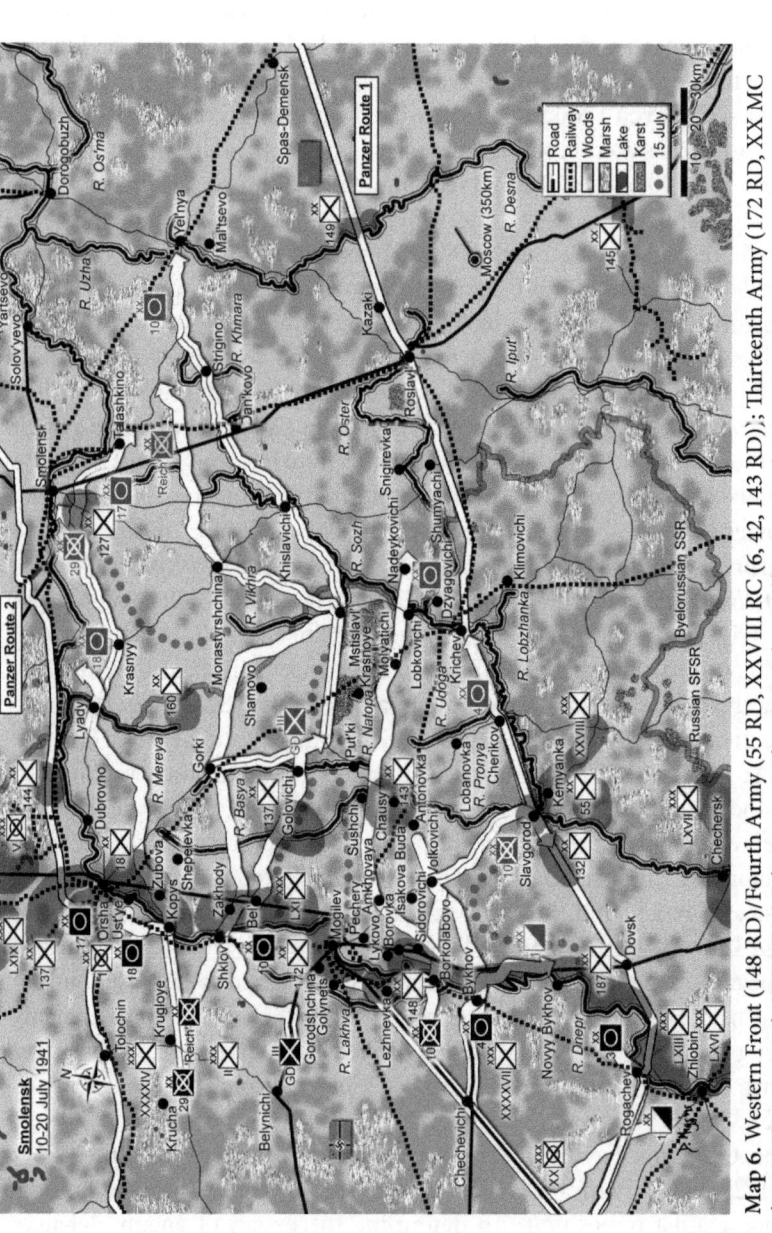

Map 6. Western Front (148 RD)/Fourth Army (55 RD, XXVIII RC (6, 42, 143 RD)); Thirteenth Army (172 RD, XX MC (26, 38 TD, 210 MD), XXXV RC (132, 187 RD), LXI RC (53 RD)); Nineteenth Army (127 RD, XXXXIV RC (64 RD); Twentieth Army (1 MD, 137, 144 RD, II RC (100, 161 RD), XX RC (18 RD), LXIX RC (73, 153, 229, 233 RD)); Twenty-First Army (LXIII RC (61, 167 RD), LXVI RC (154), LXVII (102, 132, 151)); Twenty-Second Army (160 RD); The Stavka/Twenty-Eighth Army (33 RC (145, 149 RD)). TsAMO, f.208, op.2511, d.210,l.l. During much of this period II and XXXXIV RC were spread out, bypassed, and lacking organization between the Rivers Berezina and Dnepr.

Seen here in May 1940, as a Lieutenant General (*General der Panzertruppe*), Guderian wears the 1939 Clasp for the Iron Cross 2nd Class that he earned on 17 September 1914, while serving as commander of 3rd Heavy Radio Station, and the Knight's Cross awarded on 27 October 1939 for his leadership of XIX Motorized Army Corps during the Polish Campaign. (*NAC*)

German engineers ferrying vehicles or weapon systems across the River Bug using a Bridge Equipment 'B' pontoon section affixed to what are likely pneumatic rafts. Seen just upriver from the Terespol–Brest steel truss rail bridge in I./135th Infantry Regiment's sector the men have a relaxed demeanor, but still wear helmets and carry slung rifles. Note the ammunition boxes and axe, and what looks like a damaged span on the adjacent wooden rail bridge. (*Memorial Complex 'Brest Hero Fortress'*)

A Panzer II Ausf. C (left) and a pre-production Ausf. b 18th Panzer Regiment (18 PD). Note the wrapped 20mm KwK 30 L/55 and supplemental MG-34 barrels to keep dust from fouling the weapons. (*Arne Schrader*)

10th Panzer Division personnel being ferried across the River Bug on *Barbarossatag*. Presumably the photograph was touched up for period publication and shows the men carrying their own makeshift loading ramp. The 37mm PaK 36 has a barrel cover to keep out debris until needed, while the Steib B2 sidecar has a stretcher instead of a spare tyre. (*NAC*)

17th Panzer Division vehicles waiting to head out. Considering such a formation's march column extended for dozens of kilometers along a single route, the cumulative traffic jam in constricted areas exacerbated traffic control, repairs, resupply, and a host of necessary services. The rudimentary road network throughout the Soviet Union made goggles a necessity. (*NAC*)

A Panzer II Ausf. A 'Flamingo' from 3./100th Panzer Battalion (Fl.), June 1941. A flame thrower was mounted on either front corner (seen here covered) and could respectively shoot eighty times out to 35m across a 180-degree arc. Note the five vehicle fuel containers carried on the rear deck and the lifebuoy on the railing. (*NAC*)

With Second Panzer Group having bypassed the still active Brest fortress, and its vanguards approached Minsk and the River Berezina, the predominantly foot-bound XII Army Corps was soon left well behind and reverted to Fourth Army control on 26 June 1941. Seen here two days later 12th Infantry Regiment (31 ID) passes through Rozana. Note the men using wooden poles as leverage to perform vehicle maintenance or extraction. (*NAC*)

A column of pontoon transports in June 1941 en route to some of the first of many river crossings during Barbarossa. In the distance traffic is bunching up. (*NAC*)

German soldiers on 26 June 1941, having assumed a defensive stance near a road to help block Soviet forces escaping from the Minsk Pocket. The nearest soldier (likely the squad leader) carries an MP-38/40 submachine gun, while the two-man machine-gun team uses an MG-34 on a bipod. While well-fitting jackboots were suited to marching and keeping trousers from undue wear, as temperatures dropped their trademark hobnails conducted the ground cold to the wearer's feet. (*NARA*)

A 3rd Panzer Division reconnaissance element having stopped during its advance, 29 June 1941. The combination of the Party banner and three coloured panels indicated their positions to friendly aircraft. The bicycles could carry some supplies on a rear-mounted porter, as well as the rider's small arms and grenades. The front wheel's rotation powered a headlight and each carries a tyre pump. By using a vehicle-affixed central tow rope and individual handle ropes, up to twenty bicyclists could be pulled. (*NAC*)

With Major 'Willi' Teege's Kampfgruppe having secured the Borisov Bridge at 2150hrs on 1 July 1941, the remainder of Nehring's command soon followed to push 175th Motorized Rifle Regiment (1 MD) out. Seen here two days later, motorized elements of 18th Panzer Division stream over and east of the River Berezina, where in November 1812 Napoleon I's disintegrating and desperate Grande Armée gathered to cross, but in the opposite direction. In the right distance vehicles maintain the regulation 30m separation to minimize accidents or damage if attacked, as they move across one of the waterway's tributaries. (*NARA*)

29th Motorized Infantry Division near Nieswiez, 2 July 1941. The Horch Kfz. 15 at the rear served as a sturdy, versatile light transport or command car. Civilian vehicles that had been pressed into/modified for military use generally lacked the ruggedness to survive long in the East. This Opel Admiral now serves as a staff car, with an external storage container affixed to the trunk and a mat to minimize roof damage should additional material be carried. (*NARA*)

Minsk, seen here on 8 July 1941 just before its last defenders capitulated, already had German forces moving through the heavily damaged city, such as these vehicles and bicyclists on Independence Square. Government House (right) remained largely intact, save for numerous broken windows. (*NARA*)

A Panzer III E/F upgraded with 30mm of additional glacis armour and a 50mm L/42 main gun (left), Panzer II Ausf. F, Panzer III E/F (37mm L/46.5) (centre), and a third Panzer III behind during a brief lull in the July fighting. A platoon of Sd.Kfz. 251 Ausf. Bs with early two-piece glacis are lined up along a graded, crushed stone road; each sporting a white 'G' on their wings (fenders). Seemingly alert for what is likely a forthcoming order to resume their advance, at least one tank commander and one SPW machine-gunner maintain a watchful eye starboard. To concentrate limited numbers of these SPWs 3 PD, 4 PD, 17 PD, and 18 PD respectively had one of their mounted rifle companies outfitted with the vehicles, while 10 PD had enough to fill out its entire II./69th Motorized Rifle Regiment. (*NAC*)

A typical traffic jam during Barbarossa, as two columns converge on the same route. (*NARA*)

With a vertical range of 3,700m a 20mm Flak 38 provided localized air defence against low-altitude air attacks. Seen here unhitched and positioned to defend a stretch of the River Berezina just outside of the Bobruysk Fortress, several ammunition containers, each holding a pair of twenty-round magazines are open and ready. The Osipovichi–Gomel' rail bridge's partially dropped spans are visible downriver and the crewman at the far left holds a light, Em. 1m R.36 rangefinder, suitable for tracking and triangulating moving targets. (*NAC*)

German engineers assemble portions of a Bridge Column 'K' across the River Berezina, July 1941. Unlike the 'B' variety that was better suited to regular vehicular traffic, these steel girder spans supported heavier tanks. With their squared sterns these half-pontoons could be joined back-to-back to effectively double the bridge load. (*NAC*)

Having helped eliminate an enemy pocket west of Minsk a few days previously, Second Army set off to reestablish contact with Second Panzer Group, which began crossing the River Dnepr on 10 July 1941. Three days later, 507th Infantry Regiment (292 ID) was pushing east of Borisov along Panzer Route 2. The unit's trailing 'goulash cannon' field kitchen provided German forces with at least one hot meal per day of soup or stew. Given their often tenuous logistics, looted civilian foodstuffs provided supplement, even after Kluge's September 1941 order to cease such activities under harsh penalties. (*NARA*)

Seen here at Kokhanovo on 13 July 1941, 504th Bicycle Road Construction Battalion (XXXXVII MAC) included three construction platoons and about half a dozen trucks, and performed light, quick repairs. Units like 584th Heavy Road Construction Battalion correspondingly did more substantial work involving cement and asphalt. (*NARA*)

29th Motorized Infantry Division personnel fighting for control of the extensive Smolensk rail yard on 16 July 1941, just north of the River Dnepr. Intended as a heavy complement to the T-34, the KV-1 proved much less reliable and was soon considered redundant. Note the wooden side walls on the 60-ton four-axle Flatcar Model 1934 have been removed as this KV-1A's (Model 1940) tracks exceed the platform's width. (*NAC*)

A typical haul of Soviet prisoners during the often massive German cauldron battles during Barbarossa. Seen here on 23 July 1941, such events were well suited for propaganda, as evidenced by the soldier with a camera. (*NARA*)

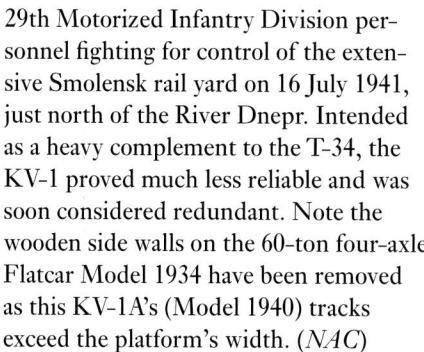

A Second Panzer Group column that includes Krupp Protze Kfz.70 6 × 4 lorries moving through another burned and bombed out Belorussian town. Considering the majority of buildings and houses in such urban areas were wooden, fires started by the retreating Soviets or advancing Germans spread quickly. (*NAC*)

A line of German infantry walking eastward in what seemed like an impossible goal to keep up with fast-moving armoured and motorized formations and help seal the many cordons thrown up around Red Army forces. (*NARA*)

Luftwaffe ground personnel from I. Antiaircraft Corps (as evidenced by the red shield, with white oak-leaf tactical symbol) in the Smolensk area, 31 July 1941. An Sd.Kfz.7 tows an 88mm Flak 18, which facing forward meant once uncoupled the weapon was already generally pointing towards its intended target. The uncensored original image included a 'WL' (Luftwaffe) licence plate and a white, arrow-tipped forward slash through a white ring unit symbol. (*NARA*)

Given these resemble Trakehner mounts, these cavalrymen, seen here in August 1941, might be from 1st Cavalry Division. Being a rest period, neither horse is fully tacked given they lack their standard M25 saddles. On the nearest animal's left an M34 saddle bag resting against the blanket held items, such as a brush, curry comb, spare horseshoe (and nails), and a (human) mess-kit tin. A slightly different version on its right contained small, personal things, like a Karabiner 98k cleaning kit, a wash kit, a second mess-kit tin, Pervitin tablets, and a heavy brush. (*NAC*)

The Mogilev Bridge seen a few weeks after Second Panzer Group crossed the Dnepr. (*NARA*)

A motorcyclist on a BMW R-12 from Second Panzer Group, as evidenced by the white 'G' on the sidecar, August 1941. The pennant with opposing black and white triangles (with a red border) indicates a member of Guderian's staff. Note the pair of Model 24 *Stielhandgranaten* wedged against the head tube for quick access. (*NAC*)

German signals personnel work to facilitate communications, both wirelessly as well as wired, as evidenced by the 500m wire spool. Note the signals patch on the right-hand soldier's sleeve. (*NARA*)

German rail workers ensuring a captured stretch adhered to the necessary wide gauge. For expediency rail lines were often left atop their original sleepers and foundation, however rudimentary. Soviet-built rail lines typically rested on a bed of sand or gravel, which under the cumulative weight of passing trains tended to shift and required regular repair to avoid a derailment. While crushed rock was preferable, given its more stable interlocking characteristics, it was also more expensive to produce and transport. (*NAC*)

A crewman from 693rd Panzer Propaganda Company uses a 35mm Askania Z film camera, with an Astro-Berlin telephoto lens. With no government desiring objective reporting of its active combat operations these military units produced content presenting German efforts in a positive light, including film (for example, *Die Deutsche Wochenschau* (*The German Weekly Review*)), print (for example, *Signal*), and photographs. To avoid lagging behind fast-moving mobile formations these units operated with armoured cars sporting an identifying 'PK' painted on the vehicles and the company symbol of a fox terrier on an inclined surface. (*Arne Schrader*)

Determined-looking SS troopers, September 1941. They wear a Type I camouflage smock (*Tarnjacke*) (and matching helmet cover pattern), which was intended to go over their assault packs. As dropping to a prone position was likely uncomfortable those with *Stielhandgrenate* have jammed them into their boots. Where the others carry 98k carbines the officer (round belt buckle) holds what looks like a Czech-made ZK-383 submachine gun. (*NAC*)

Guderian, Kluge, the commander of I. Antiaircraft Corps, Brigadier Walther von Axthelm, and an officer, August 1941. (*NAC*)

A disabled Soviet T-26 in the middle of old (southern) Smolensk's main plaza, August 1941. The signs indicate the direction for 18th Panzer Division's supply train, and where a radio can be found. The damaged *Pravda* printing press building is behind the 'G'-affixed trucks with mounted soldiers. (*NAC*)

1./213th Construction Battalion supervising Soviet prisoners (likely volunteers, given the absence of guns and except for the puttees the German drill/fatigue uniforms) building a corduroy road near Roslavl', 19 September 1941. Note the two-man saw (bottom right) and the man with an axe walking behind the group. (*NARA*)

Soviet antitank ditch just east of Krapivna, 8 October 1941. Cumulatively, such positions, along with bunkers and other built-up areas, provided a combat modifier for the weakened Red Army that slowed the German advance on Moscow. (*NARA*)

A pair of I. Antiaircraft Corps Krupp Protze lorries in Orel, 30 October 1941. (*NAC*)

As the Germans continued eastward the corresponding problems with logistics are evident. With most roads in the East unpaved, large amounts of traffic degraded what foundation they possessed that rain quickly turned into a frustrating muck. (*NARA*)

Second Panzer Army column in central Orel, 17 November 1941. A pair of 3-ton Opel Blitz 2 × 4 lorries and a Mercedes Benz 170V staff car are among the vehicles arrayed before the Church of the Transfiguration. Two more 170V staff cars (a cabriolet and a saloon version) approach on the left, having just crossed the bridge over the River Oka. (*NAC*)

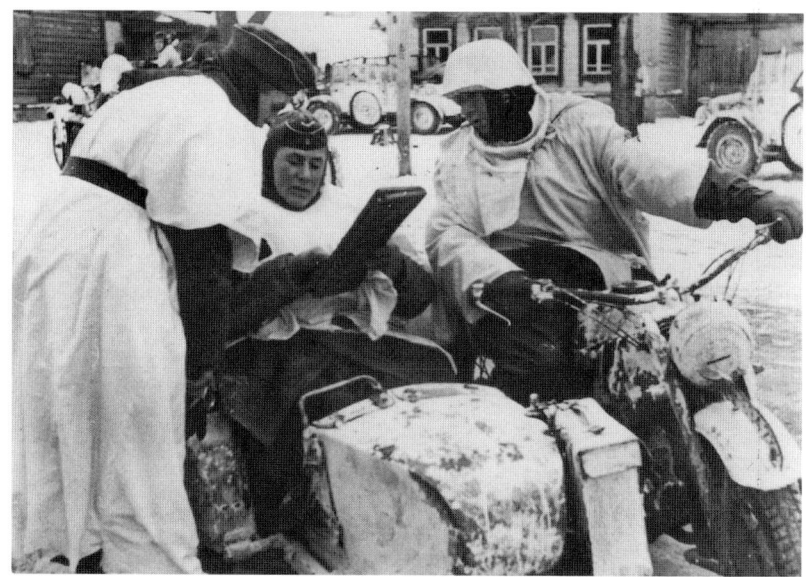

One day after Barbarossa concluded a motorcyclist team is briefed, 6 December 1941. All the vehicles have a rough coat of whitewash applied to add a degree of camouflage, much as the men wear what look like modified sheets. (*NARA*)

In a scene reminiscent of Napoleon I's Grande Armée during its 1812 withdrawal from Moscow, in Barbarossa's aftermath horses tow a German 105mm leFH18 towards an uncertain future. (*NAC*)

its 1. Motorized Rifle Company staved off a Soviet probe near Lezhnevka. To help defend the crossing for the approaching 1st Cavalry Division, 91st Light Antiaircraft Battalion and 3./704th Motorized Antiaircraft Regiment, with its 88mm guns, remained in the area temporarily under Feldt's authority. For his aggressive leadership, and the considerable success as one of Guderian's hard-charging spearheads, at 1730hrs on 10 July Model was informed Hitler had bestowed on him the Knight's Cross of the Iron Cross.

Before dawn on 11 July Weber struggled to get sufficient artillery in place on Guderian's left to support 17th Panzer Division's impending Dnepr crossing at Ust'ye. To avoid crossing supply lines, after deviating to Smolyany 18th Panzer Division had turned from Panzer Route 2 and awaited its turn a few kilometres to the west. Unlike the soft, broad floodplain downriver from Mogilev that to the north presented a more defined valley, and a narrower waterway, whose relatively steep sides presented an obstacle for vehicles and towed weapon systems, but not for foot-bound forces. As the Soviet defender along the far bank and forest beyond would have a distinct advantage in resisting an unsupported German effort, the guns from 27th Motorized Artillery, I./22nd Antiaircraft, and III./53rd Motorized Rocket Launcher Regiments were assigned, but with the morning slipping by and only two batteries of 105mm cannons from II./27th Motorized Artillery Regiment in position, at 0730hrs they opened fire.[4] As could arguably be predicted soon after the assault engineers from 6./ and 7./40th Motorized Rifle Regiment attempted to cross abreast the former was shot to pieces and the latter managed a toehold that was soon made untenable and abandoned that night.

During the morning of what promised to be yet another sunny, hot day, with the requisite amount of choking dust from multitudes of moving vehicles, Guderian left his newly located headquarters at Tolochin to observe 29th Motorized Infantry Division as its motorized infantry and assorted component units crossed the Dnepr at Kopys, where by day's end German engineers would assemble a pontoon bridge.[5] Following a brief artillery bombardment and Ju-87s having softened up Soviet defences along the far bank starting at 0500hrs Boltenstern's engineers had created and expanded a bridgehead that by midday had extended to cut the crushed rock Orsha–Mogilev road.[6] Downriver, just south of Shklov, 10th Panzer Division and Großdeutschland also made good progress having conducted a similarly timed and supported operation, as did 'Reich' crossing at the town. Having discussed XXXXVII Motorized Army Corps' situation with Lemelsen and Boltenstern, a seemingly satisfied Guderian was motored across the waterway in an assault boat to ensure his vanguard's continued success. As German forces poured across the River Dnepr the very thinly stretched Soviet Thirteenth Army resisted stubbornly in several instances. Lacking any appreciable depth, however, it steadily succumbed to the enemy's concentrated strength and subsequent disgorging of fast-moving mobile forces intent on applying maximum violence to reach the open terrain to the east.

To reinforce the space between the Dnepr and Third Panzer Group, a second Blocking Group was formed around 622nd Artillery Regiment under Colonel Christian Usinger.[7] Elements of XXXXVII Motorized Army Corps needed to hold the crossing area until Second Army's infantry moved up to replace them. To the south the German 15th Motorized Infantry Regiment overran an enemy airfield at Zubova, where German antiaircraft fire incentivised a pair of unaware Soviet staff officers to land. Upon their capture the maps they possessed provided valuable intelligence on Twentieth Army and 23rd Mixed Air Division out of Rzhev. To provide targeted, progressive ground support for XXXXVI Motorized Army Corps' advance Ju-87s struck enemy positions along the Dnepr's eastern bank between 0500and 0515hrs. Artillery then commenced to ease 10th Panzer Division's efforts, as it struck for the village of Gorki and sent elements south along the River Pronya. Nearby, Großdeutschland sent out reconnaissance units to the south-east to Bel', and readied to follow in Schaal's wake. Soviet aircraft damaged the bridges in 'Reich's' operational area, but not enough to prevent its crossing just downriver from Shklov. On reaching the far bank the majority of its units pushed to the north and east, while the still detached SS-'Deutschland' moved into the Gorodshchina area to cover the north-western portion of a forming cordon around Mogilev. To provide short-range, aerial observation Fw-189As from 6th Squadron (Army)/31st Reconnaissance Group and 3rd Squadron (Army)/14th Reconnaissance Group respectively worked with 101st Arko and 10th Panzer Division, although 'Reich' was without such services.[8] 210th Ground Attack and Antitank Wing followed with 30 minutes of bombing the Shklov bridgehead's expanding perimeter. II Air Corps then focused on the area east of the Orsha–Mogilev road between 0545 and 0730hrs.

With LIII Army Corps arriving in the Rogachev sector, and 22nd Cavalry Regiment (1 CD) having pulled out of the area south of the Drut', Feldt's horsemen moved for Bykhov and a crossing of the Dnepr. While XXIV Motorized Army Corps' armoured formations expanded their presence eastward, 1st Cavalry Division maintained a screening presence along both banks for the next ten days. At 1100hrs on 11 July 'Kampfgruppe Munzel' tried to breech Mogilev's eastern defences, but at Golynets enemy resistance and an 8km ditch that extended to the Dnepr blocked I./3rd Motorized Rifle Regiment. On the unit's left, 1./3rd Motorcycle Battalion and armour from II./6th Panzer Regiment ran into mines and trenches and was similarly stalled. Model would need to change his tack for a less direct approach. Since lead elements of XII Army Corps were approaching from the west and would be better suited to an urban fight that was shaping up to be a siege, further efforts by his I./3rd Motorized Rifle Regiment were ill advised; especially as the unit was slated to cross the Dnepr with 3rd Panzer Division. German engineers expected to have the area's damaged bridge repaired by 1600hrs; a task that took until 2115hrs to complete. To protect it 6./59th Light Antiaircraft Company was made available to 3rd Motorized Rifle Regiment, and by day's end Guderian had large portions of his three motorized corps across the Dnepr. Thirteenth and Twentieth Armies initially held firm either from stubborn resistance or ignorance of the suddenly unfolding situation, and Hoth and Guderian deftly sliced their way around and beyond such impediments.

Trapped at Mogilev

In preparation for the Smolensk offensive Army Group Centre had stockpiled 2,000m³ of fuel, 2,600 tonnes of ammunition, and two days of food rations in Minsk and towns to the east, such as Borisov.[9] On schedule Guderian's attack began at 0300hrs on 12 July, but few Soviet forces were encountered, as German aircraft, artillery, and mortars provided support along the Dnepr. Within an hour a reconnaissance plane reported all bridges in Mogilev were intact and a 50-car freight train was seen about 3km east of Amkhovaya. At 0800hrs Model was made aware of a worrying, but not unexpected, Soviet motorized column from Gomel' that had been sighted moving north past Zhlobin. Threatening to strike 4th Panzer Division's open right flank, as it crossed the river and cut across southern Sidorovichi, Langermann's fuel supplies at Bykhov were already running low. Only two weeks into the campaign the rough terrain and often rougher roads extracted a toll on German vehicle suspensions and steering components, not to mention the abundant dust that clogged engine filters and promoted overheating or worse, motor failure. Anxious to continue his rapid progress Guderian stressed the necessity that the regauging work be quickly continued to Bobruysk, but was told the stretch from Minsk remained too dangerous for the personnel to work given the still numerous groups of Red Army soldiers operating in the area.[10]

At 1920hrs on 12 July Model's Ia requested that corps reserves be released to compensate for 3rd Panzer Division's exhausted state. Initially, only III./6th Panzer Regiment was released and later, II./394th Motorized Rifle Regiment.[11] Although even a brief rest would go a long way towards refreshing and resupplying the vaunted formation the exigencies of near constant fighting dictated otherwise. Expecting to conduct pursuit more than combat operations over the coming days, fuel was prioritized over ammunition. With much of Vietinghoff's command strung out for dozens of kilometres to the west and Second Army moving eastward over the Berezina, what enemy elements that remained in the intervening area were soon crushed and scattered. In what had been a frequent activity during the rush to secure the Minsk Pocket Guderian's headquarters was relocated east of the Dnepr to Zakhody from which he could better keep an eye on his critical inner flank during the coming Smolensk encirclement.

Timoshenko's Turn

With Western Front's recently sizeable armoured force having incurred considerable losses, Timoshenko had few, if any, viable options to resist beyond the tactical level and logically concentrated his run down Twentieth and Thirteenth

Armies on defending Dnepr sectors with infrastructures capable of accommodating a large amount of traffic, such as Orsha and Mogilev, and the fresh Twenty-First Armies on Rogachev/Zhlobin. Already, by 13 July, the advance elements of 29th Motorized and 10th Panzer Divisions had advanced dozens of kilometres east of the waterway, with the latter slicing south of Shepelevka, reaching the River Pronya, and securing Gorki. What remained of V Mechanized Corps from the north and XXVII Rifle Corps out of Shamovo-Golovichi, and assorted formations from Fourth and Thirteenth Armies, counterattacked towards severing Lemelsen's spearheads. With Vietinghoff making similar headway in Guderian's centre, however, Second Panzer Group's strength east of the Dnepr and multiple advance routes proved too much for a fragmented, disorganized Western Front.

As XXIV Motorized Army Corps expanded its Bykhov bridgehead, 10th Motorized Infantry Division pushed north for Mogilev and 4th Panzer Division to the north-east. Intent on destroying the German crossing at its source, the Soviet XX Rifle Corps counterattacked towards the south-west from Sidorovichi to beyond Volkovichi to carve an 8km-wide gap between the two formations. With 6th Panzer Regiment having recently crossed east of the Dnepr and happening to be along the enemy's anticipated advance axis the onrushing Soviets soon found themselves up against seemingly greater strength than anticipated. XXXXV Rifle Corps was quickly caught between these two forces and functioned as expected. Held at the front and attacked from both flanks XX Rifle Corps proved unable to make much progress and was forced back onto Mogilev's outer entrenchments, tank ditches, and barricades that would serve as badly needed combat modifiers, alongside LXI Rifle defending the city proper and what remained of XX Mechanized Corps. Closer to the city machine guns were even reportedly positioned on roof tops, which perhaps provided greater visibility in an urban environment, the high angle preventing grazing and crossfire that would more effectively defend a given zone. With all efforts to stem the newest German flood having failed Soviet senior commanders were once again placed in unenviable positions where failure risked arrest and possible execution.[12]

Exploiting the success they had achieved since crossing the Dnepr, throughout 13 July 29th Motorized Infantry Division crossed the border into Russia for Krasnyy. Having waited west of the river for the last two days for a bridge to be completed at Kopys, and Boltenstern to move on, 18th Panzer Divisions followed behind along what were particularly poor, sandy roads.[13] For the next few days 17th Panzer Division remained affixed to the Orsha area to cover that stretch of the Dnepr and secure supplies supporting Lemelsen's drive on Smolensk. Upriver from Mogilev, Vietinghoff achieved an excellent penetration that after two days approached the River Vikhra. On Guderian's right flank XXIV Motorized Army Corps' progress had been more modest, but with 255th Infantry Division now occupying the Rogachev–Zhlobin sector, and the remainder of LIII Army

Corps moving up behind, his situation looked promising. Seemingly reflecting Timoshenko's February 1941 operational response to a potential German invasion, but given Western Front's depleted, rather disorganized state that ran counter to martial reason, Twenty-First Army counterattacked from Dovsk to Gomel'. In XXIV Motorized Army Corps' sector LXVII Rifle Corps and 50th Tank Division struck for Schweppenburg's crossing at Bykhov, with two more rifle corps further south moving on Bobruysk to sever his line of communication. As a result of this serious threat to Guderian's southern flank Bock grudgingly committed his reserve XXXXIII Army Corps (Fourth Army), which had just arrived at the River Ptich'. This, in turn, deprived Kluge of critical infantry reinforcement at a time when he moved to eliminate the Mogilev Pocket and free XXIV Motorized Army Corps to continue its eastward offensive.

Even though the Soviet LXVI Rifle Corps and supporting cavalry had travelled the 80km from around Rechitsa to establish a bridgehead over the Berezina, Timoshenko's poorly coordinated left thrust sputtered to a halt within a few days, not unlike his earlier right-hand offensive with V and VII Mechanized Corps. Although the counterattack gave Schweppenburg pause about continuing full tilt east of the Dnepr, Guderian was unswayed.[14] As Second Panzer Group continued its frequently headlong rush to the River Desna, the Soviet LXI and XXXXV Rifle Corps, and remnants of XX Mechanized Corps, became trapped in the Mogilev Pocket. In a rather confused effort to contain Guderian's fast-moving forces, many of the units under the Soviet Thirteenth Army were only made aware the Germans had crossed the Dnepr when they were being overrun or bypassed. By the end of 13 July 17th Panzer Division had taken Orsha after often bitter fighting against XXXIV Rifle Corps and unhinged Timoshenko's defences in the Dnepr bend. With half of the *Ostheer* tanks now either total losses or undergoing major repairs Halder stressed to Hitler that once the Smolensk Pocket was eliminated the continuing push for Moscow needed to be halted until Red Army forces along Army Group Centre's flanks were defeated.[15] After a period of refitting for Second and Third Panzer Groups by early August, Hoth would continue for the enemy capital, while Guderian was to be redirected to Eastern Ukraine.

To show his appreciation for all that his men had achieved in such a short period Guderian issued an 'Order of the Day' for 13 July 1941:

> Soldiers of Panzer Group 2! Three weeks ago today, on the orders of the Führer, we went on the attack. We overcame the enemy on the Bug, on the Jasiolda, the Szczara, the Berezina and now on the Dnepr. A huge booty of tanks, guns and other military equipment and tens of thousands of prisoners are the evidence of our victory. In energetically seizing opportunities, in tirelessly pursuing, in enduring all the hardships, you, my fellow soldiers, have justified the expectations that Germany and our Führer have placed in you. I thank you from

the bottom of my heart for this is a joyful duty for me. I remember those who gave their lives for the success of our great task and our wounded. Your sacrifice should be an example for us. Now let's look to the future. We want to fulfil our duty to the last and achieve the distant goals that are set for us. There is no slackening and no hesitation. Our slogan is: Forward! Hail to our Führer and to our Germany.

Once again, remaining close to his critical, inside flank Guderian accompanied XXXXVII Motorized Army Corps on 14 July, as Lemelsen worked to clear his northern flank to the Dnepr, coordinate and maintain contact with Vietinghoff, and strike for Smolensk and the River Desna. Out in front of XXXXVI Motorized Army Corps, 10th Panzer Division fought its way through XXVII Rifle Corps to approach Mstislavl', while Vietinghoff diverted follow-on forces towards Mogilev. Behind Großdeutschland, *SS-Hauptsturmführer* (equivalent to Captain) and Doctor of Engineering Wilhelm Brandt's advance detachment led 'Reich' out of Shklov, while west of the Dnepr SS-'Deutschland' remained engaged near Golynets, where 3rd Panzer Division had just called off its effort to penetrate the city from the west.[16]

Mirroring XXXXVI Motorized Army Corps' thrusts, Schweppenburg tried to push eastward, while sealing south of Mogilev. With 'Kampfgruppe Manteuffel' having crossed the Dnepr at 0930hrs, 'Kampfgruppe Kleemann' raced ahead for Chausy and in doing so cut the Mogilev–Roslavl' rail line and isolated XXXXV Rifle Corps against 4th Panzer Division to the south-east. With 3rd Panzer Division expanding beyond its bridgehead 1./403rd Bridge Column was ordered to cross the Dnepr for Sidorovichi to stay close to the front line lest its services be required. II./394th Motorized Rifle Regiment had moved into a wooded area north-west of Borovka where the tall pine and spruce helped mask their presence from Red Air Force planes. Sending a scout troop from 1st Reconnaissance Battalion north to probe the approaches to Mogilev resistance was only encountered at Pechery. II./3rd Motorized Rifle Regiment also set off from the Borovka area to reach Isakova Buda and the Mogilev–Slavgorod road. Although fighting cropped up later in the day, with 6th Panzer Regiment (minus III. Panzer Battalion) and II./394th Motorized Rifle Regiment moving up from the south, and 10th Motorized Infantry Division in tow, XX Rifle Corps risked a similar fate as XXXXV Rifle Corps. Intent on protecting his southern flank and reacquiring Panzer Route 1 Langermann sent 'Kampfgruppe Eberbach' and 7th Reconnaissance Battalion south-east to trap the long-suffering 42nd Rifle Division against Slavgorod and the River Sozh.

Assuming the recently inserted strategic reserves were the last of what the Soviets could muster, once Guderian eliminated these forces his path to Moscow would be essentially open.[17] Seemingly of a similar mind three days previously Hitler issued Directive No. 32 'Preparations for the Time After Barbarossa', which included that once the Soviets had been destroyed, 'The defence of this area, and foreseeable future offensive action, will require considerably smaller military forces than have been needed hitherto.' Already thinking about a post-conflict draw-down of German forces in the East, he provided a follow-up three days later (No. 32b), which stressed that with just Britain and potentially the United States a threat armament production and resources would soon focus on the Kriegsmarine and Luftwaffe.

Mogilev Encircled

In the pre-dawn hours of 15 July 4th Panzer Division's vanguard, II./35th Panzer Regiment, shot ahead to Slavgorod and across one of the three, timber bridges still standing over the River Pronya. Prior to pulling out of the town the Soviets set fire to several dwellings, which being mostly made of wood were soon ablaze across the town.[18] With Langermann having reached Panzer Route 1 nearly 80km to the north-east of Rogachev the Soviet LXVII Rifle Corps' extended position up to Bykhov was flanked and becoming untenable. Along his route from Volkovichi he established blocking positions to temporarily cover his exposed left flank, and continued to use the borrowed 150 K 39 cannons of 740th Motorized Antiaircraft Battalion. To mitigate friendly casualties and demoralize several nearby Soviet assembly and jump-off areas Ju-87s were requested, but only horizontal bombers were made available. At 0750hrs 'Kampfgruppe Kleemann' cleared the forests near Antonovka and to the southeast, while some 60km to the north-east 10th Panzer Division's advance detachment had reached Mstislavl', which the Soviets had recently vacated.

At noon enemy movement was reported near Chausy, where locals from Hill 172 indicated Red Army Soldiers had recently poisoned the area's wells. Undeterred, during the early afternoon 'Kampfgruppe Audörsch' pushed beyond the town for Molyatichi, with little regard for its flanks. The fragmented, largely confused and overwhelmed Soviet defence between XXXXVI and XXXXVII Motorized Army Corps meant when lingering resistance was found German mobile elements could simply bypass it and leave it for follow-on forces or to wither on the vine. In support, 51st Fighter Wing 'Mölders' created havoc among enemy ground forces. At 1500hrs 1st Motorized Reconnaissance Battalion advanced onto the Mogilev–Chausy rail line north-east of Amkhovaya and 30 minutes later 3rd Rifle Brigade elements secured the bridge just south of Sushchi. With much of his command still focused on Mogilev at 1740hrs Model asked Schweppenburg for reinforcement to enable the remainder of 3rd Panzer Division to continue to press for the River Sozh. Less than an hour later the former met with Kleemann at his forward command post 4km north-west of Chausy to discuss the present combat situation and apply III./6th Panzer and I./3rd Motorized Rifle Regiments towards clearing Soviet forces from the area. As a continuing thorn for each of the four panzer group leaders, until sufficient infantry was brought closer to the main line of battle, which in Guderian's case presently meant XII Army Corps reaching the Dnepr in strength, forces best used to provide mass to the primary eastward advance were instead siphoned off to hold captured ground or fill holes in the lines.

Over the next three days heavy fighting against what were identified as the Soviet 102nd, 151st, and 187th Rifle Divisions occurred along the road to Gomel'. During the renewed engagement along the Bobruysk–Rogachev road, on 15 July German forces entered a Komsomol house to find documents related to a Timoshenko-led, multi-day conference with senior commanders in February 1941. As part of the uncovered intelligence a map was discovered that depicted an anticipated German armoured thrust into the Rogachev area (much as what was presently occurring) and a proposed Soviet counterattack to retake the area.[19] A second Red Army thrust out of Mogilev was shown to coordinate with the first and converge on Bobruysk with the intention of severing German spearheads; much as the one the Soviet commander now unleashed.[20] A cavalry unit with three elements, committed on the west bank of the Berezina and striking northward from the Parichi area was to cut the Slutsk–Bobruysk road and the Minsk–Bobruysk rail line, and complete the enemy's defeat.[21] German forces had also uncovered documents covering broader Soviet wargaming sessions, reports, and maps that indicated a major offensive was being explored against German-held Western Poland and/or East Pomerania.[22]

At 15 July's end XXXXVII Motorized Army Corps held the southern edge of what had quickly become an elongated Soviet pocket running along the Dnepr from near Orsha, where 17th Panzer Division anchored Lemelsen's bridgehead to 29th Motorized Infantry Division at the southern approach to a burning Smolensk, just across the river. Between the two Nehring's 18th Panzer Division defended the Dnepr's left bank around Krasnyy, although most of the encircled Red Army fought north of the waterway. Along Guderian's centre XXXXVI Motorized Army Corps struggled with the same problems as Schweppenburg, in that both had to respectively siphon off valuable attack forces to man the developing Mogilev cordon in the absence of sufficient infantry.

With Hoth's 7th Panzer Division having advanced into the undulating terrain north-east of Smolensk to capture the undefended village of Yartsevo and cut Panzer Route 2, once again Guderian was losing the race to reach the area to affect an encirclement of the Soviet XX Army and assorted formations; much as the latter had been tardy at Minsk. Poised to take Smolensk, 29th Motorized Infantry Division had been reinforced with assault guns, flame-throwing Panzer IIIs from 100th Panzer Battalion (Fl.), rocket launchers, and 88mm antitank guns. Considering armour was ill-suited to operate in a confined urban area, Boltenstern sent in 15th and 71st Motorized Infantry Regiments to clear the town, where 57th Tank Regiment was deployed to defend southern Smolensk using four battalions of T-26s in blocking positions.

Considering the *Ostheer* had destroyed what pre-Barbarossa planning estimated was the bulk of the Red Army west of Moscow, and that what remained of them could be pushed into the Ural Mountains, on 15 July the German General Staff's operational department issued a memorandum outlining subsequent operations. As there was no practical way to occupy all of Russia, once the enemy had been pushed out of Eastern Europe the Germans estimated that fifty-six divisions would remain in-theatre at any one time to guard the frontier, while a contingent would move into the Caucasus–Iran region to secure its petroleum assets. A commensurately reduced Luftwaffe presence would help maintain a border zone devoid of Soviet industry and a Red Army incapable of major combat operations. With the mass of the *Ostheer* removed from duties in the East additional manpower would be allocated to the production and support of naval and air industries, which worked to make Britain's belligerent posture unsustainable and position the Reich as something of a superpower capable of a global fight.[23]

To Smolensk and the River Sozh

With Guderian having deviated from Bock's order for affecting an immediate link-up with Hoth at 0350hrs on 16 July 10th Panzer Division was, instead, directed for Yel'nya, once its vanguard of infantry and motorcyclists quickly rebuffed an unexpected Soviet attack into its assembly area. Back at Smolensk, 29th Motorized Infantry Division pushed into the narrow, occasionally burning streets of the old city and what thick, brick walls and towers remained of its early seventeenth-century fortification. As the Landsers negotiated the area's many steep ravines and hills a panoramic view of the Dnepr valley and the city's northern section awaited them, as did the commanding architectural presence of the Orthodox Dormition Cathedral, with its white, Baroque walls and golden onion towers. Although one of Smolensk's two steel arch bridges had one of its spans blown up to rest in the river at an angle, the division's forward elements secured the other in a quick strike. Later in the morning self-propelled artillery and 100th Panzer Regiment (Fl.) helped establish a toehold on the far bank. At 1600hrs 15th and 71st Motorized Infantry Regiments began crossing the Dnepr in rubber rafts under the protective fire of 29th Motorized Artillery Regiment, and soon reached the rail line some 500m to the north.[24]

While the first three weeks of Second Panzer Group's advance had been largely straightforward, as it skirted the southern edge of Minsk to the River Dnepr, Guderian's subsequent offensive around Smolensk devolved into a complicated series of attacks and counterattacks. At 0600hrs 10th Motorized Infantry Division lobbied to retain control of II./394th Motorized Rifle Regiment during the fighting around Borovka, but 4 hours later the unit was returned to 3rd Panzer Division.[25] As 10th[h] Panzer Division crossed the River Vikhra bridge east of Mstislavl' the structure soon collapsed, as did an alternate crossing to the north-west. One panzer company found and crossed a nearby ford, but it wasn't until 1030hrs that repairs to one of the bridges permitted at least lighter vehicles, such as motorcycle riflemen, to move across.[26] About 800m to the south a shallow section of the river was built up to accommodate heavier tracked vehicles. Reports from Soviet prisoners captured by Second Army confirmed that Timoshenko was in personal command of the attacks against the southern flank of Army Group Centre from Gomel'.[27]

Long at the fore of the fighting, 6th Panzer Regiment was ordered to the rail bridge over the recently repaired River Pronya crossing just south of Chausy, where 91st Light Antiaircraft Battalion had placed a light battery to protect its crossing near Put'ki. A heavy and a light battery were set to defend the airspace between Amkhovaya to Chausy. With Soviet forces along the Pronya's east bank having tapered 3rd Panzer Brigade was to secure Molyatichi, some 30km to the east, by day's end. 'Kampfgruppe Audörsch', now including II./394th Motorized Rifle Regiment, set off from the Chausy area as Model's spearhead. To maintain pressure on Model's adversary at 1435hrs 3rd Motorcycle Battalion initiated a close pursuit from its Molyatichi bridgehead. To quell the anxieties of Soviet soldiers who desired to surrender, but having seen their capitulating comrades being shot or believing their Commissars' rhetoric intended to incentivise greater resistance, Luftwaffe aircraft dropped inducing leaflets. As Model finished disengaging from the Mogilev fighting, now that XII Army Corps was filling out the lines along the city's western edge, later in the afternoon I./394th Motorized Rifle Regiment's commander Captain (commission) Günther Pape led a pursuit group 11km north-east of Chausy and reported mines and abatis. Audörsch requested to Schweppenburg that III./41st Motorized Infantry Regiment (10 MID) be transferred to his authority to secure the Amkhovaya area, with I./6th Panzer Regiment to be released as well, but this was denied. Soviet artillery in the Chausy area intensified and their reconnaissance aircraft conducted regular patrols over the battlefield, which implied Red Air Force bombers would soon target the area. To help resist a Soviet effort to retake the structure 8./75th Motorized Artillery Regiment was brought to the area where its four 150mm heavy field guns could improve the unit's chance of success. At 2100hrs locals again provided assistance to the advancing Germans by notifying 1st Motorized Reconnaissance Battalion that ten Soviet tanks were recently seen leaving Krasnoye to the north-east. About 1,000 Soviets were also reported in a forest 8km north-west of Molyatichi. At 2210hrs prisoner statements indicated that one of the surrounded Soviet units, 747th Rifle Regiment (172 RD), intended to attack the Amkhovaya area the next day, 17 July.

South of Bykhov 1st Cavalry Division operated on both sides of the Dnepr to cover XXIV Motorized Army Corps' deep southern flank, but also to maintain contact with the Soviet LXVI Rifle Corps, as it fell back onto Dovsk. For the German horsemen the often isolated, rugged battlezone in which they operated made resupply difficult; a situation exacerbated with the formation's artillery having expended more ammunition over the last three weeks than it did during the entire 1940 campaign in the West. With Second Panzer Group beginning to push beyond the Polesie Marshes 1st Cavalry Division was employed in more conventional fighting, and by 29 July it was determined to possess just 15 per cent of its *Barbarossatag* strength. With XII Army Corps once again able to directly assist Guderian the weakening formation was placed under Schroth's predominantly foot- and horse-bound command. During the night of 16/17 July 31st Reconnaissance Battalion (31 ID) moved up to the Bykhov and allowed 1st Cavalry Division to concentrate on its push southward along the Dnepr's left bank.

Having moved through Lobanovka, 4th Panzer Division arrived 3km north of Cherikov to find its bridge over the River Udoga still standing. To the rear, 39th Motorized Engineer Battalion reported moving as far as Chausy; while 40th Motorcycle Battalion (10 MID) secured the area immediately north and east of Borovka to further tighten the Mogilev cordon. Until Schweppenburg's forces arrived in strength along the River Sozh during 16 July 604th Motorized Heavy 210mm Howitzer Battalion was moved to Slavgorod to help retain the Pronya bridges against Soviet counterattacks where its 3rd Battery, still fielding 210mm guns from the previous world war, advanced towards Krichev.[28] Unconstrained with having to provide forces to contain the Mogilev Pocket, 10th Panzer Division snaked its way north-east along the River Sozh to capture Khislavichi.

At Rastenburg, Hitler laid out key objectives for the war in the East, and the area's subsequent administration and exploitation that according to his influential Reichsminister and personal gatekeeper, Martin Bormann, included:

> We ought to act here in exactly the same way as we did in the cases of Norway, Denmark, Holland, and Belgium. In these cases too we did not publish our aims . . .Therefore we shall emphasize again that we were forced to occupy, administer, and secure a certain area; it was in the interest of the inhabitants that we provided order, food, traffic, etc., hence our measures. Nobody shall be able to recognize that it initiates a final settlement. This need not prevent our taking all necessary measures – shooting, resettling, etc. . . . But we do not want to make any people into enemies prematurely and unnecessarily.

German forces were, 'To do nothing which might obstruct the final settlement, but to prepare for it in secret.' and 'To emphasize that we are liberators.' In addition to clearing areas like the Crimea for German-only settlement, 'The Russians have now ordered partisan warfare behind our front.' which had the benefit that, 'It enables us to eradicate everyone who opposes us.' Ultimately, there would be no Soviet military presence west of the Urals, and per Germany's 'iron principle', 'We must never permit anybody but the Germans to carry arms! . . . even when it seems easier at first to enlist the armed support of foreign subjugated nations. We have to create a Garden of Eden in the newly occupied eastern territories; they are vitally important to us; as compared with them colonies play only an entirely subordinate part.'[29]

1st Cavalry Division (removed from XXIV Motorized Army Corps (17 July))

While Second Panzer Group had breeched the Soviet Dnepr defences to reach Smolensk, the River Sozh, and Panzer Route 1 by 17 July a considerable number of Western Front forces remained in the field between the three armoured spearheads. With Mogilev continuing to be a thorn in Guderian's side, much as the Brest Fortress the previous month, he now needed to have XXXXVII Motorized Army Corps work with Hoth to seal off and destroy Twentieth Army along the Dnepr, while also clearing out Thirteenth Army between Lemelsen and Vietinghoff. Believing his right flank now had the most pressing issues he flew to XXIV Motorized Army Corps' sector to provide more direct leadership, as Schweppenburg contended with containing Mogilev, advancing for Roslavl', and securing the River Sozh against Twenty-First Army.

Having advanced to Krichev during the night of 16/17 July 4th Panzer Division fought through weak enemy resistance along Panzer Route 1 to take the town, but not before the Soviets blew the bridges over the River Sozh.[30] Further upriver 1st Motorized Reconnaissance Battalion scouted east of Molyatichi as far as Lobkovichi, where at 1155hrs it encountered its first notable enemy resistance of the day. Back along Model's advance 'Kampfgruppe Kleemann' (3 MRR), with support from 75th Motorized Artillery Regiment and 3rd Motorcycle Battalion took Molyatichi and numerous prisoners at 1300hrs. Although the area's bridges were generally intact and suitable for vehicular traffic, several streams and marshes meant even the best routes eastward tended to be soft and muddy and in need of regular improvement, especially to provide two-way movement. During periods of dry weather these dirt roads soon hardened and were compacted by vehicles to permit speeds comparable to paved equivalents.[31] Having recently conducted a fact-finding tour of Second Panzer Group, Major Claus von Stauffenberg (OKH Organization Department (O QIII)) determined that the formation's 'Striking power is gradually diminishing . . .' but 'self-assurance is continually growing', especially with 3rd Panzer Division.[32] As Second Army finally arrived at the River Dnepr near Mogilev, Guderian was increasingly freed to direct all his energies eastward towards finishing a flanked adversary whose disjointed elements tried to withdraw to avoid encirclement and likely destruction. More importantly to him, with its flanks increasingly secured XXXXVI Motorized Army Corps rapidly approached Yel'nya and the River Desna. While sufficient supply had been accumulated along the Dnepr to get Guderian and Hoth as far as Smolensk, the majority of the 60-tonne lorry columns making the long journey from the frontier would soon be halted, as the costs approached parity with the benefits.[33] For their battlefield successes over the last month Hitler bestowed the Oak Leaves to the Knight's Cross to Guderian, Hoth, and Lieutenant General (General der Flieger) Wolfram von Richthofen.

Back on his left flank Guderian spent 18 July with XXXXVII Motorized Army Corps, which worked its way eastward along the Dnepr's left bank. Beyond facing often strong resistance towards effecting crossings the previous evening's heavy rainfall flooded the River Mereya and washed away the crossing at Lyady, and so saturated the Dubrovno–Krasnyy stretch of the formation's main supply route as to make it unusable.[34] With Weber having been mortally wounded at Krasnyy, Brigadier Wilhelm *Ritter* von Thoma was made acting division commander; although until his arrival Licht (40 MRR) would stand in. Having set off during the early morning for Yel'nya and its surrounding high ground, at 0545hrs 7th Panzer Regiment (10 PD) reached Strigino, some 40km from its goal. No sooner had one of its tanks begun to cross the town's bridge, however, than it crashed through the structure and into the River Khmara, forcing a day's halt until a nearby alternate could be made ready. Having moved to the relative safety behind 10th Panzer Division, Nehring's 18th Panzer Division engaged enemy armour, in the customary mix of predominantly light, as well as a handful of heavier varieties. When the Red Army vehicles pressed their attack German elements simply pulled back to let their artillery and antitank assets counter the effort from a distance.[35]

At 0940hrs, 100km to the south-west, 1st Motorized Reconnaissance Battalion reported that, according to locals, Soviet forces had recently spent about 20 minutes a few kilometres west of where the two Rivers Natopa met and deposited into the Sozh before moving on. At 1030hrs XXIV Motorized Army Corps was notified that the bridgehead over the Sozh just north of Lobkovichi had been extended to 3km. With a bridge column having arrived later on 18 July it estimated constructing a 16-tonne bridge at Krichev would take until early the following morning and 'Kampfgruppe Kleemann' was forced to search for alternate routes out of the area. Just before 1100hrs 6th Panzer Regiment was ordered to further secure the area around Molyatichi and clear what had been a troublesome enemy presence occupying the forested area to the south. To establish a proper crossing of the Sozh one of Model's engineer platoons gathered what bridge supplies it could and organized a workforce from civilians and Soviet prisoners.[36]

With fighting continuing around Chausy, including a Soviet strike on the railroad bridge, 3rd Panzer Division called in an air strike to help quiet the sector. Finding it difficult to disengage from the friction of combat, at 1535hrs 394th Motorized Rifle Regiment requested its replacement be brought up to around Amkhovaya, so it could move east with the rest of the division. In one positive note 3./704th Motorized Antiaircraft Regiment shot down an enemy reconnaissance aircraft at noon. At 1610hrs 4th Panzer Division extended the bridgehead over the Sozh at Krichev, beyond which the harried Soviet XXVIII Rifle Corps had taken up a position up to the River Oster. An hour later, 1st Motorized Reconnaissance Battalion's repositioning to 3rd Panzer Division's fore reported a 4-tonne capacity bridge east of Nadeykovichi across a small tributary of the Sozh, and soon after found an 8-tonne crossing. While not strong enough for armour, lighter vehicles such as motorcycles crossed over to maintain tactical momentum. To keep up with his advance Model's forward command post was relocated from Molyatichi to Lobkovichi along a route that given recent rains was still in surprisingly good shape. The rest of his command remained strung out back to the Mogilev encirclement.

At 0715hrs on 19 July a bridge column completed a 16-tonne pontoon crossing over the Sozh at Krichev. With engineer units being brought forward to facilitate Model's crossing of the river his spearhead 1st Motorized Reconnaissance Battalion scouted eastward towards the Oster and between Shumyachi and Snigirevka. The Germans brought up II./75th Motorized Artillery Regiment should its services be needed to defend the Dzyagovichi area and the nearby crossing over the River Oster where a suspected Soviet parachute battalion operated. To alleviate strain on their ever-extending logistics at 1125hrs 3rd Panzer Division requested permission to release captive Kolkhoz farmers to bring in the harvest on their 'collective ownership' land. The guns of 2./ and 3./604th Motorized Heavy 210mm Howitzer Battalion helped defend against determined enemy attacks against the Krichev bridgehead where the German 113kg high-explosive rounds provided devastating firepower out to Klimovichi or Nadeykovichi.

Having advanced more that 30km east of the River Sozh and what represented the Russian SFSR border, throughout the afternoon 'Kampfgruppe Kleemann' cut the Khislavichi–Shumyachi road, while Luftwaffe transports offered resupply that although was no substitute for the volume land-based alternatives, still provided enough to keep Model's spearhead mobile. As had been common throughout the campaign Soviet forces opposite 3rd Panzer Division conducted determined stands, but just as often dissolved before contact in what was a general drift back onto Roslavl'. At 1730hrs I./3rd Motorized Rifle Regiment secured a position between Dzyagovichi and Nadeykovichi, with II./3rd Panzer Regiment just to the east. Soon after I./394th Motorized Rifle Regiment, its regimental staff, and other elements were ordered to move up to Lobkovichi, while I./3rd Motorized Rifle Regiment was to halt all movement south-west of Nadeykovichi in order to be at Model's disposal should a threatened area require mobile infantry reinforcement.[37] 75th Motorized Artillery Regiment's commander, Colonel Gottfried Ries, was to personally connect with his

4th Panzer Division equivalent to coordinate fire support to carve a path through which Schweppenburg's armoured and motorized forces could rush. With 35th Panzer Regiment (4 PD) having been forced to contend with often heavy Soviet resistance in securing the Krichev area, 3rd Rifle Brigade was to allocate a force to make contact and help secure one part of what remained a largely open southern flank.

With Model keeping a wary eye on his forces that were transitioning or planning to move on from the siege of Mogilev at 1900hrs on 19 July 3rd Panzer Division received a radio message that Second Army continued to hold the Dnepr line from Novyy Bykhov to Zhlobin. Having also blunted Soviet thrusts south of Rogachev and Parichi pressure was eased against Guderian's deep right flank. At 1920hrs 394th Motorized Rifle Regiment set off to assist the push on Roslavl', while leaving a security force that was low on ammunition around Amkhovaya to help protect 3rd Panzer Division's supply lines.[38] To the north-east elements of the Soviet Sixteenth Army recaptured a portion of north-western Smolensk triggering bitter house-to-house fighting over the next few days. Running low on ammunition, at 1800hrs 10th Motorcycle Battalion cleared the area north and east of Yel'nya, and later that evening its parent formation captured the remainder amid heavy enemy artillery fire. The Soviet Twenty-Fourth Army, however, prevented a German expansion of what became a salient around the town.

With 29th Motorized Infantry Division fixed in renewed combat at Smolensk and a portion of 17th Panzer Division having moved up to its immediate south Lemelsen was for the moment tied up along the Dnepr and unable to relocate any of his units to assist in linking up with Hoth. He lacked sufficient strength along the River Desna to complete the task prior to the Soviet Twentieth Army strengthening a corridor along the flat, largely treeless terrain from Yartsevo and across Panzer Route 2 to Dorogobuzh. With 10th Panzer Division holding an extended, and increasingly isolated, position at Yel'nya and 'Reich' extending back to around Mstislavl', and having outlasted 105th Tank Division's ten-day counterattack, Guderian faced reinforcing this extended bulge or helping seal the Smolensk Pocket; he chose to focus on the former. Under its recently appointed commander, *SS-Sturmbannführer* (equivalent to Major) Otto Kumm led a Kampfgruppe built around his SS-Infantry Regiment 'Der Führer' to close with 'Reich's' advance detachment, and move for Dorogobuzh towards affecting a bridgehead over the River Os'ma.[39] With the Dan'kovo Bridge having been destroyed an SS reconnaissance troop scouted for a detour, while working to improve communications with 10th Panzer Division and take an airfield just to the south where badly needed Luftwaffe support could be brought forward.

While frequently finding success using experience, intuition, insubordination, and aggression to achieve battlefield success Guderian's continuing focus on Moscow worked against his efforts to eliminate the nearly complete

Smolensk Pocket. In a phone conversation with Bock, Fourth Army's chief-of-staff, Colonel Günther Blumentritt, asked if Guderian was 'in a position to carry out the order of three days ago to link up with Third Panzer Group near Yartsevo', as otherwise Blumentritt would 'have to commit other forces to do so'. Expressing concern at Guderian's decision to strike for Yel'nya rather than linking with Hoth, Bock's probing response of 'Is everything alright with the command there?' pushed Kluge to defend the soundness of his command.[40] Although the Germans had made the capture of the Soviet capital one of its key requirements for victory, with Leningrad and Ukraine as subsidiaries, on 19 July Hitler had issued Directive No. 33 which stated that in addition, 'The aim of the next operations must be to prevent any further sizeable enemy forces from withdrawing into the depths of Russia and wiping them out.' Instead of Moscow, Bock would strengthen the offensive against Leningrad, which would open communications with Allied Finland and provide a major port through which to improve German logistics. For Guderian, overrunning of Ukraine, Russia's agricultural heartland, was to be his immediate focus, while Army Group Centre's remaining infantry formations were to continue eastward as best they could. In yet another example of Hitler interfering with what was historically the military's exclusive purview OKH expressed consternation of OKW's, and by extension, the Führer's unnecessary meddling.

Much as Guderian had done during his rapid thrust to the English Channel in May 1940, in which bridgeheads were established along the River Somme for later use in attacking France proper, the need to quickly penetrate Soviet defences along the Dnepr and advance north-eastward, crossings over the Sozh were similarly secured for a future advance on Roslavl' and points south. Along Second Panzer Group's right, having returned from 4th Panzer Division on 20 July, where its 4th Panzer Brigade had been forced to halt until more POL was brought up, Lewinski worked to block an enemy counterattack against the south-eastern section of the Lobkovichi bridgehead.[41] Due to engineers having removed the 8-tonne pontoon bridge for use further east, and its 16-tonne replacement not expected until the morning of 21 July, Langermann wanted immediate support from his rifle and artillery battalions north-west of Krichev to engage the threat. At 2040hrs Schweppenburg was notified that 33rd Motorized Rifle Regiment, on his left flank, was for the moment unable to assist until I./3rd Panzer and II./75th Motorized Artillery Regiments were made available. An hour later 1st Motorized Reconnaissance Battalion reported seeing destroyed enemy artillery, antitank, and a pair of tank groups along the Oster. Having established contact with 4th Panzer Division earlier that morning, 394th Motorized Rifle Regiment pushed on Krichev to establish a bridgehead over the River Sozh. With a Soviet IV Airborne Corps that had been worn down from its fighting withdrawal from Glusk and the River Berezina, the formation only mustered minimal resistance from behind the Sozh's marshy floodplain from Kamenka to the Oster. At 1900hrs I./394th Motorized Rifle, II./75th Motorized Artillery, II./3rd Motorized Rifle, and I./6th Panzer Regiments were subordinated to 4th Panzer Division, but remained under Audörsch's authority. Considering Langermann captured Slavgorod and spent much of the day repulsing waves of desperate enemy soldiers from the north and south, who then melted back into the forests on being checked, any assistance was appreciated.[42]

Having heard his subordinate's proposal to send 18th Panzer Division south and have the tankers relieve Großdeutschland for use near Dorogobuzh, Kluge refused approval, as IX Army Corps' forward infantry elements were still at least a day away from plugging the corresponding gap in the Smolensk cordon.[43] By day's end 'Reich' had at least moved closer to the village along 10th Panzer Division's northern flank, but German strength in the critical sector remained inadequate. With 17th Panzer Division still near Smolensk and a 40km gap remaining between XXXXVI Motorized Corps' and Hoth's forces at Yartsevo, Guderian remained unwilling to relinquish his hold around Yel'nya to commit forces towards closing the enemy pocket. Setting Licht's command and 'Reich' to the task was too risky, considering the lack of infantry, and Kluge allowed Guderian to make the determination, who opted for refraining. As had been the case at Bialystok, Minsk, and the advance to the River Dnepr, the success of Germany's mobile forces was heavily dependent on follow-on infantry moving up. Given the sheer number of divisions the Wehrmacht managed to put into the field its wave (*Welle*) approach to mobilization gave the earliest created divisions priority to the Reich's limited industrial output, petroleum reserves, and resources. While panzer and motorized divisions were capable of self-sustained operations, and relied on movement to mitigate the enemy's ability to concentrate against them, the need for established, secure supply lines was necessary to keep them combat effective. Because of insufficient mobile formations the resulting repeated stopping and restarting of offensive operations allowed the Soviets time to concentrate what seemed to the Germans like a depressing, endless amount of manpower. Although Guderian issued Panzer Group Order No. 3 on 19 July to halt his command for a badly needed rest and refit, unwilling to relinquish momentum, especially with so many 'hot' sectors within Army Group Centre that needed to be subdued, just one day later his superiors rescinded it.[44]

Chapter 6
Roslavl', 21 July–7 August 1941

After a month of hard-driving and fighting the *Ostheer* had seemingly accomplished the lion's share of the work needed to cripple the Red Army; at least as based on pre-campaign estimates, and that just one more concerted offensive would finish the matter. As Second Panzer Group moved beyond the vast Polesie Marshes subsequently reconnecting with Rundstedt would help reduce resupply and reinforcement for enemy resistance that continued to operate behind the front lines. With (full) General Maximilian von Weichs' Second Army having moved up to the Dnepr it would soon be in position to strike for Gomel' along Guderian's right, even though it would take time to fill in the 225km to Kyiv where Army Group South had only recently approached. Once completed extended flanks would be reduced and theoretically the shortened forward edge of battle would allow for the build-up of reserves and the rotation of worn down formations to the rear. Unfortunately, for the Germans geography conspired against them, as the overall lengthening of the front line from north to south, battlefield losses, and the unexpected arrival of large numbers of Soviet strategic reserves translated into a dilution of German strength and an added emphasis on resource prioritization and economy of force.[1] As additional units of Guderian's attack formations peeled away from Mogilev to join his eastward thrust, Second Army's VII and XIII Army Corps assumed these duties, while its LIII Army Corps defended the Dnepr downriver passed Zhlobin. To get badly needed infantry to the Smolensk sector Fourth Army moved up in Lemelsen's wake. Although XXXXIII Army Corps remained under Kluge's authority, its continued operations around Parichi spread his ungainly, 200km zone of control across non-subordinate lines of communication.

In the aftermath of Second Panzer Group's offensive east of the Dnepr, on 21 July its mobile divisions were strung out, having contended with the Soviet LXI and XX Rifle Corps' now faltering stand at Mogilev, and Western Front formations to their front and flanks. While XXXXVII Motorized Army Corps continued to help strangle the Smolensk Pocket out of existence, Vietinghoff's dangerously extended position around Yel'nya required assistance, given Twentieth Army's increasing attention, being along the direct route to Moscow.[2] During times of active, offensive operations, such bulges were soon swallowed in the general advance. In the steadily static situation Second Panzer Group was experiencing east of Smolensk, enemy forces made life miserable for the nearly surrounded 10th Panzer Division and much of 'Reich'. Although able to leverage interior lines, with the German position no more than 40km from north to south, Soviet artillery along the perimeter posed a serious threat, especially 122mm A-19 and 152mm ML-20 varieties whose maximum ranges approached 20km.

Remaining active among his front-line formations, Guderian met with Vietinghoff at his headquarters 8km south-west of Sazonov-Pochinok and ordered him to expand his frontage to include Dorogobuzh, which along with a bridgehead over the Dnepr would place Second Panzer Group elements in position to quickly link up with Hoth. Additional support was absent, however, as the extended formation pushed against the southern portion of the 'Smolensk Corridor' and enemy pressure correspondingly increased from the east and west and stymied the effort. To facilitate XXXXVI Motorized Army Corps' advance close-support aircraft targeted a build-up of Soviet forces well ahead of Second Panzer Group along Panzer Route 1 near Spas-Demensk that seemed poised to counterattack towards Yel'nya.[3] During the ride back to XXXXVII Motorized Army Corps, Guderian received several wireless communications from his staff that higher headquarters wanted 'Reich' moved to the Dorogobuzh fight, seemingly to reiterate the need to make contact with Hoth. Remaining focused on moving 18th Panzer Division northward towards such a link-up and sealing the nearly complete enemy pocket just outside of Smolensk, the general had little desire to reposition Hausser's command from its support position on 10th Panzer Division's northern flank. Whether concurring or looking to pick his battles Kluge settled the matter by ordering 'Reich' to remain in place.

Defeating one enemy attack just north of Amkhovaya the Germans subsequently captured 600 prisoners and further secured their own supply lines. At 0314hrs XXIV Motorized Army Corps radioed that Soviet forces had broken into Slavgorod and what was the border separating 4th Panzer Division to the east and 10th Motorized Infantry Division turning clockwise on Rogachev. Low cloud cover obscured visibility for Luftwaffe reconnaissance, although the higher terrain north of the Sozh provided the Germans with a good view of the copse-covered swampland over which their adversary approached. With his right flank covered Model continued to advance on Roslavl', while at 0715hrs Lewinski received command of what included II./6th Panzer Regiment, parts of I./3rd Motorized Rifle Regiment and a company from 521st Panzerjäger Battalion to clear similarly soft terrain south-west of Krichev and the forested area beyond. Later in the day 394th Motorized Rifle Regiment moved into this expanding Sozh bridgehead west of the River Lobzhanka, during which they captured about a hundred prisoners, of which two were found to be uniformed women. An apparent first for the shocked Landsers of 3rd Panzer Division, being well outside their patriarchal mores, this only added to their feelings that

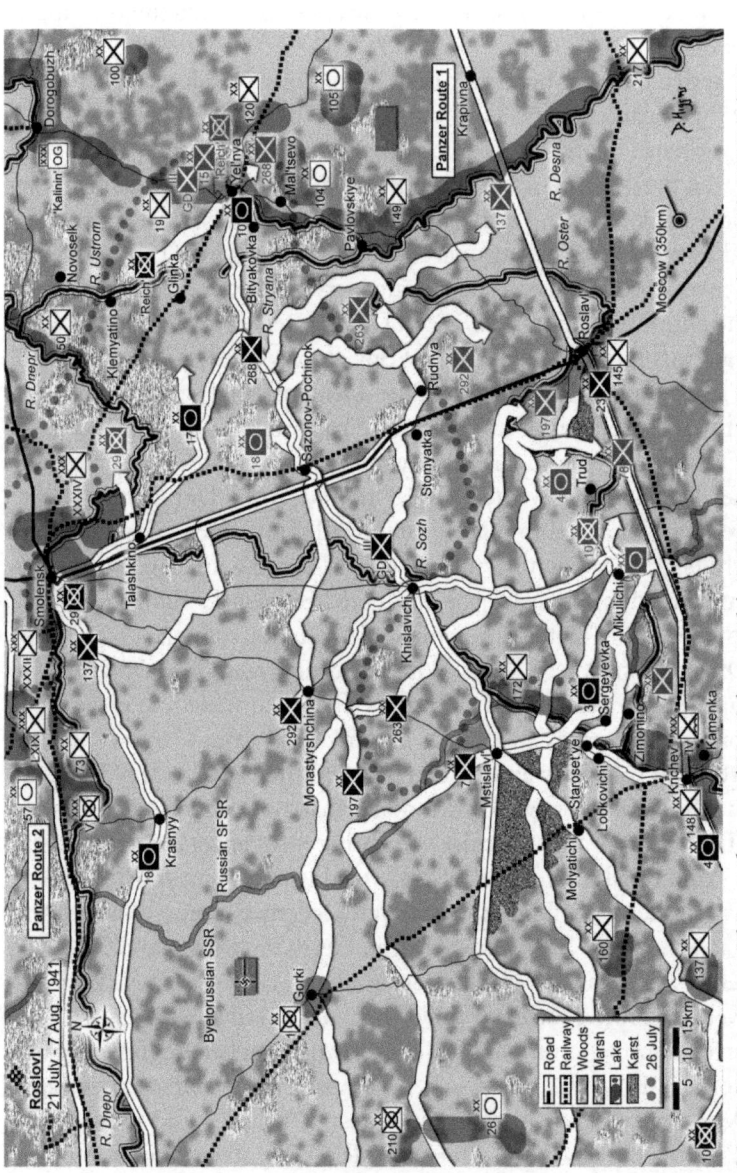

Map 7. Western Front/Thirteenth Army (IV AC (7, 8 ABde), XX RC (160 RD), XXXXV RC (148 RD), LXI RC (XX MC remnants (26 TD, 210 MD), 172 RD)); Sixteenth Army (XXXII RC (129, 152 RD)); Nineteenth Army (50 RD, XXXIV RC (38, 127, 158 RD)); Twentieth Army (73, 137 RD, 1 MRD, 57 TD, II RC (100 RD), V MC (13, 17 TD), LXIX MC (229, 233 RD)); Twenty-Eighth Army (105 TD, 'Group Kachalov' (145, 149 RD, 104 TD), XXX RC (217 RD); Reserve Army Front/Twenty-Fourth Army (19, 120 RD, 'Group Kalinin' (LIII Army Corps (107, 178 RD)). TsAMO, f.208, op.2511, d.210,l.1. TsAMO, f.358, op.5916, d.22, l.1.

they fought in an alien environment. As representative of the scorn often exhibited towards such female fighters, and what presumably reflected the extremism and degeneracy of the Communist regime, German soldiers often referred to them pejoratively as 'Gun dames' ('*Flintenweiber*').

During the afternoon of 21 July XIII Army Corps finally reached the Dnepr near Mogilev and began strengthening the shrinking southern cordon around its besieged defenders. Recent prisoners had indicated a 20,000-strong Soviet force remained in the Mogilev–River Basya Pocket and was preparing to break-out to the south-east for Klimovichi; a tall order now that Second Army occupied much of the region through which they would move. Having little time or opportunity for rest and repair over the last four weeks of fighting, 4th Panzer Division reported possessing 133 tanks, of which just 44 were operational; numbers not dissimilar to Guderian's other armoured formations.[4] While on paper these figures appeared to bode ill for Second Panzer Group, the availability of other weapon systems and veteran personnel well versed in coordinating ad hoc mixed forces to address varying battlefield situations helped compensate and maintain combat effectiveness. In this particular instance normal communication channels proved fruitless in getting spare parts and other supplies, as senior leadership had ordered such items to be presently hoarded at the depots. As withholding vital supplies from combat active formations understandably drew the ire of commanders like Schweppenburg, over the next few days spare parts and replacements were provided. Seeing 10th Motorized Infantry Division's difficulty in keeping the Soviets south of the River Sozh, Bock redirected XIII Army Corps from the Mogilev sector and along XXIV Motorized Army Corps' right flank. Weich's VII Army Corps was subsequently tasked with capturing the city alone.

Toward late morning the next day, 394th Motorized Rifle Regiment approached Panzer Route 1 between Slavgorod and Cherikov without resistance, although immobilized and abandoned enemy vehicles, equipment, and ammunition provided mute testimony to their recent activity. By early afternoon the vanguard of 34th Infantry Division (XIII AC) had arrived at Chausy to assume cordon duties for lingering elements of 3rd Panzer Division. Continuing to clear Panzer Route 1 during the afternoon, Langermann divided his attention, with part of his command striking south-west to secure Slavgorod, and in coordination with 10th Motorized Infantry Division block parts of what German intelligence believed were five Soviet rifle divisions working to break through to the south. To the north-east 33rd Motorized Rifle Regiment (4 PD) held a Sozh bridgehead at Krichev against enemy pressure from the east and south.

For all of the German Army's tremendous accomplishments during the first four weeks of Barbarossa by late July Halder's optimism about a rapid victory had waned. Having told Hitler earlier in the month that only 46 of the known 164 Soviet divisions were still combat effective, for all the destruction and losses inflicted on them the Red Army's ability to field, equip, and maintain new formations forced him on 23 July to revise the estimate to 93 divisions being in fighting shape. With the enemy possessing what seemed like an unlimited supply of manpower Halder reconsidered his belief in eliminating the Soviet army and focused instead on eliminating their industrialized areas around Moscow, in particular armaments manufacturing, and securing Ukraine.[5] With Brauchitsch and Heusinger having met Bock at his headquarters two days previously to discuss OKH's partial deviation from the Moscow advance axis, on 23 July Guderian received a communiqué addressing the change. Halder even went to the lengths of considering sending Second Panzer Group and a portion of Second Army as far as Stalingrad to cut off the enemy's major petroleum extraction and production in the Caucasus region. Even less likely Bock was to take Moscow with the remainder of Second Army and Third Panzer Group, before continuing on to secure Kazan and the River Volga![6]

On 23 July Guderian met with Thoma at Talashkino for his assumption to command 17th Panzer Division. An experienced panzer commander, the brigadier was known for steady leadership and bravery exhibited during the First World War and Spanish Civil War, and was described in a post-1945 interview as 'A tough but likeable type, [and that] he is obviously a born enthusiast who lives in a world of tanks, loves fighting for the zest of it, but without ill-feeling, respecting any opponent.'[7] For the immediate future the division acted as a link between XXXXVI and XXXXVII Motorized Army Corps, and covered the Dnepr where Kluge believed the Soviets would strike from the north. With Vietinghoff's headquarters having recently relocated to a wooded area 12km west of Yel'nya, Guderian met with the lieutenant general who told him that the Soviets were attacking the extended position from the north, east, and south. Unlike the enemy, which had a considerable amount of artillery, XXXXVI Motorized Army Corps had been running low on ammunition and often resorted to prioritizing targets. The trail connecting Glinka with Klemyatino was swampy and impassable even though on a map it was listed otherwise, and all movement had to be on foot.

In XXXXVI Motorized Army Corps' sector at 0600hrs on 23 July 10th Rifle Brigade reached Mal'tsevo, where it made contact with its 90th Motorized Reconnaissance Battalion.[8] 90th Artillery Regiment's batteries correspondingly changed positions in the area near Mal'tsevo to present a screen even though Red Army forces had seemingly vacated the areas south of Yel'nya. The attached 817th Motorized Heavy 210mm Howitzer Battalion, with its three batteries, remained in place and covered 10th Panzer Division's efforts to establish what was hoped to be a short-lived defensive position and during the afternoon both units reverted to Army control as part of 101st Arko to cover areas to the north and north-east.

During the day Guderian went to 10th Panzer Division's Bityakovka headquarters where in addition to seeing the advanced position, Schaal reported that his command had knocked out fifty enemy tanks in fighting near Yel'nya; small consolation for one-third of his armour being destroyed or undergoing maintenance after just one month. The general then went to nearby 'Reich' where he learned of the formation's recent capture of 1,100 prisoners, but also its inability to move beyond the River Uzha or reach Dorogobuzh due to several Soviet bombers targeting the area. Moving up to the front line, he met with Captain (*SS-Hauptsturmführer*) Fritz Klingenburg who three months previously had gained fame by applying bluff, improvisation, and audacity to secure the peaceful surrender of Belgrade (Yugoslavia), alongside just six of his Waffen-SS motorcycle troopers. Based in part on 2./SS-Motorcycle Battalion 'Reich' commander's appraisal Guderian determined to postpone an attack on Dorogobuzh until Großdeutschland arrived to bolster SS-Reconnaissance Battalion 'Reich', which was under infantry and artillery attack near Glinka. Further south, in an effort to beat back Nehring's rather exposed command Soviet forces struck out from the Roslavl' area and into his advance detachment. With IX Army Corps having moved into the Monastyrshchina–Mstislavl' area it would soon be able to plug the gap between XXXXVI and XXIV Motorized Corps as they held a Yel'nya-Rudnya–Krichev–Novyy Bykhov line.[9]

With the German VII Army Corps having surrounded Mogilev out to Konstantinovka the day before, at 1100hrs the formation captured the city, and with it a large number of enemy vehicles that went a long way towards replenishing its lorry losses. While the doomed pocket soldiered on to the north-east, 3rd and 4th Panzer Divisions respectively continued to the east and south-east generally along the River Sozh in strength, which helped populate Guderian's otherwise exposed right flank. At 0910hrs 1st Motorized Reconnaissance Battalion moved into a line between Zimonino and Sergeyevka, while 394th Motorized Rifle Regiment, being well to Model's rear, was temporarily placed under 4th Panzer Division during the heavy fighting around Slavgorod, where Soviet artillery fire from Kemyanka destroyed two of the three wooden Dnepr bridges. At 2310hrs Großdeutschland continued its fight that had started at 1630hrs around Stomyatka.

To reinforce the harsh Party rhetoric towards how the Barbarossa Campaign was to be conducted on 23 July 1941 Keitel, a Führer sycophant, issued a decree that German forces were to 'instil such fear as is suitable to entirely discourage any form of disobedience within the population'.[10] Two days later OKH supplemented the order with 'the required ruthlessness is not being applied in all quarters'. As could be expected the results worked against the Wehrmacht by disincentivising Soviet prisoners and civilians from proactively aiding the German cause, if not galvanizing active resistance against it. Even if applied in isolated instances Soviet propaganda would incorporate such kernels of truth into a broad countering campaign to further erode enemy efforts at the front line, and behind it.

IX Army Corps (137th, 263rd, and 292nd Infantry Divisions) (to Second Panzer Group (24 July))

At 1030hrs the commander of 33rd Motorized Rifle Regiment (4 PD) reported a large enemy force moving south-east of the Krichev bridgehead. Considering a Soviet reconnaissance-in-force, with tank support, struck the area the previous afternoon, Luftwaffe observation was required to better ascertain the threat's size and intention than that from the ground provided. As a precaution III./75th Motorized Artillery Regiment was ordered to deploy just south of the town. At 1100hrs 33rd Motorized Rifle Regiment sent out reconnaissance towards Trud, and within a few minutes 1./521st Panzerjäger Battalion was inserted into the bridgehead should enemy armour make an appearance. Although the makeshift vehicles had high silhouettes and thin armour, their 47mm main guns possessed a 1,200m effective range that could typically outdistance their adversaries. To assist in blocking the Soviet counterattack 4th Panzer Division contacted XXIV Motorized Army Corp to request an airstrike on the forest edges east and south-east of the Krichev bridgehead. With VII Army Corps' duties at Mogilev nearly concluded it would soon be available to move to the south-east and free up XXIV Motorized Army Corps to focus on taking Roslavl'. By 1350hrs 33rd Motorized Rifle Regiment reported that Trud and Kemyanka were enemy-free, and within 2 hours 394th Motorized Rifle Regiment was released from 4th Panzer Division back to Model.

Due to the newly-arriving infantry divisions from XII and XIII Army Corps' filling in the front line south of Novyy Bykhov the adjacent XXIV Motorized Army Corps was free to once again continue offensive operations. Down to just 28 per cent of its *Barbarossatag* complement of tanks operational, Guderian's manpower had dropped by nearly 10 per cent.[11] After six days of heavy fighting on 25 July the Soviet Sixteenth Army recaptured the part of Smolensk north of the Dnepr. Able to reinforce XXXXVI Motorized Army Corps' beleaguered defence of Yel'nya at 0300hrs 17th Panzer Division entered firing positions 50km to the south-east, where the area's hilly terrain, poor roads, and numerous waterways hindered movement. To help plug Vietinghoff's still open right flank 18th Panzer Division reoriented its advance axis across his supply lines to the south-east. Starting at 0300hrs enemy artillery subjected II./SS-'Deutschland' to over 12 hours of sustained, accurate artillery fire. Over this period Soviet infantry conducted four attacks only to have 8./SS-'Deutschland' rebuff each one using small arms and antitank guns to knock out or destroy what supporting Red Army tanks broke through their lines.[12] During the last two days of defensive fighting 'Reich' claimed to have destroyed at least fifty enemy tanks, including eight multi-turret T-28s.¹³ In recognition of his men's accomplishments during their participation in the Yel'nya fighting Hausser expressed:

> For four days we have been in one of the decisive battles of this campaign. It has continuously demanded of you all the highest that can be demanded of a soldier. The entire German Fatherland looks with pride and admiration on the men of the front, who now struggle for the decision against the Bolshevik world enemy. The fact that we advanced the furthest east of all the Army's divisions must be our duty. The casualties and severity of the struggle will not be in vain. We hold the ground we have won because we know that we will win.¹⁴

137th Infantry Division (IX to XXXXVII Motorized Army Corps (26 July))

Throughout the next day little of the front line changed. Heavy fighting ensued along the Soviet corridor and Smolensk, where 137th Infantry Division had been allocated to XXXXVII Motorized Army Corps to provide more suitable forces for the urban environment Lemelsen worked to pacify. While its 449th and 448th Infantry Regiments (137 ID) bolstered the city's northern defence, alongside 71st Motorized Infantry Regimen (29 MID), Guderian requested that 268th Infantry Division (VII AC) be brought up from the Monastyrshchina area to allow his armoured elements to pull back from their combat positions for some badly needed rest, resupply, and maintenance.¹⁵ As was a common occurrence for follow-on German infantry, the neighbouring 463rd Infantry Regiment (263 ID) fought off Soviet forces in battalion strength at Khislavichi just before dawn on 26 July to keep the popular road hub clear and keep the division's lorry transports moving forward.¹⁶ With Hoth effectively sealing the pocket east of Smolensk and trapping 10 Soviet divisions, 200km to the southwest lingering clusters of resistance from what had recently been the Mogilev Pocket were cleared on 26 July, with some 35,000 soldiers falling into German captivity. What formations that retained a semblance of cohesion moved for Guderian's still porous enemy lines from Mstislavl' south past Krichev.¹⁷

On 27 July Guderian's chief-of-staff, Lieutenant Colonel Kurt Baron von Liebenstein, flew to attend a meeting at Army Group Centre's headquarters at Borisov to report on Second Panzer Group's status and to discuss Bock's future intentions. Expecting to hear that he was to continue eastward for Moscow or at least Bryansk, as per Army Command's Directive No. 21 that called for 'the prompt seizure of the economically important Donets Basin' and a 'rapid arrival at Moscow', Hitler's orders were for a disgusted Guderian to, instead, strike in the opposite direction to subdue Gomel' in coordination with Second Army. Given the unknowns of the Führer's operational redirection that seemed fixed on mitigating what he felt were the three army groups' lengthy flanks and preserving logistic security, the general continued to focus on first taking

Roslavl'. Having heard his subordinate's proposal to send 18th Panzer Division south and have the tankers relieve Großdeutschland for use near Dorogobuzh, Kluge refused approval.[18] To effectively implement his new mission Guderian received Bock's approval to have VII (Fourth Army) and XX Army Corps (Ninth Army) placed under his control, which given Second Panzer Group's increased size it was renamed Army Group Guderian and transferred back to Army Group Centre.

Army Group Guderian (Fourth Panzer Army to Army Group Centre (28 July))
VII Army Corps (15th, 78th, and 197th Infantry Divisions) (to Army Group Guderian (28 July))
137th Infantry Division (XXXXVII Motorized to IX Army Corps (29 July))

As an example of Army Group Centre's considerable success, during the fighting between the Dnepr and Desna, by 29 July what had recently been Second Panzer Group had captured 76,570 Red Army soldiers, as well as 903 armoured vehicles, 661 artillery pieces, and 163 aircraft.[19] On 29 July seemingly an effort to assuage any ill feelings his hard-charging general may harbour over the dramatic change in operational priorities Hitler sent Chief Adjutant of the Army of the Führer and Commander-in-Chief of the Wehrmacht, Colonel Rudolf Schmundt, with Guderian's Oak Leaves to his Knight's Cross. Although Guderian, Hoth, and Bock held to the view that capturing the enemy capital would unhinge Soviet forces opposite Army Group Centre and make available the city's considerable road and rail system, each commander needed to resign themselves to the new reality and work towards the quick conclusion of their respective tasks. However maddening Guderian's operational deviation was to him, given Army Group Guderian's declining strength, setting off towards the comparatively less defended south offered a renewal of deep manoeuvre.[20] Considering the distances between Brest and Minsk and from there to Smolensk were respectively 330 and 310km, covering the remaining 370km to Moscow seemed entirely feasible, and at least for Hitler, once the *Ostheer*'s flanks could be secured.

268th Infantry Division (to XXXXVI Motorized Army Corps (30 July))

With Army Group Guderian and Third Panzer Group having finally made contact at Solov'yevo the previous day and cleared the Dnepr's west bank, Red Army forces opposite the waterway for now prevented the Germans from establishing a bridgehead. On 30 July some 15km downriver from the village 'Operational Group Yartsevo' broke through to the encircled, greatly beaten down Sixteenth and Twentieth Armies struggling to maintain combat effectiveness.[21] In the ensuing rush to get east of the Dnepr the recently trapped Soviet forces abandoned large amounts of weapons and equipment, desertions were rampant, and cases of self and mutual mutilation to get out of the fight rose precipitously.[22] When the Germans destroyed the crossing the pullout switched to Solov'yevo, where the river was only a metre deep and could be crossed with some difficulty. With what were considered a sufficient number of German infantry formations surrounding Smolensk to ensure economy of force 137th Infantry Division had been pulled the previous day and relocated 70km to the south-east where IX Army Corps awaited the order to move on Roslavl'. Since 258th Infantry Division had taken over 4th Panzer Division's positions along Panzer Route 1, the latter was freed up to strike for the city as well.

In XXIV Motorized Army Corps' sector Soviet bombers had repeatedly struck positions along the River Sozh; a situation made worse as Luftwaffe intervention failed to materialize in spite of clear skies.[23] That day, Hitler issued his Directive No. 34 ordering Soviet forces fighting north-west of Kyiv to 'be brought to battle west of the Dnepr and annihilated.' and Army Group Centre was 'to go over to the defensive.' to retain its recently hard-won gains. Although the Germans had seemingly achieved sufficient battlefield success over the last few weeks to herald the enemy's imminent destruction, many Landsers undoubtedly wondered where the Russian soldiers of 1917 who had capitulated or dissolved en masse had gone, as Soviet ideology, propaganda, and a knowledge of what surrender entailed now helped bolster their encountered resistance.

7th Infantry Division (to XXIV Motorized Army Corps (31 July))

Roslavl'

With Second Army presenting a solidified, southern facing between Novyy Bykhov and Krichev, at 0400hrs on 1 August 4th Panzer Divisions finally got its chance to act as Schweppenburg's vanguard. Bursting beyond a security screen Model had established at his Staroset'ye bridgehead over the Sozh, Langermann initially skirted the River Oster's northern edge before turning south to reach Panzer Route 1. As 4th Panzer Division now struck directly for Roslavl', Eberbach, now in command of 5th Panzer Brigade, whose personnel had recently been decimated by friendly fire and the command remnants transferred from Model to Langermann, and a Kampfgruppe built around Colonel Oswlin Grolig's 33rd Motorized Infantry Regiment, respectively paved the way on the right and left. Just to the north, Guderian visited VII Army Corps' sector, which was positioned to pin Twenty-Eighth Army's forward elements, behind which the more mobile Schweppenburg was readying to cut off.[24] Finding neither the corps' headquarters nor that of its subordinate 23rd Infantry Division the general went to the 3rd Panzer Division, whose artillery had conducted a softening bombardment at 0345hrs that morning, as part of Model's return to offensive action. To further support his getting through a particularly active enemy forward defence, and be in position to support 4th Panzer Division to his east, at 0700hrs Luftwaffe bombers targeted the rail depot at Krichev and along the line to at least Roslavl'.[25] That afternoon, I./394th Rifle Regiment fought off enemy cavalry to take the 50m-long Oster Bridge at Mikulichi and secure a bridgehead to the south.[26]

Comprising its original three motorized and two newly-added infantry corps, by 2 August Army Group Guderian contended with three fights along what was becoming a frustrating, increasingly sluggish front line extending for 300km. During what was a complex, often chaotic period of adjustment, German infantry divisions took over from Guderian's mobile formations when possible to free them up for badly needed rest and refitting, or reallocation south for the planned thrust into Ukraine. For 18th Panzer Division, having been pulled back to the relatively quiet Sazonov-Pochinok area since late July, it was ready to transition to combat operations once again.

While Thoma's 17th Panzer Division plugged the distance between Großdeutschland's anchoring position along XXXXVI Motorized Army Corps' left and Smolensk, 'Reich' continued to hold back repeated Soviet attacks. In what had become a magnet for Soviet attention XXXXVI Motorized Army Corps' components weathering multiple, daily attacks at Yel'nya suffered casualties and materiel losses it could ill afford, lest its ability to continue as an armoured vanguard be compromised. Adding to German difficulties, a few kilometres to the north Luftwaffe reconnaissance reported the Soviets had built a bridge east of Smolensk and that large numbers of the enemy were pouring out.[27]

While the introduction of 268th Infantry Division into the fight helped reinforce the German defence, Guderian was willing to pull his men back from the extended position to remove any flanks that would weaken his important position. While exposed flanks were a natural result of a war of movement in static fighting in which Vietinghoff now found himself such a protrusion provided few long-term benefits. At 1400hrs on 2 August the Soviets attacked towards Mal'tsevo in roughly regimental strength. Just over an hour later 268th Infantry Division reported rebuffing one such assault during the morning, although heavy enemy artillery continued to target them with what one battalion recorded of upwards of 400 rounds into its sector in just an hour. At 1530hrs the Ia from 'Reich' indicated a serious situation that involved enemy attacks from the north and north-east. The Soviets had broken through 11th SS-Infantry Regiment near Novoselk, but as was a typical reaction the Germans quickly cobbled together a counterattack that ejected them. If 'Reich' remained in its present position for an extended period it risked destruction, as its rifle companies had each been fought down to between sixty and seventy men. On 2 August Wolfgang Fischer, who had been promoted the previous day to brigadier, assumed command of 10th Panzer Division when Schaal was transferred to OKH Leader Reserve. A decorated First World War veteran and member of the inter-war Reichswehr, Fischer had served as a motorized regimental commander under

Guderian's XIX Army Corps during the Polish Campaign and afterward led 10th Panzer Brigade.

Working his way north-east through his newly allocated infantry formations along his right flank, Guderian spent the morning of 2 August back with IX Army Corps. As could be expected given the Soviets continued to stitch together a relatively organized defence, XXIV Motorized Army Corps was opening a sizeable gap between Roslavl' and Krichev, and correspondingly Twenty-Eighth and Thirteenth Armies. From 509th Infantry Regiment's (292 ID) command post Guderian watched the Soviets withdraw southward onto Roslavl'. The remainder of IX Army Corps followed in what was a southward thrust between Rudnya and Pavlovskiye towards cutting Panzer Route 1 astride the River Oster. He was then driven to where 507th Infantry Regiment was advancing on Kazaki. Although the foot-bound division risked leaving an open left flank during its advance on Roslavl', with so much of the Soviet Twenty-Eighth Army's attention focused on Yel'nya the German effort would likely reach a successful conclusion before significant, or at least organized, enemy forces could be brought against it. Caught between VII Army Corps pushing into the western part of the city and IX Army Corps threatening it from the north-east, Army Group Guderian worked to encircle and eliminate as much of Twenty-Eighth Army as possible and secure the area's road and rail network. Back at his headquarters he learned that the former had recently reported taking 3,700 prisoners, and several artillery guns and tanks.[28] Some 20km outside of Roslavl' examples of the Red Army's newly-fielded Ilyushin Il-2 ground-attack aircraft conducted low-altitude strafing of German positions, but the seemingly tentative attack runs produced few results.[29] A German 20mm quad antiaircraft gun scored some hits that ominously appeared to cause little meaningful damage to the armoured fuselage.

Army Group Guderian Reverted to Second Panzer Group (3 August)

As the fighting to eliminate the nearly complete Smolensk Pocket neared its conclusion in early August the German logistics system showed renewed signs of strain.[30] For many, including Halder, the problem was with the railway engineer troop leadership opting to quickly get low-capacity lines regauged and functioning. While this expediency can be understood given the *Ostheers* rapid advance across Belorussia, once beyond the Dnepr the Germans needed to continue the process. To build the necessary stockpiles of fuel, ammunition, food, and other materiel to support another 300km advance three times as many trains needed to operate along the lines than the dozen that typically ran each day at present. With their hands full just repairing and reinforcing frequently neglected structures and bridges, they left less immediate work to others, such as to add sleepers and repair or install the necessary signals, workshops, depots, and other infrastructure necessary to facilitate higher capacity lines. While many in senior German leadership felt the fighting in the East would conclude before the onset of winter, in his role as major general within OKH's Administration Division, Franz Kleberger indicated to Halder that sufficient supplies of winter clothing would be available by October 1941, including 'woollen vests, toques, earmuffs, gloves, scarves, [and] chest warmers'. To provide shelter some 300,000 wooden barracks were to be made available, complete with water basins, blankets, lamps, bed linen, and other necessities to ensure protection from the elements and hygiene.[31]

23rd Infantry Division (to VII Army Corps (4 August))
15th Infantry Division (to Second Panzer Group (4 August))

Although IX Army Corps had come close to severing Panzer Route 1 east of Roslavl' the previous day, due in part to sloppy road conditions, on 4 August 'Kampfgruppe Eberbach' lead 4th Panzer Division through the city to make contact and trap an estimated two Soviet rifle and one tank division. With the pocket soon collapsing, the German formation captured 38,500 prisoners, as well as much of Western Front's remaining armour. A lack of reserves and a shortage of ammunition hindered Guderian's ongoing efforts, but he reported to Halder that 50 per cent combat effectiveness was available and sufficient for further offensive operations.[32] During what was Hitler's first trip to the Eastern Front, under a partly cloudy sky nearly 300km to the east, he and Schmundt met with Bock at his Borisov headquarters, with Guderian and Hoth brought in to provide status reports and address future operations. One of the discussed subjects included exploiting the deep hatred large parts of the population had towards the Communists and their abusive system of forced collectivizations, state-mandated atheism, repression, and the widespread NKVD-administered Gulag work camps and penal colonies. Having held serious concerns about the likelihood of Barbarossa's ultimate success, Army Group Centre's typically humourless commander positively viewed using this potentially considerable manpower to the Germans' advantage; even though pride and contempt combined with what had fast lived up to the 'war of annihilation' mantra increasingly turned these enthusiastic assets into implacable enemies.

For the Führer capturing the Crimea was necessary to remove the threat of Soviet bombers targeting their partner Romania's vital oil resources, specifically in Ploesti. The subject of impending offensive operations was also naturally covered. Hitler made taking Leningrad the priority due in large part to its industry, but seemingly remained undecided on whether to strike for Kyiv, where Army Group South created the conditions for what promised to be a massive cauldron, or Moscow. Whether due to wishful thinking or a flawed OKH assessment, Guderian continued to lobby for the latter where he stressed the last remaining large grouping of Red Army forces stayed in the field. Bock and Hoth concurred, and expressed their respective intentions to be ready to initiate what Clausewitz envisioned as the great decisive battle (*Entscheidungsschlacht*) by 20 August.[33] Both panzer commanders stressed several days were first needed to rest and refit, to which Hitler agreed. Guderian further emphasized his need for new tanks and tank engines to replace what dust and other sources had damaged, and was promised the release of 300 new tank engines for the entire Eastern Front; a wholly inadequate number given the losses to date. Replacement tanks would not be forthcoming, and as per the German emphasis on removing fought-down units from the fighting for refitting and replenishment, as opposed to relying on a trickle of replacements, the long distances to the front line, overburdened rail services, and sustained enemy pressure complicated implementing such efforts. In addition to congratulating Bock on his 'unprecedented success' the Führer spoke of 'an attack to the east', something with which Army Group Centre's commander 'happily agreed and said that in this way we should surely meet the Russian strength and decision against what was probably his last forces to be hoped for there'.[34] To illustrate what was a common disconnect between those serving at the front and senior leadership hundreds of kilometres to the west on being told about the masses of Soviet armour being encountered around Yel'nya and elsewhere Hitler told Bock and Guderian that, 'Had I known they had as many tanks as that, I'd have thought twice before invading.'

In the absence of orders from OKW at the meeting's conclusion Bock, and those with whom were in agreement, got the impression that 'it appears that he [Hitler] is not yet clear on how the operations should now proceed'.[35] Given that front-line senior German commanders often tolerated the Führer's interference in their domain during what had been a string of successes into Soviet territory, Guderian viewed the matter as more of a mission-type instruction (*Weisung*) than a direct order (*Befehl*). Due to his penchant for massaging orders to fit his own interests and a disregard for higher authority when his understanding of a battlefield situation differed it risked adding uncertainty and confusion into the decision-making process. On his flight back to his headquarters based on the day's meeting and his success in capturing Roslavl', Guderian determined to continue to push east for Moscow until forced to desist and set his staff in motion towards that end.

Fall of Smolensk

Although the Soviet V Mechanized Corps had moved into the Solov'yevo area to hold open a corridor that permitted large numbers of their trapped comrades to escape the doomed Smolensk Pocket during the night of 3/4 August, one day later Guderian finally linked up with Hoth to trap and defeat the defending Soviet Sixteenth and Twentieth Armies and assorted units. After what had been a costly, grinding, and largely self-inflicted struggle for the Germans, their elimination of 309,110 prisoners, 3,205 tanks, and 3,120 artillery pieces from the Red Army's ranks dealt a serious blow to Soviet strength standing between Bock and his direct route to Moscow. With his Second Panzer Group credited with taking 97,040 prisoners, early on 5 August a satisfied Guderian visited VII Army Corps to discuss strengthening his southern border, which extended back to Krichev.[36] Guderian then visited 197th Infantry Division's commander, Brigadier Hermann Meier-Rabingen, north of Roslavl' where VII and IX Army Corps squeezed the exhausted, depleted remnants of the city's recent defenders into seeming oblivion, only to have some slip through the cordon to briefly take Kazaki the next day.[37] Meeting next with 4th Panzer Division, the general learned that 35th Panzer Regiment had been pulled from the front line, given that its immediate task had been completed, but with the escaping Soviets needing to be countered he wirelessly contacted XXIV Motorized Army Corps towards securing Panzer Route 1 east of Roslavl'. Guderian then returned to VII Army Corps, which already had 23rd Infantry Division send out its 23rd Reconnaissance Battalion to quickly throw up a screen at the gap and buy time for other blocking forces to arrive. After moving among VII Army Corps' subordinate divisions to occasionally issue tactical-level orders, he instructed the formation's 7th Arko, Brigadier Robert Martinek, to keep tabs on trouble spots along Panzer Route 1.[38]

Having eliminated Soviet resistance around Smolensk and Roslavl' to help secure Guderian's flanks, over the next few days Second Panzer Group reorganized for subsequent operations. During the night of 5/6 August 15th Infantry Division began replacing the hard-pressed 'Reich' along the northern sector of the increasingly pointless Yel'nya bulge between 17th Panzer and 268th Infantry Divisions. With the need to secure Rogachev and Gomel', on 6 August Halder suggested Guderian release one of his panzer divisions to temporarily assist Second Army's efforts. Professing XXIV Motorized Army Corps required rest and refurbishment, although a nearly pathological need to retain forces allocated to him was perhaps more to the truth, Guderian vociferously rejected the idea. According to his intelligence hardly any Soviet forces remained in the Roslavl' area, or for a 40km stretch towards Bryansk; a situation Halder inferred as Guderian looking to conduct an offensive against the latter before turning to help take Gomel'.[39] Instead, on 7 August Guderian asked Bock to allow him to direct 3rd and 4th Panzer Divisions to the south-west and along the River Iput' towards Chechersk and Gomel'. Such a professed compromise would seemingly allow the general to avoid relinquishing control, and on completing that task, simply redirect the formations eastward once again. While IX Army Corps reorganized west of the River Oster following their role in eliminating enemy forces north of Roslavl', the adjacent VII Army Corps would set off to take Bryansk before Soviet forces gathered to stop them. With the infantry of

XXXXIII Army Corp still west of the Dnepr and unable to immediately lend support from the west the field marshal quashed any such movement for the time being. However much Bock desired to break through the hardening enemy crust and push for Moscow, and beyond, he felt, 'The situation is extremely tense . . .' and that, 'I don't know exactly how a new operation is to take place . . . with the slowly sinking fighting strength of our . . . forces'.[40]

Chapter 7

Turning from Moscow, 8–26 August 1941

15th Infantry Division (Second Panzer Group to XXXXVI Motorized Army Corps (8 August))
268th Infantry Division (XXXXVI Motorized to XX Army Corps (8 August))

For all his desire to co-lead Army Group Centre in one final encirclement battle (*Kesselschlacht*) that would capture Moscow, and with it the enemy's political heart and major communications and infrastructure hub, forced to adhere to 19 July's Directive No. 33 Guderian could now only hope to quickly complete his new mission to ensure as much time as possible remained before the advent of winter. With Soviet strategic reserves having gathered along the most direct route to Moscow, at the expense of other sectors, the sudden, unexpected change in the German advance axis caught Soviet senior leadership off guard.

Over the last few days, on Guderian's north 17th Panzer and elements of 29th Motorized Infantry Division continued to man a largely static front line east of Smolensk to where XX Army Corps now held XXXXVI Motorized Army Corps' vacated positions around Yel'nya. Early on 8 August a Soviet grouping of 102nd Tank Division, 3 rifle divisions, and 230 artillery pieces struck elements of 15th Infantry Division along the salient's central perimeter. Ordered from the fighting the German formation began pulling out to the south-west, while just to the north 10th Panzer Division took a welcome respite having been similarly withdrawn a few days prior; although it remained as a potential reinforcement. With IX and VII Army Corps' having moved up to the front line around a newly conquered Roslavl' much of Guderian's armoured and motorized forces had been withdrawn from the combat zone for a few days rest and refit, but were now back in the line between Krichev and Roslavl'. With 10th Motorized Infantry Division having advanced to Khislavichi on 1 August before turning south, it spent the next few days positioning itself between 3rd and 4th Panzer Divisions in preparation for further offensive operations.[1]

292nd Infantry Division (to XX Army Corps (9 August))
29th Motorized Infantry Division (XXXXVII Motorized Army Corps – at the disposition of Second Panzer Group (9 August))
15th Infantry Division (XXXXVI Motorized to XX Army Corps (9 August))

Back at what was his new critical front on 9 August Guderian joined 4th Panzer Division, where Colonel (Graduate Engineer) Erich Schneider's 103rd Motorized Artillery Regiment softened enemy positions along Langermann's slated advance axis. Having remained behind a protective screen of 7th and 78th Infantry Divisions for the last two days, XXIV Motorized Army Corps now struck southward, where for the last two days the bulk of Second Air Force had been softening up XXVIII and XL Rifle Corps. As its armoured and motorized divisions poured across Panzer Route 1 the infantry divisions made way to respectively reorient to the west and east to protect Schweppenburg's flanks. As part of Guderian's effort to switch out XXXXVII Motorized for VII Army Corps occupying the Roslavl' area, Boltenstern's 29th Motorized Infantry Division progressively pulled out of its positions near Smolensk and was sent south. Perhaps leveraging the Führer's recently rekindled interest in striking for the enemy capital, during the evening Guderian pitched rather farcically having his XXIV Motorized Army Corps turn 180 degrees from its south-western advance on Klimovichi and instead make for Vyaz'ma, over 200km to the north-east. Exaggerating to Bock the lack of enemy forces in the Roslavl' sector in which Schweppenburg now advanced, the field marshal quashed any such repositioning due to the Red Army's strong presence east of Smolensk that looked to block the most direct German advance axis against Moscow.[2]

Having written optimistically in his diary on 3 July 1941 that the war in the East had been won in two weeks, on 10 August Halder expressed that, 'At the outset of the war we reckoned with about 200 enemy divisions. Now we have already counted 360.' and that 'if we smash a dozen of them, the Russians simply put up another dozen'. Later that day he added, 'Our last reserves have been committed.' and that, 'What we are now doing is the last desperate attempt to prevent our front line from becoming frozen in positional warfare . . .'.[3] For Bock, the deficient number of men and materiel replacements coming from Germany and the enemy's numerical strength and incessant attacks hindered rotating his forces through forward combat positions and quiet rear areas to help maintain their battlefield effectiveness. After a 90km drive to reach Roslavl' on 10 August 29th Motorized Infantry Division sent out an advance detachment to lead its way towards Mglin. Between Smolensk and Yel'nya 17th Panzer Division pulled from its front-line positions and alongside the nearby 18th Panzer Division, which had been kept from the fighting for a brief period.

To express his gratitude for recent battlefield success Guderian issued a rather detached 'Group – Order of the Day' that read:

> Soldiers of the Army Group! The struggle for the Roslavl' area has ended victoriously. A large territorial gain was achieved. More important, however, is the destruction of the enemy encountered in this area: 38,561 prisoners were brought in, and numerous other military equipment was captured, 250 tanks, 359 artillery guns, 163 antitank

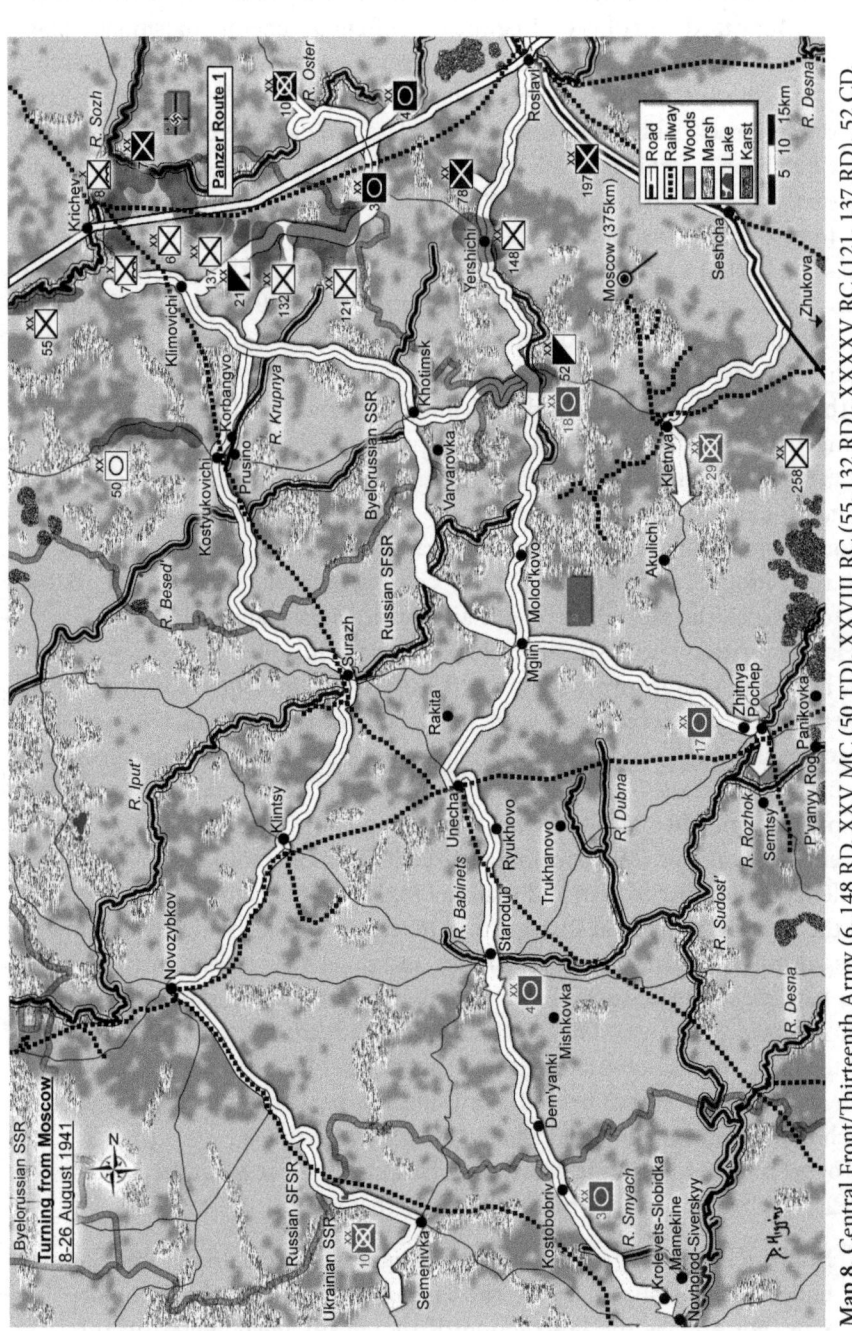

Map 8. Central Front/Thirteenth Army (6, 148 RD, XXV MC (50 TD), XXVIII RC (55, 132 RD), XXXV RC (121, 137 RD), 52 CD, 21 MCD, IV AC (7, 8 Abde)); Reserve Army Front (II RC (258 RD)). TsAMO, f.226, op.648, d.6, l.61.

guns, 91 antiaircraft guns, 1,000 M.G. and numerous other military equipment. In this way, a hole was punched in the enemy front, which the opponent tried to patch in vain. A new German strike is underway, another in preparation. Soldiers of the army group! I thank you for the dedication with which you have solved the task set to you. And if I now call you not to slacken in spite of all your efforts in the future, I am sure of your help and understanding. The enemy must not close his ranks again, he must not come to rest. We want an early German victory! Therefore forward for our Germany and for our Führer Adolf Hitler!

29th Motorized Infantry Division (Second Panzer Group to XXXXVII Motorized Army Corps (11 August))

Gomel'

With Fourth and Second Armies having moved up to the Rivers Dnepr, Pripet, and Sozh, and German forces now issuing forth from a bridgehead near Cherikov, Gomel's defence was threatened from the west and north. In concert with these predominantly infantry formations, Guderian's XXIV Motorized Army Corps for once had strong flank protection as it sliced across Thirteenth Army. To initially protect Schweppenburg's expectedly lengthy left, 78th and 197th Rifle Divisions sent out advance elements to facilitate their respective southward advances along the River Iput' and the Roslavl'–Bryansk road. While the 78th simply bulled its way through a blocking position at Yershichi, the 197th turned inward for Kletnya.[4] Over the last few days 4th Panzer Division had swung clockwise passed Klimovichi to near Krichev to encircle a sizeable portion of XXXXV Rifle Corps defending that stretch of the River Sozh.[5] With its ongoing role as Langermann's vanguard completed by 11 August, 'Kampfgruppe Grolig' (33 MRR) turned to rejoin 'Kampfgruppe Eberbach' in its southward advance.[6]

As 4th Panzer Division approached Kostyukovichi the next day, at 1743hrs the formation encountered a cluster of T-26 tanks some 600–800m off its left. One of the light vehicles emerged from a wooded area near Prusino to fire on the advancing German panzern, striking one.[7] To provide a clearer picture of what awaited his comrades on the ground an observing Luftwaffe pilot dropped smoke to indicate enemy positions. Just over 10 minutes later 6km north-east of Kostyukovichi seven more Soviet T-26s were seen, of which four soon crossed a bridge over the River Krupnya to cautiously enter Korbangvo. With additional enemy armour emerging from a nearby grove the aircraft fired on a fleeing enemy tank in Korbangvo's square between 1828. and 1848hrs. German tanks engaged their Soviet counterparts where the road crossed the rail line, scoring two hits.[8] During the shooting four more Soviet tanks arrived near the road/

rail intersection and engaged those from 35th Panzer Regiment pulled back on Kostyukovichi, and 15 minutes later the unit's left-hand marching group was around Korbanovo near the still undamaged bridge. At 1932hrs additional Soviet tanks were spotted on the road about a kilometre north of Kostyukovichi, and another to the north-east at the River Krupnya. Amid the confused fighting a white flare arced skyward indicating the German front line at Kostyukovichi Train Station. At about 2200hrs the right battle group near the village and the left-hand one 3km to the north-east fought with eight Soviet tanks in a wheat field and two others to the north. Muzzle flashes from larger calibre, presumably Soviet, guns were seen at two locations 3km west of Kostyukovichi. During the engagement the Soviets claimed three of their tanks hit four German ones, three tankettes, two armoured vehicles, and shot down an enemy aircraft with rifle fire for the loss of one tank and one armoured vehicle. Upon the Soviet exit the Germans found several abandoned light tanks awaiting repair.[9]

18th Panzer Division (XXXXVII to XXXXVI Motorized Army Corps (14 August))

With XX Army Corps stretched thin along the northern salient around Yel'nya, and frequently hammered by Soviet artillery, its commander, Lieutenant General (*General der Infanterie*) Friedrich Materna, flew to meet Guderian on 14 August to plead for a shortening of that sector or for reinforcement.[10] Finally willing to relinquish the protrusion the general avoided a commitment and afterward telephoned Bock to stipulate conditions for maintaining what by now was little more than a casualty-inducing appendage. After getting bumped up to Halder, who expressed an uninspired belief that the enemy suffered greater losses in trying to take the salient than the German defenders, the decision was left to Bock, who left things unchanged.

78th Infantry Division (VII to XX Army Corps (15 August))

By 15 August Second Army's right flank had burst across the Dnepr south of Zhlobin, which in concert with its left along the River Sozh to Chechersk, attempted to seal a nearly complete pocket around the Soviet LXVI Rifle Corps. Twenty-First Army's continued possession of Gomel' seemed in doubt and Guderian's desire for a quick conclusion to his southern foray seemed in the offing. On XXIV Motorized Army Corps' left, on 15 August, 78th Infantry Division was transferred from VII to XX Army Corps to beef up its defence around Yel'nya. To weight this static battlefield with his less mobile formations Guderian also ordered IX Army Corps north to replace Großdeutschland and 'Reich'. With the general continuing to lobby for a resumption of an eastward offensive OKH considered putting him under Kluge once again to impart an additional level of control and oversight, but refrained.

137th Infantry Division (IX Army Corps to XXXXVI Motorized Army Corps (16 August))

With 3rd Motorcycle Battalion (3 PD) haven taken the bridge over the River Besed' at Khotimsk and had established a position beyond, between 0750 and 0920hrs on 16 August the unit pushed on to Varvarovka. Forced to contend with extensively wooded and marshy terrain bordering the Iput' and its many tributaries, Model's men were perhaps reminded of their struggles to get east of the Bug. Forced to contend with 4th Panzer Division attempting to push south out of Kostyukovichi and its own crumbling front, the Soviet Thirteenth Army was unable to offer much resistance or prevent 3rd Panzer Division from reaching the River Iput' later in the day. On finding a nearby ford to accommodate the heavier German vehicles Model's advance detachment drove on for another 4 hours to reach Molod'kovo, and the firmer, more open terrain beyond. With few Red Army forces in its way, and little immediate threat to its flanks, the unit pressed its luck to capture Mglin at 1900hrs.[11]

Continuing its pace the following morning, Model's vanguard reached Rakita, while II./3rd Motorized Rifle Regiment approached Unecha at about 1000hrs in what was shaping up to be another hot, dusty day. Soon after German scouts observed enemy engineers laying mines, and antiaircraft and antitank guns distributed as a blocking force before the town. After receiving some threatening fire from a Soviet anti-aircraft battery, 7./6th Motorized Rifle Regiment soon eliminated the threat. At about 1300hrs on 17 August 'Kampfgruppe Manteuffel' and II./6th Panzer Regiment fought a brief firefight against Unecha's defenders before taking its northern edge. Unwilling to concede the entire town, stiffening Soviet resistance slowed further German progress, and it would take another 2 hours of house-to-house fighting for 3rd Panzer Division to cut the Gomel'–Bryansk railway and deny the Soviets operational-level, east–west resupply and casualty evacuation.[12] With II./3rd Motorized Rifle Regiment and III./6th Panzer Regiment expected to arrive at Unecha at 1700 hrs, but delayed by Red Air Force interdiction, German reconnaissance elements set off to the south-east to scout new advance routes. Finding the bridge over a River Dubna tributary at Trukhanovo destroyed, 'Kampfgruppe Manteuffel' struck instead for Starodub and the River Babinets. To shore up the gap with 4th Panzer Division, which worked to penetrate XXXXV Rifle Corps' defences along the River Besed', 10th Motorized Infantry Division deviated from following 3rd Panzer Division to reach Surazh. With Second Army having reached Gomel' and XXIV Motorized Corps achieving similar progress 100km to the east, the intervening Soviet Thirteenth Army was forced to disengage from its positions between Kostyukovichi and Chechersk or risk encirclement.

18th Panzer Division (XXXXVI to XXXXVII Motorized Army Corps (18 August))

Having produced an operations plan on 18 August, Halder laid out limited goals for Hoth and Guderian to respectively secure Army Group Centre's northern and southern flanks to facilitate a renewed push eastward involving their commands, with Ninth and Fourth Armies sandwiched in-between. Where the Army Chief of Staff had previously envisioned Bock and Rundstedt coordinating towards capturing Ukraine, now Second Panzer Group was to redirect just 3rd and 4th Panzer Divisions at a right angle to the advance on the enemy capital, with a constraint that they advance only as far south as Novhorod-Siverskyy.[13]

137th Infantry Division (Removed from XXXXVI Motorized Army Corps (19 August))

In response to the seemingly endless Soviet forces Goebbels noted in his diary on 19 August that, 'Obviously we underestimated the Soviet thrust and, above all, the equipment of the Soviet armies.' And, 'Inwardly the Führer is very angry with himself that he was so deceived by the reports from the Soviet Union about the potential of the Bolsheviks.'[14] For Guderian's XXXXVI Motorized, and XX and IX Army Corps still fighting in and around the Yel'nya bulge, such words would certainly resonate. Hard-pressed to maintain the extended position against masses of Twenty-Fourth Army personnel was unsustainable. With much of his reorganization complete the general could better focus on his southward offensive. While XXXXVII Motorized Army Corps finished its week-long takeover of the Bryansk thrust from VII Army Corps, which was sent north, the much more mobile 29th Motorized Infantry Division now served as vanguard. With Second Army taking Gomel' on 19 August, and with it some 50,000 prisoners, the already faltering Twenty-First and Thirteenth Armies scrambled to evacuate the area and withdraw southward.[15]

'Reich' (Removed from XXXXVI Motorized Army Corps (20 August))

As much as Guderian might wish to exploit the relative absence of enemy forces and have 17th Panzer Division push on to the River Desna and strike Bryansk from the south, Bock was of a different mind. Desiring to instead have XXXXVI and XXXXVII Motorized Army Corps withdrawn to the Roslavl' area to rest and refit in preparation for an anticipated renewal of the Moscow offensive, the latter was to push no farther than Pochep and the River Sudost'.

In adherence, throughout the morning of 20 August 'Kampfgruppe Licht' (40 MRR) travelled the Mglin–Pochep road across flat, very open farmland and pastures that almost invited enemy aerial interdiction. Fighting through a Soviet counterattack from the north and north-east the spearhead reached Zhitnya and the comparatively higher terrain beyond, before taking Pochep the following day. Likely too weak to hold a bridgehead over the Sudost', additional elements from 17th Panzer Division were moved through Mglin to assist. Others remained near Unecha to cover Thoma's still active western flank. 29th Motorized Infantry Division performed similar patrolling and clearing along XXIV Motorized Army Corps' right to around Akulichi and later Kletnya, which well illustrated the large number of Red Army forces still operating in the area. Ground and aerial reconnaissance indicated the enemy was strengthening a stretch of the Desna 10km south of Zhukova.

Remaining intent on keeping the Führer's mind on Moscow, on 18 August OKH submitted a memorandum that laid out compelling arguments that Army Groups North and South were capable of successfully carrying out their operational missions without Bock's assistance. Stressing that time existed for only one more major offensive before the onset of the bi-annual rainy season and frigid autumn and winter, Halder and Chief of the Wehrmacht's Operations Staff, Lieutenant General (*General der Artillerie*) Alfred Jodl, sweetened the proposal in that not only Moscow could be captured, but Kyiv as well. Brauchitsch even argued a maxim of Hitler's role model, Friedrich II (the Great), about eliminating the enemy's army being a prime consideration and how Army Group Centre's efforts reflected this, as opposed to Army Groups North and South's focus on Soviet industry and resources. Remaining adamant, on 21 August Hitler stated that, 'The army's proposal for the continuation of the operations . . . does not correspond with my plans'. Among the actions to be undertaken, 'The most important objective to be achieved before the onset of winter is not the occupation of Moscow, but rather . . . the occupation of the Crimea and the industrial and coal region of the Donets, together with the isolation of the Russian oil regions in the Caucasus and, in the north, the encirclement of Leningrad and link-up with the Finns.' With Army Group Centre to be stripped of its offensive capabilities its Ninth and Fourth Armies were to maintain their present embattled front lines. Many remained against relinquishing the hard-won, operational momentum that had been achieved, and deviating from the Soviet capital now that enemy forces were believed to be in some disorder along that advance axis. Among them, Hitler's Wehrmacht adjutant, Major Gerhard Engel, noted in his diary that after Halder and Brauchitsch had refrained from tending their resignations over the matter it remained a 'black day for the German Army'.[16]

XX Army Corps (15th, 78th, and 268th Infantry Divisions) (removed from Second Panzer Group (23 August))

VII Army Corps (23rd and 197th Infantry Divisions) (removed from Second Panzer Group) (23 August))
IX Army Corps (removed from Second Panzer Group (23 August))

To officially address forthcoming operations, during the afternoon of 23 August Halder arrived at Borisov to meet with Bock and his army commanders, where he dourly conveyed the stunning news that Hitler had decided to deviate from his envisioned thrust on Leningrad and Moscow, and instead focus on Ukraine and the Crimea. Not caught entirely unawares, as an apparently informed Greiffenberg had called earlier to present the possibility as a likely hypothetical, to which Guderian threatened resignation should such a scenario be enacted, now that it had the general changed tactics. Joining Halder's post-meeting flight to the Wolf's Lair, Guderian presented an impassioned, reasoned argument for keeping the focus on Moscow and his command intact. After listening respectfully to his 'front soldier' an unswayed Führer then listed his reasons for holding firm on the new southern thrust. Lacking further recourse, the normally headstrong field commander had little recourse save acceding to Hitler's wishes, who as if to soothe the sting agreed to his general's request to keep his command together for the forthcoming offensive.[17] Surprised and dismayed Bock wrote that, 'They apparently do not wish to exploit under any circumstances the opportunity decisively to defeat the Russians before winter!' and later added, 'the objective to which I devoted all my thought, the destruction of the main strength of the enemy army, has been dropped'.[18]

With Second Panzer Group's front coalescing along a Novozybkov–Starodub–Pochep–Seshcha front line over the last few days, on 23 August VII, IX, and VII Army Corps were assigned to Fourth Army. Both infantry-based formations would maintain positions in the Yel'nya sector and become too difficult for Guderian to effectively control during his southern thrust; although with Kluge ill the general retained command for three more days.[19] Still in the Starodub area 3rd Panzer Division readied to renew its advance, even though a report from the previous day listed just twenty Panzer IIIs and five panzer IVs operational, as well as thirty-four Panzer IIs, which were ill-suited for front-line combat given their light armour and 20mm main gun. Eighty tanks were in various stages of repair.[20] After advancing 40km to the south-east over particularly primitive, dirt roads that sapped POL as much as the drivers' patience, 'Kampfgruppe Lewinski' began crossing the Ukrainian SSR border at about 1000hrs.

Due to the steadily declining numbers of available motor transport heavier loads were often carried on those vehicles that remained functional, which further reduced speed and limited ranges to little more than 70km on a full tank. After a brief halt in the early afternoon the unit set off once again with 7./6th Panzer Regiment as a vanguard. On approaching the heights along the Desna's western bank near Novhorod-Siverskyy at 1730hrs the company detected strong Soviet defensive positions. For several kilometres up and downriver the waterway broke up into several oxbow lakes and meanders along its broad, clover- and bluegrass-covered floodplain. With Model riding immediately behind the point company and the remainder of II./6th Panzer Regiment ready for rapid committal he discussed the threat with Lewinski and his company officers and decided on a course of action against an enemy that seemed largely unaware of its presence.[21] Soon after a Soviet artillery gun crew observed the gathering and fired a projectile into the officers' midst killing one, severely wounding two others, and lightly wounding the battalion commander, but Model again escaped untouched. At 2100hrs on 23 August 394th Motorized Rifle Regiment reported having sent reconnaissance east to Ryukhovo found the area enemy free. Having been similarly hindered by the area's poor roads, follow-on German motorized infantry only arrived after dark and were unable to fully discern the terrain over which they advanced against the Soviet positions. Now lying approximately 7km from Novhorod-Siverskyy the division organized to secure it and open the way south.

XXXXVI Motorized Army Corps (removed from Second Panzer Group (24 August))

With 10th Motorized Infantry Division having covered the 40km of largely open country from Klintsy to capture Novozybkov, Guderian focused on taking Konotop, which from Novhorod-Siverskyy represented roughly the halfway point to his anticipated meet-up with Army Group South. XXIV Motorized Army Corps would operate on Guderian's right, where its 4th Panzer Division would follow Model from Ryukhovo. On Schweppenburg's left-rear, 17th Panzer Division led XXXXVII Motorized Army Corps into the area west of the Desna, where Soviet forces tried to block the approaches to Bryansk. Further upriver, 29th Motorized Infantry Division protected an 80km sector, with 18th Panzer Division moving behind, having just passed Roslavl'. With German intelligence continuing to struggle with ascertaining enemy strengths and intentions Guderian was concerned as to whether all of XXXXVII Motorized Army Corps would succumb to the friction of war and get too entangled with Red Army forces near the Desna, or whether it could help carve a path southward. Just as troubling, the general's supplies were barely sufficient for another lengthy foray across often rough terrain.[22]

By 25 August all of Second Panzer Group was south of Roslavl'. Along its right Guderian visited 17th Panzer Division's headquarters 5km north of Pochep, where the formation contended with several of Thirteenth Army's formations between it and the Desna. Toward effecting a crossing, Thoma moved on Trubchevsk but the mass of the division was unable to relieve the Kampfgruppe under 18th Rifle Brigade's commander, Brigadier Max Fremerey, until noon when enemy activity abated. Having spoken with Thoma and Lemelsen, Guderian went to 63rd Motorized Rifle Regiment (17 PD) to gain firsthand insight into the front line-fighting.[23] The remainder of Lemelsen's command extended north to Roslavl', while 258th and 34th Infantry Divisions moved up to the Desna most of 29th Motorized Infantry Division continued to hold its forward combat positions. Advance elements of all three of XXXXVII Motorized Army Corps' divisions, however, were active along the Kosovskiye–Kletnya road and east to the Desna. With 10th Motorized Infantry Division having made contact with Second Army near Novozybkov XXIV Motorized Army Corps now had unified flank protection extending beyond Gomel'. As Guderian's spearhead for his southern strike Schweppenburg could focus on his attack axis as his command moved through Kholmy and Avdiyivka, just across the Ukraine border. Off his left flank Model's 'Kampfgruppe Lewinski', with I./3rd Motorized Rifle Regiment and 6th Panzer Regiment, with its sixty tanks in the field, led 3rd Panzer Division's push through Kostobobriv–Novhorod-Siverskyy to the Desna. To the rear 4th Panzer Division resumed its follow-on role having moved into Starodub and cleared the western bank of the Sudost'. One worrisome concern was the supply of valuable lubricating oil, considering the region's rugged, dusty environment, damaged crankshafts, and fatigued gaskets increased vehicle consumption by two-thirds.[24]

Behind 6th Panzer Regiment its parent formation moved across the River Desna at Novhorod-Siverskyy to punch through Twenty-First Army's withdrawing front line.[25] Thirteenth Army similarly pulled back and 3rd Panzer Division cut the Kyiv–Moscow rail line at Shostka. Taking advantage of the Soviet retreat, Second Army struck out along Guderian's western flank, and along the Dnepr towards Kyiv.[26] At 0705hrs on 25 August 39th Motorized Engineer Battalion reported weak enemy resistance just north of Dem'yanki and within the hour 3rd Motorized Rifle Regiment secured Model's left by taking Mishkova. Just before 1000hrs 3rd Panzer Division's spearhead reached Kostobobriv, while a Luftwaffe reconnaissance plane reported the lengthy bridge at Novhorod-Siverskyy was undamaged, which given the Desna's broad floodplain made its intact capture critical for XXIV Motorized Corps' continued southern thrust. Throughout the afternoon Soviet pressure around Pogar increased, as 6th Panzer Regiment moved through enemy infantry and artillery fire to establish a position on the high, largely treeless ground west of Novhorod-Siverskyy. As motorized infantry was ordered forward from Kostobobriv, 1st Motorized Reconnaissance Battalion reported enemy lorry traffic along the Mamekine–Novhorod-Siverskyy road indicating the Soviets were evacuating the area west of the Desna, and that the latter's crossing remained operational. To best ensure success and bring additional forces forward, with which to establish a presence beyond the Desna a raid on the Novhorod-Siverskyy Bridge was slated for after dark.

At 0300hrs, on 26 August 604th Motorized Heavy 210mm Howitzer Battalion and 623rd Motorized Artillery Regiment were subordinated to Model, although it would take time for them to move up. Once again, 3./39th Motorized Engineer Battalion was at the forefront of a critical operation having established a position near the Desna Bridge at Pyrohivka, as rain replaced dusty roads with mud. With his lead elements across the River Smyach, and not wanting to wait for 4th Panzer Division's promised artillery support to move up, at 0710hrs Model initiated his attack on Novhorod-Siverskyy. As 'Kampfgruppe Kleemann' (3 MRR) fought off enemy resistance south of Krolevets-Slobidka a Soviet artillery round killed Ries at his 75th Motorized Artillery Regiment command post. Just over 150km to the north, starting at 0800hrs Ju-87s supported 17th Panzer Division's move away from the relatively hilly terrain west of the River Sudost' and into the flatter, more wooded territory south of Pochep. En route, the formation fought through often heavy enemy resistance before forcing a crossing of the River Rozhok at noon. Thoma captured Semtsy and the adjacent high ground to the east and west 2 hours later; and in the process 800 prisoners, 4 guns, and assorted weapons and materiel. Violent Soviet counterattacks from the west continued to hinder both 17th Panzer and 10th Motorized Divisions' progress, which was typically bypassed and unhinged for the sake of maintaining momentum. As a rough comparison of time and effort, as the latter passed through Kholmy the distance from there to Yel'nya equalled the 315km from Yel'nya to downtown Moscow.

Although Model had worked to secure the Novhorod-Siverskyy Bridge earlier in the morning, by 1000hrs on 26 August 'Kampfgruppe Kleemann' had ejected the Soviet 143rd Rifle Division from its defence of the area. Less than an hour later 'Kampfgruppe Lewinski' moved into the town's eastern edge along the Desna, where assault engineers from 394th Motorized Rifle Division's headquarters company rushed the nearby 800m crossing over a section where the river briefly splits into two paths. Under protective fire from 6th Panzer Regiment a two-group German assault worked to pin and prevent a contingent of 171st NKVD Regiment from detonating explosives on the structure. By 1130hrs German forces had crossed the waterway and fought to establish a bridgehead that soon encompassed Ostroushky. Believing expanding the foothold on the Desna's eastern bank outweighed waiting for additional elements of 3rd Panzer Division to arrive, 'Kampfgruppe Audörsch' was soon advancing to the south and south-east. 'Kampfgruppe Kleemann' was ordered to strike into the Voronizh–Hlukhiv area, with 3rd Motorcycle and 1st Motorized Reconnaissance Battalions positioned to cover 3rd Panzer Division's open left flank.[27] Soon after an appreciative Model arrived at the bridge he put in for the engineer platoon leader responsible for the audacious bridge capture, Second Lieutenant of Reserves Georg Störk, for the Knight's Cross.

Having been ordered to strike for Voronizh at 1400hrs on 26 August a section of 'Kampfgruppe Lewinski' engaged in fighting at Pyrohivka, just south of the River Shostka. Within 3 hours 6th Panzer Regiment elements crossed a damaged bridge over the Desna, downriver from Model's recent bridgehead, and took the village. Just over an hour later 3rd Motorcycle and 1st Reconnaissance Battalions pushed as far as Prokopovka, but found no enemy. At 2000hrs II./3rd Motorized Rifle Regiment reported that only a small bridgehead had been created, but strong Red Army forces that included artillery and snipers in the forest west of Pyrohivka hindered the effort. With no option to construct a bridge Lewinski pulled what forces that had crossed the Desna back across the waterway, save one platoon, which could facilitate a future crossing attempt or be withdrawn without undue trouble.[28]

As 29th Motorized Infantry Division trailed Thoma's slogging, southward advance over muddy roads, at about midday the formation's 29th Motorcycle Battalion and I./71st Motorized Infantry Regiment moved into Pochep and worked to extend the bridgehead over the Sudost' immediately north-east of the town. Considering that throughout the day the Soviet 55th Cavalry Division worked to delay XXXXVII Motorized Army Corps' push through the heavily forested area west of Kletnya the nearby 18th Panzer Division was telephoned a 'heads-up', as it moved into the area. To check on one of his two exposed flanks Guderian visited 17th Panzer Division on 26 August before being driven to Mglin where Nehring was operating, and finally to his command post at Unecha. During the drive he received word of Model's capture of the lengthy Desna Bridge east of Novhorod-Siverskyy, which would greatly facilitate Second Panzer Group's continued rush southward.[29]

Chapter 8

Capping History's Largest Encirclement, 27 August–23 September 1941

Whittled down to just two corps for his sudden reorientation southward, on 27 August Guderian's XXIV Motorized Army Corps continued to hammer its way forward towards further splitting the Soviet Thirteenth and Third Armies and eventually linking up with Army Group South. With his leading elements having driven nearly 300km along the new advance axis, perhaps concerningly, Rundstedt had yet to even reorient his command from its extensive, 800km frontage along the Dnepr's right bank from just north of Kyiv, past Dnipro, and down to the Black Sea. Even though the further south Guderian needed to move meant a lengthier advance to Moscow when the time came, the inability of Central Front to block him presented an excellent opportunity to vigorously exploit.[1] Continuing to apply his aggressive, risky, but successful leadership Model's crossing of the Desna at Novhorod-Siverskyy undermined what defence the Red Army endeavoured to make along the waterway, and gave him considerable latitude on how best to continue the advance. To the west, 10th Motorized Infantry Division maintained advance parity, with 4th Panzer Division following as reserve, while covering Model's deep left flank. With XII Army Corps having taken over XXXXVII Motorized Army Corps' positions west of Bryansk, Lemelsen peeled away from his southern advance axis towards covering Schweppenburg's lengthening left flank and establishing jump-off positions beyond the Desna for the upcoming Moscow offensive.

Although Guderian loudly complained that the recent removal of so much of his subordinated formations allowed enemy forces withdrawing from Gomel' and new ones arriving from the east to repeatedly strike his flanks and impede operations, little could be done until LIII Army Corps completed its relocation to Fourth Army, and allowed XII Army Corps to shift southward. Still concerned that the general would go off on his own, Halder stressed to Bock that he keep his subordinate 'on short reins and move the rear divisions of XXXXVII [Motorized Army] Corps behind XXIV [Motorized Army] Corps, as soon as 31st and [1]67th [Infantry] divisions have arrived, and not behind Seventeenth Armoured Division, which had bogged down'.[2] At 0400hrs 'Kampfgruppe Audörsch' continued in its spearhead role, with its II./394th Motorized Rifle

Regiment establishing a bridgehead over the River Ivotka just south of Ivot before turning for Voronizh. About 3 hours later 'Kampfgruppe Lewinski' (I./3 MRR and 6 PR) was ordered to push the enemy out of Pyrohivka and clear the area to the east, while additional formations from 3rd Panzer Division, including 'Kampfgruppe Manteuffel', continued to move through Novhorod-Siverskyy. Starting at 1100hrs Red Army aircraft conducted several low-altitude attacks against the town and bridge, to which I./11th Antiaircraft Regiment offered resistance with two heavy and one light battery.[3] To the south-west 10th Motorized Infantry Division was given 8th Antiaircraft Company to help defend its crossing of the Desna before Korop.

At 0800hrs on 27 August a column from 3rd Panzer Division reached the northern outskirts of Shostka, where the town's Powder Plant No. 9, a facility the Germans hoped to secure for their own use, burned to the ground, while dispensing a yellowish pall across the area. Leveraging the visibly obscured environment, Model's advance detachment captured that part of the town before the enemy became aware of the danger. Advancing south to the nearby railway, Schmidt-Ott's I./6th Panzer Regiment ambushed a Soviet locomotive, set it alight, and prompted enemy soldiers to bail from their freight cars and seek shelter in the nearby forest. 29th Motorized Infantry Division extended its Pochep bridgehead, which enemy aircraft subjected to attacks throughout the day, out to Panikovka and P'yanyy Rog along the River Rozhok. The formation's 29th Reconnaissance Battalion and I./71st Motorized Infantry Regiment overcame sloppy roads to the south where they used an armoured element from 17th Panzer Division that had passed a burning Semtsy during the afternoon to open a corridor between the River Sudost' and extensive woodland to the east. The former then raced through the area to take Kambovka at 2030hrs, and before day's end, Lyubets along the Desna. Although the division would take Parovichi the next day, it bypassed Trubchevsk, while leaving a contingent to contain any enemy in the sector. Extending for several kilometres to the south and west, terrain that centuries of rain and groundwater had long seeped into and dissolved the underlying carbonate bedrock formed ravines, underground cavities, and sinkholes over which vehicle movement was conducted with caution. Atop this karst a layer of fertile, yellowish loess soil and vegetation had formed into a grassy steppe, which ancient, nomadic, Scythian tribes had covered with numerous burial mounds.

To address Guderian's incessant calls for reinforcements Paulus had arrived at Second Panzer Group's headquarters the previous day, only to find its commander away at the front. Given Army Group Centre's lengthening and thinning front line, and increasing difficulty in maintaining reserves, let alone sending support to its southbound right flank, the Quartermaster instead broached the subject of transferring infantry formations from the neighbouring Second Army to the general's control with Liebenstein, and later OKH. The inability of

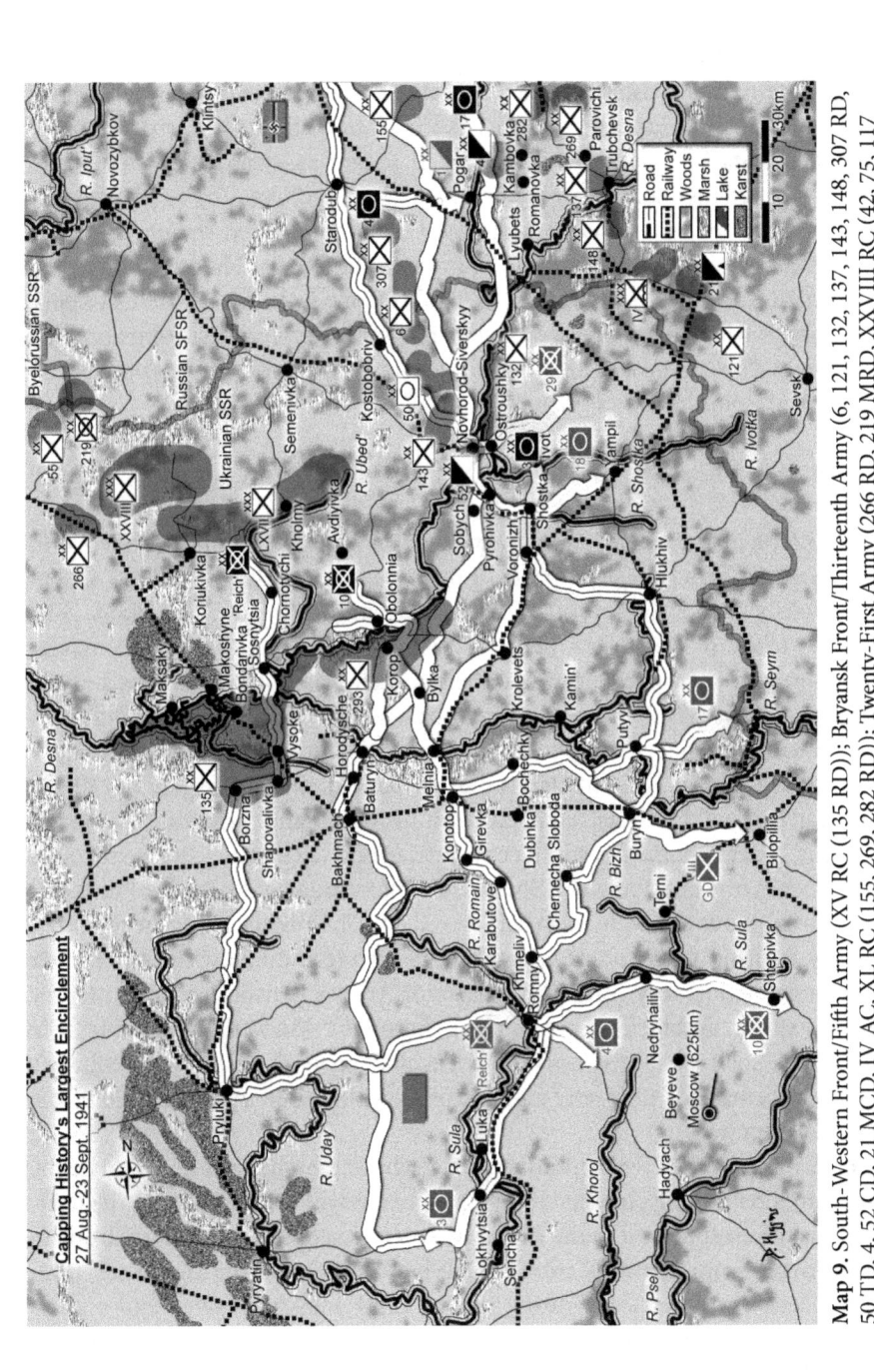

Map 9. South-Western Front/Fifth Army (XV RC (135 RD)); Bryansk Front/Thirteenth Army (6, 121, 132, 137, 143, 148, 307 RD, 50 TD, 4, 52 CD, 21 MCD, IV AC, XL RC (155, 269, 282 RD)); Twenty-First Army (266 RD, 219 MRD, XXVIII RC (42, 75, 117 RD), LXVI RC (55 RD), LXVII RC (187 RD)). TsAMO, f.361, op.6079, d.26.

Army Groups North and South to encircle and eliminate large numbers of Red Army troops had left both of Bock's flanks vulnerable, and drew attention and resources away from the primary thrust eastward. Given Hitler's increasing say in front-line matters, the seemingly constant Red Army counterattacks shook his confidence. As Guderian's former XVI Motorized Army Corps Chief of the General Staff he held the man in high regard as a clever and intelligent commander; feelings seemingly reciprocated given Paulus acting as advocate for his acerbic former subordinate.[4] Although Guderian stressed the need to clear his exposed left flank, as he sent forces towards the Desna, Halder, annoyed by this deviation from Second Panzer Group's planned southward thrust, spoke via telephone with a hard-pressed Bock to recommend refraining from acceding to the general's demands; at least not until LIII Army Corps moved up from its location between the Rivers Sozh and Iput'.[5]

7th Infantry Division (removed from XXIV Motorized Army Corps (28 August))

After a month of attritional, largely static combat reminiscent of the First World War's Western Front major, repeated Soviet attacks against the Yel'nya salient had seriously weakened several of Kluge's defending infantry divisions. The repeating tactic of Red Army artillery saturating an area into which masses of infantry and occasionally cavalry then rushed was typically stopped at the main line of resistance, or soon after a penetration, but with increasing difficulty. Having assisted Schweppenburg's initial breakthrough south of Krichev earlier in the month, 7th Infantry Division had since been largely out of the fight near Roslavl' and was removed from his command. 3rd and 4th Panzer Divisions 200km kilometres south continued to once again cut a swathe through Thirteenth Army and force the Soviets to allocate men and resources to counter it. Throughout the 28th, 10th Motorized and 3rd Panzer Divisions engaged in heavy fighting to get south of the Desna, while the follow-on 4th Panzer Division worked its way through Thirteenth Army's rearmost enemy infantry that now threw up blocking positions at Starodub.[6] Much like the 1914 'Race to the Sea', such sustained operations resulted in both of Schweppenburg's armoured formations to briefly run out of fuel; this time in the middle of the Ukrainian steppe!

For as much as the Germans attempted to eliminate what was hoped to be the Red Army's remaining strategic reserves more always seemed to be on the horizon. What often appeared to the *Frontsoldaten* to be continuous activity from an ever-present enemy not only from ahead, but with disturbing frequency from behind, such asymmetrical fighting robbed the Landsers of sleep and a sense of security that eroded morale and health. On a relatively positive, but almost criminally tardy note, OKH finally exhibited concern for those serving at the front lines by authorizing the distribution of winter clothing SS and Luftwaffe leadership had stockpiled. Under either a lingering delusion or motivated to adhere to the official narrative, with autumn approaching many within the department believed that between sixty and eighty of the divisions allocated in the East could be brought back to Germany before winter for rest and refurbishment to then return to the front the following spring. With much weight being given to one of Germany's leading meteorologists, Franz Bauer had predicted a mild to average winter, even though it was based on little more than a belief that the last three had been unusually cold (January 1940 hit a record low of -42 °C) and this would probably not be repeated in 1941–2.[7]

During the evening of 30 August a Soviet armoured and motorized group conducted a reconnaissance-in-force towards Pogar, but lacking adequate screening and scouting the force seemed to unintentionally split into two parallel advance routes before Kambovka.[8] From obscured, woodland positions along the lesser grouping's march route panzern from the awaiting 39th Panzer Regiment suddenly shot up five T-40 light tanks and considerably disrupted the column. Ju-87s that were subsequently called in targeted the accompanying Soviet artillery, while heavier T-34s and KV-1s were engaged at uncomfortably close ranges to improve the chances of immobilizing or destroying them. A few kilometres due south the accompanying, primary Soviet column moved through Romanovka, with its one-storey, aging wooden farmhouses and walled courtyards. Similarly struck by other elements of the German regiment and what had seemingly presented a serious threat to Guderian's lengthy eastern flank had been rebuffed by day's end. As had been drilled into the German military Arnim quickly moved to exploit the enemy's disorganized state. Over the next four days 39th Panzer Regiment and dive-bombers roughly handled what was soon found to be an unsupported 108th Tank Division, as it withdrew between Bryansk and Trubchevsk.[9]

By 31 August Model had carved out a sufficiently large bridgehead beyond Novhorod-Siverskyy, such that 4th Panzer Division crossed the Desna and advanced south. To the west 10th Motorized Infantry Division finally moved over the Desna near Korop, but heavy enemy counterattacks forced Löper's men to return to the north bank. As evidence of the desperate fighting that finally halted the Soviet threat, even a German field bakery company was thrown into the fray.[10] Having been providing reconnaissance for the division Major Kurt Plagemann's Kampfgruppe (40th Motorcycle Battalion) became encircled at Konotop prompting elements of its parent division to relieve them. With XXXXVI Motorized Army Corps having been relocated behind the front lines south of Smolensk, Guderian naturally wanted Bock to return the formation to Second Panzer Group, as well as 7th Panzer and 14th Motorized Infantry Divisions from Hoth and Rundstedt's 11th Panzer Division to assist his southward advance. By framing Hitler's order for a southern thrust as an avenue towards circumventing the chain of command Guderian's increasing vitriol towards Halder, Brauchitsch, Kluge, Bock, and others for what was seen as their lack of adequate support naturally prompted reciprocal friction. Having his hands full fighting 'Army Group Timoshenko' (Western Front), and the need to keep an armoured and motorized force in a centralized, reserve position, only Großdeutschland was initially provided on 30 August. With Guderian's offensive slowing from exhaustion and inadequate logistic support, and Timoshenko's repeated hammer blows against Army Group Centre threatening to unhinge its flagging defence, Hitler considered renewing the Moscow offensive; something Halder was now loathe to support until the present commitment to the Kyiv Campaign was successfully concluded. Although Rundstedt had finally established two bridgeheads over the lower Dnepr in preparation for his planned thrust northward, should Second Panzer Group and Second Army be halted the intervening 250km gap would not only prevent the capture of potentially massive numbers of Red Army men and materiel, but would ensure the Germans having to occupy an extended frontage running around Ukraine's capital. Bock was understandably dumbfounded by the frequent alterations of operational focus, as evidenced by his writing in his diary that, 'the Supreme Command's sudden change of opinion has come too late to force a decision against the main body of the Russian Army . . .'.[11]

1st Cavalry Division (at the disposition of Second Panzer Group (31 August))

Since *Barbarossatag* 1st Cavalry Division reported capturing 13,872 Soviet soldiers and a respectable amount of enemy equipment, including 48 tanks, 73 heavy guns, 230 machine guns and 11 aircraft by their 'rapid exploitation of favourable opportunities'.[12] After two months of hard campaigning, however, and with replacements not keeping pace with losses, Feldt believed his command was presently unfit for further combat service. Two weeks later, in an OKH requested assessment, the cavalry leader stressed that the formation had proven successful at rapidly closing gaps in the front line, screening flanks, and conducting defensive operations, and that even though expansion to a corps would enable it to contribute in more direct offensive operations, the dominance panzer divisions had shown on a contemporary battlefield was a better alternative.[13] Even though the horsemen needed a period of rest and rehabilitation, on 31 August Bock officially reallocated the formation to Second Panzer Group. Soon pulled from the area north-west of Semenivka, where the formation anchored Guderian's and Weichs' shared boundary, 1st Cavalry Division was redirected to the north-east to relieve 18th Panzer Division, which in turn moved on to Yampil. The horsemen would then provide screening and security duties along the Desna from Novhorod-Siverskyy, across the hills and marshy valleys near Trubchevsk, and up to Pochep. Adopting a defence of strongpoints to maintain a degree of concentration in select areas and create mobile reserves,

Feldt spent the next several days rebuffing Red Army probes seemingly intent on reaching the River Sudost' and disrupting Guderian's supply lines. At the end of 31 August 4th Panzer Division was notified that Großdeutschland would take over what elements of Langermann's command remained in Novhorod-Siverskyy. The arrival of the crack regiment also freed up 3rd Motorcycle Battalion from screening Model's eastern flank, and allowed it to be put to better use scouting his southward advance.

'Reich' (at the disposition of Second Panzer Group (1 September))

On 1 September XXXXVII Motorized Army Corps occupied positions running south of Pochep and along the River Desna, with its 29th Motorized Infantry Division acting as a reserve. Unable to practically disengage from active Soviet forces to its east until Bock's most recent reorganization got sufficient infantry formations into the numerous gaps along his lengthy front line, Lemelsen remained in place for the next few days fending off enemy attacks. Having protected the corps' left flank during the River Bug crossing on *Barbarossatag*, 167th Infantry Division now reprised the role off Lemelsen's northern edge. Further south XXIV Motorized Army Corps continued to pummel its way forward, with 3rd Panzer Division striking out from its bridgehead around Ostroushky, 'Kampfgruppe Lewinski' outflanked lingering resistance at Pyrohivka to broaden Model's bridgehead. This allowed 4th Panzer Division to cross the Desna and strike south through Sobych and into a wooded area beyond the Soviet 293rd Rifle Division's positions. Destroying or evicting enemy forces along its advance axis that skirted the Desna's eastern bank Langermann covered nearly 40km by the next day, with its lead elements reaching Bylka; even though both German formations fielded a mere eighty-six tanks between them.[14]

XXXXVI Motorized Army Corps (to Second Panzer Group (3 September))

With Kesselring having visited Guderian the previous day with welcome words that Rundstedt had finally affected crossings over the Dnepr, on 3 September the general went to 10th Motorized Infantry Division, as it held a section of the Desna near Korop. Amid what was a confusing time for Bryansk Front to accumulate forces and coordinate an effective defence, Model's men captured NKVD Major of State Security Pavel Chistov as he was driven to Konotop, unaware the Germans already possessed the area. Sent from Moscow with the Herculean task of creating major defensive positions along the Desna's eastern bank the loss to the Soviets was a boon for German intelligence. As the recently arrived 'Reich' provided badly needed assistance to the north-west of Löper's rather stationary position Guderian met with Hausser to discuss the SS troopers striking for Sosnytsia and coordinating with 5th Motorized Machine-Gun

Battalion, which had also recently arrived from Roslavl'. Torrential rain during that day and the next, however, made roads nearly unusable, but 'Reich' managed to solidify its position along Guderian's right.

During the early afternoon of 4 September high- and low-altitude Soviet aircraft struck Krolevets, where Model had established his command post at School No. 1, with its brick exterior and standing seam metal roof.[15] Following German antiaircraft fire shooting down one of the planes and the pilot parachuting to the ground, only to be killed while trying to evade capture, the documents on the body presented 3rd Panzer Division's Ic with maps depicting Soviet forces arrayed against XXIV Motorized Army Corps, and the boundary of the Soviet Twenty-First and Thirteenth Armies running through Sosnytsia.[16] As an attack into such a dividing line promoted confusion between the two groups and disrupted their command and control Schweppenburg adjusted his attack axis more to the south-west to pry open a gap through which he could more easily continue his southward advance. Unwilling to accede to Hitler's wishes to maintain concentration with Weichs' infantry, as they moved up to the River Seym, Guderian continued to operate parts of XXXXVII Motorized Army Corps east of the River Desna, and away from helping encircle and destroy the intervening Soviet Twenty-First Army.[17] Sharing Halder's irritation at the general allowing himself to be bought with keeping his command intact in return for a major thrust away from Moscow, Bock unsuccessfully requested OKH relieve his headstrong subordinate.[18]

Guderian spent the day at the front with 4th Panzer Division, which was attacking towards the Korop area, where he met with Schweppenburg. With 3rd Panzer Division having pushed up to the River Seym, the general ordered Model to continue beyond to the Konotop–Bilopillia rail line, and once again cut off a major lifeline to much of the Soviet South-Western Front. Two battalion-sized Kampfgruppen respectively built around I./6th Panzer Regiment and 1st Motorized Reconnaissance Battalion set off at 1140hrs from Krolevets and across the hilly terrain to the south.[19] Likely to Guderian's irritation OKW forwarded its dissatisfaction with Second Panzer Group's advance through Bock. In particular XXXXVII Motorized Army Corps' unsupported efforts east of the Desna and Schweppenburg having pushed too far to the south-east allowed considerable enemy forces to operate in the corresponding gap with Second Army.[20] With Leningrad put under siege on 4 September, and Army Groups Centre and South having sealed the northern, western, and southern approaches to Kyiv, all that remained was to close the resulting salient into a massive pocket and eliminate it. Although the subordinate formations under the newly established Bryansk Front had suffered considerable losses in men and materiel over the last several weeks, they continued to maintain sufficient pressure on Guderian's left flank to tie up German forces that would otherwise have been added to his southward offensive.

With the Soviet Twenty-First Army's northern, right wing hanging before Second Army, Schweppenburg moved to strike behind it to unhinge the larger Soviet defence. While Weichs then exploited the resulting disruptions to enemy command and control to continue his southward push, it would also negate much of the Soviet strength along the neighbouring XXIV Motorized Army Corps' right flank and facilitate the latter's effort to link up with Rundstedt. Per Schweppenburg's 0100 hrs order on 4 September a Kampfgruppe under 41st Motorized Infantry Regiment's commander, Colonel Hans Traut, spearheaded 10th Motorized Infantry Division's thrust south-west out of the Obolonnia area and along the Desna's right bank towards Sosnytsia.[21] Löper's 20th Infantry and III./41st^t Infantry Regiments, with I./10th Motorized Artillery Regiment and the heavy antiaircraft batteries from II./11th Antiaircraft Regiment in support, coordinated with 4th Panzer Division to expand a bridgehead beyond Korop. Although the oncoming 'Reich' was strung out over 100km of rain-soaked roads, by 0600hrs II./ and III./'Der Führer' Regiment were moving through the Avdiyivka area, respectively on the left and right.[22] Intent on clearing the intervening area to the River Ubed', Soviet forces occupying the soft, wooded area to the north remained largely inactive and could be delt with by follow-on units.

At 0800hrs several hundred Soviet soldiers disembarked from light lorries, and along with four batteries tried, unsuccessfully, to counter the German thrust. 'Reich' approached the Chornotychi area 4 hours later, having reportedly killed 120 Red Army soldiers and captured some 500 along the way. Continuing bad weather meant by day's end only a strong reconnaissance element made it as far as the low hills south-west of the Ubed'.[23] Achieving similar results, 'Kampfgruppe Traut' swung around enemy resistance 15km upriver from Sosnytsia to pin it against the Desna's right bank, and to the east, 10th Motorized Engineer Battalion repaired its crossing at Korop to allow part of its parent division to cross to the south bank. Although stubborn enemy resistance during the late afternoon prevented Löper and Langermann from cleaning the area to the River Sejm, its often broad floodplain and few crossings would help prevent the Soviets from leaving the area in a controlled manner.

Throughout much of 5 September Guderian remained with 'Reich', whose military bearing elicited the general's admiration. With SS-11th Regiment having arrived in the contested sector to support 'Der Führer', the division took Sosnytsia at 1630hrs, and moved for the rail bridge at Makoshyne, and later Maksaky.[24] Across the Desna, 4th Panzer Division tried to get past what had been 293rd Rifle Division's irritating stand before the River Seym's crossing at Baturyn, but as Langermann's men reached the waterway the Soviets blew the bridge. Further east, Model struck out from Krolevets to affect his own crossing at Melnia using 'Kampfgruppen Munzel' and a Bridge Column 'B'.[25] On approaching the Seym at 1120hrs 'Kampfgruppe Manteuffel's' 7. and

8./3rd Motorized Rifle Regiment, each with a company of SPWs, respectively split off to the right and left near Mutin, where a liberal spreading of Soviet landmines required the assistance of 3./39th Motorized Engineer Battalion. Early in the afternoon German reconnaissance discovered that with no crossing at Kamin' XXIV Motorized Army Corps would need to allocate a bridging unit to construct one. Lacking the strength to affect tangible results, and increasingly flanked between Second Army and Second Panzer Group, Twenty-First Army subsequently began pulling out and largely removed any immediate threat to Guderian's advance.[26]

Halder and Brauchitsch had met with Bock three days previously to determine that no renewed offensive on Moscow would occur before late September at the earliest. As such the casualty-inducing Yel'nya salient was to be evacuated. Kluge oversaw logistics, as non-combat personnel withdrew under the cover of darkness on 4/5 September. The easternmost German formations pulled out the following night, and the remaining Landsers the night after that. Heavy rain and cloud cover obscured much of the activity and kept losses unexpectedly low, during what was often more disorganized abandonment than coordinated withdrawal onto defensive positions incorporating the Rivers Stryana and Ustrom. This shortening of the front line allowed for the creation of limited reserves and a degree of tactical flexibility to counter any renewed enemy pressure in the sector. With heavy rain continuing into 6 September to make life and movement for the Landsers just that much more difficult, at the Wolf's Lair Hitler issued Directive No. 35 to lay out what was to be expected for the offensive against Moscow; a massive undertaking that was to include seventy-eight German divisions, with roughly one-third being motorized and armoured.

'Reich' (at the disposition of Second Panzer Group to XXIV Motorized Army Corps (7 September))

With XXIV Motorized Army Corps having carved out a 50km gap between South-Western and Bryansk Fronts, Model believed an opportunity existed to achieve a major breakthrough. On 7 September 3rd and 4th Panzer Divisions succeeded in establishing bridgeheads across the Seym, in spite of the efforts of the Soviet 293rd and 135th Rifle Divisions' efforts. Guderian went to the latter's sector to observe its 12th and 33rd Motorized Rifle Regiments spearhead the advance on Horodysche, which included Ju-87s attempting to clear a path to facilitate 35th Panzer Regiment's southward advance. In the late afternoon the general went to XXIV Motorized Army Corps' headquarters where Schweppenburg told him that prisoners indicated the Soviet Fortieth Army had been inserted between Thirteenth and Twenty-first Armies; a location directly ahead of XXIV Motorized Army Corps' expected advance. For all the shortcomings of German logistics, especially fuel, ammunition was at least available in quantity.[27]

That evening Guderian flew back to his headquarters where Bock had sent a message indicating that 1st Cavalry Division was to be relocated north to replace 18th Panzer Division and provide security duties along the Desna between Novhorod-Siverskyy and Trubchevsk. Considering mounted forces were well suited to operate in the area's wooded ravines and marshland, much as he had done along the Dnepr in early July, Feldt again relied on establishing strongpoints and mobile units to best conduct his mission.[28] With several Soviet rifle formations across the Desna, many of which possessing sizeable artillery and mortar support, the horsemen kept busy warding off enemy raids intended to get a Red Army presence to the River Sudost'. While this freed up valuable armour to help Guderian's thrust towards Romny, Model lacked the time or inclination to await the assistance. By the evening of 8 September 3rd Panzer Division had elements 25km south of the River Seym and was in a position to bypass any potential holdup around Konotop and break out farther south. Understanding that delay allowed the enemy forces to concentrate against him, 3rd Panzer Division's commander opted for what had proven so successful during the campaign to complete his part in what promised to be a major encirclement and defeat of enemy forces east of Kyiv; audacity, speed, and aggression. By conducting as rapid a tempo as was possible, given the circumstances of his fatigued men and machines, it would help compensate for the lack of flank and rear support for what would essentially be an angry, roving German pocket cutting through enemy territory.

As perhaps a natural by-product of a war of annihilation, especially one in which Germany was seemingly on a path to victory in the East and likely not to be held to any account, the head of OKW's General Office of the Armed Forces, Major General Hermann Reinecke, provided direction on 8 September towards the treatment of Soviet prisoners. In addition to what was 'as a rule, to be regarded as legal' he stipulated that, 'The war between Germany and Russia is not a war between two states or two armies, but between two ideologies . . . The Red Army [soldier] must be looked upon not as a soldier in the sense of the word applying to our western opponents, but as an ideological enemy. He must be regarded as the archenemy of National Socialism and must be treated accordingly.' The result of such decrees not only added to the already heavy psychological and moral burden Landsers carried through the combat zone, they were in contrast to Section 47 of the 1872 German Military Penal Code (1872). It included:

> If through the execution of an order pertaining to official duties, a penal law is violated, then the superior giving the order is solely responsible. However, the subordinate who obeys shall be punished as a participant: (1) if he exceeded the order he received, or, (2) if he knew that the order of the superior concerned an act which constituted a civil or military crime or offence.[29]

A German soldier's pay book also spelled out ten commandments of 'proper' battlefield behaviour, but these, too, were incompatible with how the fighting in the East was to eliminate a 'subhuman' fighting for a Jewish/Bolshevik/ Communist system intent on conquering and subjugating the West. The resulting breakdown of established rules of war caused concern among German leadership, and that without maintaining checks such actions would have a negative impact on combat effectiveness; a sentiment even shared among many Waffen-SS commanders due to the unnecessary problems it created.[30]

17th Panzer Division (XXXXVII to XXXXVI Motorized Army Corps (9 September))

Having decided to restore primacy to an offensive against Moscow at the conclusion of the Kyiv fighting, on 9 September OKH correspondingly instructed Bock to begin preparations to that end. Until then Guderian was to continue southward against the newly positioned Soviet Fiftieth Army, whose constituent remnants proved unequal to the task of blocking him. In preparation for what was understood to conclude his part in Second Panzer Group's push south Model and his Ia organized the division to the task. With 'Kampfgruppe Kleemann' up front, perhaps due to a temporary lack of fuel, a seemingly small advance detachment of motorized infantry, artillery, armour, antitank, and engineers was created under 521st Panzerjäger Battalion's commander, Major Heinz-Werner Frank.[31] As indicative of the kind of seemingly vague, but understood oral mission order that provided a commander's intent, Model simply directed them 'to thrust forward as far as possible'.[32] During the morning Red Army aircraft flying at high and low altitudes targeted the German-held bridge at Melnia, which given the area's marshy floodplain made the crossing critical to 3rd Panzer Division's continued advance. While 'Kampfgruppe Aürsorch' built up its artillery north-west of Konotop and awaited the rain to clear to permit close air support, II/394 penetrated to the town's western edge. With the weather improving by noon, Ju-87s targeted enemy positions around the town. Soon after, 3rd Panzer Division advanced through Konotop against surprisingly minimal resistance. Poor roads remained a problem, and prevented 1st Reconnaissance Battalion from establishing contact with 4th Panzer Division's advance elements that had employed armour to cross the Seym the night before to take Baturyn.

By 1600hrs 'Kampfgruppe Frank' skirted to the west of Konotop to defeat an enemy cavalry contingent along the road to Romny and secure the route as far as Girevka, while 3rd Motorized Rifle Regiment covered its right out to a few kilometres against little resistance. Over the next 3 hours his command had taken the intact Karabutove Bridge over the River Romain's marshy origin, and seemed in an excellent position from which to push ahead. Towards securing the important crossing at Romny 40m³ of fuel were stockpiled in north-western Konotop along the rail line to Krolevets. 4th Panzer Division added 200m³ more that it had recently captured, along with 50m³ of oil.³³

With 1st Cavalry Division's duties of capping the northern edge of a Soviet bulge near Koriukivka completed, due to the front line moving south of the River Desna, the formation made its way north to the Starodub area along XXXXVII Motorized Army Corps' left. In its place 'Reich' filled the gap between XXXV High Command (for special purposes) and XXIV Motorized Army Corps, as they respectively advanced to the south-west and south. On 9 September 'Reich' followed up its Desna crossing by turning to the south-east to maintain contact with Schweppenburg to provide the necessary concentration to hammer the Soviet Twenty-First Army, as it struggled to disengage from the fighting. III./SS-'Deutschland' and II./SS-Artillery Regiment operated west of Bondarivka, while Hausser's forward command post crossed a bridge over the waterway and relocated to Makoshyne.³⁴ During the morning German observation and reconnaissance indicated a strong enemy presence in the woods north-east of Vysoke, including heavy artillery. To clear the threat a Kampfgruppe that included SS-Motorized Reconnaissance and SS-Motorcycle Battalions, and 11th SS-Infantry Regiment, with SS-'Deutschland' providing reinforcement captured the area at 1415hrs. During the night of 9/10 September the attack continued during the morning of what was another rain soaked day, with III./SS-'Der Führer' and I./SS-'Deutschland' respectively advancing along the west and east against Shapovalovka and beyond.³⁵

Taking advantage of his lead units making the enemy's stance around Konotop untenable, Model rushed the bulk of his command along the main road to Romny that often cut through the region's low hills. With heavy rain commencing at 0900hrs the area's clay and blackish soil threatened to confound the efforts of 'Kampfgruppe Frank' as his Panzerjäger and supporting units arrived along the high ground north of the town. Surprisingly, Soviet forces before their goal seemed unaware of the nearby German presence, while 'Kampfgruppe Türckheim' reported the southern portion as 'enemy free'. Not wanting to squander such an opportunity Frank led most of his command into the River Romain valley to take its bridge intact. With the defenders taken by surprise the small, mixed group pressed through the town to take another undamaged crossing over the nearby River Sula. Gradually overcoming their shock Soviet resistance solidified within Romny and near the bridges, which Frank managed to quell. Red Army aircraft conducted twenty-five attacks against 3rd Panzer Division that along with muddy roads temporarily severed the formation's resupply link, save for a few fuel lorries that engineer tractors managed to get forward.³⁶

Driven to Lemelsen's headquarters, Guderian received a status update on XXIV Motorized Army Corps' progress south of the Seym, including Model's recent success that brought Second Panzer Group to within 50km of its anticipated link-up with Rundstedt. Subsequently going to Romny, Soviet bombers struck Guderian's convoy as it crossed the river, but emerging unscathed he reached his destination later in the day. At the town Model provided an appraisal of the situation, including that enemy stragglers were still active in the area and that armoured transport was necessary to move around in relative safety. Working his way down the ranks the general also spoke with Kleemann, who along with other staff officers expressed concern for enemy air attacks; a problem compounded by localized Soviet and Luftwaffe airfields respectively being in comparatively dry and saturated areas. Guderian then sent a wireless message to his staff that starting on 11 September strong fighter support was to be provided for 3rd Panzer Division, and that XXXXVII was to advance into the Putyvl area. Keeping close to his primary sector the general stayed a very rainy night at Model's headquarters at Khmeliv.[37] Well to the north-west, 4th Panzer Division secured Bakhmach at 1830hrs and made contact with 15./SS-'Deutschland', while the remainder of 'Reich' continued its advance to the south-west for the Borzna area to widen XXIV Motorized Army Corps' breach and remain close to Second Army.

On 11 September Bock informed Guderian that Kleist was experiencing similar torrential rain that all but negated Luftwaffe support or easy overland travel. That night, 180km south of Romny, 16th Panzer Division crossed the Dnepr and into the Kremenchuk bridgehead before striking northward. With several infantry divisions also across the river in a congested space they were similarly ready to burst forth to run roughshod across South-Western Front's rear. With the weather having cleared on 12 September 3rd Panzer Division reorganized its Kampfgruppen towards quickly getting a German presence south. Even though the Soviet Thirty-Eighth Army greatly outnumbered Model's very isolated command, getting a small force like 'Kampfgruppe Frank' into Lokhvytsia would disrupt enemy command and control, as well as their east–west road and rail movements. Although Army Groups Centre and South finally neared a linkup gaps remained along the fledgling German perimeter. Once again many Soviet elements worked to extract themselves from the increasing chaos and disorganization within the cauldron to continue the fight.[38]

As a result of Guderian's lengthy thrust southward by 13 September, the lack of sufficient infantry formations along his left flank meant XXXXVII Motorized Army Corps' 18th Panzer and 29th Motorized Infantry Divisions had assumed an eastward facing to anchor defensive positions from Pochep to near Shostka. 17th Panzer Division and Großdeutschland (both XXXXVI MAC) continued the line down to Putyvl and along the River Seym. While, perhaps, not an optimal situation, given the lack of Soviet forces east of 3rd Panzer Division, the roughly 50km to Romny seemed manageable over the near term. More importantly, along the front line of Second Army and XXIV Motorized

Army Corps, even though the enemy made determined stands, German forces were pushing hard between and around such obstructions at several locations, and leaving them for friendly elements moving up behind. Notable among these penetrations, while the bulk of 3rd Panzer Division solidified its gains around Romny, Model's vanguard made a determined dash across sloppy roads to reach Lokhvytsia.

During Luftwaffe reconnaissance ahead of Model's advance, Red Army columns were sighted heading from the south-west of Lokhvytsia towards the east and south in an effort to escape the closing pocket. Although 'Kampfgruppe Frank' used its meagre artillery to force one to turn back, additional formations were needed to properly seal the area. With 16th Panzer Division now just 45km from 3rd Panzer Division's forward most units the Germans once again raced to throw up a solid cordon and prevent what were believed to be forty enemy divisions from escaping destruction. With Ju-87s having broken up a Soviet armoured column approaching Frank's small command at about 1530hrs on 13 September the arrival of 6th Panzer Regiment nearly 2 hours later provided the necessary firepower to counter what enemy forces might be anticipated in the short term. Although 'Kampfgruppe Lewinski' had recently arrived across the Sula from Lokhvytsia, as it began its attack on the town at 1815hrs Soviet resistance and the approaching darkness precluded further progress until the morning.[39]

At 0600hrs on 14 September Captain Gustav Peschke and his 3./3rd Motorized Infantry Regiment stormed across the Sula Bridge at Lokhvytsia's northeastern edge and into the town to capture it, along with six Soviet antiaircraft guns.[40] Following Model's path through Konotop, 10th Motorized Infantry Division pushed to the south and east. Although seemingly little different than other German penetrations along the Kyiv Pocket's northern sector, with the Soviet Fortieth Army outside of the cordon Schweppenburg's left flank would be exposed. Spending the night of 14/15 September there, Guderian ordered Löper to quickly move to Romny, while his headquarters relocated to Konotop to keep up with the advancing front line. Quickly exploiting its success, 3rd Panzer Division established expanding bridgeheads at Lokhvytsia and Luka. To coordinate with close support between Ju-87s and 3rd Panzer Division white sheets were laid out on the ground to indicate the direction (arrow) and distance (accompanying vertical line (1,000m), triangle (500m), and triangle and line (100m)) of enemy forces.[41] For as much success as the German mobile divisions had achieved the effort came at a considerable cost in armoured vehicles. While Second Panzer Group's artillery allotment had remained between 75 and 90 per cent, 3rd, 4th, 17th, and 18th Panzer Divisions respectively had just 20, 29, 21, and 31 per cent of their tanks presently operational, with the remainder undergoing repairs or designated a loss.[42] While many of these vehicles could be fixed near the combat zone, those with more severe issues needed to be sent back to Germany.

Having endured weeks of hard fighting, maintenance, and a host of martial exertions over 400km of primitive roads and often poor weather at 0910hrs on a dry and windy 15 September 1941, elements of 3rd and 9th Panzer Divisions (XXXXVIII MAC) established contact with each other at Lokhvytsia and Sencha, trapping five Soviet field armies to their west. As agreed upon a few days earlier the former issued the codeword *Tannenberg* to indicate the achievement. As 17th Panzer Division advanced for Putyvl, Arnim returned to the formation having recovered from his wounds and Thoma was correspondingly placed into OKH Leaders Reserve. In the afternoon Guderian went to Konotop to meet with Liebenstein who had recently arrived from Army Group Centre with instructions on the coming thrust on Moscow, and Bock's operational directive. Although Hitler intended for Second Panzer Group to remain in action well to the south in Ukraine, and possibly assist in securing the eastern, Donbas region, the field marshal's concern for what would be a lengthy right flank and desire for as much armoured support as possible meant Guderian was re-included. Even though the elimination and capture of vast numbers of enemy personnel from the Kyiv Pocket forced a significant deviation (1,170km connecting Smolensk–Lokhvytsia–Moscow) it straightened the German front line to improve force density and created a sizeable rupture in the enemy ranks that the Soviets were unable to quickly close.

To coordinate the solidification of the Kyiv Pocket, hold off Soviet forces in the east, and prepare Second Panzer Group for its strike for the enemy capital Guderian's headquarters moved to Romny. With the Kyiv perimeter solidifying and the pocket shrinking, Second Army was withdrawn from the front line and sent north to be in a more centralized position for Army Group Centre's part in the forthcoming offensive on Moscow. Much as during the fighting in the Minsk–Bialystok Pocket Soviet desperation increasingly translated into unco-ordinated rushes to escape entrapment that often degraded to human waves intended to overwhelm localized German defences.[43] While terrifying to those subjected to such wasteful tactics they served to reinforce a widely held Landser opinion that their adversary was less than human and something to be hated and feared. Reflective of this attitude, in response to a comment made by Hitler on 16 September regarding the quashing of fledgling enemy partisan activity, Keitel stated that, 'It should be taken into account that in the countries con-cerned individual human life is widely felt to be worth nothing, so a deterrent can only be achieved through unaccustomed severity.'[44]

In the aftermath of enclosing the Kyiv Pocket, in contrast to the southern arm that largely hugged the River Dnepr, Soviet forces facing Second Panzer Group and part of Sixth Army in the north presented little semblance of a solid front line, as they hurriedly retreated. While Schweppenburg coordinated with more of Kleist's panzer divisions to contain the pocket's eastern edge, Guderian focused on what he expected to be his culminating achievement in the East;

the renewed offensive against Moscow.[45] For now, XXXXVII Motorized Army Corps was essentially in position for subsequent action to the north-east, but Vietinghoff still needed to clear up ongoing fighting around Putyvl and along the Seym.

Defending Romny

After a quiet night, early on 17 September 17th Panzer Division continued to push east of Konotop to take Dubinka, since Kleist had pushed up as far as Lokhvytsia and Army Group South having taken over control of the shrinking Kyiv Pocket. Closer to the River Seym, Großdeutschland attacked Bochechky from the south and pushed the enemy back into the nearby forests. Although 'Reich' had been anchoring XXIV Motorized Army Corps' western flank, and had taken Pryluki the day before, Schweppenburg solidified his gains to Pyryatin and along the River Uday, as Army Group South's forward armoured elements moved up to cover his outside, eastern flank. With the majority of 10th Motorized Infantry Division hard-pressed in an isolated stand at Romny where remnants of several enemy rifle divisions worked to exit their untenable positions and Soviet cavalry had pushed to within a few kilometres of Guderian's headquarters, on 18 September Schweppenburg acted. Having to contend with localized Soviet air superiority that hindered Luftwaffe reconnaissance the town was subjected to a heavy bomber strike. With their work in the Kyiv fighting concluded 3rd and 4th Panzer and SS-Motorized Division 'Reich' began transitioning from their forward positions and heading to the north-east.

At 1100hrs 20th Motorized Infantry Regiment (10 MID) reported the area just west of Buryn was enemy-occupied. At 1307hrs 41st Motorized Infantry Regiment reported a force of some 500 cavalrymen, with heavy and light artillery, east of Romny. Just over an hour later Luftwaffe reconnaissance sighted lengthy enemy columns moving on Nedryhailiv, Beyeve, and Hadyach, with the intent of converging on Löper towards forcing a breach in his lines through which to free their trapped comrades. At present 40th Motorcycle Battalion operated in the threatened area, having recently moved down from Konotop to clear the area east of the route to Romny. To preserve this critical logistics corridor, especially given 3rd and 4th Panzer Divisions once again needed fuel, and block likely determined Soviet attacks from the east and west, Schweppenburg assigned Löper to the task. During the late afternoon II./41st Motorized Infantry and III./10th Artillery Regiments were sent to bolster 'Kampfgruppe Traut' as it prepared defences along the River Bizh south-west of Terni down to Nedryhailiv. To add to Löper's troubles at 1545hrs XXIV Motorized Army Corps reported that it would be unable to assist for at least a day being too far to the south-west.

With Traut soon reporting constant attacks on his position, at 1740hrs the commander of II Air Corps' close-support airplane group (*Nahkampfgruppe*), Brigadier Martin Fiebig, provided a briefing on the approaching Soviet columns. While the northernmost one had apparently taken refuge within a wooded area, as aerial visibility had been lost for the last 3 hours, Luftwaffe continued to watch the centre column, but avoided engaging due to its numerous antiaircraft guns. Instead, Ju-87s concentrated against the southern line of enemy vehicles.[46] With a strong Soviet force in the forests north of the road to Konotop Löper maintained a wary eye in that direction towards repelling the enemy relief force. At 1830hrs 'Kampfgruppe Plagemann' provided intelligence from enemy prisoner statements that Löper faced two Soviet cavalry and two rifle divisions, as well as two tank brigades, with forty tanks intent on retaking Romny. For its attack on Chernecha Sloboda and points south, 20th Motorized Infantry Regiment was assigned to XXXXVI Motorized Army Corps and provided with additional artillery. As a final reorganization for the approaching fight, 'Kampfgruppe Traut' was subordinated to 'Reich', and 20th Motorized Infantry Regiment was positioned on the right, with Großdeutschland and 17th Panzer Divisions respectively in the centre and on the left.[47] Implying this sector just south of the Seym was to be reinforced, German reconnaissance aircraft relayed sighting nineteen enemy trains heading north towards Sumy.[48]

As a result of all the scrambling to organize a defence of Romny, during 19 September most of 17th Panzer Division, with part of 10th Motorized Infantry Division on its right, pushed south of the Seym and into the advancing enemy's right flank, 15km south-east of Buryn. Since 'Reich' had moved up around noon to reinforce the bulk of Löper's command the Soviet relief was effectively blocked. Having been carved up into a pocket around the Soviet Thirty-Seventh Army's defence of Kyiv and another to the east that trapped Fifth, Twenty-Sixth, and Thirty-Eighth Armies, the Germans captured the Ukrainian capital. With the Soviet pressure around Romny easing Guderian's headquarters returned to Konotop where the location was better positioned to orchestrate Second Panzer Group's upcoming assault on Bryansk and Orel.[49] Although the formation's 300km southward drive into Ukraine had helped destroy South-Western Front and straightened the front line the time taken to see the mission to completion meant only a few weeks remained before the biannual period of heavy rain and mud commenced, followed by the notoriously bitter Russian winter. Considering Guderian's panzer divisions had upwards of just 30 per cent of their organizationally allotted tanks operational, with only eleven days until the Germans unleashed their attack on the Soviet capital, these and numerous other deficiencies would be difficult to correct. Much of the blame stemmed from Hitler's belief that the Red Army would soon be defeated and thus newly produced tanks were to be kept within the Reich's borders. Once victory in the East had been achieved these valuable, but depleted formations were then to be amalgamated and their assets and surplus crews returned to Germany to populate new ones.

On 19 September the Moscow offensive received the moniker 'Typhoon', although unlike Hitler's Directive No. 35 that was to employ Third and Fourth Panzer Groups, Bock also incorporated Second Panzer Group from the southwest. With Bock concerned that large enemy forces might opt to trade space for time and evade a large German encirclement, after arguments with OKH about where to close Army Group's pincers it was decided on Vyaz'ma; being a comparatively modest encirclement that could be better sealed off and destroyed.

1st Cavalry Division (Second Panzer Group to XXXXVII Motorized Army Corps (20 September))
17th Panzer Division (XXXXVI Motorized Army Corps to the disposition of Second Panzer Group (23 September))
XXXXVI Motorized Army Corps (removed from Second Panzer Group (23 September))
XXXXVIII Motorized Army Corps (to Second Panzer Group (23 September))

At the start of 23 September the Kyiv Pocket had lost any defined form having broken down into small clusters that Army Group South would soon eliminate. With the German Fourth and Ninth Armies having established strong defensive positions during Guderian's and Hoth's absence to weather determined Soviet efforts to eject them from the Smolensk and Yel'nya areas, now that its encirclement duties had ended Second Panzer Group transitioned to an eastward facing front line through Pochep–Pogar–Hlukhiv–Romny–River Khorol. Having weathered strong Soviet forces attempting to penetrate west of Romny XXXXVI Motorized Army Corps firmed up their designated jump-off sector between the town and Hlukhiv, just across the River Bereza. To bulk out Bock's forces south of Smolensk XXXXVI Motorized Army Corps was pulled from Guderian's control and sent north. To compensate for the loss, and as Sixth Army's advance axis diverged to the south-east, Second Panzer Group was given Lieutenant General (*General der Panzertruppe*) Werner Kempf's, XXXXVIII Motorized Army Corps along the general's otherwise hanging right flank.

In recognition of his command's recent successes, on 23 September Guderian issued a 'Group – Order of the Day' that read:

> Soldiers of Second Panzer Group! On August 25, you launched an attack in a southerly direction to destroy the enemy held at the Dnepr. In fierce battles the front of the enemy was penetrated, the course of the Desna and Seym was overcome and on September 13 the ring around the enemy east of Kyiv was closed by union with a tank group from the south. All attempts to break through and relieve the opponent were rejected. The booty during this time amounts to:

86,000 prisoners. 220 tanks. 850 artillery guns. The commander-in-chief of the Russian 5th [Fifth] Army fell into our hands. The entire Russian southern front is thus shattered and the way to new, decisive steps is paved. In these weeks you have again done your duty in full measure and taken all efforts upon yourselves, although you have not been able to be granted a rest since 22.6. You have gained new fame with your often proven fighting and attacking spirit. Thank you for that. Now it is necessary to gather all strength once more into this eventful year of war in order to achieve the goal of the campaign in a tremendous effort. I know that I can rely on you and that we will fulfil the orders of our leader. I use this occasion to express the best wishes for their future to the associations leaving the group after three months of armed comradeship with my special recognition. Heil Germany and Heil our Führer Adolf Hitler!

While Germany's captured battlefield adversaries up to *Barbarossatag* had been accorded treatment of varying degrees in keeping with established laws of war, Norwegians, Danish, Dutch, and British were best off. Considering the long, vitriolic history with France its soldiers were arguably worse off, but not as bad as the Poles, or at the very bottom of the scale Red Army prisoners, being labelled as 'subhuman' and unworthy of care or concern. According to Supplement No. 1 Soviet military service was not considered military duty, which due to the murders committed in its name on and off the field of battle their armed forces were deemed criminal in its entirety. Considering the unprecedented barbarism on the Eastern Front even though Germany had signed and ratified the 1929 Geneva Convention that stipulated rules for the treatment of prisoners of war that included providing medical care and Red Cross access to their opponents, the Soviet Union's refusal to do so provided both sides licence to quickly devolve into extralegal, reciprocating violence and cruelty. To add to the burden under which Red Army personnel struggled was an official Soviet mindset that those who surrendered were traitors and subsequently disowned by their government, which then placed relatives in jeopardy of imprisonment or worse. In response to OKW's issuance of ruthless regulations for the treatment of Soviet prisoners earlier in the month, on 23 September Keitel wrote that, 'The objections arise from the military concept of chivalrous warfare. This is the destruction of an ideology. Therefore I approve and back the measures.' A week earlier he ordered that attacks on soldiers in the East should be met by putting to death 50 to 100 Communists for each German soldier killed, with the comment that human life was less than nothing.

Chapter 9
Orel, 24 September–31 October 1941

9th Panzer Division (XXXXVIII to XXIV Motorized Army Corps (24 September))
'Reich' (removed from XXIV Motorized Army Corps (24 September))

Following the elimination of the Kyiv Pocket, by late September the German front line from the Baltic to Black Sea had been considerably straightened, and in a much better position to increase reserves and concentrate at the planned advance axes slated for Typhoon. On 24 September Guderian flew to Bock's headquarters at Smolensk for a final conference on the operation that would include three-fourths of the *Ostheer*'s strength! With Brauchitsch, Halder, Kluge, Weichs, Hoth, and Generals Erich Höpner (Fourth Panzer Group) and Adolf Strauss (Ninth Army) in attendance it was decided that Second Panzer Group would begin its attack on 30 September as the right wing of Army Group Centre. With poor roads throughout most of the intended battlespace Guderian hoped to at least get to the better transportation networks around Orel and Bryansk before the expected rainy season began. With the difficulty in getting the necessary number of trains to support Army Group Centre, given the large number of participating panzer and motorized divisions, prioritization of fuel was implemented to build stockpiles. The general also desired for his superior to allocate Luftwaffe support intended for other Army Group Centre formations to his own considering Second Panzer Group was to begin its attack along a 300km frontage two days before its peers.[1]

9th Panzer Division (XXIV to XXXXVIII Motorized Army Corps (26 September))

With Army Group Centre's advance at least as far as Moscow having been put on hold for the last seven weeks Guderian was finally given the opportunity for which he long desired. Had Bock been permitted to strike for the enemy capital in mid-August, what tantalizingly appeared to have been a beaten, disorganized enemy mob was in reality a much stronger force than anticipated. Although Second Panzer Group had advanced roughly 600km from the River Bug to just beyond the Dnepr in about six weeks, to cover a similar distance necessary to complete its part in encircling the enemy capital it would now operate with its key mobile formations in a much more depleted state and increasingly beyond the range that logistics could be adequately provided. With four Soviet Armies having been destroyed and two more crippled, and some 665,000 of its soldiers captured in the Kyiv Pocket, Red Army leadership scrambled to address the impossible; stabilize the huge void in its lines, while maintaining the necessary defensive strength along Bock's direct route to Moscow.[2] Although the Soviets conducted several localized counterattacks towards this end, little was accomplished. On 26 September Bock signed off on Typhoon.

In response to the seemingly unstoppable German advance that in the early autumn had approached the River Desna in strength most Soviet authorities had left the Orel and Bryansk areas in anticipation of their coming fall. With rear areas devoid of political authority disorganized groups of Soviet soldiers frequently entered villages and urban areas in search of food. Having suffered under Stalin's repressive collectivization policies that ran the gambit of executions, mass deportations, starvation, and forced labour much of the area's subsequently impoverished inhabitants were naturally less than enthusiastic. Such feelings were only exacerbated when Red Army personnel had the time to remove livestock, machinery, fuel, and anything else of value, and burning or destroying the rest to deny it to the enemy; actions that typically left the unfortunate civilians to face starvation, exposure, and other deprivations. As German forces moved into these areas civilians often returned to their property hoping to restart an existence approximating their former lives. Before too long, however, as front-line German forces moved on and were replaced by security and Party administrative personnel the reality of a war of annihilation became quickly apparent.

In preparation for an offensive along a Hlukhiv-Orel advance axis, on 27 September Guderian's 14 1/2 divisions were organized along the River Desna between LIII Army Corps, which had been positioned across from Bryansk to the north, and what was a sparsely occupied enemy sector to the south, into which Sixth Army now advanced. Once again XXXXVII Motorized Army Corps comprised Second Panzer Group's left flank, which for little over a week included 1st Cavalry Division. While of minimal use in a stand-up, conventional fight, the formation was positioned along a 50km stretch of the River Desna where it would attempt to fix as much of the Soviet Third Army and keep it from peeling off to interfere with Lemelsen's 29th Motorized Infantry and 17th and 18th Panzer Divisions, as they struck for Orel.[3] In his centre Guderian positioned XXIV Motorized Army Corps to reinforce his southern prong against Bryansk, while still well to the south, and out of the general's initial offensive, XXXXVIII Motorized Army Corps would hopefully keep Soviet Major General Arkadii Ermakov guessing as to the intended German advance axis and consequently spread his limited forces

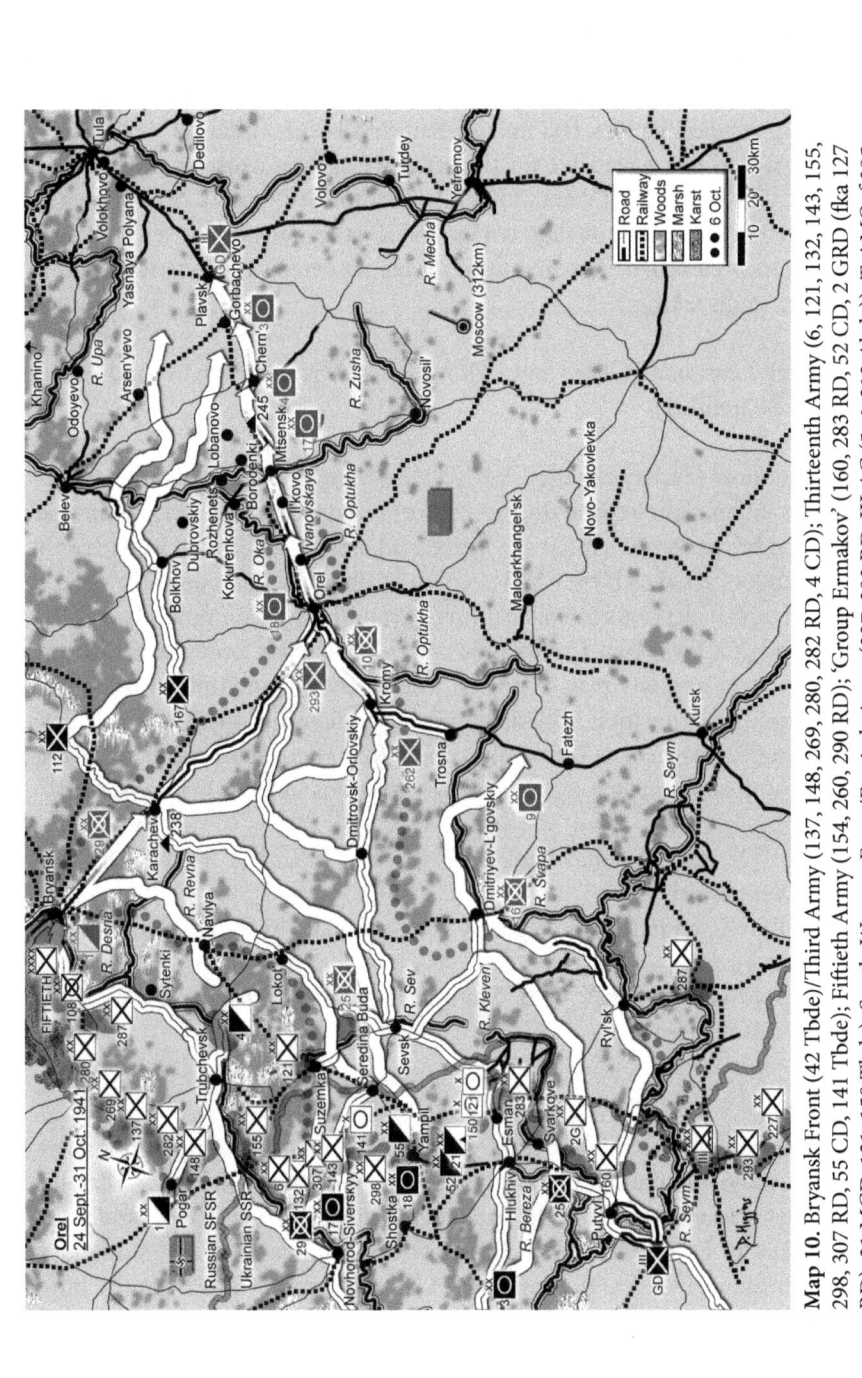

Map 10. Bryansk Front (42 Tbde)/Third Army (137, 148, 269, 280, 282 RD, 4 CD); Thirteenth Army (6, 121, 132, 143, 155, 298, 307 RD, 55 CD, 141 Tbde); Fiftieth Army (154, 260, 290 RD); 'Group Ermakov' (160, 283 RD, 52 CD, 2 GRD (fka 127 RD), 21 MCD, 121, 150 Tbde); South-Western Front/Fortieth Army (227, 293 RD, III AC (5, 6, 212 Abde)). TsAMO, f.395, op.9136, d.30. TsAMO, f.202, op.5, d.169, l.16.

to address the perceived threat. Once Second Panzer Group's part in Typhoon commenced, Kempf would progressively disengage and relocate closer to Schweppenburg to maximize concentration at the critical penetration. As part of the preparations for Typhoon, Second Panzer Group had only been given 124 newly produced Panzer IIIs and 25 Panzer IVs, of which 50 were sent to Orsha and would be unavailable for the offensive against Moscow until at least 1 October. This meant XXIV and XXXXVII Motorized Army Corps possessed a combined 94 Panzer IIIs, 36 Panzer IVs, and 57 other tanks.[4] Worse, stockpiled fuel was in less than sufficient quantities to sustain what was Guderian's part of the massive undertaking.[5]

XXXV High Command (293rd and 296th Infantry Divisions) (to Second Panzer Group (28 September))

On 28 September Guderian halted XXXXVIII Motorized Army Corps' foundering attack on his right beyond the recently captured town of Putyvl, and instead directed the formation to exploit the successful assault on Shtepivka where the Soviet defenders acted as if they had been taken unaware. To reduce the need to siphon off combat elements to hold captured ground the predominantly infantry XXXIV and XXXV High Commands were respectively brought up in echelon on his right and left rear. With the former comprising only two infantry divisions and the latter four, with a combined modicum of support units, both corps seemed capable of successfully conducting their semi-static roles that freed veteran formations for active combat operations in more critical sectors.

17th Panzer Division (Second Panzer Group to XXXXVII Motorized Army Corps (29 September))
XXXIV High Command (for Special Purposes) (to Second Panzer Group (29 September))
1st Cavalry Division (XXXXVII Motorized Army Corps to XXXV High Command (30 September))

Typhoon
Eager to complete the monumental undertaking of organizing and orchestrating his massive command Bock worked to mitigate deficiencies that had dogged the *Ostheer* throughout the campaign. Concentration, shock, and speed remained key in keeping the Red Army off balance, reactive, and susceptible to being outmanoeuvred and eliminated. Unanticipated delays from the bitter Smolensk–Yel'nya fighting, the 400km drive southward to seal Kyiv's fate, and all the incurred losses in personnel, vehicles, and equipment weighed on an increasing number of senior German commanders who questioned whether ultimate success could be achieved by the New Year. To destroy the three enemy

fronts defending their capital Bock was given Fourth Panzer Group from Army Group North. With Army Group Centre only barely able to provide the minimum amount of supplies it seemed entirely probable the formation lacked the range and endurance to encircle the enemy capital.

With Second Panzer Group having essentially maintained its 280km front line from near Pochep to east of Lokhvytsia, since completing its part of defeating the Kyiv Pocket a week earlier, only some intervening reorganization was needed to optimally position Guderian's command for its thrust towards Orel and Tula. In what was to be a modified version of the successful wedge and cauldron-style pincer operations to date, 3rd and 4th Panzer Divisions were to help encircle what was expected to be the bulk of enemy forces assigned to block the most direct route to Moscow. In the wake of the Soviet South-Western Front's recent catastrophic losses in the Dnepr bend the formation had limited means to plug the resulting 300km gap in its front line or allocate formations to the threatened Moscow sector. Having gone to his newly established command post at Hlukhiv early on 30 September to more centrally conduct his part in the operation at 0500hrs Eberbach assembled his Kampfgruppe in its jump-off positions across the low, rain-soaked hills and farmland around the town, and along the main route to Sevsk. Fog obscured visibility on the ground and prevented air support, as he led a southern grouping of his force, and Munzel a smaller, northern one, both possessed a mix of armour, antiaircraft, motorcycle, and engineers to address most contingencies. Immediately following a 30-minute German preparatory bombardment, at 0635hrs the southern group set off to the north-east without enemy contact, while some continuing artillery fire supported its right flank.[6] Although the northern group was momentarily held up, as II./6th Panzer Regiment proved unable to cross an emergency bridge over a Bereza tributary north of Hlukhiv, 'Kampfgruppe Munzel' conducted a rapid advance that soon cut though the defending 283rd Rifle Division and weakened what defensive stance it had mustered.

With the Soviet infantry and artillery finally reacting to 4th Panzer Division's spearheads just west of Esman village, at about 0715hrs I./35th Panzer Regiment knocked out a handful of light enemy tanks.[7] Half an hour later its II. Panzer Battalion comrades and guns from II./11th Antiaircraft Regiment reported knocking out nine more enemy tanks near the village, in spite of the reduced visibility. Considering the Panzer IIIs and IVs lacked sufficient firepower to effectively engage the heavier enemy tanks at typical ranges German crews often resorted to firing inside of 200m to quickly achieve a knockout and hopefully prevent the stricken vehicle from returning the favour. Unwilling to then remain in place and slug it out to their eventual disadvantage the German drivers often pulled back or relocated to repeat the process from another position. While capable of firing their main guns while on the move, the absence of stabilizers all but eliminated the accuracy a stopped platform on level ground provided. As the only real impediment to Langermann's progress a pair of KV-2s defiantly held their positions along the advance road. Even though the fog was slowly burning away with the dawn, with poor visibility confounding longer range targeting, two assault engineer parties were tasked with eliminating the high-silhouette behemoths. During the ensuing game of cat-and-mouse, each time the tanks were threatened they progressively fell back to a mined location where the main road crossed over the rail line running past Esman. With I. and II./35th Panzer Regiment respectively directed to the north-east and south of the obstruction the addition of German artillery and Luftwaffe support finally drove the enemy tanks off and reopened the route.

Off to an auspicious start Second Panzer Group's drivers kept a watchful eye on their fuel gauges, and unlike Höpner's essentially full-strength panzer divisions, Guderian's were on average just 50 per cent.[8] Having advanced some 50km since setting off the day before, they left the requisite wreckage of enemy tanks and other vehicles in their wake. Once again, counterattacking Soviet tanks in brigade strength created some temporary discomfort near Stepnoye, but were soon caught up in the torrent of German forces and swept aside.[9] Now on 1 October 4th Panzer Division nearly destroyed the oddly idle Soviet 121st Tank Brigade and captured a bombed out and smoking Sevsk and its surprisingly undamaged bridge over the Sev. As seeming evidence of the difficulty in organizing much beyond hindering the German advance along the front line and declining Soviet tank numbers these sub-division sized units were increasingly used to bolster slow-moving friendly infantry instead of being concentrated alongside similarly mobile support units for maximum effectiveness; tactics that disastrously undercut France's battlefield efforts the previous year. Intent on being up front with his vanguards as they quickly laid the groundwork for a more substantial penetration into 'Group Ermakov' and the adjacent Thirteenth Army to the north, Guderian met with Schweppenburg and Langermann to discuss subsequent combat operations. Although limited fuel quantities elicited talk of temporarily halting to ensure adequate amounts were made available, on speaking with an optimistic Eberbach, as to the feasibility of pushing on to at least Dmitrovsk-Orlovskiy to more fully exploit their early successes, Guderian naturally determined to forge ahead.[10] To express his gratitude and be seen among his men at an active front line, during his stay the general visited Langermann's spear tip, II./35th Panzer Regiment. To Schweppenburg's left, XXXXVII Motorized Army Corps similarly burst through weak resistance from south of Pogar to Yampil and was soon several kilometres to the north-east. On Guderian's right, XXXXVIII Motorized Army Corps' struggled against strong Soviet forces south-west of Sumy and along the River Psel, including an enemy counterattack from across the River Kleven' beyond Svarkove, as 9th Panzer and 25th Motorized Infantry Divisions continued to redeploy northward and beyond the River Seym.

16th Motorized Infantry Division (to XXXXVIII Motorized Army Corps) (2 October))

As Bryansk Front recoiled before Guderian's offensive, on 2 October Fourth Panzer Army unleashed its attack along the Soviet formation's northern wing. Reflective of similar scenarios over the last few months understrength and equipped Red Army forces were hard pressed to contain the enemy along their concentrated breakthrough sectors. Forced to place their limited power forward to maintain a cohesive front line it was at the expense of providing reserves necessary for creating a defence-in-depth.[11] For all their comrades' struggles on the ground, Soviet aircraft had recovered to a considerable degree from their drubbing on *Barbarossatag* and were able to provide a certain level of support. With 4th Panzer Division taking Dmitrovsk-Orlovskiy, and its advance elements reaching Kromy by day's end, Langermann had arrived at the paved stretch of road leading to Orel. Under the reasonable assumption that the city would soon fall and provide the Germans with a critical logistics hub in which to stockpile the materiel necessary to propel Second Panzer Group forward, Guderian's right hook would continue.

Mtsensk
45th Infantry Division (to XXXIV High Command) (3 October))

Having led 4th Panzer Division over the last three days, by 3 October a Kampfgruppe built around II./35th Panzer Regiment had advanced 240km to reach Orel.[12] Taking advantage of an adversary not expecting German elements so far into their rear areas, Second Lieutenant Artur Wollschlaeger rushed his 6./35th Panzer Regiment into the undefended city. For the cost of three panzern being knocked out, his capture of the city not only resulted in acquiring what enemy supplies, weapons, and equipment remained, but denied Bryansk Front a major road and rail conduit, and forced them to use lesser quality, alternative routes to keep its combat elements effective. With the bulk of 4th Panzer Division strung out along the Dmitrovsk-Orlovskiy–Orel road, 6./35th Panzer Regiment reportedly shot up twenty enemy antitank guns that were being removed from the area, as part of the larger Soviet effort to disassemble and relocate industrial assets and other materiel eastward to keep them from falling into German hands.[13] Pushing through an area where much of this work was still in progress, with machinery and equipment in various stages of disassembly or transport, Wollschlaeger engaged elements of V Airborne Corps that TB-3 bombers were landing at one of the city's airfields.[14] Strung out over more than 100km Breith's 3rd Panzer Division advanced in 4th Panzer Division's wake as far as Dmitrovsk-Orlovskiy before turning to the north and inward towards encircling Red Army forces around Bryansk. Already, both formations neared the end of their fuel and soon called a halt until more was brought up. Taking advantage of XXIV Motorized Army Corps' suddenly stalled situation, Soviet armour quickly concentrated on ejecting the enemy from Orel. With 18th Panzer Division already approaching Karachev, however, Bryansk Front's stitched-together defence appeared ready to unravel. Seemingly not willing to let an opportunity for authoritarian bombast to pass by, Hitler, having left Rastenburg for Berlin, gave a public address that included, 'I declare today . . . that the enemy in the East has been struck down and will never rise again . . .' and that, 'Behind our troops there already lies a territory twice the size of the German Reich when I came to power in 1933.'

Second Panzer Group redesignated Second Panzer Army (5 October)
25th Motorized Infantry Division (XXXXVIII Motorized Army Corps to XXXIV High Command (5 October))

With the bill coming as a result of its rapid *coup de main* against Orel, as II./35th Panzer Regiment pushed its luck and headed for Tula, enemy resistance finally began to coalesce against the exposed unit. Having made contact with Major Meinrad von Lauchert's I./35th Panzer Regiment on 5 October, a day after Soviet T-34s momentarily halted his advance at Ivanovskaya, II. Panzer Battalion and the regimental staff were to remain in the area. The remainder of the Kampfgruppe merged with Lauchert, who then muscled his way forward once again.[15] At 1030hrs Guderian visited Lemelsen's headquarters at Lobanovo to discuss his subordinate's progress, as 18th Panzer Division advanced across the Orel–Bryansk highway towards Karachev, and 17th Panzer Division moved purposefully along its left rear with the goal of striking the Bryansk defenders from behind their strong, largely westward facing defences.[16] The general then flew to XXIV Motorized Infantry Corps' headquarters at Dmitrovsk-Orlovskiy, where he contacted Second Air Fleet about having 100,000 gallons of fuel flown in to Orel, which would avoid the ongoing problem of traffic congestion.[17]

25th Motorized Infantry Division (XXXIV High Command to the disposition of Second Panzer Army (6 October))

With 7./12th Motorized Rifle Regiment tasked with guarding the River Optukha Bridge, at 0830hrs on 6 October 'Kampfgruppe Lauchert' became entangled with Soviet armour from the Il'kovo area, NKVD personnel, and Katyusha rocket launchers to the north-east of Mtsensk and west along the rail line running parallel with the Oka. Although Eberbach reinforced his forward elements with a battery of 88mm antiaircraft guns, and one each of 100mm and 105mm cannons, the heavier enemy tanks made for a rather unequal tank duel that halted the German push as it approached Mtsensk.[18] As evidence of the often fierce, sustained fighting in the East, Lauchert and First Lieutenant Helmut Krause from the 'yellow bears' of 3rd Panzer Company were the regiment's only tank commanders from the Polish Campaign still in action. Four days later Krause would be killed in combat.

As Guderian's headquarters moved to Sevsk from which to coordinate his renamed command, now Second Panzer Army, 190km to the north-east advance elements from 4th Panzer Division tangled with a Soviet blocking force that included numerous Soviet T-34s that had been placed south of Mtsensk. Using proven tactics the Germans worked to separate any accompanying Red Army infantry before concentrating antitank fire on vulnerable tracks and finishing off the immobilized vehicles, the numbers now encountered proved more than a handful. Although the vehicles possessed an excellent balance of armoured protection, firepower, and manoeuvrability for 1941, they lacked refinement, safety features, and any concept of ergonomics that overburdened what were commonly minimally trained crews; those with experience had largely become casualties. The absence of a turret basket meant the loader needed to physically adjust to any rotation, and the cramped internal space, made worse by the sloped armour, meant that penetrations commonly struck ammunition or critical mechanical components. With 76.2mm armour-piercing rounds in short supply, poor visibility, and propensity for spalling, superior German gunsight optics, and crew training and experience promoted quicker and more accurate targeting that removed some of the shine from these otherwise well-designed Soviet vehicles. Barring the availability of devastating 88mm antitank guns, the German 47mm Czech-manufactured and newer 50mm varieties being allocated to infantry divisions offered a chance of defeating the heavier Soviet vehicles, given short engagement ranges or against thinner sections of armour. Since the fielded numbers of these vehicles was sure to increase, Guderian called for representatives from the Army Ordnance Office, Armaments Ministry, and related personnel to come to the Mtsensk area to assess the situation and begin the process of formulating an armoured solution. According to a report from 4th Panzer Division's Ia:

> Time and again our tanks have been split right open by hits from the front and the commander's cupolas on the Type [Panzer] III and IV tanks have been completely blown off, proof that the armour plating is inadequate and that the fastening on the cupolas is faulty, and also proof of the great accuracy and penetration of the Russian (T-34) 7.62cm tank cannon.[19]

With Second Army having acted as an anvil upon which XXXXVII Motorized Army Corps turned and fell, on 6 October Weichs' infantry crossed the River Desna towards making contact with 17th Panzer Division. On Guderian's comparatively quiet southern flank XXXXVIII Motorized Army

Corps pushed beyond the Ryl'sk area, with 9th Panzer and 16th Motorized Infantry Divisions coordinating to secure the Dmitrovsk-Orlovskiy sector, and 25th Motorized Infantry Division moving up from Putyvl as a reserve. The Soviets had logically weighted their resources west of Moscow, and along Army Group Centre's most direct advance axis. Correspondingly the Vyazemskaya Defensive Line presented three, roughly parallel belts of trenchworks, bunkers, and gun emplacements that incorporated the River Dnepr. The Mozhaisk Defensive Line comprised two more belts that extended in an arc nearer the capital and south to Tula, with additional positions filling in the area to Moscow. These locations included a host of defensive combat modifiers, such as minefields, remote flamethrowers, chevaux-de-frise made from trios of welded rail ties, and rows of ground-protruding, tank-deterring logs set vertically that the Landsers referred to as 'asparagus beds'.[20]

As much as the Germans had hoped to conclude Barbarossa before the onset of cold weather during the night of 6/7 October the first snow of autumn began to fall. While it did little more than further dampen the already wet roads that the sun would soon dry out its occurrence portended worse was close behind. While Bock's armoured and mobile vanguards had maintained a rapid battlefield tempo over the last several days capturing Moscow seemed a long way off. On Army Group Centre's northern wing Third Panzer Group's LVII Motorized Army Corps and Fourth Panzer Group's XXXX Motorized Army Corps met around Vyaz'ma to encircle a massive number of enemy men and materiel from the defending Nineteenth, Twentieth, Twenty-Fourth, Thirtieth, and Forty-Third Armies on a scale rivalling that of Kyiv. As a result of Guderian mirroring the success in the south Second and Fourth Armies were able to exploit the resulting gap in the middle towards both assisting in cutting off additional enemy formations and advancing straight at Moscow from the south-west. Even with so many resources allocated to Typhoon, Hitler was already looking to Leeb to capture Leningrad, whose port facilities promised to dramatically improve Army Group North's logistics, establish contact with the Finns, and cut the railway to the ice-free port of Murmansk leading to the Barents Sea. Apparently dissatisfied with striving for realistic goals, the Führer also wanted Rundstedt to clear the Black Sea coast, take important urban centres, such as Kharkiv, Rostov-on-Don, and Stalingrad, and strike into the Caucasus to capture the oil fields south of Maikop. Although Guderian had professed requesting winter clothing numerous times, with the pressing needs of Typhoon ammunition remained prioritized for rail transport at the expense of other considerations.[21]

Having led 17th Panzer Division to approach Karachev from the south Major Hans Gradl's I./39th Panzer Regiment was made aware of the light enemy presence in the extensive woodland separating him from Bryansk. After working with 63rd Rifle Regiment to overcome a Red Army position on Hill

238, 13km south-west of Karachev, he formed what seemed a ludicrously small Kampfgruppe of a handful of tanks, motorized infantry, and a pair of 20mm antiaircraft guns and rushed off through the forested marshland. Along the Desna's eastern bank on 6 October 'Kampfgruppe Gradl' destroyed a substantial enemy supply dump before making a bold thrust on nearby Bryansk. In a move reminiscent of Klingenburg's capture of Belgrade, the major pushed through surprised enemy forces to secure the 250m timber trestle road bridge leading into the city. The bold, aggressive move helped cut off a critical logistics hub for the nearly surrounded Soviet Third and Thirteenth Armies. The bulk of 17th Panzer Division fought through often heavy resistance from 154th Rifle Division along Fiftieth Army's southern flank, but within a day had arrived at Bryansk.[22] Advancing on Arnim's heels, 29th Motorized Infantry Division pivoted at Navlya to face inward against the forming pocket around the city's defenders. Boltenstern's advance element continued on to reach the River Revna and down to where it flowed into the Desna.

95th Infantry Division (to XXXV High Command (7 October))

With OKH and Bock desiring Second Panzer Army continue for Tula and capture critical crossings over the River Oka roughly 100km beyond lingering Soviet resistance at Mtsensk first needed to be cleared. For now, XXXXVII Motorized Army Corp would tighten its encirclement towards eliminating the Bryansk defenders, while a relatively fresh 3rd Panzer Division moved additional forces into the Orel area to provide the increased punch to get Schweppenburg across the intervening 180km to Tula.[23] With Guderian's penchant for trying to leave cleaning up surrounded enemy forces to follow-on infantry, in this case Second Army, his wishful thinking that the Soviets were on their last legs was offset by the reality of his insufficient logistics. With Weichs taking Kozel'sk on 8 October to help secure Second Panzer Army's northern flank along the River Zhizdra that evening XXXV High Command reported increased enemy activity north of Suzemka.[24] Guderian correctly interpreted this as enemy forces south of Bryansk trying to break out to the east, and after ordering 1st Cavalry Division to cross the Sudost' and move on Trubchevsk he returned to Orel to convene a meeting with Schweppenburg about clearing Mtsensk to resume the German offensive.[25] In an optimistic attempt to weaken Soviet resolve during 8 October 3rd, 28th, and 53rd Bombardment Wings, and II./210th Ground Attack and Antitank Wing dropped a combined 267,000 propaganda leaflets over Red Army lines to induce their surrender.[26]

On the receiving end of the expected southward Soviet breakout from the nearly closed Bryansk Pocket on 9 October 293rd Infantry Division (XXXV HC) fell back on Suzemka and to the south-east to better absorb the blow. Along with 29th Motorized Infantry Division's position just 45km to the north-east Soviet movement along the Desna was increasingly restricted. Heavy Soviet pressure cropped up along the roads connecting Trubchevsk with Sevsk, Orel, and Karachev, but only a few trapped elements broke free across the Seredina Buda–Sevsk road, including the staff of Thirteenth Army. Keeping close to its extending front line, Second Panzer Army's headquarters relocated to Dmitrovsk-Orlovskiy during a heavy snowstorm that foreshadowed the terrible weather to come. In spite of the area's frequently atrocious roads that hindered wheeled and tracked vehicles, 3rd Panzer Division's advance element managed to take Bolkhov. In parallel to its west Nehring closed with XXXXIII Army Corps to shut the Bryansk encirclement, but also made contact with 3rd Panzer Division east of Karachev.[27] To provide dedicated air support Guderian was allocated 265 attack and dive-bomber aircraft, 144 single-engine fighters, and 13 reconnaissance planes.[28]

1st Cavalry Division (XXXV High Command to XXXXVII Motorized Army Corps (10 October))

Even though Soviet forces were frequently forced to leave vehicles and heavy weapons behind due to their having become stuck in the viscous, muddy terrain between Trubchevsk, Lokot, and the Desna's left bank, they continued to hammer 29th Motorized and 293rd Infantry Divisions that attempted to block their southward escape from Bryansk.[29] With thousands soon succeeding in pushing through 293rd Infantry Division's zone of control west of Sevsk, the recently arriving 25th Motorized Infantry Division was tasked with helping plug the offending gap in the cordon.[30] With large portions of Guderian's command temporarily immobile until drier conditions returned, a situation to which the enemy similarly suffered, XXXV High Command was at least able to move up to assume the southern perimeter.[31]

With 1st Cavalry Division having worked to clear its sector west of the River Desna over the last three days, on a snowy, rainy 11 October its 1st Bicycle Battalion established a bridgehead and physically contacted 29th Motorized Infantry Division near Sytenki. During the next nine days the mounted regiments and the division's cyclists fought hard against the retreating Soviet forces and collected a respectable amount of booty in the process.[32] In just a few short weeks, Feldt would receive orders that his cavalrymen were to be reorganized as a panzer division as soon as possible. Although the horsemen performed their peripheral combat, reconnaissance, and security operations well, the formation proved difficult to maintain, and lacked the ability to take on more direct, mobile missions. To retain a degree of its former self following the transition to 24th Panzer Division, Feldt's recommendation that its personnel retain their golden-yellow uniform piping and insignia was approved, as opposed to the official pink used with other armour personnel.

Working to crack the unexpectedly stiff enemy resistance around Mtsensk and clear the main road to Tula, to which Ju-87s added their targeted attacks, often flying through heavy Soviet ground fire, on 11 October 12th Motorized Rifle Regiment (4 PD) managed to enter the town from the west. While additional German units respectively approached the Zusha to the west and east, I./ and III./103rd Motorized Artillery Regiment, and the long-range guns from 604th Motorized Heavy 210mm Howitzer Battalion, engaged enemy forces beyond. Over the next few days Langermann fought to expand his bridgehead beyond the river against a stubborn enemy defence along the high ground to the town's north-east. Able to see several kilometres beyond their enemy who held the lower, bowl-like terrain around Mtsensk, the 6th Guards Rifle Division and a reinforcing airborne brigade applied their larger calibre, more numerous artillery guns to harry 4th Panzer Division's positions day and night. German artillery was correspondingly coordinated through 324th Panzer Observation Battery, which used sound-listening and flash-ranging to facilitate counter-battery fire.[33]

Having all but eliminated the Vyaz'ma and Bryansk Pockets by 12 October, and the eighty-six Red Army divisions originally trapped within, Bock could now focus on a final strike against Moscow, without concern for his rear areas. In the aftermath of such seemingly catastrophic losses, for German leadership it once again seemed difficult to conceive that the Soviets now possessed the requisite strength or endurance to offer an effective defence; this time before their capital.[34] Confident of victory, that day Hitler had OKW issue an order that, 'The Führer has reaffirmed that the surrender of Moscow will not be accepted, even if it is offered by the enemy . . .' and that, 'Everyone who tries to leave the city and pass through our positions must be fired upon and driven back . . . It would be utterly irresponsible to risk the lives of German soldiers to save Russian towns from fires or feed their populations at Germany's expense.'

As Second Panzer and Sixth Armies respectively continued to advance to the north-east and south-east the gap between their inner flanks commensurately widened. Even though Soviet forces in the area remained weak following the Kyiv Pocket's destruction the unavoidable gaps in the lengthening German line required XXXXVIII Motorized Army Corps to help shore them up. With the shrinking perimeter east of Trubchevsk no longer requiring 16th and part of 25th Motorized Infantry Divisions both were essentially freed to follow 9th Panzer Division, as it crossed the Svapa and struck for Fatezh. Compounding the continuing problems with keeping Guderian supplied over poor roads, on 13 October Red Army forces that had recently escaped the Bryansk Pocket struck 9th Panzer Division's administrative and supply services south of Sevsk. Without the accompanying butcher and bakery units, and no flour to be found in the Dmitriyev-L'govskiy area, personnel were sent further afield to confiscate quantities from civilians and mills, and take them to makeshift ovens to at least temporarily provide 9th Panzer Division with bread. Local meats and produce were to be similarly taken as an expedient. Unlike XXIV and XXXXVII Motorized Corps' need for large quantities of fuel to maintain their advance tempos and keep the enemy off balance, XXXXVIII Motorized Corps' more limited role of flank protection meant the 60m^3 of fuel located a few kilometres south-west of Dmitriyev-L'govskiy, however small, allowed 9th Panzer Division to continue at least as far as Fatezh.[35]

25th Motorized Infantry Division (at the disposition of Second Panzer Army to XXXXVIII Motorized Army Corps (15 October))
95th Infantry Division (XXXV to XXXIV High Command) (16 October))

Following the collapse of the Vyaz'ma Pocket on 14 October the bulk of the German Ninth Army was freed to reinforce Fourth Panzer Army, whose forward elements approached to within 70km of downtown Moscow. Further south along the River Oka, Fourth Army had already moved past Kaluga, while Guderian, having the furthest to travel to encircle the enemy capital, continued to struggle to advance beyond Mtsensk, some 300km from its goal.[36] With Bock moving into the Mozhaisk Line, however quickly constructed, it served to slow his advance as much as days of cold rain and soft terrain, and helped the enemy compensate for its largely depleted state.[37] While Army Group Centre made slow, but steady progress its Second Army finally crushed what remained of the encircled Soviet Fiftieth Army north-east of Bryansk on 17 October. In an effort to break 4th Panzer Division's impasse at Mtsensk, at 0900hrs 'Kampfgruppe Kleemann' (3 PD) sent armour and mounted riflemen through the Dubrovskiy area towards the River Oka, which 'Kampfgruppe Schmidt-Ott' had reached the previous day. In something of a mixed blessing Luftwaffe reconnaissance sighted long lines of Soviet forces withdrawing to the north-east of Mtsensk, and although this would enable Langermann to finally get moving, it only delayed fighting them again during the battle for Tula. Over the next few days, Second Panzer Army worked to reorganize now that the trapped remnants of the Soviet Third and Thirteenth Armies teetered on oblivion east of Trubchevsk and Lemelsen reoriented his entire command to a north-east advance axis.[38]

LIII Army Corps (56th, 112th, and 167th Infantry Division) (to Second Panzer Army (19 October))
95th Infantry Division (Removed from XXXIV High Command (19 October))
XXXXIII Army Corps (31st Infantry Division) (to Second Panzer Army (19 October))

Much as OKW communiqués would include that Typhoon was progressing according to plan (*planmaessig*), months of hard campaigning, insufficient replacements, a homeland economy that had yet to transition to a wartime footing, and a host of other factors had eroded the *Ostheer*'s sharp edge. For Army Group Centre the return of operational movement once the ground hardened and a noticeable decline in their adversary's numbers gave many Landsers optimism. With any offer to surrender Moscow to be rejected in favour of encircling and starving the city into submission, planning for any subsequent action remained nebulous and rather inconceivable to the victor; as if the Red Army would simply see the supposed futility of continuing and give up.

XXXXIII Army Corps (31st Infantry Division) (removed from Second Panzer Army (20 October))

Although largely freed up to direct all its energy towards its primary task, weather and poor terrain stymied Second Panzer Army's best efforts to quickly capture Tula. Instead, over the last few days the formation's frontage had changed little, with XXXXVII and XXXXVIII Motorized Army Corps reorganising from north of Kursk to Orel, and LIII Army Corps moving on an advance axis that would take them between Kaluga and Orel. Key to the offensive, XXIV Motorized Army Corp remained held up at Mtsensk, which Guderian attributed to a lack of German armour/artillery coordination.[39] As 3rd Panzer Division elements continued to work on unhinging the northern flank of these stubborn defenders, as a reward for all his achievements across Eastern Poland, Belorussia, Ukraine, and Russia, at 1250hrs on 21 October Model received word of his promotion to command XXXXI Motorized Army Corps under Hoth.[40] Retroactively made a Lieutenant General (*General der Panzertruppe*) to 1 October, he would remain to complete the present action (appropriately coined 'Final Hunt' ('*Schlußjagd*')) until his replacement, Brigadier Hermann Breith, arrived from his position as General of Mobile Troops within OKH.

17th Panzer Division (XXXXVII to XXIV Motorized Army Corps (22 October))
296th Infantry Division (removed from XXXV High Command (22 October))

Having reoriented to the east along a broad frontage, 18th Panzer Division took Fatezh on 22 October to cut the Kursk–Orel road, but its 18th Panzer Regiment remained north of Mtsensk to assist Model. Divided into a northern Kampfgruppe under Eberbach (4 PD) and a southern one based around 3rd Rifle Brigade, 3rd Panzer Division pushed up to assembly positions along a moderately defended River Zusha. Since 39th Engineer Battalion repaired the recently collapsed bridge about 6km downriver from Mtsensk, and 8./ and 6./394th Motorized Rifle Regiment had respectively established a bridgehead at Rozhenets and Kokurenkova, Model's positions beyond the rivers expanded and joined with 4th Panzer Division's left. With road conditions exacerbating limited fuel supplies a lorry convoy in Glausunovo was tasked with getting more from 18th Panzer Regiment, which was temporarily allocated to Eberbach's 5th Panzer Brigade at 1400hrs and ordered to follow 6th Panzer Regiment's lead.[41] With a prime mover carrying seventy-five 20l canisters assigned to each of the participating panzer battalions, and one towing a trailer of four-times the amount for each panzer regiment, Model had some insurance as he advanced to clear enemy forces north of Mtsensk and reach the Chern' area and re-establish his primary supply route back through Orel.[42]

Following a German bombardment early on 23 October that targeted the Zusha's far bank both groups set off during what was to be the beginning of nearly a week of overcast, rainy weather that saturated the already soft surrounding farm and grassland. On crossing the Belev–Mtsensk road III./6th Panzer Regiment ran into Soviet tanks, artillery, and infantry around Borodenki. As additional elements of 'Kampfgruppe Eberbach' arrived more Red Army armour and supporting units continued to hinder his eastward advance into the next day. II./3rd Rifle Regiment had at least advanced 20km to secure the high ground north-east of Lobanovo.

1st Cavalry Division (removed from XXXXVII Motorized Army Corps (24 October))

On a foggy, near freezing 24 October the Orel–Tula Rollbahn remained in good condition compared with the surrounding secondary routes, which frequently needed corduroy support from the region's abundant birch trees. With Breith now in command, 3rd Panzer Division negotiated enemy minefields to capture Chern' and finally undercut the Soviet hold on Mtsensk. During the night of 24/25 October III./6th Panzer Regiment established positions south of the village where Soviet forces pulled out of the area to the accompaniment of often heavy skirmishing. Although Second Air Fleet got 662 aircraft into the fight on 24 October, lingering bad weather and difficulty getting fuel shipments to the various Luftwaffe airfields hamstrung replicating these numbers for future actions.[43] With XXIV Motorized Army Corps freed to resume its advance, vehicles throughout the *Ostheer* neared the end of their operational lives, as mechanisms wore out from prolonged operation in poor weather, worse terrain, and towing stricken comrades. Considering the widespread use of numerous captured and militarized civilian vehicles to provide mobility on the battlefield and compensate for insufficient domestic production, the vast number of incompatible parts proved insurmountable. With many of the panzern having exceeded 5,000km of use, and were thus due for engine replacement, the time available to achieve victory in the East became ever more acute.[44]

10th Motorized Infantry Division (XXIV to XXXXVII Motorized Army Corps (25 October))

XXXXVIII Motorized Army Corps (removed from Second Panzer Army (25 October))
XXXIV High Command (removed from Second Panzer Army (25 October))
XXXV High Command (removed from Second Panzer Army (25 October))
293rd Infantry Division (removed from XXXV High Command (25 October))
25th Motorized Infantry Division (XXXXVIII Army Corps to XXXXVII Motorized Army Corps (25 October))

Attempting to make stands, however brief, as the depleted Red Army fell back onto Moscow, options to trade space for time in which to bring on reinforcements were narrowing.[45] On 25 October Guderian watched Großdeutschland advance on Chern' and join 'Kampfgruppe Eberbach' as vanguard. Continuing to struggle with insufficient fuel shipments, as German armour required the 'eyes' and support of accompanying infantry one battalion from Großdeutschland rode into the combat zone atop the tanks, and would dismount to fight.[46] During its withdrawal Fiftieth Army had established a defensive line connecting the village with Arsen'yevo–Odoyevo–Khanino, and along Second Panzer Army's path to Tula.

Moving on Tula
134th Infantry Division (to XXXIV High Command (26 October))
XXXXIII Army Corps (31st Infantry Division) (to Second Panzer Army (26 October))

By the end of October LIII Army Corps reached the roughly 90m-wide River Oka between Orel and Belev, while downriver XXXXIII Army Corps moved along the waterway's left bank before turning to the north-east on reaching the confluence with the Upa. To Guderian's north, however, Fourth Army's seemingly unstoppable advance was being ground down in Soviet defences stretching south to Serpukhov. Over the next two days Typhoon ground to a halt along lengthy stretches of the front line due to stiffening Soviet resistance, mud, and a host of other issues that cumulatively caught up with the Germans. Even though masses of traffic had by now considerably degraded the Orel–Tula road, with no better option XXIV and XXXXVII Motorized Army Corps' were forced along the congested, constraining route.[47] With reports of additional Soviet forces arriving to the east, on 27 October Guderian ordered LIII Army Corps to cut across his primary line of advance to establish a presence on his right between Yepifan' and Stalinogorsk.

After what seemed like a never-ending string of cold, rainy days that frustrated movement and made everything that much more miserable, a freeze on 29 October at least helped solidify the roads, although drivers needed to take heed of the resulting ice. As indicative of the heavy, typically chaotic fighting many of the Soviet rifle divisions before Tula fought on as pitiful fragments of their previous strength.[48] Recently arriving Red Army reinforcements, however, were at least roughly full strength, as evidenced when 413th Rifle Division detrained at Stalinogorsk that day.[49] In an effort to take Tula without delay at 0530hrs the next morning German artillery engaged the city's defences amid another cold rain. A 6km-long antitank ditch that the area's mostly women and non-military age civilians had dug across Guderian's most likely advance axis proved to have an unfinished section about 3km south of the town centre. Großdeutschland and armour from 3rd Panzer Division followed up with an attack on these trenches and barricades at the bombardment's conclusion.[50] With surprise lost 'Kampfgruppe Eberbach' advenced from the high ground along the city's southern edge against NKVD and minimally trained workers from Volokhovo to the north-east.[51] Soviet artillery from north of Tula and armour from 32nd Tank Brigade added to their platoon and company-sized infiltrations to eject the Germans, who later applied their own artillery from Kosaya Gora to finally force Red Army forces to withdraw. Lacking reinforcement, worn out, and often sick, Eberbach's men were soon forced to pull back. Struggling to get his subordinate formations forward in strength, and unable to take Tula in a *coup de main*, Schweppenburg proposed a temporary halt to reorganize and replenish until colder weather firmed up the battlezone and improved mobility. The city would simply be bypassed and enveloped from the west during the drive on Moscow; actions with which Guderian concurred.

Chapter 10

Tula, 1 November–5 December 1941

By the beginning of November 1941 Army Group Centre's successes at Vyaz'ma and Bryansk and the approach to Moscow meant that Bock appeared to be on the precipice of securing what many believed was the campaign-winning prize. As much as the Germans capturing the capital would likely not force the Red Army into a general surrender, considering they could simply continue to fall back on the Ural Mountains where their industry was relocating alongside existing factories and continue the fight, it would provide the attacker with the nation's largest road, rail, and telephone communications hub, not to mention potential housing over the winter. At the southern end of Bock's front line that now ran from Kalinin on the River Volga down to Volokolamsk, Naro-Fominsk, Serpukhov, to near Tula, the final location's industrial assets and infrastructure made its capture a prerequisite for Guderian continuing his part of the offensive.[1] In spite of German efforts to prevent often sizeable portions of the Soviet Fiftieth, Third, and Thirtieth Armies from escaping encirclement and annihilation, many of these formations' personnel rejoined the Moscow defence.[2]

On a misty 2 November XXIV Motorized Army Corps continued its painfully slow push on Tula through the morass that had recently been considered roads. With Großdeutschland already at the city's doorstep to cover Schweppenburg's right, 17th Panzer Division's advance detachment moved off to the south-east towards Stalinogorsk. Until the heavily backed up traffic along the Orel–Tula road could be thinned, 18th Panzer Division remained around the former. To help ensure the necessary movement of combat, communication, and logistics elements along this vital artery, Reich Labour Service (*Reichsarbeitsdienst*)/RAD personnel worked tirelessly to improve it. With the Soviet Twenty-Sixth Army organizing to block Guderian's advance axis, during the night of 5/6 November temperatures dropped to a frigid -29 °C. Later that day he was flown through the wet snow to his front line.[3] With the Germans at the end of overextended supply lines, short on supplies and resources, and lacking the necessary industrial output and access to raw materials to compete in a lengthy, attritional war, such an opportunity might not present itself again. While Bock's men pressed on Army Group Centre's requirements for thirty-one trainloads of supplies each day to remain combat effective had by 11 October dropped to twenty, and then to sixteen on 6 November.[4] With Second Panzer Army's front line between Orel and Tula changing little over the last few days, XXXV and XXIV High Commands, and XXXXVIII Motorized Army Corps, worked to shore up Guderian's weak right flank as far south as Kursk. Temporarily unable to conduct wide-ranging operations due to road conditions, 25th Motorized Infantry Division spent the time cleaning the area around Sevsk of lingering enemy forces, including shooting fifty people deemed to be partisans on 6 November.

With the season's first significant freeze occurring on 7 November, and improving movement for both sides, the first cases of frostbite among Guderian's ranks followed, which if untreated risked bone and muscle necrosis. While German winter clothing was available in rear area warehouses distribution to those who needed it was as hamstrung by over-extended logistics that had prioritized fuel and ammunition shipments. Wool greatcoats were dolled out to provide welcomed resistance to rain, wind, and cold temperatures common in Western Europe, but their recipients in the East soon found them insufficient. Continuing the previous day's overcast mix of rain and light snow, on 9 November Guderian sent 'Kampfgruppe Eberbach' to assist LIII Army Corps and assumed a defensive stance to absorb what he expected were imminent enemy counterattacks east and west of Tula.[5] In what was a necessity German forces were often shuffled to ensure the best men and equipment were at the fore, and sufficiently armed and fuelled. As such, 17th Panzer Division was attached to XXIV Motorized Army Corps and moved to Plavsk, but with fresh Soviet forces appearing east of Chern', Arnim was reinforced with parts of XXXXVII Motorized Army Corps. As an indication of available German numbers increasingly being insufficient, four battalions from 4th Panzer Division were forced to hold a 32km stretch of front to maintain contact with LIII Army Corps and 3rd Panzer Division.[6] With the Soviet Twenty-Sixth Army offering a determined stand west of Tula, Guderian, unwilling to incur unnecessary losses that would sap Second Panzer Army's endurance, adjusted his attack axis around the troublesome area and set off to the north-east. Considering the snowy, often frigid weather in which his men now fought, Lemelsen issued Corps Order No. 46 that included the need to provide accommodations to ensure his advancing command's success; a rather unrealistic decree given how stretched and harried Guderian's command was.[7]

By mid-November Second Panzer Army was a rather ungainly grouping considering its seven subordinate corps were distributed along a 380km frontage. As Guderian struggled to keep moving, and in the necessary strength, in the critical Tula sector XXXXIII Army and XXIV Motorized Army Corps respectively continued to make steady progress to its north-west and south. On Second Panzer Army's still fluid right flank, LIII Army Corps had moved up to cover what had been Schweppenburg's hanging right flank. Similarly filling in the newly captured territory XXXXVII Motorized Army Corps advanced

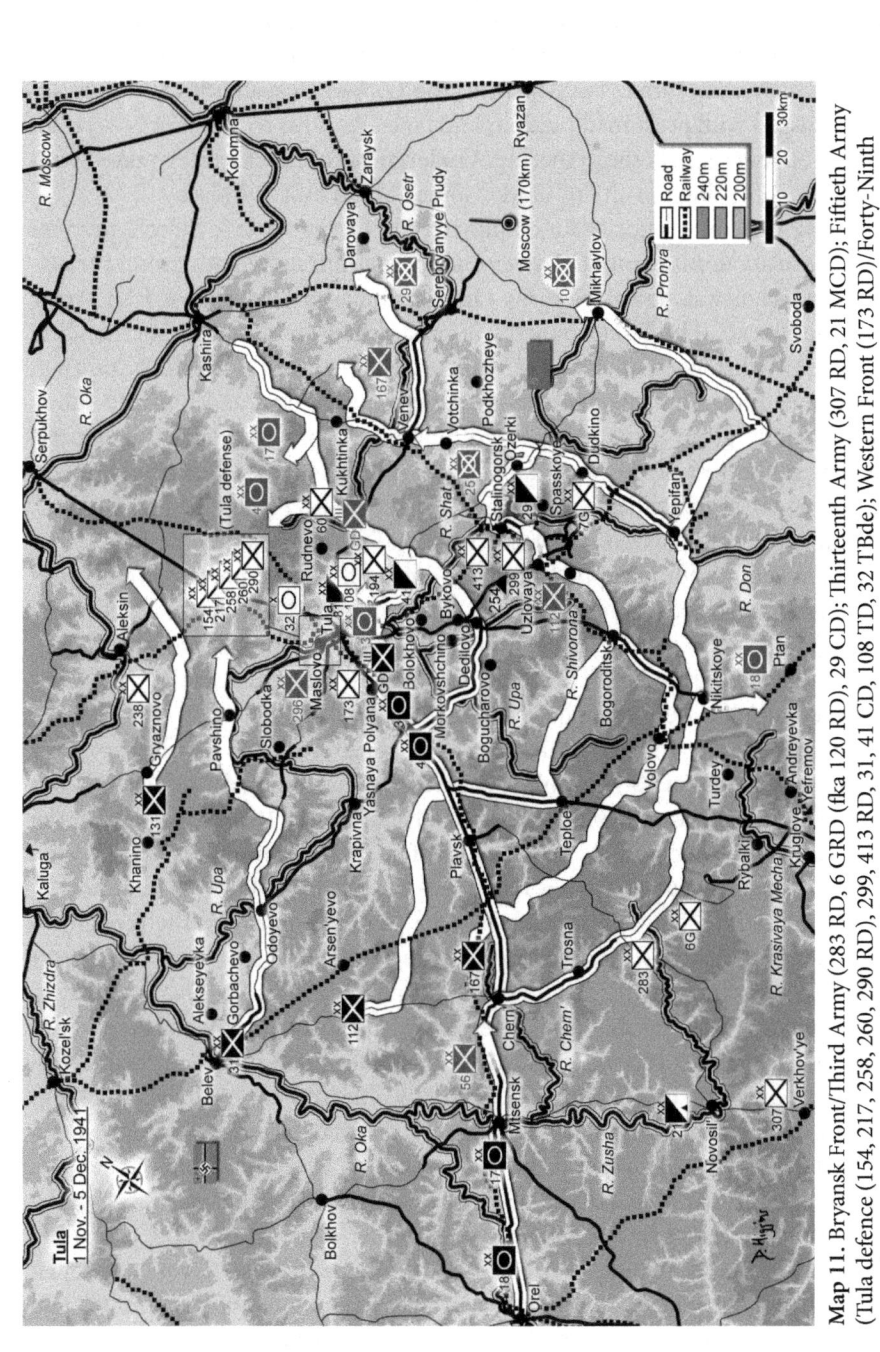

Map 11. Bryansk Front/Third Army (283 RD, 6 GRD (fka 120 RD), 29 CD); Thirteenth Army (307 RD, 21 MCD); Fiftieth Army (Tula defence (154, 217, 258, 260, 290 RD), 299, 413 RD, 31, 41 CD, 108 TD, 32 TBde); Western Front (173 RD)/Forty-Ninth Army (60, 194, 238 RD, 7 GRD (fka 64 RD)). TsAMO, f.202, op.5, d.64, l.402a.

along the Orel–Tula road before turning to the south-east as far as Turdey, along the River Mecha. Even though the chiefs-of-staff of the three army groups, their respective army corps, and Second Panzer Army met on 13 November in Orsha, during which an accurate assessment of the *Ostheer*'s capabilities and logistics was discussed with presumed candour and facts. As if his recent efforts were not difficult enough during the gathering, Guderian was unrealistically tasked with ultimately capturing the city of Gorki, some 400km east of Moscow![8]

During this time, once again employing his Fiesler Fi-156 'Storch' to more easily move about his command given the present difficulty with ground transport, Guderian was flown from his Orel headquarters for that of LIII Army Corps at Plavsk. The lightweight plane, renowned for its very short landing and take-off distances, was well suited for reconnaissance, artillery spotting, and liaison duties, but not the sub-freezing temperatures and blustery snowfall; especially given its valuable cargo. Forced to land at Chern', the general was driven the rest of the way across the white landscape. During the meeting the corps commander, Lieutenant General (*General der Infanterie*) Karl Weisenberger, summarized the successful fight for Teploe and Guderian offered for him to keep 'Kampfgruppe Eberbach' during his slated push on Volovo and Stalinogorsk. As a consequence of this weakening of XXIV Army Corps, and with only a one-day supply of fuel on hand, Schweppenburg expressed his inability to advance beyond his Tula–Bogoroditsk line for at least six days, until the necessary supplies were brought forward.

25th Motorized Infantry Division's spearhead reached the Kromy area during the evening of 13 November. Schweppenburg ordered Munzel's II./6th Panzer Regiment-based Kampfgruppe to advance to the River Upa and cut the Orel–Tula road.[9] The unit cleared the hilly, forested area from Yasnaya Polyana to the north-west, but the going remained frustratingly slow.[10] While most of the group returned to its original positions from the morning the reconnaissance battalion continued northward to secure the airfield at Maslovo against negligible resistance. Being just downriver from Tula, however, its proximity to Soviet forces prevented its immediate use by the Luftwaffe. With the bulk of 17th Panzer Division renewing its advance on Tula, and Großdeutschland having moved up to the city's southern edge alongside 3rd Panzer Division as far as the Upa reality soon snuffed out the flicker of German progress. Once again, no sooner had XXIV Motorized Army Corps started to regain some momentum than it was forced to spend the next two days reorganizing and resupplying for another lurch eastward. During an even colder morning than the preceding one, on 14 November Guderian visited 167th Infantry Division, which had just inserted itself between 112th Infantry Division pushing out of Bogoroditsk and 18th Panzer Division to the south-west. After the usual queries regarding its battlefield situation and capabilities, and responding with insight and direction, Guderian repeated his fact-finding at about noon with 112th Infantry Division, which had recently had several hundred of its soldiers removed from front-line duties with frostbite.

With Eberbach down to just fifty active tanks every effort was made to keep them serviceable. Considering the difficulties of labour-intensive maintenance, heavy spare parts, engine replacement, and a myriad other components and services on a good day, the extreme cold made misery out of such activities. Several weeks previously three Central Replacement Lagers had been respectively established for Army Groups North, Centre, and South at Pskov, Borisov, and Berdychiv, but breakdowns in the necessary lorry transports hampered getting these critical spare parts to where they were needed. For the crews operating during such cold daytime temperatures, let alone those at night, 'poor circulation in the extremities increases the danger of cold injury', such as numb fingers adversely impacted fine manual dexterity.[11] For the tankers, supplies of track cleats and salve to keep telescopic gunsights from frosting over had yet to arrive in quantity. Condensation on the uninsulated vehicle ceilings produced water that dripped onto crews and equipment which added to their discomfort, as did having to wear heavier clothing inside their already cramped fighting compartments.

On a frigid, clear 15 November Bock initiated what was essentially Typhoon's second, and hopefully final, stage. Instead of the seventy-two divisions that quickly crushed Red Army forces around Vitebsk and Bryansk just six weeks ago, thirty-six now continued the offensive against Moscow, with the remainder having transitioned to defending the new front line and mopping up lingering fighting to the west. Along Guderian's left the Soviets resumed their attacks on XXXXIII Motorized Army Corps, which struck eastward between Alekseyevka and Aleksin, and into what was a land bridge separating the Rivers Oka and Upa. Short on fuel, Lemelsen spoke with Guderian and decided to take Yefremov, believing its capture would unhinge the Soviet defence in the sector. Back at Rastenburg, Hitler continued to question the almost singular importance Guderian, and others, placed on capturing Moscow, and gravitated towards replacing Brauchitsch with the Führer's ardent supporter, Schmundt.[12]

296th Infantry Division (to Army Group Centre Reserve (Second Panzer Army sector) (17 November))

With the Orel–Tula road having sufficiently firmed and been shored up to again enable the reasonable flow of supplies, over the last few days 18th Panzer Division had maintained a steady, eastward pace across the monotonous, largely colourless landscape. In reaching the River Krasivaya Mecha near Yefremov to cover LIII Army Corps' hanging southern flank until Second Army arrived, on 18 November Nehring's advance element scouted north towards a crossing at Rybalki, where enemy defences were found to be weak. On approaching the waterway its 18th Panzer Regiment encountered entrenched enemy forces in the strength of two regiments backed with artillery, but with the bridge damaged and unsuited to heavy vehicular traffic the Germans avoided forcing the issue for now. To protect the right flank 88th Motorized Reconnaissance Battalion went as far as the hills west of Krugloye, while 5th Motorized Machine-Gun Battalion moved up to provide welcomed defensive firepower. Much as with the broader *Ostheer* at this time, Lemelsen continued to make progress below the surface supply problems, bitter winter weather, sickness, exhaustion, injury, and the seemingly endless fighting and manoeuvring cumulatively eroding his men's morale and resolve.

With Fourth Army moving parallel to the north the inability of the Germans to achieve deep, converging forces meant its tactically frontal attacks served more to push Soviet forces back rather than cut them off from resupply and defeat them at comparatively less cost. What appeared on Hitler's map tables as the same German formations that had cut an impressive swathe across Belorussia, Ukraine, and Western Russia were in reality now suitable for defence only. Although the time for the *Ostheer* to intentionally transition from the offensive, while they still retained sufficient strength to hold their positions and apply a limited, scorched earth withdrawal to create a buffer and hinder enemy counterattacks had arguably passed, the advance trudged on. With many Landsers perhaps reassuring themselves that the Red Army might finally be on its last legs, they redoubled their resolve to complete what promised to be the campaign's final offensive, and possibly that of the war.

In LIII Army Corps' sector a seemingly minor, but ominous event occurred, when 112th Infantry Division encountered fresh enemy forces near Uzlovaya. Faltering before what was identified as 238th Rifle Division out of Central Asia, and its forty tanks, the adjacent German 167th Infantry Division had to divert elements from the main thrust to help stabilize the sector. During the afternoon LIII Army Corps headquarters notified that of 4th Panzer Division about the incident, and later discovered the Soviet 817th Rifle Regiment (239 RD) was quickly moving southward, and that other Red Army units should be expected to arrive and detrain, including 269th Rifle Division around Nikitskoye.[13] To address the new threat 29th Motorized Infantry Division deviated from its advance towards Serebryanyye Prudy and Zaraysk for the west and into 239th Rifle Division's rear.[14] On the strategic level, with Japan having signed the 'Berlin Pact' on 27 September 1940 that obligated them to attack whoever attacked Germany, Stalin was presented with a boon that may not have been immediately apparent. Combined with Japanese representatives later signing a neutrality treaty with Moscow in April 1941, the need to maintain a strong Red Army presence in the East was diminished and focus could be maintained in the Western Russian Theatre.[15]

At 0545hrs on 18 November the renewed German offensive commenced during yet another uncomfortably cold day where the hardening ground made digging trenches and defensive positions using hand tools very difficult. With what had devolved into a test of endurance and willpower Guderian believed his improperly clothed and supplied men were unable to march more than 10km each day, as Grolig's 33rd Motorized Rifle Regiment-based group advanced across the low, mostly treeless hills to the east to reach Dedilovo at about 0730hrs. Under a partly cloudy sky Ju-87s tried to aid the ground offensive by targeting the village's western edge, but the Soviets had already pulled back from the area. After a 5-hour fight that regularly devolved into close-combat to clear its wooden and thatched roof structures the Germans secured a now burning Dedilovo.[16] As part of 4th Panzer Division's effort to secure Stalinogorsk, during the early afternoon 'Kampfgruppe Eberbach' advanced on Morkovshchino, although without 17th Motorcycle Rifle Regiment, and elements of 27th Motorized Artillery Regiment, as they were returned to XXIV Motorized Army Corps' control. Overcoming several of its tanks breaking down in the icy waters of the high-banked River Shivorona to approach the village as dusk descended, eight tanks from the group's 39th Panzer Regiment deviated for a bridge 16km upriver that the Soviets pre-emptively blew up. Further east II./12th and 33rd Motorized Rifle Regiments established positions approaching Uzlovaya, while nearly 100km to the south 18th Panzer Division hustled to get as many of its worn out and broken down vehicles as possible operational for its assault on Yefremov. What Second Panzer Army fuel that remained, after ensuring Nehring was fully supplied, went to 10th Motorized Infantry Division, as it struck out eastward for Yepifan'.

While the predominantly infantry formations that had eliminated the Bryansk and Vyaz'ma Pockets had been granted time in which to move up to the present front line, the Soviets reciprocated as Guderian's advance axis became apparent. During a heavily overcast 19 November XXIV Motorized Army Corps took Bolokhovo. As German strength was whittled down, and the breadth of the attack frontage correspondingly narrowed, to maintain the sharp points necessary to punch through the similarly solidifying enemy defences German units were hurriedly shuffled and adjusted as circumstances warranted. At about 1100hrs, 'Kampfgruppe Eberbach' struck from the east, along with 33rd Motorized Rifle Regiment and II./12th Motorized Infantry Regiment on its left, now down to just 120 men. Weathering enemy fire from both sides his advance took on a wedge shape that managed to hack out a respectable gap in the enemy lines. To combat the cold, which sapped Guderian's strength and exacerbated logistics difficulties, even though 4th Panzer Division reportedly had sufficient amount of winter clothing available, suitable housing was in short supply.[17] Just a week previously, Wagner had notified Halder that no logistical infrastructure could be quickly created for Army Group Centre, or even its attached armies before late November 1941, and that winter clothing for Bock's command was only scheduled to start arriving at Second Panzer Army's sector in late January 1942![18]

Hugging Tula's outskirts, 3rd Panzer Division went on the offensive in the industrial and residential area near Bolokhovo, where Soviet infantry and armour put up sufficiently tough resistance to halt Breith's drive by the evening.[19] Throughout a cold, intermittently light snowfall on 20 November about 500 Soviet soldiers penetrated into an area 5km north-west of Uzlovaya where just one company from I./33rd Motorized Rifle Regiment was on hand to present a defence. To assist, while II./12th Infantry Regiment was to cover the northern flank 8km north-east of downtown Tula, Schweppenburg ordered a group of heavy field guns moved so far forward that together with 210mm heavy howitzers they could conduct a sustained barrage on the threatened area. Eberbach's 5th Panzer Brigade reported enemy infantry advancing in parallel with the direction of the attack with a force of one battalion on Hill 254, but without reconnaissance elements.[20] Responding to the threat, Langermann set his three Kampfgruppen to action, one of which through Bykovo, with its 34th Motorcycle and 7th Motorized Reconnaissance Battalions, to secure the division's northern flank, although delays resulted due to the intersection with columns from 17th Panzer Division. At 1100hrs the Kampfgruppe set around the monocled Colonel Dietrich von Saucken's 4th Motorized Rifle Brigade struck out eastward, with its newly attached II./12th Motorized Infantry Regiment, and into strong enemy forces and sustained combat south-east of Bogucharovo. In the centre, 'Kampfgruppe Eberbach' engaged in fierce tank fight near Dedilovo that included KV-1s, and recently arrived Soviet medium artillery.

Yefremov

With 293rd Infantry Division covering its right, 18th Panzer Division moved to Yefremov's western edge on 22 November. During what was another cold, snowy day German forces made progress but there always seemed to be depressingly more terrain and enemy combatants to conquer beyond the horizon. Even though part of 10th Motorized Infantry Division operated 80km to the northeast its 41st Motorized Infantry Regiment, having been temporarily attached to Nehring, took the town's northern half, including one of the country's three synthetic rubber production factories. With a Soviet train having arrived along the adjacent rail line, infantry, with supporting armour from 150th Tank Brigade, attempted to oust the German incursion. Even though the Germans succeeded in overcoming often bitter street fighting to rebuff the attack, converging threats to their hold on Yefremov remained. Just before noon word arrived that a large column of Red Army motorized and horse-drawn traffic was making its way south from Andreyevka, with the seeming intent of intervening, while Luftwaffe aircraft engaged a second large column advancing along the rail line towards Yefremov. As a result, 52nd Motorized Rifle Regiment (18 PD) was to secure a bridgehead over the River Krasivaya Mecha prior to any enemy build-up, from which further eastward progress could be made. 18th Panzer Regiment proved unable to join with 88th Panzer Reconnaissance Battalion and was momentarily tasked with protecting the division's supply line. Once the road north of Yefremov was opened 41st Motorized Infantry Regiment would then rejoin its parent 10th Motorized Infantry Division, although its 20th Motorized Infantry Regiment and 40th Motorcycle Battalion were only now approaching Teploe and would be out of any immediate fight.

Even though Second Panzer Army continued to make progress near Venev, Stalinogorsk, and Uzlovaya, from Bock's broader vantage the battlefield looked anything but positive, given his largely stalled lines before Moscow. The Soviets leveraged interior lines that included paved, all-weather roads radiating from the capital to provide regular resupply to their front line, although the lack of suitable alternatives regularly snarled traffic by channelling march columns through the city's centre. With Guderian intent on reinforcing his northward thrust between Tula and Yepifan' and bypassing the Soviet Fiftieth Army, as much as every German unit was needed on the front line he sent 35th Motorized Infantry Regiment (25 MID) to the Plavsk–Krapivna area, where the bridge over the nearby reservoir's dam was found to have been blown up by the withdrawing Soviets. With the move enabling a reinforced 71st Motorized Infantry Regiment to move up to Mtsensk–Gorbachevo, both units were subsequently designated as Second Panzer Army reserves. A Red Army penetration of 5th Motorized Machine-Gun Battalion's lines south of Yefremov gave the Germans little respite, as they tried to secure Guderian's right flank and allow XXIV and XXXXVII Motorized and LIII Army Corps to focus on completing Tula's encirclement and pressing for crossings over the River Oka. Due to the declining strength of German formations, and their correspondingly thinning attack sectors, the need to concentrate at the point of impact and maintain momentum at this critical stage of the campaign grew increasingly difficult.

On a partly sunny, but still freezing 23 November, according to Lieutenant Colonel Wolf von Kahlden, High Command liaison to Hoth and Guderian, the latter planned to use Tula as Second Panzer Army's winter quarters after first laying waste to the area to its east to provide a buffer.[21] Guderian visited Bock to personally lobby to have his orders changed to assume a defensive posture, to which the field marshal agreed to forward the request to OKH. At 1515hrs XXIV Motorized Army Corps reported that 'Kampfgruppe Eberbach', which included a pair of 88mm guns, was to be subordinated to Licht, who although still a colonel had been promoted to command 17th Panzer Division on 11 July 1941. Arnim, in turn, was tasked to lead XXXIX Army Corps (AG North).[22] With one battery of III./103rd Artillery Regiment disbanded for lack of prime movers, 5 hours later II./63rd Motorized Infantry Regiment (17 PD) pushed into Venev, having recently ejected Red Army forces from Votchinka. As the division moved across the region's low, snow-covered hills, with their now leafless birch and ash trees, it notified XXIV Motorized Army Corps that its present fuel, oil, and lubricant amounts would only allow for 33rd Motorized Rifle Regiment, with two light artillery elements to continue. At 2115hrs the regiment's adjutant reported that due to lack of transport, 2./ and one platoon of 7./33rd Motorized Rifle Regiment remained footbound. 12th Motorized Rifle Regiment would need two days of reorganization to be made combat capable.[23] To maximize availability the participating vehicles were to avoid moving during the night.

As part of a string of overcast days, with intermittent snow, on 24 November most of the Soviets opposite 18th Panzer Division had withdrawn to the east and north-east, although they remained along the southern bank of the River Krasivaya Mecha and intermittently shelled Yefremov. To the north, with Langermann having recently overcome strong enemy defences and armour in the Uzlovaya area, 4th Panzer Division now crossed the River Shat towards sealing Tula to the east. Ever vigilant about capturing bridges before the retreating Soviets could blow them up, the formation's 2./79th Engineer Battalion removed 300kg of explosives from the nearby depot along the Venev–Uzlovaya rail line, and soon after 610kg from the still-active railway bridge nearby. No Red Army forces were reported in the area, although what were described as two partisan groups were eliminated. While the Germans typically applied the designation broadly to quickly remove a threat, however real or professed, the lack of official uniforms with such combatants conveniently removed what laws of war might otherwise have been accorded to them, however minimal.[24]

With Second Panzer Army having moved up to the Tula sector in strength, XXIV and XXXXVII Motorized, and LIII Army Corps spread out to the north and north-east towards securing the area up to the Oka. Along Guderian's left, Fourth Army was intended to advance north of the waterway, and in doing so cover his flank, while the general continued on to connect with Third Panzer Group and encircle Moscow. Until then, as 167th Infantry Division fought its way into Stalinogorsk explosions were heard, as Red Army and NKVD personnel blew up or burned industrial facilities, mines, cultural institutions, schools, hospitals, and houses to deny them to the advancing Germans. Further north 'Kampfgruppe Eberbach' operated with 17th Panzer Division, which took Venev. While 56th Infantry Division largely sat out the Tula offensive between Bryansk and Orel, 112th Infantry Division relocated to a position a few kilometres east of Uzlovaya. With 29th Motorized Infantry Division advancing off to the right and expected to encircle the industrial Stalinogorsk area and the defending Soviet 239th Rifle Division, however, these two infantry divisions were to temporarily halt their offensive actions until the matter became more settled. In the relative absence of Soviet resistance east of Stalinogorsk, 10th Reconnaissance Battalion (10 MID) sprinted ahead to secure Mikhaylov to get a crossing over the River Pronya (different from the Mogilev sector). Along Guderian's far left flank XXXXIII Motorized Army Corps approached the River Upa, but its ability to actively assist with Tula's encirclement was waning. On the centre and right LIII Army Corps and XXXXVII Motorized Army Corps finally broke through the Soviet Fiftieth Army and were respectively advancing to the north-east and east.

As the majority of 18th Panzer Division solidified its position near Yefremov, its 18th Motorized Reconnaissance Battalion reached south-eastern Svoboda. Fanning out behind, and into the sparsely defended east and north-east, 10th Motorized Infantry Division's advance detachments created a loose front line for XXXXVII Motorized Army Corps and captured Mikhaylov, whose road hub and rail line would serve to facilitate badly needed logistics close to the fighting. Capitalizing on Löper's success, Guderian ordered him to sever the rail line running south from Ryazan, some 60km distant, as well as the much less realistic one east of Moscow. Likely feeling optimistic about their rapid advance Licht's 17th Panzer Division struck along the Kukhtinka–Kashira road for the River Oka. To the rear, 104th Antiaircraft Regiment assets were brought up to help protect captured crossings over the Shat, and maintain the logistics flow. In what was yet another troubling sign for the Germans reports throughout Second Panzer Army increasingly referenced its soldiers were becoming 'resentful', with much of this feeling stemming from a lack of sufficient, dedicated antiaircraft weapons with which to effectively engage the growing enemy air threat.[25] While the bulk of 29th Motorized Infantry Division remained around Podkhozheye its reconnaissance elements moved on for Zaraysk and a crossing over the River Osetr. Just before midnight on 25/26 November its I./15th Motorized Infantry Regiment was driven back just north of Dudkino by reportedly large enemy forces with heavy losses.[26] As much as Second Panzer Army's efforts seemed to be making headway the difficulty in getting supplies to where they were needed and in the necessary quantities forced the formation to temporally halt its advance to the River Oka.

While 17th Panzer and 10th Motorized Infantry Divisions struggled to reach the River Oka, LIII Army Corps moved into the Stalinogorsk area towards providing infantry to add bulk to Guderian's offensive and help hold captured territory. Just downriver from its Stalinogorsk reservoir origin, 167th Infantry Division crossed the River Don to inflict reportedly high casualties against 239th Rifle Division. With the formation forcing the Soviets from the area Guderian stopped at the nearby 71st Motorized Infantry Division, as it moved through the area heading north.[27] Having been recently ejected from Spasskoye, 4th Panzer Division continued its anticlockwise push around Tula's north-east. To keep newly arriving Soviet forces at bay, at 0040hrs on 26 November Langermann ordered part of I./33rd Motorized Rifle Regiment, a contingent of armour, a sixunit battery from 53rd Motorized Rocket Launcher Regiment, and all his available artillery to orient eastward. 12th Motorized Infantry Regiment deviated to its right to help hold Venev 2 hours later. At 0930hrs the commander of the 4th Motorized Rifle Brigade reported that its attack advanced up to the town against heavy defences.[28] During the morning the Germans inserted a dozen tanks that engaged the enemy at about half a kilometre, the latter lacking antitank guns with which to balance the fight.[29] At 1325hrs a radio report indicated that Red Army elements were returning to Stalinogorsk; presumably from 239th Rifle Division. Decreasing German strength, draconian resource prioritization, and numerous Soviet attacks along Second Panzer Army's front took a cumulative, unsustainable toll.

Further to the north, communication was finally established with 63rd and 40th Motorized Rifle Regiments (17 PD), as they looked for an opening on their left into which they would try to establish contact with XXXXIII Army Corps and seal off Tula, while also making for Kashira. To reinforce 29th Motorized Infantry Division's roughly parallel advance on the right towards Kolomna, at 1830hrs 'Kampfgruppe Saucken' was attached to the formation's II./71st Motorized Infantry Regiment. During the clearing up of its recently hit southeastern flank, the division's signals personnel intercepted an order from the Soviet Fiftieth Army to remove 239th Rifle Division through Ozerki, which implied its work of hindering German progress had ceased for the moment. With *Ostheer* dead and wounded numbering 743,112 out of the 3,200,000 that started *Barbarossatag*, on 26 November 1941 German front-line soldiers and officers were increasingly convinced of the futility of continuing their offensive against Moscow.[30] Seemingly no exception, should Guderian's push beyond the Oka prove unfeasible the now iced up barrier would provide a frozen, but still defensible buffer north and east of Tula, following its seemingly imminent fall.[31]

On an overcast 27 November at about 1100hrs a Soviet breakthrough near Kashira caught 17th Panzer Division rather flat-footed, and forced many of its artillery crews to fire over open sights to restore order. Similar resistance cropped up along Guderian's eastern and south-eastern sectors. To hinder any further enemy interference south of the Oka, 29th and 10th Motorized Infantry Division forward detachments respectively sent engineers ahead to blow up the Kolomna road bridge and a section of the rail line to Ryazan. A strong Soviet presence, however, prevented the actions. In an attempt to halt yet another Red Army counterattack, Schweppenburg struck the area near the Ptan rail station. 18th Panzer and 25th Motorized Infantry Divisions (minus 35th Infantry Regiment still in reserve) were ordered to stabilize the area within two days. With much of 293rd Infantry Division (Second Army) having reached Yefremov, it worked to strengthen its position to relieve 18th Panzer Division and 5th Motorized Machine-Gun Battalion for action in the more critical sector.

To directly assess the situation at 29th Motorized Army Division, Guderian met with Boltenstern at about midday on 27 November, before moving on to Dudkino. While in the area he met with the men of 15th Motorized Infantry Regiment, who had recently been subjected to bitter, night-time fighting and high casualties, with rather less-than-comforting words that included, 'Sometimes these things happen.' Compounding the fight's adverse psychological impact on the Landsers, the bodies of fifty of their comrades were found, with wounds commensurate with having been brutally mutilated. While such events commonly occurred in any war, and perhaps more so on the Eastern Front, the culprit was often the by-product of a vicious, chaotic, close-combat fight using bayonets, shovels, and anything else on hand to eliminate the opponent. Regardless of what really happened the scene provoked a grim, brutal visual that prompted the men of 29th Motorized Infantry Division to take out their frustrations on the roughly 1,500 Soviet prisoners taken after the fight. As a typical repercussion for such matters, a few days later fifteen 'Asiatic' Red Army soldiers were executed and left to hang from a nearby village's entrance beam alongside a sign that read, 'These beasts mutilated and murdered wounded German soldiers on the night of 25/26 November 1941.' A steady dose of propaganda, personal experience, groupthink, fear, duty, and self preservation within the context of a war of annihilation not surprisingly promoted a reciprocal cycle of violence and extralegal actions for both sides.[32]

By the end of November 1941 reports from German front-line ground and air assets were indicating that several enemy formations were bulking up for what could only be assumed were forthcoming offensive operations. During the afternoon of the 27th, 63rd and 40th Motorized Rifle Regiments (17 PD) revealed that strong Soviet forces were being unloaded south-east of Kashira, a sector of the Oka XXIV Motorized Army Corps resolved to shore up as soon as possible. Among Licht's three Kampfgruppen only Eberbach's had the fuel to undertake offensive operations, alongside a smaller grouping formed around II./35th Panzer Regiment.[33] At 2330hrs the inevitable happened, as the Soviets unleashed a large offensive from the east to 63rd Motorized Rifle Regiment. Having moved sufficiently north, 33rd Motorized Rifle Regiment helped repulse the threat, after which dispersed, company-sized groups, several pulling sleds to better traverse the snowy terrain, withdrew northward. Although a German fuel and ammunition shipment arrived before midnight on 27/28 November, it did little more than resupply II./103rd Motorized Artillery Regiment. As such, when 'Kampfgruppe Saucken' advanced the following day its 5./ and 11./33rd Motorized Rifle Regiment remained idle for lack of fuel.

296th Infantry Division (Army Group Centre Reserve to XXIV Motorized Army Corps (29 November))

With the Soviet 269th Rifle Division having pushed 18th Motorized Reconnaissance Battalion from its forward position at Skopin the previous day, on 30 November a much more worrisome situation far to the south occurred. With Rundstedt having taken Rostov-on-Don the extended position invited a concentrated enemy response much like that at Yel'nya. Unwilling to sacrifice his men and materiel so that his superiors could leave a marker on their maps in place, the field marshal prudently pulled his over-extended First Army back. Being contrary to Hitler's wishes of physically holding conquered territory (at the expense of mobility) the venerable Prussian commander, and man who helped coordinate the largest encirclement in recorded history, offered his resignation, which was accepted on 1 December 1941. Facing a similar situation, OKW expressed concern about Second Panzer Army's ability to complete its part of Moscow's encirclement.

29th Motorized Infantry Division (XXXXVII Motorized to LIII Army Corps (1 December))

On what was a cloudy, bitterly cold 1 December heavy snow and strong winds made any activity physically and mentally exhausting.[34] Although Guderian was tasked to initiate an attack in coordination with Fourth Army to cave-in Soviet defences immediately south of Moscow the following day, Kluge stressed his need for four more days of preparation.[35] Given that idling invited defeat, XXIV Motorized Army Corps continued offensive operations between Tula and the River Oka, providing the supplies and reinforcements expected on 3 December were brought forward. 29th Motorized Infantry Division had reached the Serebryanyye Prudy area and engaged in heavy fighting to take Darovaya on 3 December.[36] To reinforce Schweppenburg's efforts, LIII Army Corps' artillery that comprised a mortar battalion and a heavy artillery battalion and 25th Motorized Infantry Division were placed under XXIV Motorized Army Corps' authority. For what was to be the final assault on Tula the sustained cold temperatures caused water to form and freeze in fuel lines, motor oil to thicken, and tank and artillery gun recoil mechanisms jammed. Fires were commonly lit under vehicles to warm engines, although this ate up valuable fuel even when not in use. Batteries subsequently suffered reduced effectiveness and many German crews brought up landlines so their wireless radios could be turned off. Landsers had to keep their rifle bolts in comparatively warm areas, such as their uniform pockets and not insert them until the enemy had closed to within 50m lest the frozen component fail at the moment of truth. In such dangerously cold conditions, German units typically occupied trenches and firing lines during the day, and left only token forces during the night. Generally housed in nearby settlements, rats, disease, lice, and other vermin brought a whole new level of discomfort. The absence of appropriately warm, layered, and breathable clothing promoted dehydration, hypothermia, and slurred speech, as well as degraded judgement and coordination, and impeded maintaining proper hygiene. Eating poor quality food and snow only worsened these cold-weather maladies. To avoid unnecessary exposure during elimination Landsers were known to cut flaps into their trouser rears. With heavy physical exertion that included digging trenches from the hard, frozen earth German soldiers soon became emaciated. Once proper winter clothing was issued, like sheepskin, quilted jackets, it was possible to sleep in the field and near weapons.

Under clear skies on 2 December, with a northerly wind and temperatures that dropped to -20 °C, Guderian visited his forward command post at Yasnaya Polyana, some 7km south of Tula, to receive a status report that included Schweppenburg's 3rd and 4th Panzer Divisions and Großdeutschland had broken into surprised, forward enemy positions on the city's outskirts, but failed to fully penetrate its defences. To provide a modest, but centralized reserve half of 25th Motorized Infantry Division was immediately transferred to Stalinogorsk, while XXIV Motorized Army Corps' solidified its gains along the road to Venev, in spite being down to just sixty tanks in operation. Perhaps expressing an opinion shared among many of his comrades, for Lemelsen 'the German sacrifice in this titanic struggle between two worldviews was necessary to free the world from Bolshevism, [and that] this danger cannot be overestimated. It is impossible to imagine what would have happened if sooner or later these hordes had invaded our dear German fatherland and lived there like beasts.'[37]

Continuing to leverage the flexibility Kampfgruppen offered to address the myriad issues now impacting its numbers, Second Panzer Army's declining strength meant instead of being able to dictate the flow of battle, it was now increasingly forced into reactive stances and as fire brigades to shore up threatened sectors. Unfortunately, dedicated positions onto which German forces could fall back and await more favourable campaigning conditions had yet to be established, as efforts focused on the offensive against the enemy capital. Toward finally severing Tula's remaining supply line to the north, 4th Panzer Division's vanguard arrived at the Serpukhov–Tula road and approached to within 15km of XXXXIII Army Corps, but the latter frustratingly lacked the strength to move forward to meet Langermann. Intent on affecting this critical meet-up, while his command still had the time and strength, Guderian travelled to Gryaznovo. Receiving a positive response from the rank and file with whom he met would ensure a second attempt set for 5 December would be successful.

At 0600hrs on 4 December 4th Panzer Division repulsed an enemy attack from the north of Rudnevo, but the end of Second Panzer Army's offensive was in sight given temperatures had dropped to -32 °C. To help his threatened, northern flank Guderian approved inserting 25th Motorized Infantry Division to bulk up his position. Even though XXIV Motorized Army Corps had captured 1,175 enemy soldiers, destroyed or captured 7 guns and 25 tanks over the last 2 days, it amounted to little in the broader theatre.[38] At 1500hrs Schweppenburg proposed postponing XXXXIII Army Corps' attack by an extra day to 6 December, but Guderian held firm to the already revised timetable. In a foreboding message at 2010hrs the *Flivo* reported that the temperature during the attack would be little different from 4 December. With German-produced locomotives having their piping arranged towards their exterior they were more susceptible to the effects of extreme cold than their Soviet counterparts. What supplies that got as far as Orel still needed to be driven to the front, which if XXXXVII Motorized Army Corps' managing to bring up around 1,000l of fuel over the last eight days was any indication, 'difficult' was an understatement.

By 0600hrs on 5 December 3rd and 4th Panzer Divisions were under attack during an even more frigid day than the last. With Soviet pressure building along Second Panzer Army's perimeter, and the larger, envisioned encirclement of Tula unlikely to offer enduring success given the available time and resources, Guderian soon favoured a more modest undertaking, in which 3rd Panzer and 296th Infantry Divisions would converge on an area a few kilometres northwest of Rudnevo. At noon, after initial successes towards helping seal the Tula gap, 31st Infantry Division's southern flank became bogged down in combat. Against the repeated warnings and requests of his army group commanders and Halder's advice, Hitler, increasingly inserting himself into operational level decisions, and even the tactical on occasion, forbade a broad disengagement of German forces. Stemming from a malignant narcissism and hubris that prevented him from taking responsibility for his own shortcomings and failures, the Führer's distrust of his generals and consolidation of power within the chain-of-command led to his decision to hold the captured territory before Moscow at all costs, rather than relying on movement and flexibility to achieve battlefield success.

Along XXIV Motorized Army Corps' left the Soviets had been attacking the right wing of 17th Panzer Division since the afternoon. 4th Panzer Division was similarly struck along the Serpukhov–Tula railway, and 3rd Panzer Division from the forest north-east of Tula.[39] 31st Infantry Division made a determined advance against heavy resistance, and although casualties were sustainable numerous cases of frostbite ultimately doomed the effort. Lieutenant General (*General der Infanterie*) Gotthard Heinrici urgently requested a division be allocated to get his XXXXIII Army Corps moving, but none could be spared. For as much effort Guderian's men were exerting into eliminating Tula's defenders, German intelligence reported that 20 Soviet locomotives and 2,000 cars had moved into the Ryazan area. Similarly 15 more engines with 900 cars pulled up to the south. While they had respectively not disembarked their contents of Red Army soldiers, weapons, and equipment it was only a matter of time until these reinforcements made their presence felt. With 3rd Panzer Division encountering increasing enemy pressure and penetrations of its front line, Guderian conferred with Schweppenburg who indicated that, 'Since yesterday, the situation has changed fundamentally. Fourth Army had already transitioned to the defence and at 2130 hrs. Guderian moved to follow suit. In order to prevent Tula from being cut off, the enemy moved his forces from the front of the 17th Panzer Division to the south-west against the north flank of the 4th Panzer Division . . .' XXXXIII Army Corps reported at 2135hrs that it was no longer capable of warding off strong attacks. Should the Soviets penetrate the sector in sufficient strength to take Orel, the logistics base for two field armies, German senior leadership needed to act quickly to prevent a catastrophe. Having assumed command a few days previously when his predecessor, Weisenberger, was placed into Leader Reserve, Lieutenant General (*General der Infanterie*) Walther von Weikersthal expressed that his LIII Army Corps 'stands there and held the shield forward, but the shield is fragile in places'.[40] With Lemelsen and Liebenstein in agreement, during the night of 5/6 December Guderian worked on his own authority to pull his forward units back to more defensible positions roughly along the Rivers Don, Shat, and Upa to wait out the winter. In spite of Hitler's continued refusal reality had other ideas. With providence indeed always on the side of the last reserve Barbarossa was officially concluded.

Aftermath

With Army Group Centre's over-extended offensive around Moscow having ground to a standstill, a steady, loosely orchestrated Soviet counteroffensive coincided with a drop in temperatures to -35 °C during the night of 5/6 December. For the next two days both sides largely hunkered down to await something of a warming. On 8 December a low-pressure ridge brought above-freezing temperatures and rainfall that quickly turned snow-swept, dirt roads back to a familiar mush. As Red Army forces renewed their efforts to expel German forces threatening Moscow, Bock desperately reported that his command would be unable to hold them back; a sentiment with which Guderian concurred regarding his own command. Having so recently maintained an optimistic view that all their sacrifices would still bear fruit, the seemingly sudden reversal of fortune shocked most German civilians who were well away from the combat zone and had little idea of the conditions in which their physically and psychologically exhausted *Frontsoldaten* fought. Demoralized and angered by the lack of adequate supplies, winter uniforms, felt-lined boots, and foresight to have avoided such a situation, what began for the *Ostheer* as a general withdrawal became increasingly frantic after 18 December, as a Red Army counteroffensive along the Moscow front gained momentum.

On 19 December Hitler informed Halder that the position of Commander-in-Chief of the Army was to be integrated into that of Führer. Just over four months later, such centralizing of power and abdication of the General Staff's authority to a political agitator being seemingly insufficient, the former corporal was granted:

> ... all the rights postulated by him which serve to further or achieve victory. Therefore – without being bound by existing legal regulations in his capacity as Leader of the nation, Supreme Commander of the Armed Forces, Head of Government and supreme executive chief, as Supreme Justice and Leader of the Party – the Führer must be in a position to force with all means at his disposal every German, if necessary, whether he be common soldier or officer, low or high official or judge, leading or subordinate official of the party, worker or employer – to fulfil his duties. In case of violation of these duties, the Führer is entitled after conscientious examination, regardless of so-called well-deserved rights, to mete out due punishment and to remove the offender from his post, rank and position without introducing prescribed procedures.

The Red Army's counteroffensive around Moscow gained steam and continued to push an exhausted *Ostheer* back across a frigid landscape of windswept snow dunes, where the sick and wounded soon perished. With fuel gone, roads buried under deep snow, and inoperable weapon systems and equipment correspondingly abandoned, on 26 December 1941 Hitler issued a blanket, one-size-fits-all 'Halt Order' (*Haltebefehl*). For all the problems and lack of success a static defence typically meant for its participants, the adoption of numerous, independent 'hedgehog' positions around built-up villages, helped erode the Soviet advance and arguably prevented a greater catastrophe.

Heady with military success in the West, and in particular against its vaunted nemesis, France, and in control of much of Continental Europe when Brauchitsch initiated planning for Barbarossa per Hitler on 22 July 1940, German senior military leadership had been placed in a position of conforming reality to match a flawed narrative of the Soviet Union's depth of resources and resolve. Under pressure to pre-emptively defeat the Red Army before their wary ally struck them in possibly overwhelming force, a not invalid assumption given the Soviet military build-up and reorganization along their western border, a very secretive, brutal, and fear-based Leninist-Stalinist political system greatly hindered outside reconnaissance and intelligence gathering. Hubris and the prevalent belief in Slavic inferiority resulted in self-inflicted wounds for the Germans, as was neglecting to adequately prepare for the possibility of the fighting progressing well beyond the River Dnepr. Once committed, given existing resources and capabilities meant that German logistics functioned optimally out to about 300km, with the distance from Brest to Moscow over three times further, and the Ural Mountains 1,000km beyond that, major problems were unavoidable. Hitler and his OKH planners had underestimated the enemy's existing and potential size and capabilities, and never seemed to consider their mass dismantling and relocating of much of its industry beyond the range of the Luftwaffe.

Overriding all other decisions the need for a comparatively quick battlefield solution, like that against France and the West, meant Halder, and others, were often pressured to or wilfully ignored or disregarded intelligence and circumstances that ran contrary to the groupthink. This lack of operational and strategic-level insight on the enemy throughout Barbarossa often forced the Germans into reacting to major, unforeseen battlefield situations. As the campaign lingered and the stakes grew, the centralization of power into the person and personae of the Führer all but removed debate, separation of duties, and flexibility from the decision-making process. Worse, the governing dynamic in which Hitler's senior henchmen like Göring, Himmler, Bormann, and others operated intentionally promoted conflict among the echelon, where members machinated and fought internally to gain favour and grow their positions and wealth at the expense of their peers and others. While such a framework kept Hitler in control and insulated him from reproach it made for a schizophrenic approach to formulating and executing operational and strategic matters across German manufacturing, economic, financial, and military spheres, and severely undercut the capabilities and endurance of what in June 1941 was arguably the most dominant military in the world.

In 'Interdependence of the Elements of War', a chapter in his magnum opus *On War*, Clausewitz wrote that:

> Within the concept of absolute war, then, war is indivisible, and its component parts (the individual victories) are of value only in relation to the whole. Conquering Moscow and half of Russia in 1812 was of no avail to Bonaparte unless it brought him the peace he had in view. But these successes were only a part of his plan of campaign: what was still missing was the destruction of the Russian army. If that achievement had been added to the rest, peace would have been as sure as things of that sort ever can be. But it was too late to achieve the second part of his plan; his chance had gone. Thus the successful stage was not only wasted but led to disaster.

Appendix A
Second Panzer Group, 22 June 1941[*1]

Commander-in-Chief:	General Heinz Guderian
Chief-of-Staff:	Lieutenant Colonel Kurt Baron von Liebenstein
Operations Officer (Ia):	Lieutenant Colonel Fritz Bayerlein

113,500 personnel, 1,058 tanks (exc. Panzer Is)
2nd Motorized Signals Regiment Staff

302nd Harko (Major General Erich Heinemann)
740th Motorized Heavy Artillery Battalion (150mm K 39)
159th Bridge Construction Battalion
2./3rd Railroad Engineer Regiment
5th Motorized Machine-Gun Battalion (1.-3./ (16 × MG ea.), 4./ (12 × 37mm AT))
602nd Self-Propelled Light Flak Battalion (Sd.Kfz. 10/4)
693rd Panzer Propaganda Company

Koluft Second Panzer Group (Colonel Karl von Gerlach)
3.(F)/31st Reconnaissance Group (Bf-110F)
1.(H)/21st Reconnaissance Squadron (XII AC) (Hs-126)
10th Luftwaffe-Army Cooperation Staff (XXIV MAC)
- 7.(H)/32nd and 6.(Pz)/41st (4 PD) Reconnaissance Groups (Hs-126); 9.(Pz)/2nd Instruction Wing (3 PD) (Fw-189A)

14th Luftwaffe-Army Cooperation Staff (XXXXVI MAC)
- 6.(H)/31st; 3.(Pz)/14th (10 PD) Reconnaissance Groups (Hs-126)

31st Luftwaffe-Army Cooperation Staff (XXXXVII MAC)
- 5.(H)/23rd; 6.(Pz)/13th (18 PD); 6.(Pz)/32nd (17 PD) Reconnaissance Groups (Hs-126)

---

* Considering the complexity of Second Panzer Group's subordinate formations what's presented is abbreviated, but should provide sufficient insight into its organizational structure for *Barbarossatag*. Anlage 2 zu Pz.Gr.2, Ia Nr.301/41 g.Kdos. vom 8.6.41.

Courier Flight (3 × Ju-52/3m)
I./26th Motorized Antiaircraft Regiment (XII AC)
I./704th Motorized Antiaircraft Regiment (XII AC)
94th Motorized Light Antiaircraft Battalion
2nd Motorized Signal Communication (Luftwaffe) Operating Company (H)

I. Antiaircraft Corps (Brigadier Walther von Axthelm)[2]
- 101st Motorized Antiaircraft Regiment (Lieutenant Colonel Johann-Wilhelm Doering-Manteuffel) (I./12th and I./22nd Antiaircraft Regiments, 91st Light Antiaircraft Battalion)
- 104th Motorized Antiaircraft Regiment (Colonel Hermann Lichtenberger) (I./, II./11th Antiaircraft Regiment, 77th Light Antiaircraft Battalion)

XXXXVII Motorized Army Corps (Lieutenant General (*General der Panzertruppe*) Joachim Lemelsen)
447th Signals Battalion

100thPanzer Battalion (Fl.)
Panzern (82): II (67) (25, 42 (Fl)); III (5 × 50mm); Pz.Bef. III (1); MK.IV 744(e) (9)[3]
611th Panzerjäger Battalion (9 × 47mm Pak(t) (Sfl) auf Fgst.Pz.Kpfw.35 R 731(f))
413th Engineer Regiment Staff ('for special use' (no subordinate units))
42nd Motorized Engineer Battalion
238th Engineer Battalion
27th, 29th, 98th, 42nd, 2./422nd Bridge Columns 'B'
504th Bicycle Road Construction Battalion
213th Construction Battalion[4]
584th Heavy Road Construction Battalion[4]

2./402nd Motorized Bridge Column 'B'[5]
71st, 72nd Bridge Columns 'B' (Unit Assemblage)[5]
902nd Assault Boat Detachment (81 craft)[5]

17th Panzer Division (Major General Hans-Jürgen von Arnim)
Panzern (190): II (44); III (106 × 50mm); IV (30); Pz.Bef. III (10)[3]
27th Motorized Mapping Detachment
39th Panzer Regiment(I.–III. (1 med., 2 light panzer companies ea.))
17th Rifle Brigade
- 40th Motorized Rifle Regiment (I. (one company armoured), II.)
- 63rd Motorized Rifle Regiment (I., II.)
- 17th Motorcycle Battalion

27th Motorized Reconnaissance Battalion
27th Antitank Battalion
- 1./66th Light Self-Propelled Antiaircraft Company (20mm)
27th Motorized Engineer Battalion
27th Motorized Signal Battalion
27th Motorized Supply Battalion
27th Replacement Training Battalion

101st Arko[5]
Panzer Observation Battery
616th Motorized Artillery Battalion Staff
- III./53rd Motorized Rocket Launcher Regiment (18 × 150mm launchers)
- 616th Motorized Heavy 210mm Howitzer Battalion (6 × 210mm M18)[16]
- 400th Artillery Battalion (7./ (150mm sFH18), 8./, 9./ (105mm leFH18))[6]
29th Motorized Artillery Regiment Staff (I./, II./ (105mm leFH18), III./ (150mm sFH18))[7]
- 238th Artillery Regiment Staff (I./–III./ (105mm leFH18), IV./ (150mm sFH18))[8]
27th Motorized Artillery Regiment Staff (I./, II./ (105mm leFH18), III./ (150mm sFH18))

18th Panzer Division (Brigadier Walther Nehring)
Panzern (212): II (50); III (114) (99 × 37mm, 15 × 50mm); IV (36); Pz.Bef. III (12)[3]
88th Motorized Map Detachment
18th Panzer Brigade
- 18th Panzer Regiment (I.–III. (1 med. (Tauchpanzer IV), 2 light panzer companies ea. (Tauchpanzer III)))
18th Rifle Brigade
- 52nd Motorized Rifle Regiment (I. (one company armoured)/, II./)
- 101st Motorized Rifle Regiment (I., II.)
- 18th Motorcycle Battalion
88th Motorized Reconnaissance Battalion
88th Antitank Battalion
- 631st Light Self-Propelled Antiaircraft Company (20mm)
98th Motorized Engineer Battalion
88th Motorized Signal Battalion
88th Motorized Supply Battalion
88th Replacement Training Battalion

146th Arko
Panzer and 20th Artillery Observation Battalion Staff Batteries

II./53rd Motorized Rocket Launcher Regiment (18 × 150mm launchers)
88th Motorized Artillery Regiment Staff (I., II. (105mm leFH18), III. (150mm sFH18))[9]
792nd Artillery Regiment Staff
- 616th Motorized Heavy 210mm Howitzer Battalion (3 × 210mm M18)[16]
- 817th Motorized Heavy 210mm Howitzer Battalion (9 × 210mm M18)
- II./71st Mixed Heavy Artillery Regiment (7. (105mm K18), 8., 9. (150mm sFH18))
- 422nd Heavy Field Howitzer Battalion (150mm sFH18)
- 631st 100mm Cannon Battalion (105mm K18)

90th Motorized Artillery Regiment Staff (I., II. (105mm leFH18), III. (7. (105mm K18), 8., 9. (150mm sFH18)))[14]

29th Motorized Infantry Division (Brigadier Walter von Boltenstern)
15th Motorized Infantry Regiment (I.–III.)
71st Motorized Infantry Regiment (I.–III.)
29th Motorcycle Battalion
29th Reconnaissance Battalion
29th Antitank Battalion
- 1./59th Light Self-Propelled Antiaircraft Battalion

29th Motorized Engineer Battalion
29th Motorized Signal Battalion
29th Motorized Supply Battalion
29th Replacement Training Battalion

167th Infantry Division (Major General Hans Schönhärl)[5]
315th Infantry Regiment (I.–III.)
331st Infantry Regiment (I.–III.)
339th Infantry Regiment (I.–III.)
238th Reconnaissance Battalion
238th Antitank Battalion
238th Signals Battalion
238th Replacement Training Battalion

XII Army Corps (Lieutenant General (*General der Infanterie*)) Walther Schroth 52nd Signals Battalion

507th Motorized Engineer Regiment Staff
215th, 750th Engineer Battalion (horsedrawn)
4th, 593rd Bridge Construction Battalions
17th, 31st, 34th, 81st, 131st, 2./409th, 1./41st Bridge Columns 'B'

24th Commander of Construction Troops
11th, 46th, 402nd Construction Battalions
313th RAD Group K
5./312th, 6./312th, 5./318th, 2./314th RAD Battalions
654th Panzerjäger Battalion (minus one coy)
610th Light Antiaircraft Battalion (minus one coy)
3./31st Light Self-Propelled Antiaircraft Battalion
I./26th Mixed Antiaircraft Battalion
Armoured Trains Nos 27 and 28

31st Infantry Division (Brigadier Kurt Kalmukoff)
12th Infantry Regiment (I.–III.)
17th Infantry Regiment (I.–III.)
82nd Infantry Regiment (I.–III.)
I./67th Artillery Regiment
31st Reconnaissance Battalion
31st Antitank Battalion
31st Engineer Battalion
31st Signals Battalion
31st Replacement Training Battalion
1., 3./192nd Assault Gun Battalion[10]

112th Arko
8th Observation Battery
31st Artillery Regiment (I.–III. (105mm leFH18), IV. (150mm sFH18)
617th Motorized Artillery Regiment Staff (on special assignment)[10]
- II./66th Motorized Heavy Field Howitzer Battalion (150mm sFH18)[10]
- 845th Motorized Heavy Field Howitzer Battalion (150mm sFH18)[10]
- 854th Motorized 210mm Howitzer Battalion (12 × 210mm M18)[10]
- 709th Motorized 100mm Gun Battalion (105mm K18)[10]
- 101st Motorized Balloon Battery

6th Motorized Rocket Launcher Battalion (9 × 105mm launchers)[11]

34th Infantry Division (Major General Hans Behlendorf)
80th Infantry Regiment (I.–III.)
253rd Infantry Regiment (I.–III.)
107th Infantry Regiment (I.–III.)
I./70th Artillery Regiment
34th Reconnaissance Battalion
34th Antitank Battalion
34th Engineer Battalion

34th Signals Battalion
34th Replacement Training Battalion

148th Arko (Colonel Hans Schlemmer)
34th Artillery Regiment (I.–III. (105mm leFH18), IV. (150mm sFH18))
788th Motorized Artillery Regiment (on special assignment)[10]
- II./109th Motorized Heavy 210mm Howitzer Regiment (9 × 210mm M18)
- 430th Motorized 100mm Gun Battalion (105mm K18)
- 17th Artillery Observation Battalion Staff Battery
- 100th Motorized Balloon Battery

6th Motorized Rocket Launcher Battalion (9 × 105mm launchers)[11]

45th Infantry Division (Brigadier Fritz Schlieper)
130th Infantry Regiment (I.–III.)
133rd Infantry Regiment (I.–III.)
135th Infantry Regiment (I.–III.)
I./99th Artillery Regiment
45th Reconnaissance Battalion
45th Antitank Battalion
81st Engineer Battalion
65th Signals Battalion
45th Replacement Training Battalion
2./192nd Assault Gun Battalion[10]
201st Assault Gun Battalion (Major Heinz Huffmann) (3 btrys)

27th Arko[11]
98th Artillery Regiment (I./, II./, III./ (105mm leFH18), IV./ (150mm sFH18)
4th Motorized Rocket Launcher Regiment Staff (for special use)[11]
- 8th Motorized Rocket Launcher Battalion (18 × 280/320mm launchers)[11]
- 105th Motorized Decontamination Battalion[11]

2./833rd Heavy Artillery Battalion (600mm Karl-Great 040)[11]
3 × 210mm howitzer batteries (M16, stationary)[11]

XXIV Motorized Army Corps (Lieutenant General (*General der Panzertruppe*) Leo *Reichsfreiherr* Geyr von Schweppenburg)
424th Signals Battalion Staff

515th Motorized Engineer Regiment Staff
45th Motorized Engineer Battalion

69th, 70th Bridge Columns 'B'[12]

10th, 39th, 79th, 2./403rd, 1./404th, 1./405th, 2./408th, 606th Bridge Columns 'B'
503rd Bicycle Road Construction Battalion
97th, 133rd Construction Battalions
21st Bridge Construction Battalion
136th Construction Battalion (255th Infantry Division)
521st Panzerjäger Battalion (3 btrys) (27 × Panzerjäger Is (47 mm))
515th Engineer Regiment Staff

3rd Panzer Division (Major General Walter Model)
Panzern (215): II (58); III (110) (29 × 37mm, 81 × 50mm); IV (32); Pz.Bef. III (15)[3]
5th Panzer Brigade
- 6th Panzer Regiment (I., II. Panzer Battalions (1 med., 2 light panzer companies ea.), III. Panzer Battalion (1 med. (Tauchpanzer IV), 2 light panzer companies ea. (Tauchpanzer III)))

3rd Rifle Brigade
- 394th Motorized Rifle Regiment (I., II.)
- 3rd Motorized Rifle Regiment (I. (one company armoured), II.)
- 3rd Motorcycle Battalion

1st Motorized Reconnaissance Battalion
543rd Panzerjäger Battalion (37mm PaK 36/37), 1 antitank company (28mm)
- 6./59th Light Self-Propelled Antiaircraft Company (20mm quad, 20mm)

39th Motorized Engineer Battalion
39th Motorized Signals Battalion
83rd Replacement Training Battalion

143rd Arko
75th Motorized Artillery Regiment Staff
- I./53rd Motorized Rocket Launcher Regiment (18 × 150mm launchers)[13]
- II./42nd Motorized Artillery Regiment (150mm sFH18)
- II./75th Motorized Artillery Regiment (150mm sFH18)
- 714th Motorized Battalion (leFH18)

623rd Motorized Artillery Regiment Staff
- Panzer Observation Battery (for special use)
- II./69th Motorized Artillery Regiment (105mm K18)
- 7./75th Motorized Artillery Regiment (105mm K18)
- II./75th Motorized Artillery Regiment (105mm leFH18)

10th Motorized Artillery Regiment Staff (I./, II./ (105mm leFH18), III./ (150mm sFH18)[14]
- 604th Motorized Heavy 210mm Howitzer Battalion (9 × 210mm M18)[13]

4th Panzer Division (Brigadier Willibald Baron von Langermann and Erlencamp)
Panzern (177): II (44); III (105) (31 × 37mm, 74 × 50mm); IV (20); Pz.Bef. III (8)[3]
35th Panzer Regiment (I., II. (1 med., 3 light panzer companies ea.)
4th Motorized Rifle Brigade
- 33rd Motorized Rifle Regiment (I., II.)
- 12th Motorized Rifle Regiment (I. (one company armoured), II.)
- 34th Motorcycle Battalion

7th Motorized Reconnaissance Battalion
49th Antitank Battalion
- 5./66th Light Self-Propelled Antiaircraft Company (20mm quad, 20mm)

79th Motorized Engineer Battalion
79th Motorized Signal Battalion
84th Motorized Supply Battalion

103rd Motorized Artillery Regiment Staff
Panzer Observation Battery
III./103rd Motorized Artillery Regiment Staff
- I./, II./ (105mm leFH18), III./ (150mm sFH18)

SS Artillery Regiment 'Reich'[15]
- I./, III./SS Artillery Regiment 'Reich' (105mm leFH18)

II./SS Artillery Regiment 'Reich' (105mm leFH18)
IV./SS Artillery Regiment 'Reich' (150mm sFH18)

10th Motorized Infantry Division (Major General Friedrich-Wilhelm von Löper)
20th Motorized Infantry Regiment (I.–III.)
41st Motorized Infantry Regiment (I.–III.)
40th Motorcycle Battalion
10th Motorized Reconnaissance Battalion
10th Antitank Battalion
10th Motorized Engineer Battalion
10th Motorized Signals Battalion
10th Replacement Training Battalion

255th Infantry Division (Major General Wilhelm Wetzel)
455th Infantry Regiment (I./, II./, III./)
465th Infantry Regiment (I./, II./, III./)
475th Infantry Regiment (I./, II./, III./)
255th Reconnaissance Battalion (3 x 37mm)
255th Antitank Battalion (2 coys (3 × 47mm, 8 × 37mm ea.), 1 coy (12 x 37mm))
255th Engineer Battalion (1./404th Motorized Bridge Column 'B')

255th Signal Battalion
255th Replacement Training Battalion

255th Artillery Regiment (I./, II./, III./ (105mm lFH18), IV./ (150mm sFH18)

267th Infantry Division (Brig Friedrich-Karl von Wachter)[12]
467th Infantry Regiment (I.–III.)
487th Infantry Regiment (I.–III.)
497th Infantry Regiment (I.–III.)
267th Reconnaissance Battalion
267th Antitank Battalion
267th Engineer Battalion
267th Signals Battalion
267th Replacement Training Battalion

1st Cavalry Division (Brigadier Kurt Feldt)
1st Cavalry Brigade
- 1st Cavalry Regiment (I., II.)
- 2nd Cavalry Regiment (I., II.)

2nd Cavalry Brigade
- 22nd Cavalry Regiment (I., II.)
- 21st Cavalry Regiment (I.)

1st Bicycle Battalion
40th Motorized Antitank Battalion (37mm)
40th Motorized Engineer Battalion
86th Motorized Signals Battalion
Panzer Reconnaissance Instruction Battalion[16]

1st Horse Artillery Regiment Staff
- 10./1st Motorized Horse Artillery Regiment (105mm lFH18))
- II./, III./267th Artillery Regiment (105mm lFH18)
- IV. 267th Artillery Regiment (150mm sFH18)
- III./1st Horse Artillery Regiment (75mm FK 16 nA)

267th Artillery Regiment[17]
- I./267th Artillery Regiment (105mm leFH18)
- 1st Horse Artillery Regiment (I.–III.) (75mm FK 16 nA)

XXXXVI Motorized Army Corps (Lieutenant General (*General der Panzertruppe*) Heinrich von Vietinghoff *genannt* Scheel)
446th Signals Battalion Staff

513th Engineer Regiment Staff (for special use)[5]

85th Engineer Battalion[5]
49th, 'Reich', 22nd, and 85th Bridge Columns 'B'[5]

10th Panzer Division (Major General Ferdinand Schaal)
Panzern (182): II (45); III (105 × 50mm); IV (20); Pz.Bef. III (12)[3]
90th Motorized Map Detachment
4th Panzer Brigade
- 7th Panzer Regiment (I./, II./ (1 medium, 3 light panzer coys ea.))

10th Rifle Brigade
- 69th Motorized Rifle Regiment (I./, II. (armoured)/)
- 86th Motorized Rifle Regiment (I./, II./)
- 10th Motorcycle Battalion

90th Motorized Reconnaissance Battalion
90th Motorized Antitank Battalion
- 3./55th Light Self-Propelled Antiaircraft Company (20mm quad, 20mm)

49th Motorized Engineer Battalion
90th Motorized Signal Battalion
90th Motorized Supply Battalion
90th Replacement Training Battalion

SS-Motorized Division 'Reich' (Major General (*SS-Gruf.*) Paul Hausser)
SS-Infantry Regiment 'Deutschland' (I.–III.)
SS-Infantry Regiment 'Der Führer' (I.–III.)
11th SS-Infantry Regiment (I.–III.)
SS-Motorcycle Battalion 'Reich'
SS-Antiaircraft Battalion 'Reich'
SS-Reconnaissance Battalion 'Reich'
SS-Antitank Battalion 'Reich'
SS-Engineer Battalion 'Reich'
SS-Signals Battalion 'Reich'
SS-Training Replacement Battalion 'Reich'
SS-Assault Gun Battery (7 × StuG IIIB)

Großdeutschland Motorized Infantry Regiment (Brigadier Wilhelm-Hunold von Stockhausen)
- I.–III. Motorized Infantry Battalions
- IV. Motorized Infantry Battalion (13th Heavy Motorized Infantry Gun (150mm), 14th Motorized Antitank (50mm), 15th Motorized Infantry Gun (75mm), 16th Assault Gun (7 × StuG IIID) Companies)

- V. Infantry Battalion (17th Motorized Reconnaissance, 18th Motorized Engineer, 19th Motorized Signals, 20th Medium Self-Propelled Antiaircraft Companies)
- 400th Motorized Supply Battalion

Second Panzer Group Luftwaffe Support

Second Air Force (*Luftflotte 2*) (Field Marshal Albert Kesselring) (1,480 combat aircraft/1,065 serviceable)[18]

II Air Corps (Air Marshal (*General der Flieger*) (Luftwaffe) Bruno Loerzer)

210th Ground Attack and Antitank Wing
- Staff (4 × Bf-110D); I. (40 × Bf-110D); II. (40 × Bf-110D) (all Radzyn)

3rd Bombardment Wing 'Blitz'
- Staff (6 × Do-17Z, 4 × Ju-88A); I. (40 × Ju-88A); II. (4 × Do-17Z, 36 × Ju-88A) (all Deblin-Irena)

53rd Bombardment Wing 'Legion Condor'
- Staff (4 × He-111H) (Radom); I. (40 × He-111H) (Grojec); II. (40 × He-111H); (Radom); III. (38 × He-111H, 2 × He-111P) (Radzyn)

77th Dive-bomber Wing
- Staff (4 × Ju-87B, 6 × Bf-110) (Biala Podlaska); I. (40 × Ju-87B) (Biala Podlaska); II. (36 × Ju-87B, 4 × Bf-110) (Woskrzenice); III. (40 × Ju-87B) (Woskrzenice)

51st Fighter Wing
- Staff (4 × Bf-109F) (Siedlce); I. (40 × Bf-109F) (Starawies); II. (40 × Bf-109F) (Siedlce); III. and IV. (in Hungary)

53rd Fighter Wing (79 Bf-109F on call from Second Air Force)

1.(F)/122nd Reconnaissance Group (7 × Ju-88A/D, 3xBf-110) (Warsaw)
102nd and 105th Bombardment Groups 'for special use' (53 × Ju-52 ea.) (Warsaw)

32nd Aviation Signal Regiment

Notes

Introduction

1. Seeckt's H. Dv.487, *Führung und Gefecht der verbundenen Waffen* (1921, 1923) and Bock's *1933 German Regulation 300, Truppenführung* quantified the lessons of the First World War towards conducting a modern, conventional conflict.
2. Adolf Hitler, *Mein Kampf* (Houghton Mifflin Company, 1998), 84.
3. 303 Red Army divisions existed on 22 June 1941. David Glantz and Jonathan M. House, *When Titans Clashed: How the Red Army Stopped Hitler* (rev. and expanded edn, Lawrence: University Press of Kansas, 2015), 11.
4. Although the Soviet Chief of the General Staff, Marshal Boris Shaposhnikov, had worked to reconstitute and streamline the military in the leadup to Barbarossa, and anticipated the main German offensive would be along the Minsk–Moscow axis, when the moment arrived Stalin and the Soviet General Headquarters (*Stavka*) issued conflicting orders that greatly undercut Red Army efforts.
5. Although the Soviet Tyr ('rear services') was intended to centrally control and coordinate a host of logistics-based services, including farm food production, railway construction, and even furniture making, Stalin's purges and the Red Army's inconsistent battlefield performance over the last two years had exposed considerable shortcomings in the supply system.
6. General of Signals Troops Alert Praun, German Radio Intelligence (Unpublished Foreign Military Studies Typescript #P-038 Historical Division USEUCOM, 1950), 148.
7. In mid-June 1941 the Soviet General Staff planned for 237 divisions to serve in their West, of which 186 were to comprise the first echelon and the remainder a strategic reserve; 31 more divisions were deployed to the Southern and Eastern fronts, 3 to the Crimea, and 1 to the Arkhangel'sk area. David Glantz, *Barbarossa Derailed. The Battle for Smolensk, 10 July–10 September 1941, Vol. 1* (Warwick: Helion, 2010), 22.
8. Charles Burdick and Hans-Adolf Jacobsen (eds), *The Halder War Diary, 1939–1942* (Novato, CA: Presidio, 1988), Vol. VI, 160.
9. At Barbarossa's start, with 170 divisions in their Western Theatre the Soviets were short of expectations by some 1.5 million men (see V.A. Zolotarev, *The Great Patriotic War 1941–1945, Book 1* (Moscow: 'Nauka', 1998), 108–9).
10. Stunned by the rapid German victories in the West, Stalin steadfastly refused to prematurely provoke a war with Hitler until the Soviet military was sufficiently strong and trained to actively defend its western border. As one of several pleas from senior commanders advocating for a pre-emptive strike, on 13 June 1941 the People's Commissar of Defence and Marshal of the Soviet Union S.K. Timoshenko phoned Stalin to stress placing their border military district forces on alert. The Premier responded with simply, 'We'll think about it.' Bernd Wegner (ed.), *From Peace to War: Germany, Soviet Russia, and the World, 1939–1941* (Providence, NY and Oxford: Berghahn Books, 1997), 392.
11. American and British general staffs held a similarly poor view of the Red Army's capabilities and resolve. On 27 December 1939 the German Ministry of Transportation incorporated occupied Western Poland's rail network into the Reichsbahn.
12. Paul Wohl, 'Transport in Development of Soviet Policy', *Foreign Affairs*, April (1946).

13. Major Lonnie O. Ratley III, 'A Lesson of History: The Luftwaffe and Barbarossa', *Air University Review*, XXXV, No. 2 (January–February 1984), 53.
14. Williamson Murray, *Strategy for Defeat: The Luftwaffe 1933–1945* (Maxwell AFB: Air University, 1983), 78.
15. Dr Russel H.S. Stolfi, 'A Bias for Action: The German 7th Panzer Division in France & Russia 1940–1941', Faculty and Researcher Publications, 1991, 82.

Chapter 1

1. BA-MA RH 21-2/927, KTB Nr 1, Pz.Gr. 22.6.41.
2. Destroyed/unusable Bug bridges (road): Legi, Terespol-Brest Fortress, Terespol-Rzeczyca, 'Volyn' fortification, 45 ID/34 ID border, Slawatycze (Sławatycze) and Włodawa; (rail): Orchowo. AOK 4 Koluft Stabsbildmeldung. I Bild, Nr.B.Nr.15/41, g.Kdos. and period photos.
3. Official German military time coincided with Central European Time.
4. Soon after midnight on 21/22 June 1941, per Stalin's authorization, the codeword 'Thunderstorm' was issued for senior Red Army commanders along the western border to open their sealed 'red packages', which provided rather outdated instructions for holding the frontier during what was originally assumed to be a period of mutual mobilization.
5. Panzerjäger I's 47mm main gun was housed in a seven-sided gun shield that provided the crew with a degree of protection from shrapnel and small arms. While the overburdened chassis was prone to breaking down and hindered crew visibility to the outside, the cannon could penetrate 52mm at 30° from 1,000m, making it sufficient to defeat its primary Soviet T-26 and BT-7 contemporaries' respective 15mm and 40mm maximum armour thickness. Lorrin Bird and Robert Livingston, *World War II Ballistics: Armor and Gunnery* (Albany, NY: Overmatch Press, 2001), 61.
6. Gerd Habedanck, 'Bei Brest-Litovsk über die Grenze', *Die Wehrmacht* (1941): 233.
7. On 19 June 1941, Soviet People's Commissar of Defence Marshal Semyon Timoshenko and Red Army Chief of Staff General Georgy Zhukov ordered that by 15 July 1941 Soviet airfields were to be better camouflaged, including planting foliage and painting buildings that blended with each location's environment, constructing fake airfields and aircraft, and prohibiting planes from being arranged in linear fashion. Dmitri Volkogonov, *Stalin: Triumph and Tragedy* (London: Grove Weidenfeld, 1991), 393.
8. When brigade level artillery worked with that of corps an artillery commander (Arko) and his headquarters coordinated assets and observation. A high artillery commander (Harko) performed the same function at division level with that at army.
9. Within the German General Staff only the Ia (chief-of-staff) and Ib (chief supply officer) were true staff officers who had been selected to and graduated from the War Academy.
10. In the Brest area the Soviets had 10th Mixed Air Division airfields with modern aircraft just north of the city (123rd Fighter Aviation Regiment (10 Yak-1s)); east of Wolczyn (74th Assault Aviation Regiment (49 I-15s, 8 Il-2s)); and north of Kobryn (123rd FAR (10 Yak-1s and 61 I-153s)).
11. Based largely on the rough treatment Finnish forces subjected the Soviets to during the Winter War (1939–40), the Red Army General Staff worked to better respond to a German offensive by strengthening frontier forces to wear down, disrupt, and fix initial enemy actions and permit strong mechanized forces to conduct rapid counterattacks deep into the opponent's rear areas. Toward this end during March and April 1941 the Soviet Fourth Army participated in Western Military District's operational map game in Minsk, which emphasized such a thrust west along the Bialystok–Warsaw axis.

12. SD-2s possessed 225kg/Fp 60/40 (TNT/Ammonium Nitrate) Amatol of explosives and fuse settings for impact, air burst, long delay, and anti-handling that were armed after roughly ten rotations unscrewed a threaded arming spindle.
13. While the Ju-88 and Do-17 possessed bomb bays capable of incorporating SD-2 racks, He-111s lacked them, and instead likely carried SD-10 fragmentation bombs.
14. By the morning of 22 June, 39th Bomber Regiment (10th Mixed Air Division) was bombed 4 times in which 43 SBs and 5 Pe-2s were destroyed on the ground, with the Western Military District losing 48 per cent of its 1,540 aircraft. Evan Mawdsley, *Thunder in the East: The Nazi-Soviet War, 1941–1945* (London: Bloomsbury Publishing, 2015), 54.
15. Considering the difference in latitude, Army Group North, and Third Panzer Group and Ninth Army (AGC) were scheduled to attack at 0305hrs on 22 June 1941. Army Groups South, and Second Panzer Group and Fourth Army (AGC) would do so 10 minutes later to accommodate for dawn at different latitudes; OKH believed the risk to the latter being justified. (See Klaus Gerbet, *Generalfeldmarschall Fedor von Bock: The War Diary, 1939–1945* (Atglen, PA: Schiffer, 1996), 222.)
16. The Soviets had planned to develop defences that extended much further eastwards, but this hadn't been accomplished by June 1941.
17. On 22 June 1941 the Brest fortress garrison comprised at least 8,000 soldiers within 5 rifle battalions (6 RD), 2 rifle battalions (42 RD), 33rd Independent Engineer Regiment, 132nd Independent NKVD Battalion, and a detachment of 17th Border Guards.
18. In addition to the 210mm Mörser 18's 113kg high-explosive round a 121.4kg anti-concrete option was well suited for destroying built-up positions.
19. Army Group Centre Ic's documents, 22–9 June 1941.
20. On 22 June ninety-two Soviet bunkers had been constructed along 62nd Fortified Region's (Brest) 170km frontage; roughly 30 per cent of the planned number. A. Krupennikov, *In the First Battles (A Collection of Articles and Drafts on the Initial Period of the Great Patriotic War)* (Krasnogorsk, 1998).
21. BA-MA MSg 1/1147: *Tagebuch* Lemelsen, 21.6.41.
22. In addition to 17th 'Red Banner' personnel at their Outpost No. 2, the Soviet 3./18th Separate Machine-Gun and Artillery Battalion had a presence at Nowosiolki. The latter unit's 1st and 2nd companies respectively fought from defensive positions that integrated the outlying Brest forts north and south of the main fortification.
23. BA MA RH 27-18/20, Ia KTB, 18.Pz.Div., 22.6.41.
24. Elements of the Soviet 131st Light Artillery Regiment were located in this area near the River Bug.
25. Beilage 4 zu Pz.Gruppe 2, Ia Nr 300/41, g.Kdos.v.8.6.41.
26. 2nd Border Commandant's Office of 17th Red Banner Brest Border Detachment was at Outpost No. 5 just east of Czelejewo, and was responsible for protecting about 6km of the River Bug.
27. Ia, KTB 1 and 2, 25 May–13 July 1941, XXIV Armeekorps (mot.), NARA, series T-314, Roll 718.
28. Korpsbefehl Nr 1 für den Angriff, XXXXVII Armeekorps (mot.), NARA, series T-314, Roll 1097.
29. Between June and October 1940, 160 Panzer III Ausf. F, G, H, and 8 Panzer III Ausf. E command vehicles were converted to Panzer III Ausf. H(U) Tauchpanzer IIIs. Forty-two Panzer IV Ausf. D models were transformed into Tauchpanzer IVs. On 18 August 1940 they had been organized into four battalions of three companies each.
30. Mil.-Geo.-Karte, Ausgabe Nr 1. Brest-Litovsk. Sonderausgabe! III. 41.
31. BA-MA RH-27-18/20, Ia KTB, 18.Pz.Div.

32. Newer front-line Red Army rifle divisions (Shtat 04/400-416 (5 April 1941)) had a 14,483-man paper strength that included 3 rifle, 1 light artillery, and 1 howitzer regiment, as well as a reconnaissance, antiaircraft, engineer, signals, and antitank battalion. With an official strength of 10,549 personnel a Soviet tank division (Shtat 010/10 (9 June 1940)) possessed some 300 tanks and 100 armoured cars, and comprise 2 tank, 1 motorized rifle, and 1 motorized artillery regiment, with support from a reconnaissance, antiaircraft, motorized pontoon, maintenance, medical, and transport battalion.
33. In actuality the Soviet 6th and 42nd Rifle Divisions (XVIII RC), and other units, occupied the city and fortress of Brest. Misidentifying the actual 54th Tank Brigade may have originated from its subordination to XXVIII Mechanized Corps.
34. Eight assault boats, and ninety small and forty large pneumatic rafts were used. (See Friedrich Hossbach, *Infanterie im Ostfelzug* (Osterode: Giebel & Oelschlägel, 1951).)
35. III./17th Infantry Regiment had been attached to 82nd Infantry Regiment.
36. I./ and III./31st Artillery Regiment; II./66th Artillery Regiment; I./67th Artillery Regiment; 854th Mortar Group; and 833rd Battery. Stug.Abt. 192. Ia/34 N° 267/41 Secret. (Issued 13 June 1941).
37. As part of the artillery branch assault gun battalions were under army control and not organic to divisions.
38. Jean Restayn, 'Les Sturmgeschutz III Du 192. Abteilung', *Steel Masters*, No. 20, April–May 1997, 36–41.
39. Per Zhukov's 2 May 1941 order, Soviet forward defences that were garrisoned in some strength in April 1941 were relocated to barracks, with food and ammunition sent to warehouses.
40. Pre-war, NKVD Border Guards occupied forward positions along the 1939 frontier. Rifle and tank divisions were located just to the east, with mechanized corps further still. On 22 June 1941 the Soviet Western Front (ZOVO) had 671,165 men under arms.
41. MS # D-239. Forced Crossing of the Bug River, Advance through the Russian Border Defenses and Capture of the Fortress Brest-Litovsk.
42. 'Track gauge' indicated the width between the tracks, with 'loading gauge' referring to the volume rolling stock occupied, which determined the size of tunnels, station overhangs, and how close other equipment could be placed to the rail line.
43. Pz.Gr.2, Ia Nr 301/41 g.Kdos. vom 8.6.1941.
44. On 19 June, 22nd Tank Division had 256 tanks (148 T-26 linear, 81 T-26 radium, 6 T-26 twin turret, 16 flamethrower T-26s, and 5 T-37A/38).
45. Rostislav Aliev, *The Siege of Brest 1941: A Legend of Red Army Resistance on the Eastern Front* (Barnsley: Pen & Sword, 2013), 72.
46. The Soviet tanks were from 44th Tank Regiment (22 TD) which was assisting its brethren 22nd Motorized Rifle Regiment.
47. BA-MA RH 20-4/192; BA-MA RH 26-45/20, KTB 45.Inf.Div., 22.6.41.
48. German Brandenburgers cut Soviet phone lines at Zaprudy and Zabinka at about 0100hrs on 22 June 1941; which the Soviets repaired by 0230hrs. (See L. Akhmetova, 'Kazakhstan Citizens in the 455th Rifle Regiment. The Brest Fortress, June–July, 1941', *European Journal of Natural History*, No. 6 (2015): 32.)
49. Sergeant V.F. Osaulenko (62nd Frontier Region (Brest)). (See Alexey Isaev, Artem Drabkin, *June 22. Black Calendar Day* (Yauza: Eksmo, 2008).)
50. The civilian People's Commissariat for Communications operated Soviet military wired/telephone lines, which included the Brest hub and its connections to Maloryta and Zabinka, and a third to the north-west along the River Bug that turned north for Bialystok.
51. BA-MA RH 20-4/192; BA-MA RH 26-45/20, KTB 45.Inf.Div., 22.6.41.

52. Only 75th Rifle Division occupied the position and included 34th Rifle Regiment (Miedna-Rogozno), 28th Rifle Regiment (left flank of Fourth Army), 115th Rifle Regiment (wooded area east of Maloryta), and division headquarters (Maloryta).
53. MS # B-701, Summary of A Gp B Engagements, Appendix I, Oberst a.D. Reichhelm, 29 November 1947, 62.
54. The 'B' variety of pontoon bridge equipment accommodated 8t (<83m long) and 16t (<54m long). (H.Dv. 220/3b.) The steel truss 'K' versions were more of an assault bridge that supported up to about 20 tonnes. (H.Dv. 220/3c).
55. German engineers comprised varieties that included combat (*Pioniertruppen*); construction (*Bautruppen*); railway operating (*Eisenbahntruppen*); and technical.
56. These units were actually from 22nd Rifle Regiment, with 22nd Reconnaissance Battalion and sixteen T-26s from I./43rd Tank Regiment arriving a bit later to offer support. Prior to hostilities, 22nd Tank Division's two tank regiments were to conduct gunnery exercises in the area during 22 June 1941. TsAMO, f.38, op.11373, d.67.
57. Of the roughly 22,000 tanks the Soviets possessed on *Barbarossatag* only about 14,700 were combat-ready, with the remainder being under repair or possessing only a machine-gun armament. (See Yuri Kirshin, 'The Soviet Armed Forces on the Eve of the Great Patriotic War', in Bernd Wegner (ed.), *From Peace to War: Germany, Soviet Russia, and the World, 1939–1941* (Providence, NY and Oxford: Berghahn Books, 1997), 385.)
58. III./115th Rifle Regiment (75 RD) occupied positions that included Stradecz.
59. A Soviet 122mm battery from 68th Artillery Regiment (75 RD) occupied the position near Gora Majakowa.
60. The Soviet 34th Rifle and 68th Artillery Regiments provided support.
61. Wlodawa station water level report, 22 June 1941. Institute of Meteorology and Water Management – National Research Institute, Warsaw, Poland.
62. 'Terrain factors in the Russian campaign', Office of the Chief of Military History, Special Staff, US Army, in November 1950, 13.
63. Yevgeniy Drig, *Mechanized Corps of the Red Army in Battle: The History of the Armored Forces of the Red Army in 1940–1941* (Moscow: ACT, Transitkniga, 2006), 379.
64. KTB Nr 8, RH 20-4/1199.
65. Kenneth Macksey, *Kesselring: The Making of the Luftwaffe* (New York: David McKay Co., 1978), 83.
66. Joachim Neumann, *Die 4. Panzer-Division 1938–1943, Bericht und Betrachtung zu zwei Blitzfeldzügen und zwei Jahren Krieg in Rußland* (Bonn: Selbstverlag, 1989), Vol. 1, 195.
67. zu Pz.Gr.2, Ia Nr 301/41 g.Kdos. vom 8.6.1941.
68. III./125th Rifle Regiment (6 RD).
69. The formation was responsible for 182km of the border, including the two rail and four vehicle bridges in the Brest sector, but had no order regarding destroying the structures once fighting commenced.
70. What intelligence the Soviet's possessed, analysed, and applied proved understandably poor and resulted in slow responses that often bore little resemblance to reality when implemented.
71. The Soviet II./34th Rifle Regiment occupied positions in the marsh and woods near Rogozno and Lake Biale.
72. Adapting to his force's withdrawal the Soviet Fourth Army commander reallocated 22nd Tank Division from XIV Mechanized to XXVIII Rifle Corps.
73. A Soviet Mechanized Corps (1941) comprised about 37,000 men and nearly 1,000 tanks and armoured vehicles deployed in 2 tank and 1 mechanized division, and a motorcycle regiment, with very few at official strength. Soviet Rifle Corps included some 26,500 men organized into 2 rifle divisions.

74. Per the 1936 PU-36 (Provisional Field Service Regulations) if the Soviet commander's mobile antitank and tank assets failed to block such an enemy armoured thrust, or be deemed unsuited for a counterattack, the subordinate division officers could request permission to withdraw to a more advantageous position.
75. At 1155hrs the Soviet Fourth Army's headquarters sent 'Combat Report No. 05' to Western Front, which stated that 6th Rifle Division had been forced to surrender Brest (VIZH. 1989. No. 5).
76. This force was from 61st Tank Regiment. What units within its 30th Tank Division that had yet to receive vehicles, along with 30th Artillery Regiment (which lacked ammunition), remained to prepare defences around Pruzana.
77. Colonel General Leonid M. Sandalov, CoS of Fourth Army, produced a brochure stamped 'Secret' with limited distribution and indicated that 30 of 30th Tank Division's remaining 120 T-26s had been destroyed.
78. On 19 June, 30th Tank Division had 211 tanks (124 T-26 linear, 57 T-26 radial, 8 T-26 twin turret, 8 flamethrower T-26s, and 14 tractor T-26 variants), of which 174 T-26s under Colonel Semyon Bogdanov had operated around Pruzana since February 1941. During the night of 21/22 June the formation conducted nighttime firing exercises near Poddubno.
79. The Soviet Fourth Army commander ordered a counterattack for 0600hrs on 23 June.
80. Heinz Guderian, *Achtung Panzer!* (London: Arms and Armour Press, London, 1995), 176.
81. BA-MA RH 20-4/192; BA-MA RH 26-45/20, KTB 45.Inf.Div., 22.6.41.
82. BA-MA RH 27-18/20, KTB 18. Pz. -Div., 23.6.41.
83. Hans-Joachin Röll, *Oberleutnant Albert Blaich: Als Panzerkommandant im Ost und West*, 42–43 (Dresden: Flechsig, 2009).
84. Hossbach, *Infanterie im Ostfelzug*.
85. Richard Freiherr von Rosen, *Panzer Ace: The Memoirs of an Iron Cross Panzer Commander from Barbarossa to Normandy* (London: Greenhill, 2018), 34.
86. Sixty-one of these planes were lost to combat. BM-MA RL 2/1185.
87. Donald Nijboer, *Flak in World War II* (Mechanisburg, PA: Stackpole, 2018), 124.

Chapter 2

1. Having been established on 23 June 1941 to orchestrate its war effort, the *Stavka*, under Timoshenko, provided little direction to those fighting along its Western borders, save for what in practice were often poorly executed, high-casualty counterattacks. (See Gerhard Weinberg, *Global History of WWII* (Cambridge: Cambridge University Press, 2006), 279–80.)
2. Paul Carrel, *Hitler Moves East* (New York: Ballentine, 1941), 22.
3. KTB. 4th Panzer Division's supply group of staff sections battalion (25.5.41–31.3.42).
4. The Soviet XIV Mechanized Corps' HQ, and that of Fourth Army, were located at Kobryn. Red Army command centres up to around battalion level were often difficult for the enemy to find being rather primitive and relying on runners and visual signals. Radios were usually provided at division level and higher, although tank divisions had them at lower commands. Unlike their opponents Soviet air-to-ground radio communications was rare.
5. The Soviet Fourth Army's commander issued a private order No. 04 to 75th Rifle Division that it was to conduct a fighting withdrawal towards Pinsk.
6. In accordance with USSR NKO's 'Directive No. 3' (and his own sealed 'Red Packet'), the commander of the Soviet Fourth Army, Major General Alexander Korobkov, was to have his XIV Mechanized and XXVIII Rifle Corps engage the German onslaught to buy time for Red Army forces to the east to move towards the frontier. Initially intent on using the former's two tank divisions, as they were immediately available, his staff and corps commander

convinced him to include 205th Motorized Division. (See Leonid Sandalov, *The Experience* (Moscow: Voenizdat, 1961), 71–2.)
7. 30th Tank Division possessed roughly 120 T-26s and was reinforced with 1 battalion from 205th Motorized Infantry Division. The latter also sent its 127th Tank Regiment to assist XXVIII Rifle Corps. (See Vladimir Martov, *Belarusian Chronicles (1941)* (http://www.idiot.vitebsk.net/i41/mart41.htm, 2011).)
8. BA-MA RH 27-18/20, KTB 18.Pz.-Div., 23.6.41.
9. On 19 June 205th Motorized Division had 61 tanks (37 T-26 linear, 17 T-26 radial, 2 T-26 twin turret, and 5 T-37A/38).
10. Lieutenant General Max Bork, a.D., 'Comments on Russian Railroads and Highways', US Dept of the Army, 1953.
11. Drig, *Mechanized Corps of the Red Army in Battle*, 384.
12. Unable to counter the enemy's rapid battlefield tempo the Soviet Fourth Army commander stressed to his Western Front superior the need to focus air assets in the Pruzana–Bereza Kartuska sector to help blunt the advance of 17th and 18th Panzer Divisions.
13. Ilya Ehrenburg and Vasily Grossman, *The Complete Black Book of Russian Jewry* (London: Routledge, 2003), account of Dr Olga Goldfain.
14. During the action to retake Pruzana 30th Tank Division possessed eighty T-26s. Soviet intelligence believed twenty German tanks had been destroyed.
15. BA-MA RH 20-4/1199, KTB AOK 4, 23.6.41.
16. KTB Nr 1, RH 21-2/927.
17. Western Front possessed 2,251 tanks. Robert Forczyk, *Tank Warfare on the Eastern Front, 1941–1942: Schwerpunkt* (Barnsley: Pen & Sword, 2014), 46.
18. With the Brest–Minsk rail line terminating in Moscow it, along with three others (River Neman – Leningrad; River Bug – the Donets Basin; and River San – Odesa), represented the primary east–west routes across Soviet territory.
19. KTB, RH 26-29/6.
20. Neumann, *Die 4. Panzer-Division 1938–1943*.
21. Red Army soldiers and NCOs carried a 'gold book' that contained information such as weapons and uniforms issued, which was intended to help ensure such items were cared for, and provided a control mechanism under threat of leadership revoking them.
22. 22nd Tank Division's commander, Major General V.P. Puganov, was killed during the fight that reduced his operational tanks to just forty.
23. L.M. Sandalov, *Combat Operations of the 4th Army Troops in the Initial Period of the Great Patriotic War* (Moscow: Voenizdat, 1961).
24. The northern group included elements from 84th and 333rd Rifle Regiments, while the other contained a horse-drawn battalion from 204th Howitzer Artillery Regiment.
25. Over the course of 22 and 23 June 1941 Second Panzer Group was credited with destroying 220 Soviet tanks. RH 21-2/927.
26. KTB Nr 1, RH 21-2/927.
27. 'Kampfgruppe Beigel' comprised 2./ and 3./39th Rifle Battalion, 39th Engineer Battalion, 6./75th Motorized Artillery Regiment, 1./3rd Motorcycle Battalion, (one platoon)/543rd Panzerjäger Battalion, and two twin antiaircraft guns from 91st Light Antiaircraft Battalion.
28. Seeing the operational and strategic consequences of a German offensive that showed few signs of tapering, on 24 June 1941 an Evacuation Council was established in Moscow to organize the deportation of Soviet citizens and eventually the relocation of more than 1,500 factories to the safety of the Urals, River Volga region, and Siberia. Six days later Stalin established the State Defence Committee (GKO) that centralized all facets of the war effort.
29. Operational summary of the headquarters of Western Front No. 5 by 2200hrs on 24 June 1941.

30. KTB, RH 26-45/20.
31. Thomas Jentz, *Panzer Tracts. Bertha's Big Brother* (Darlington, MD: Panzer Tracts, 2001), 33.
32. T-315 Roll 115. 3.Panzer.Division ktb 24.6.41.
33. The Pinsk Naval Flotilla had been dispersed along the main waterways to the east and west of its namesake city. The Pinsk airfield had been repeatedly bombed and made unusable, along with the aircraft already there.
34. In 1938 the Soviet Union (Eastern Europe) and Germany respectively had 1.8 and nearly 20 rail miles per 100 square miles. 'Comments on Russian Railroads and Highways'.
35. Abt.Gef.Stand, d.26.6.1941, II.Abteilung Flak-Regiment 11 (mot. gl.), Abt.Ia Az.13/41.
36. German divisional and higher staffs comprised a tactical group of general staff sections (*Fuhrungsabteilung*), corps or division quartermaster (*Quartiermeister*), and Adjutant's Office (*Adjutantur*).
37. Veterans of the 3rd Panzer Division, *Armoured Bears Volume One: The German 3rd Panzer Division in World War II* (Mechanicsburg, PA: Stackpole, 2013), 149.
38. During such advances under fire German tank crews typically employed fire and movement, in which one vehicle(s) would assume a stationary firing position while others would advance. On reaching a point roughly half the effective range of the overwatch tank's main gun the process would be reversed.
39. Elements of the Soviet 55th Rifle Division.
40. These 30th Tank Division forces were subsequently withdrawn east of Slutsk to concentrate around Podores'ye, Voloshevo, and Sorogi. TsAMO f.4a, op.4613, d.20, l.318-319.
41. KTB. 4th Panzer Division's supply group of staff sections battalion (25.5.41–31.3.42).
42. BA-MA RH 27-18/20, KTB 18 PD, 24.6.41. Kreuter, Georg Christian (SR 101/18 PD), 2007. Craig W.H. Luther papers.
43. German intelligence had correctly identified the Soviet 121st and 143rd Rifle Divisions (XXXXVII RC), and the independent 155th Rifle Division. 143rd Rifle Division, however, actually operated in the Kyiv sector.
44. T-315 Roll 115. 3.Panzer-Division ktb 25.6.41.
45. David Stahel and Craig Luther (eds), *Soldiers of Barbarossa: Combat on the Eastern Front* (Mechanicsburg, PA: Stackpole, 2020).
46. Heinz Guderian, *Panzer Leader* (Bsoton, MA: Da Capo Press, 2002), 130.
47. Franz Götte (ed.), *Die 29. Falke-Division: 1936–1945; 29. I.D.29. I.D. (Mot.)–29. Pz.-Gren.-Div.; eine Dokumentation in Bildern* (Eggolsheim: Ed. Dörfler im Nebel-Verl, 2004).
48. At this time, with no connection with his superiors, the commander of the 205th Motorized Rifle Division, believing the front had already moved far to the east, at 0900hrs abandoned the River Jasiolda and made for Slonim to join the main army.
49. Of the 170 Soviet divisions located in the western frontier zone, 48, 64, and 56 were respectively 10–50km, 50–150km, and 150–500km from the frontier. (Militärgeschichtliches Forschungsamt (Research Institute for Military History), *Germany and the Second World War*, 10 vols (Oxford, 1990–2012), Vol. IV, *Attack on Soviet Union*, 85–6; David Glantz, III, 21–2.)
50. Report, 'Air Staff Post Hostilities Intelligence, Requirements on G.A.F. Tactical Employment-Liaison Operations', Call # 519.601B-4, Section IV H, 7, 12–13, in the USAF Collection, AFHRA, Maxwell AFB Alabama; Oral Interview, 'Lt Gen Heinz Gaedcke', U.S. Air Force Oral History Program, 12 April 1970, Call # K239.0512-1180, 5, in the USAF Collection, AFHRA, Maxwell AFB Alabama; Report, 'Air Staff Post Hostilities Intelligence Requirements on G.A.F. Tactical Employment', Call # 519.601 B-4 Section IV E Part 1, 60, in the USAF Collection, AFHRA, Maxwell AFB Alabama.
51. Report, No. VII/34, 'Air Operations on the Russian Front in 1941', 3.

52. 512.621 VII/34, in the USAF Collection, AFHRA, Maxwell AFB Alabama; 'Conduct of the Air War in the Second World War', 439.
53. General der Flieger a. D. Paul Deichmann, 'German Air Force Operations in Support of the Army', USAF Historical Division, 1962, 131–3.
54. Report, Air Staff Post Hostilities Intelligence Requirements on G.A.F. Tactical Employment, Call #519.601 B-4 Section IV E Part 1, 63, in the USAF Collection, AFHRA, Maxwell AFB Alabama.
55. KTB Nr 8, RH 20-4/1199.
56. The Soviets were similarly guilty of shooting prisoners, although official efforts were made to cease such actions and ensure relatively proper interrogation, feeding, and care policies were maintained. BA-MA RH 19 III/444, folders 207–14.
57. Abt.Gef.Stand, d.26.6.1941, II.Abteilung Flak-Regiment 11 (mot. gl.), Abt.Ia Az.13/41.
58. KTB Nr 1, RH 21-2/927.

Chapter 3

1. On 26 June 1941 senior Soviet leadership in Belorussia ordered the creation of 14 guerrilla units totalling 539 NKGB (People's Commissariat for State Security) and 623 NKVD personnel, as well as Red Army soldiers. Once in action, however, these groups were soon destroyed.
2. Von Rosen, *Panzer Ace*, 56.
3. TsAMO, f.208, op.2526, d.27, l.214–219.
4. Model's spearhead included I./6th Panzer Regiment, I./394th Rifle Regiment, and part of 3rd Rifle Regiment.
5. The Soviet Slutsk fortified districts totalled 129 defensive structures constructed in 1938/39, and organized into six Battalion Defence Areas (part of 63rd Fortified Region extending to Minsk). What heavier weapons systems they initially incorporated were mostly relocated to outfit newer 1939 border defences that ran along German-occupied Poland. Belorussia's remaining defensive zones included Polotsk, Minsk, and Mozyr'; four of twenty-three such sectors that comprised the 'Stalin Line'. S.A. Pivovarchik, *Belarusian Lands in the System of Fortification Construction of the Russian Empire and the USSR (1772–1941)* (Grodno: Grsu, 2006).
6. XIV Mechanized Corps was considered to have lost 75 per cent of its effectiveness, since the start of hostilities, according to the 'Operational summary of the headquarters of the 4th Army No 1 on June 24, 1941'. The formation would soon be withdrawn to Dovsk before relocating to Smolensk to refit.
7. Drig, *Mechanized Corps of the Red Army in Battle*, 390.
8. Unlike the German/European model where resupply requisitions were made to replace what had been expended, which resulted in a relatively equal distribution, the Red Army prioritized logistics to active formations. 'Handbook on USSR Military Forces', Chapter VII: Logistics. War Department (USA).
9. KTB Nr 3, RH 27-3/14.
10. The Soviet VI Mechanized Corps (4 TD, 7 TD) tried to force a breakout north of Baranowicze.
11. KTB, RH 27-18/20.
12. Gerbet, *Generalfeldmarschall Fedor von Bock*, 165.
13. Having met with Stalin on 30 June, Zhukov garnered the Premier's approval to establish an emergency defensive line running from near the Latvian border, and connecting Polotsk, Vitebsk, Orsha, Mogilev, and Mozyr'. Another would extend along Selizharovo–Smolensk–Roslavl'–Gomel'.

14. Brigade Commissar Ivan S. Tkachenko (75 RD).
15. KTB Nr 1, RH 21-2/927.
16. Colonel Ostashenko (800), Colonels Pimenov and Berkov (600 each), and Major Dmitriev (400) from XXVIII Rifle Corps HQ, with some personnel from XIV Mechanized Corps.
17. With Pavlov's Western Front having been roughly handled and operating in an increasingly chaotic battlespace he relocated his headquarters to Mogilev to presumably better orchestrate his rather fragmented command.
18. T-315 R-706 18.Pz.-Div. 27 June 1941.
19. R.L. Swank and W.E. Marchand, 'Combat neuroses: development of combat exhaustion', *Archives of Neurology & Psychiatry*, 55 (1946), 236–47.
20. Larger German projectiles possessed sufficient mass to jam the turrets of KV-1s and 2s, which suffered from over-stressed clutches and engines that limited 'life expectancy' to some 100 hours before major maintenance was required. 37mm guns could penetrate the much lighter T-34s out to some 400m, and even 20mm AP rounds if given a sufficiently short range and effective armour thickness. For all the benefits of a vehicle balanced among firepower, protection, and mobility, its glacis-mounted driver's hatch and 'waffle'-pattern tracks proved weak points. Collection of combat documents of the Great Patriotic War, issue 33 (Moscow: Voenizdat, 1957), p. 207, Declassified. Military-scientific Directorate of the General Staff.
21. KTB, RH 26-29/6.
22. In Guderian's path the Minsk fortified region No. 63 was 140km long and comprised 327 pillboxes.
23. Soviet commanders favoured using schools, factories, and administrative buildings for command posts, as they had the necessary amount of room for communications, etc., equipment and personnel. Private homes were avoided due to the prevalence of lice and other infestations. Russel Stolfi, Lonnie Ratley, III, and John O'Neill, Jr, 'German Disruptions of Soviet Command, Control, and Communications in Barbarossa, 1941', Naval Postgraduate School, 1983, 54.
24. KTB Nr 1, RH 21-2/927.
25. Already, Hoth's 20th Panzer Division was moving into the Kurapaty Forest on Minsk's northern edge where NKVD personnel (per Order Nos 00447 and 00485) had murdered and buried tens of thousands of ethnic Belorussian, Pole, Finn, Balt, and German civilians since 1937, as part of widescale Soviet political repression. January 1989 findings from a Belorussian SSR Public Prosecutor's Office criminal investigation headed by the Deputy Chairperson of the Council of Ministers, Nina Mazaï.
26. G. Aronson and A. Goldstein, *Russian Jewry, 1917–1967* (New York: 1969), 88–122, 171–208.
27. KTB, RH 27-18/20.
28. 1,700km to the west, British cartographers at Bletchley Park broke a German Army Enigma key (Vulture I) being used on the Eastern Front, intelligence they soon provided to Stalin, who for the foreseeable future lacked the means to exploit it.
29. OKW ktb, 27 June 1941.
30. At 2200hrs on 27 June the Soviet Fourth Army commander ordered engineers from 121st Rifle Division to detonate explosives on all three structures. A report from the Soviet commander of XXXXVII Rifle Corps to that of Fourth Army, Corps Control Department, 23 June to 3 July.
31. BA-MA RH 27-3/14, KTB 3. Pz.-Div., 28.6.41.
32. On 28 June 1941, in his political capacity as head of the Borisov District, and tasked with organizing a defence of the town and garrison two days previously, Corps Commissar 1st Rank Ivan Susaykov reported to the commander of Western Front that what forces that had been thrown together near the town (save for the 1,400-odd cadets of the Borisov

Automobile and Tractor School No. 17/101) were 'incapable of combat' and comprised a mix of panicked, demoralized 'rabble' from the rear areas. F. 208, op. 3038ss, house, ll. 41, 42.
33. The Soviet armour was from 26th Tank Division; although the numbers appear to be inflated given the formation started the war with forty-four tanks and 38th Tank Division operated to its south.
34. Ob.d.L. Abt. Ic, g.Kdos., Lagebericht Nr 660, 30.6.1941.
35. BA-MA RH 26-45/20 KTB 45. Inf.-Div., 29.6.41.
36. KTB Nr 4, SS-Rgt 'Deutschland', 25.5.1941–31.8.1941.
37. Guderian, *Panzer Leader*, 131.
38. White Star Line, 1912. 'The Wehrmacht – Complete Series', 54, 23–54: 32.
39. KTB, RH 27-18/20.
40. The T-34/76s and KV-1 were from I./13th Tank Regiment (7 TD). Drig, *Mechanized Corps of the Red Army in Battle*, 239.
41. With the fall of Minsk just a week into the conflict between 28 June and 2 July 1941 the *Stavka* worked to build up its presence across Bock's advance axis to Moscow, including Twenty-Fourth and Twenty-Eighth Armies (nineteen divisions) between the capital and Smolensk, and Nineteenth Army (nine divisions) and Sixteenth Army (six divisions) from Front Reserve to the Smolensk sector. Timoshenko arrived at Western Front on 4 July 1941, who as the People's Commissar of Defence worked to integrate the retreating Fourth and Thirteenth Armies, and the remnants of Third and Tenth Armies along the Berezina River.
42. KTB Nr 1, RH 21-2/927.
43. During Barbarossa's planning daily fuel consumption was estimated at 9,000m^3. By 1 July it averaged 11,500m^3, a 128 per cent increase. (See Burdick and Jacobsen (eds), *The Halder War Diary*, Vol. VI, 193.)
44. Just before noon on 29 June 1941 the Soviet 36th Cavalry Division pushed into the Slonim area, as did 29th Mechanized Rifle and 7th Tank Divisions in an attempt to breakout.
45. Red Army soldiers referred to the Wolkowysk–Slonim road as 'The Road of Death'. Drig, *Mechanized Corps of the Red Army in Battle*, 238.
46. KTB, RH 27-18/20.
47. KTB Nr 3, RH 27-3/14.
48. US Military Intelligence Service, 'Notes on German Artillery', *Tactical and Technical Trends*, No. 6, August 27, 1942.
49. On 29 June 1941 Moscow issued a general directive calling for Soviet forces to conduct scorched earth tactics before any withdrawal to deny food, fuel, shelter, and other assets to the Germans, and further hinder their overburdened logistics.
50. SS-Division 'Reich' Ia, Div.Gef.St., 29 June 1941.
51. KTB 10. Infanterie Division, 29.6.41.
52. I./Schützen-Regiment 12. O.U., den 1.7.1941.
53. Major I.N. Rukhle. 'On the Nature of the Initial Period in the Two World Wars', *Military History Journal*, No. 4 (1960).
54. KTB Nr 3, RH 27-3/14.
55. 2nd [II] Rifle Corps Combat Log on the Combat Actions of the 100th Rifle Division (20 June to 6 July 1941).
56. Martin Gilbert, *The Second World War: A Complete History* (Bloomington, IN: Indiana University Press, 2009), 15.
57. Guido Knopp, *Die Wehrmacht: Eine Bilanz* (Munich: Goldmann Verlag, 2007), 150.
58. On 24 June 1941 a 'Council of Evacuation' was formed to implement the relocation of Soviet industry from Western Russia to the relative safety of the Urals, Volga, and Siberia. Six days later Stalin established the State Defence Committee (GKO) that centralized all facets of the war effort.

59. Given their country's respective, post-First World War standing, the Germans and Soviets used the secret facility near Kazan, Russia to their mutual benefit between 1926 and 1933.
60. BA-MA RH 27-18/20, KTB 18. Pz.-Div., 1.7.41.
61. Soviet armoured train No. 47, which had recently moved through Orsha and Borisov. (See M.V. Kolomiets, *Armored Trains in Battle 1941–1945* (Weston-super-Mare: Aviapress, 2018).)
62. Having failed to hold the River Berezina in the Borisov sector, on 2 July 1941, Susaykov provided a report that elements of 1st Moscow Motor Rifle Division refused to fight in the town's defence; a situation no doubt due to lack of communications, weapons, and information on the fast-approaching enemy, in addition to both commands operating rather independently. (See S.S. Zakharevich, *Considerable Blood: How the USSR won the war of 1941–1945* (Minsk: Sovremennaia Shkola, 2009).)
63. As what occasionally happened during the chaos of combat Tser wished to keep the Borisov Bridge open as long as possible to allow Soviet forces filtering out from around Minsk an escape, only to have fast-moving German elements catch the town's defenders by surprise. (See Yakov Kreizer (Colonel commanding 1st Moscow Motorized Rifle Division), 'In the Battles Between the. Berezina and the Dnieper', *Military History Journal*, No. 6 (1966).)
64. Albert Schick, *Die Geschichte der 10. Panzer-Division 1939–1943* (Winnipeg: J.J. Fedorowicz, 2013), 279–80.
65. KTB Nr 3, RH 27-3/14.

Chapter 4

1. To replace battlefield losses the Presidium of the Supreme Soviet of 22 June 1941 decreed that with the classes of 1919–23 already serving those from 1905–18 would follow suit (including 800,000 women), while a broader manpower pool of males aged 16 to 50 were to receive pre-military training. (See Horst Boog et al., *Germany and the Second World War, Vol. IV: Attack on Soviet Union* (Oxford: Clarendon Press, 2015), 839.)
2. Guderian, *Panzer Leader*, 135.
3. 'In the Battles between the Berezina and the Dnieper', *Military History Journal*, No. 6 (1966).
4. Having secured air superiority, largely free-ranging Luftwaffe aircraft inflicted a considerable psychological, as well as physical, toll on Red Army soldiers, as evidenced by their use of the term 'aeroplane panic' (*'samoletoboiazn'*). (See Mawdsley, *Thunder in the East*, 55, 58.)
5. Having recalled General of the Army, Dmitriy Pavlov, to Moscow for eventual court marshal and execution, as a scapegoat for failing to stop Army Group Centre's offensive, on 2 July Stalin placed Timoshenko, in command of Western Front.
6. SS-Division 'Reich', NAM T-354 R-121.
7. SS-Division 'Reich', Div.Gef.Std., 2–4 July 1941.
8. A study on US veterans that fought at Normandy discovered that after sixty days of continuous combat 98 per cent became 'psychiatric casualties' and the remainder 'aggressive psychological casualties'. (See Dave Grossman and Bruce K. Siddle, 'Psychological Effects of Combat', *Encyclopedia of Violence, Peace, and Conflict* (San Diego, CA: Academic Press (2000).)
9. By now, the Soviet Twentieth Army had moved up to the River Dnepr to begin fortifying its eastern edge, save for 137th and 172nd Rifle Divisions respectively west of the waterway at Mogilev and Orsha. TsAMO, f.208, op.2511, d.434.
10. The Borisov Automobile and Tractor School comprised four training tank battalions. 1st Moscow Motorized Rifle Division had recently been brought up to full strength and comprised 225 BT-7M light tanks, plus 10 KV-1s and 30 T-34s.
11. Combining a lack of military experience, an overinflated sense of self importance, and Stalin's favour, the head of the Main Political Directorate of the Red Army, Lev Mekhlis,

was sent to the front tasked with finding those leaders considered responsible for Soviet retreats and failures, and if necessary have them labelled 'traitor' and summarily executed.
12. Von Rosen, *Panzer Ace*, p. 62.
13. 2300hrs, the bridge over the Drut' at Kolosy is finished, using Brücko B403 and Brücko 606.
14. The Soviet armoured train No. 50 had come up from Gomel' to the south of Bobruysk. (See Kolomiets, *Armored Trains in Battle*.)
15. KTB 3PD 5 July 1941. In response to the rapid German advance along the frontier the GKO began to mobilize, name, and number one volunteer division from each of the Moscow area's twenty-five administrative districts (Raions). Overwhelmingly lacking military experience, uniforms, and generally relying on aging foreign small arms, they were tasked with digging trenches. (See Rodric Braithwaite, *Moscow 1941: A City and its People at War* (London: Profile, 2006), 117.)
16. KTB 3PD 3 July 1941.
17. Röll, *Oberleutnant Albert Blaich*, 82.
18. *Geschichte der 3. Panzer-Division Berlin-Brandenburg 1935–1945* (Berlin: Günter Richter, 1967), Traditionsverband der Division (Hg), 125.
19. Von Rosen, *Panzer Ace*, 91.
20. Illustrating the damage Red Army forces had sustained over the last two weeks, 6th, 42nd, and 55th Rifle Divisions numbered just 340, 4,000, and 800 personnel, respectively. TsAMO: f.208, op.2511, d.429.
21. Oberstlt Joseph Dinglreiter, *Die Vierziger. Chronik des Panzer-Grenadier-Regiments 40* (Augsburg: Kameradschaft Regiment 40, 1955), 40–4.
22. SS-Division 'Reich', Div.Gef.Std., 4 July 1941.
23. XX Mechanized Corps (26 TD, 38 TD, 205 MRD) was tasked with blocking the most direct enemy attack axis against Mogilev, which included the River Drut', and a defensive line that ran through Krasnaya Sloboda and Tverdovo.
24. Having moved up from Krasnyy, during 4/5 July, 73rd Rifle Division took over from 137th Rifle Division, which withdrew from its defence of Orsha and Vysokoye to the Dnepr's east bank.
25. Jan Grabowski and Barbara Engelking, *Night Without End: The Fate of Jews in German-Occupied Poland* (Bloomingotn, IN: Indiana University Press, 2022).
26. In what was the intended role for such formations the Soviet V (including 13 TD, 17 TD, 109 MRD (974 tanks)) and VII Mechanized Corps (with 14 TD and 18 TD (571 tanks)) each struck for the Vitebsk and Lepel areas with the intention of delivering a crippling blow to Bock's offensive. Drig, *Mechanized Corps of the Red Army in Battle*, 189, 247.
27. Daily Report from 6.7.1941. Attachment Nr 201 to the War Diary Nr 2 XXXXVII.Pz.Korps.
28. TsAMO, f.38, op.11353, d.5, l.79.
29. Timoshenko, Zhukov, and Twentieth Army's recently allocated commander, Lieutenant General Pavel Kurochkin, were unaware 17th Panzer Division's advance element had recently arrived at Senno. (See Glantz, *Barbarossa Derailed*, Vol. 1, 73.)
30. Kurochkin reported to Timoshenko that the lack of coordination among Red Army armour, artillery, and air support undercut V and VII Mechanized Corps' effectiveness. (See *Donesenie komanduyushchego 20-oi armii narodnomu komissaru oborony Soyuza SSR ot 6 iyulya 1941 g. o boevykh 5-go I 7-go mekhanizirovannykh korpusov* (Sbornik), 33.)
31. Stalin's execution, imprisonment, and expulsion of nearly 55,000 Soviet officers between 1937 and 1941, the Red Army's massive expansion during the Five-Year Plan (1937–42), and the transfer of veteran officers to fill out new formations broadly undercut Soviet combat capabilities that had yet to be rectified by Barbarossa. To compensate for the dearth of qualified personnel Soviet senior leadership often had to insert partially formed, trained, and equipped formations into the field, which further degraded quality, morale, and discipline.

32. Grufl. 21 Command Post (7.7.41), RG242 T313 R222, F7486800.
33. Indicative of Kurochkin's poor command and control that adversely affected Soviet performance at 2300hrs on 7 July he sent out Combat Order No. 16 that grossly misstated that XX Mechanized Corps was 'inflicting a successful strike on the enemy'. (See *Boevoi prikaz komanduyushchego voiskami 20-I armii No. 16 ot 7 iyulya 1941 g. na oboronu rubezha Gnezdilovichi, Bogushevskoe, Orsha.*)
34. BA-MA MSg 1/1147: Tagebuch Lemelsen, 10.7.41.
35. Guderian, *Panzer Leader*, 136. Nineteenth Army had recently moved into the line from the Soviet strategic reserve. TsAMO, f.208, op.70438, d.1, l.14.
36. SS-Division 'Reich' Ia, Div.Gef.Std., 4 July 1941.
37. Artillerie-Regiment 103 Ia. Rgts.Gef.Std., 5.7.41 0500hrs.
38. The Soviet 117th Rifle Division (LXVI RC) had recently moved up from Gomel'.
39. 3. Pz. Div. Abt. Ia. Anl. Nr 1 zum KTB Nr 3, 6.7.41.
40. SS-Division 'Reich', Div.Gef.Std., 8 July 1941.
41. Attachment Nr 217 to the KTB XXXXVII.Pz.Korps. 7.6[8.7].41.
42. Surprisingly, Stalin was only convinced of the reality and magnitude of the German offensive on 7 July 1941, having previously believed the reports of fighting over the last two weeks were panic mongering and German SD security personnel conducting provocative actions much as they had done in Poland and the West.
43. To address the lack of coordination between V and VII Mechanized Corps, and their respective subordinate units, Lieutenant General Andrey Eremenko stressed establishing a mechanized army command, with its own headquarters. (See Andrey Eremenko, *At the Beginning of the War* (Moscow: Nauka, 1965).)
44. The engineers were from 316th Rifle Regiment (18 RD).
45. For the loss of 12,157 personnel (out of an initial 750,000) Army Group Centre inflicted 417,729 Soviet casualties, and destroyed or captured between 1,177 and 1,669 aircraft, 4,799 tanks, and 9,427 guns and mortars. Heeresgruppe Mitte. Ic/A.O., H.Qu. den 15.7.41.
46. Timoshenko mistakenly believed XXIV Motorized Army Corps would try to cross the Dnepr at Rogachev and not Bykhov. Glantz, *Barbarossa Derailed*, Vol. 1, 94.
47. Burdick and Jacobsen (eds), *The Halder War Diary*, Vol. VI, 52.
48. Guderian, *Panzer Leader*, 140.
49. During this period Soviet rifle divisions occupied frontages upwards of 25km, which for a defensive stance was more than double its doctrinally intended distance. The recent damage the Germans had inflicted on the armour-heavy Soviet mechanized corps greatly reduced the number of tanks available.
50. Between the opening of hostilities and 9 July 1941 the Soviet Western Front suffered 417,790 casualties and the loss of 4,799 tanks. G.F. Krivosheev (ed.), *Rossiia i SSSR v voinakh XX veka: Poteri vooruzhennykh sil* (Moscow: OLMA-PRESS, 2001), 267–8, 484.

Chapter 5

1. Although Soviet intelligence had kept Timoshenko informed about the German build-up there was little time to bring up reinforcements from Nineteenth Army (regrouping from around Kyiv) and XXIII Mechanized Corps (Orel).
2. Pz AOK 2, KTB, 10 July 41.
3. KTB. 4th Panzer Division's supply group of staff sections battalion (25.5.41–31.3.42).
4. T-314, R 1098. KTB Nr 3. XXXXVII Pz.Korps.
5. Pz AOK 2, KTB. 11 July 41.

6. The Soviet 316th Rifle Regiment (18 RD) suffered heavy losses during the barrage and offered no initial resistance against 29th Motorized Infantry Division's crossing at Kopys. Veniamin Kazantsev, *The Eighteenth Division* (Kazan: Tatnigoizdat Publishing, 1968).
7. Corps Command for the Attack over the Dnejepr (Dnepr). Anlage Nr 238, KTB Nr 2, XXXXVII.Pz.Korps.
8. 3./(Pz)/14 attached to Headquarters XXXXVI (Motorized Army) Corps from 10.7.41.
9. O.Qu., Anlagenband 2 z. KTB, 4 May 1941–28 April 1942, Panzerarmee 4, NAM, series T-313, Roll 335, Frame 8617204.
10. Second Panzer Group, 'KTB I', Vol. I 25034/1.
11. 3rd Panzer Division, KTB, 12.7.41.
12. As what often occurred during desperate wartime situations in which senior leadership made major decisions, while far removed from the crisis, at 1545hrs the *Stavka* ordered Timoshenko to attack all along his front from Polotsk to Zhlobin.
13. 18. Panzer-Division, Abt. Ia. KTB Teil I vom 22.6–20.8.41 (inclusive).
14. Panzer Group 2, 'KTB Nr I', Vol. I, 16 July 1941, T-313/80/7318639-7318640.
15. Burdick and Jacobsen (eds), *The Halder War Diary*, Vol. III, 74.
16. SS-Rgt 'Deutschland' was without its I. and Reconnaissance Battalions at the time.
17. Desperate to fill the gap the German Army Group Centre created after crushing Western Front, on 14 July 1941 the *Stavka* created the Front of the Reserve Armies, with Twenty-Ninth and Thirtieth Armies generally across from Hoth's sector and Twenty-Fourth and Twenty-Eighth Armies focusing on Guderian's.
18. Von Rosen, *Panzer Ace*, 106.
19. Komsomol was a youth division of the Communist Party of the Soviet Union. Second Army, Ia., 'KTB Teil I', 15 July 1941, 16690/1, National Archives Microfilm Publication T-312, roll 1654 (T-312/1654/00038).
20. Speeches Stalin made on 13 January 1941 before army commanders and 8 February 1941 at the Party Central Committee synced with Red Army's State Defence Plan to conduct what they believed would be decisive counterattacks against a German invasion. BA-MA, RH 24-24/335, 24 September 1941. Map exercises emphasized Soviet attack axes from Leningrad to Helsinki, Grodno–Brest towards East Prussia, Western Ukraine to Warsaw–Lodz, and south of the Polesie Marshes to the Carpathian Mountains. BA-MA, RH 21-1/472, 27 August 1941.
21. LIII Army Corps 'KTB I', 15 July 1941, T-313/1310/000086.
22. BA-MA, RH 20-4/672, n.d.; BA-MA, RH 24-48/198, 1 July 1941.
23. Due to heavy losses among the tank-heavy, Soviet mechanized corps, and disruptions to armour production, as facilities were relocated eastward, on 15 July 1941, the *Stavka* ordered these formations dissolved.
24. 10th Panzer Division, Ia., 'KTB Nr 5', 16 July 1941, 22340/1, T-315/561/000325.
25. III./394th Motorized Rifle Regiment, half of 3./ and 7./75th Motorized Artillery Regiment, 543rd (minus 2. Company), and the rest of 521st Panzerjäger Battalion were also brought back under Model's authority.
26. Schick, *Die Geschichte der 10. Panzer-Division*, 310.
27. 'KTB Teil I', 16 July 1941, T-312/1654/0041.
28. On 16 July 1941 the GKO ordered the construction of the Mozhaisk defensive line about 170km outside of the Moscow reservoir and the creation of the Reserve Front. The formation comprised five NKVD divisions and ten of the new volunteer divisions. Braithwaite, *Moscow 1941*.
29. Aktenvermerk vom 16. Juli 1941, in Der Prozess gegen die Hauptkriegsverbrecher vor dem Internationalen Militärgerichtshof. Nürnberg 14. November 1945–1. Oktober 1946.

30. Hans Schäufler (ed.), *Knight's Cross Panzers: The German 35th Panzer Regiment in WWII* (Mechanicsburg, PA: Stackpole, 2010), 89–90.
31. Dept of the Army, 'German Armored Traffic Control During the Russian Campaign', 1962, 3.
32. Burdick and Jacobsen (eds), *The Halder War Diary*, Vol. VI, 250.
33. Ibid., 248.
34. KTB Nr 2 XXXXVII Pz.Korps. T-314/1097.
35. 'Operational Group Kachalov' included 104th Tank Division, with a dozen KV-1s, 30 T-34s, and 180 BTs and T-26s. Forczyk, *Tank Warfare on the Eastern Front*, 86.
36. The national directives for partisan activity, issued on 18 July 1941, stated that partisan members were to include only 'participants in the Civil War and those comrades who have already showed their worth in the destruction battalion [NKVD – the Soviet Secret Police and State Security Organization – sabotage units], the people's militia, and also workers from the NKVD'. Outside instruction called not so much for openly fighting the Germans, but helping reinstate and uphold Soviet authority in the occupied territories.
37. Lewinski allocated I./6th Panzer, II./75th Motorized Artillery, and I./3rd Motorized Rifle Regiments, and 521st Panzerjäger Battalion to the task. 3rd Panzer Division, KTB, 19.7.41.
38. Panzer Group 2, 'KTB Nr I', Vol. I, 19 July 1941, T-313/80/7318678.
39. SS-Division 'Reich' Ia, Division Command Post, 18 July 1941, 2330hrs.
40. Gerbet, *Generalfeldmarschall Fedor von Bock*.
41. 10th Panzer Division, 'KTB Nr 5', 21 July 1941, T-315/561/000394.
42. On 20 July 1941 Stalin ordered that all Red Army units 'should be purged of unreliable elements'. Gilbert, *The Second World War*, 214.
43. Panzer Group 2, 'KTB Nr I', 20 July 1941, T-313/80/7318684.
44. To help stem Army Group Centre's progress on 20 July 1941 the *Stavka* threw together five operational groups from its Front of the Reserve Armies; four each from one of its armies and one of cavalry. The one from Lieutenant General V.Y. Kachalov's Twenty-Eighth Army included two rifle and one tank division and was sent to the west of Roslavl'.

Chapter 6

1. As a rough example of the expanding front line on *Barbarossatag* the *Ostheer* (excluding Axis Allies) was distributed along a 712km stretch between Nimmersatt and Sianki (General Gouvernment (German-occupied Poland)). One month later (22 July 1941) the distance had increased to 1,381km (Narva to Chisinau (Chişinău) (Moldavian SSR)).
2. The Soviet 152nd Rifle Division's initially successful efforts to wrest Smolensk from the Germans soon evaporated, as 129th Rifle Division proved unable to provide coordinated support, and XXXIV Rifle Corps was slow to react. Sixteenth Army's Journal of Combat Operations, TsAMO, f.358, op.5916, d.22.
3. As part of Front of the Reserve Armies, Twenty-Eighth Army was placed under Western Front on 21 July 1941.
4. At this time 35th Panzer Regiment possessed 44 Panzer IIs (20 operational, 13 under repair, 11 total loss); 31 Panzer III 37mm and 74 Panzer III 50mm (2/18, 16/42, 13/14); 20 Panzer IVs (7, 9, 4); and 6 command tanks (2, 3, 1). A lack of replacement parts, and especially engines and transmissions presented a considerable problem. 4. Panzer-Division command post. Ia status report to Schweppenburg on the division's personnel and materiel.
5. Ian Kershaw, *Hitler: A Biography* (New York: W.W. Norton & Company, 2010), 409.
6. Burdick and Jacobsen (eds), *The Halder War Diary*, Vol. III, 100.
7. B.H. Liddell Hart, *The German Generals Talk* (New York: W. Morrow, 1971).
8. Schick, *Die Geschichte der 10. Panzer-Division*.

9. To help resist Army Group Centre, Red Army personnel and requisitioned civilians were used to construct trenches, weapons emplacements, and other defences before Ostashkov, Rzhev, Yel'nya, and Bryansk.
10. *Berück Süd Befehl* 23.8.41, Military Tribunal V of the United States of America (Case 12).
11. Bock, 'Tagebuchnotizen Osten I', 24 July 1941, T-84/271/000375.
12. II./SS-Rgt 'Deutschland', Battalion Command, 27.7.41.
13. XXXXVI Panzer (still Motorized Army) Corps, Corps Command Post, 25.7.41.
14. SS-Division 'Reich' Ia, Division Command Post, 25 July 1941.
15. KTB, 137. Infanterie Division, 26.7.1941. T-315, R-1413. 18507/1.
16. KTB, 263. Infanterie Division Ib, 26.7.1941. T-315, R-1835.
17. Second Army, 'KTB Teil I', 24–6 July 1941, T-312/1654/000070-0074.
18. Panzer Group 2, 'KTB Nr I', 20 July 1941, T-313/80/7318699.
19. Abt. Ic /A.O. 30.7.1941. Since the start of Barbarossa, 18th Panzer Division captured or destroyed 633 Soviet armoured vehicles, 141 artillery guns, and 5,500 Red Army soldiers. T-315 R-706 18.Pz-Div, 28 June 1941.
20. David Stahel, 'And the World held its Breath. The July/August 1941 Crisis of Army Group Centre and the Failure of Operation Barbarossa', 203–17; VIII, 99–103.
21. Rokossovsky's 'OG Yartsevo' became operational on 22 July 1941. TsAMO, f.208, op.2511, d.210.
22. Boris Sokolov, *Marshal K.K. Rokossovsky: The Red Army's Gentleman Commander.* (Warwick: Helion, 2015), 88, 89.
23. On 30 July 1941, Zhukov was placed in charge of Reserve Front, which included constructing what became known as the Mozhaisk Defensive Line to protect Moscow.
24. T-315, Roll 196. KTB Panzer-Division 4 (23479/6).
25. By 1 August the Soviet Air Force had lost some 10,000 aircraft, since the campaign's commencement; four times the number the Luftwaffe had on the Eastern front. TsAMO, f.35, op.11333, d.23.
26. KTB Nr 3, 3. Panzer-Division. 1.8.1941.
27. K.K. Rokossovskii, *Soldatskii dolg* (Moscow: Eksmo, 1968), 31–39.
28. Guderian, *Panzer Leader*, 152.
29. The pilots had little training beyond how to take off and land. TsAMO f.319, op.4799, d.25. The Il-2 possessed homogeneous steel protecting important components, such as the gear box, cockpit, and fuel tanks.
30. Rudolf Hofmann and Alfred Toppe, 'Consumption and Attrition Rates of Army Group Centre in Russia (22 Jun.–31 Dec. 1941)', NARA M1035, Chapter 6, P-190.
31. Burdick and Jacobsen (eds), *The Halder War Diary*, Vol. VII, 8.
32. Ibid., 18.
33. In a post-war interview, Kleist felt that, 'Clausewitz's teachings had fallen into neglect by this generation', being 'regarded as a military philosopher, rather than as a practical teacher'. Instead, Schlieffen 'received much greater attention'. B.H. Liddell Hart, *The Other Side of the Hill* (London: Pan Macmillan, 1993), 203.
34. Gerbet, *Generalfeldmarschall Fedor von Bock*, 272.
35. Ibid., 4 August 1941.
36. Abt.Ic/A.O. 28.9.41.
37. IX Army Corps, 'KTB 7', 5 August 1941, T-314/80/7318845.
38. Guderian, *Panzer Leader*, 154.
39. Warlimont wrote a memorandum doubting the German forces' ability to reach the Arkhangel'sk–Astrakhan line.
40. Bock, 'Tagebuchnotizen Osten I', 7–8 August 1941, T-84/271/000397-000398.

Chapter 7

1. On 8.8.41 the Soviet 258th Rifle Division (Orel Military District) had moved up from near Bryansk to establish a blocking position just west of Zhukova. Map No. 3, Thirteenth Army, 1300hrs 8.8.41.
2. Bock, 'Tagebuchnotizen Osten I', 10 August 1941, T-84/271/000400-000401. The Soviet Central Front was created on 24 July 1941 to sit between Bock and Moscow, and included Thirteenth and Twenty-First Armies.
3. Burdick and Jacobsen (eds), *The Halder War Diary*, Vol. VII, 36.
4. These were the Soviet 148th (Yershichi) and 258th Rifle Divisions (south-east of Seshcha).
5. Including the corps' 121st Rifle Division, parts of its 137th, 160th, and 132nd Rifle Divisions.
6. 'KG Eberbach' (33 MRR; Staff, 2./35 PR; I./103 MAR (minus 2./); one coy. 49 ATB; and 45 MEB) – cooperating with II./43 AR; I./53 RLR (minus one bty.). 'KG Grolig' (5 PBde; 35 PR (remainder); 34 MCB (minus one platoon); 12 MRR; II./ and III./103 MAR; one bty. I./53 RLR; 1./ and 3./79 MEB; one coy. 49 ATB; 2. lt. ptn./1./84 Medical Coy.) – cooperating with II./69 AR. KTB 4.Panzer-Division Ia, Division order for the attack on 9.8.41.
7. These vehicles were from the Soviet 50th Tank Division (XXV MC), and parts of 137th Rifle Division.
8. Luftwaffe pilot report (6./(N) 41) based on radio communications during the enemy tank raid.
9. Commanding General XXIV Pz.K., Corps Command Post, 13.8.1941.
10. XX Army Corps, 'KTB I', 14 August 1941, 000198.
11. In an attempt to check widespread Red Army desertions and surrenders on 16 August 1941 Stalin issued Order No. 270 to promote greater resistance and authorize senior commanders and commissars to demote, replace, or summarily execute those deemed in violation.
12. Guderian, *Panzer Leader*, 196.
13. KTB OKW, Vol. I, p. 1059.
14. Elke Fröhlich (ed.), *The Diaries of Joseph Goebbels*, Part 2, Vol. 1 (Munich: K.G. Saur, 1993), 260.
15. Having stressed Army Group Centre's high combat losses around Smolensk and a lack of large reserves, Zhukov tried unsuccessfully to get Stalin to reposition formations from the Moscow front to more threatened sectors, but the Soviet Premier, having recently assumed the position from Vyacheslav Molotov, remained firmly convinced that Moscow was the primary German goal.
16. Gerhard Engel and Hildegard von Kotze, *Heeresadjutant bei Hitler* (Stuttgart: Deutsche Verlags-Anstalt, 1974), 110.
17. Guderian, *Panzer Leader*, 162.
18. Gerbet, *Generalfeldmarschall Fedor von Bock*, 292.
19. IX Army Corps, 'KTB 7', 22 August 1941, T-314/405/000636.
20. Four Panzer IIs, fifty-nine Panzer IIIs, and seventeen Panzer IVs were being repaired. 6th Panzer Regiment Transcript, 24.8.41. Having been involved in continual action for two months 3rd and 4th Panzer Division's were both down to just 15 per cent of their original tank strength, with 17th, 18th, and 10th Panzer Divisions respectively reduced to 42, 60, and 90 per cent. Memorandum of the combat readiness of mobile units of Army Group Centre, 08.22.1941.
21. Bryansk Front and Thirteenth Army had indeed lost contact with 3rd Panzer Division at this time. TsAMO RF, Military History Department No. 15, Op. 67/2, Box No. 493/527, No. 114, Journal of combat operations of the Bryansk Front in the Patriotic War from 16 August to 12 November 1941.
22. KTB Nr 1, Part 2, Panzergruppe 2, 21 Aug.–31 Oct., 1941. NAM, series T-313, Roll 86.
23. Guderian, *Panzer Leader*, 164.
24. 3. Panzer-Division Ia, Division Command Post, 25.8.1941.

25. The Soviet Twenty-First Army's commander, Major General Vasiliy Gordov, had thought Guderian's advance was directed more to the south-west and Kyiv. Once the German intentions became clear he moved quickly to rectify the very serious threat to his Soviet northern shoulder.
26. The frequent reorganization of Red Army divisions among parent corps and armies, as evidenced in several TsAMO documents during this period (i.e., f.361, op.6079, d.26) implied considerable chaos, as Guderian tore up Central Front.
27. 3. Panzer-Division, ktb. Nr 3., Abt.Ia 1. 26.8.41.
28. Believing Guderian would soon turn back on Moscow, Stalin broke up Central Front and sent its forces to Bryansk Front (the *Stavka* directive No. 0012554), which weakened Red Army strength along Second Panzer Group's unchanged, southward advance axis.
29. Guderian, *Panzer Leader*, 164.

Chapter 8

1. The Soviet 6th (Thirteenth Army) and 55th Rifle Divisions (Twenty-First Army) attempted to block their way. Suffering heavy losses Central Front had been disbanded on 25 August and its Thirteenth and Twenty-First Armies were added to the recently created Bryansk Front.
2. Burdick and Jacobsen (eds), *The Halder War Diary*, Vol. VII, 69.
3. T-315, R-115 3rd Panzer Division.
4. David Stahel, *Kyiv 1941: Hitler's Battle for Supremacy in the East* (Cambridge University, 2013), 124.
5. Burdick and Jacobsen (eds), *The Halder Way Diary*, Vol. VII, 69.
6. The Soviet 155th and 307th Rifle Divisions presented blocking positions, respectively facing the town from the east and south. TsAMO, f.361, op.6079, d.26.
7. J. Neumann and H. Flohn, 'Great Historical Events that were Significantly Affected by the Weather: Part 8, Germany's War on the Soviet Union, 1941–45', *Environmental Science* (1 June 1987), 620–1.
8. 141st Tank Brigade. TsAMO, f.202, op.5, d.63, i.92.
9. TsAMO, f.3195, op.1, d.2, l.7.
10. Guderian, *Panzer Leader*, 165.
11. Gerbet, *Generalfeldmarschall Fedor von Bock*, 299.
12. David R. Dorondo, *Riders of the Apocalypse: German Cavalry and Modern Warfare, 1870–1945* (Annapolis, MD: Naval Institute Press, 2012), 156–63.
13. Returning to Germany in November 1941, 1st Cavalry Division was officially remade as 24th Panzer Division on 28 November 1941.
14. Ia, KTB 1, Part 2, Panzergruppe 2, 21 Aug.–31 Oct. NAM, series T-313, Roll 86. Of these 4th Panzer Division had 16 Panzer IIs, 26 Panzer IIIs, and 7 Panzer IVs operational. KTB, 4th Panzer Division, 31.8.41.
15. KTB 3, Panzer-Division. 4.9.41.
16. Veterans of the 3rd Panzer Division, *Armoured Bears Volume One*, 728.
17. Panzer Group 2, Ia., 'Aniage zum KTB vom 4 Sept. 1941', T-84/271/000438.
18. Burdick and Jacobsen (eds), *The Halder War Diary*, Vol. VII, 82.
19. I./6th Panzer (with 6./3rd Rifle and 5./75th Motorized Artillery Regiments (half battery), 3./39th Panzer Engineer Battalion and one platoon from 521st Panzerjäger Battalion). 1st Reconnaissance Battalion (with 1./521st Panzerjäger and 3./39th Panzer Engineer Battalion (one recon. troop), and I./6th Panzer (three tanks) and I./75th Motorized Artillery Regiment (minus one battery)). 3. Panzer-Division KTB, 4.9.41.
20. Guderian, *Panzer Leader*, 166.

21. 'Kampfgruppe Traut' included I./ and II./41st Motorized Infantry Regiment and 40th Motorcycle Battalion. KTB 10th Motorized Infantry Division, 4.9.41.
22. Otto Weidinger, *Comrades to the End: The 4th SS Panzer-Grenadier Regiment 'Der Führer' 1938–1945: The History of a German-Austrian Fighting Unit* (Atglen, PA: Schiffer Military History, 1998), 80.
23. KTB 10th Motorized Infantry Division, 4.9.41.
24. KTB 'Reich', 7.9.41.
25. 'KG Munzel' (II./6th Panzer, I./75th Motorized Artillery, and II./3rd Motorized Rifle Regiments, with 1st Motorized Reconnaissance Battalion) and 'KG Kleemann' (I./394th Motorized Rifle and III./6th Panzer Regiments). KTB, 3rd Panzer Division, 4.9.41. Guderian, *Panzer Leader*, 166.
26. The Soviet Twenty-First Army commander, Lieutenant General Vasily Kuznetsov, had thought Guderian's advance was directed more to the south-west and Kyiv. Once the German intentions became clear he moved quickly to rectify the very serious threat to the Soviet northern shoulder. TsAMO, f.202, op.5, d.20, l.21; TsAMO RF, f.96a, op.2011, d.5, l.74-85.
27. The *Stavka* had recently created Fortieth Army from the depleted Twenty-Sixth and Thirty-Seventh Armies defending the Kyiv sector.
28. The Soviet 6th, 155th, 137th, and 269th Infantry Divisions and elements from 282nd Infantry Division and remnants of 4th Cavalry Division were arrayed across from Feldt's sector.
29. C. Keller, *Militär-Strafgesetzbuch für das Deutsche Reich*, trans. United States Holocaust Memorial Museum (Berlin: Weidmann, 1873).
30. Most Red Army soldiers came from rural backgrounds with little exposure to technology, aside from perhaps farm or industrial machinery. Years of oppressive Communist doctrine had produced a sense of fear, and collectivism, in which private property was illegal, and this made for widespread poverty, famine, unrest, and hardship. A steady dose of commissar ('political leader') (an entity officially reintroduced on 16 July 1941) rhetoric worked to exhort the largely under-trained and equipped Soviet soldiers to greater resistance. With so many Red Army personnel surrendering or exploiting the chaos of battle and abandoning their positions, especially those hailing from Soviet-occupied territories that had been conscripted, NKVD personnel roamed the rear areas with orders to arrest and/or shoot anyone leaving the battlefield without permission.
31. 'KG Frank' comprised 1./3rd Motorized Rifle Regiment, 6./75th Motorized Artillery Regiment, one company each from 6th Panzer Regiment and 543rd Panzerjäger Battalion, and an engineer platoon. KTB, 3rd Panzer Division, 9.9.41.
32. Dr Russel H.S. Stolfi, 'The Greatest Encirclement in History: Link up of the German 3rd and 9th Panzer divisions on 15 September 1941 in the Central Ukraine', *RUSI Journal* (December 1996), 63–72.
33. KTB, 3rd Panzer Division, 9.9.41.
34. KTB 'Reich', 9.9.41.
35. Ibid., 10.9.41.
36. KTB, 3rd Panzer Division, 10.9.41.
37. In response to Model taking Romny, Stalin ordered South-Western Front to send 90 per cent of its air missions against 3rd Panzer Division, and the major threat it posed to its deep northern flank.
38. Tasked with holding Kyiv at all costs, when Semyon Budyonny's failure became imminent, Stalin flew him from the area and replaced him as the South-Western Front commander with Timoshenko.
39. KTB, 3rd Panzer Division, 13.9.41.
40. Ibid., Stolfi, 'The Greatest Encirclement in History'.

41. *Flivo*, 3rd Panzer Division KTB. Div.Gef.Std, 14.9.1941.
42. Burdick and Jacobsen (eds), *The Halder War Diary*, Vol. VII, 101.
43. Faced with the result of his unwillingness to pull Soviet forces from its extended Kyiv position when time was available Stalin now belatedly ordered a breakout of South-Western Front from what was now a pocket.
44. Gerd Ueberschär and Wolfram Wette, *Der deutsche Überfall auf die Sowjetunion – Unternehmen Barbarossa 1941* (Frankfurt am Main: Fischer Taschenbuch, 2011).
45. Guderian, *Panzer Leader*, 171.
46. 10. Infanterie-Division (mot.) KTB. Stab Ic, 18.9.41.
47. Ibid., 18.9.41.
48. Heeresgruppe Mitte, Ic/A.O., 18.9.41.
49. Guderian, *Panzer Leader*, 172.

Chapter 9

1. Guderian, *Panzer Leader*, 172.
2. KTB OKW, Vol. II, 661, 26.9.41.
3. According to a 27 September 1941 'Reference Report of Bryansk Front's Artillery Headquarters on the Likely Actions of the Enemy and the Necessary Change in the Artillery Grouping of Bryansk Front's Troops', Soviet intelligence gleaned from aerial observation, prisoner interrogation, and agents that Bock was preparing an attack against Moscow (along Panzer Routes 1 and 2, being logical considering the quality of the respective roads). Should this effort stall it was believed the Germans would encircle Bryansk Front from the north and south towards removing a sizeable portion of the capital's defenders and materiel.
4. KTB No. 1, Part 2, Panzergruppe 2, 21.8.41–31.10.41. T-313, R-86.
5. On 1 October Army Group Centre was distributed along a 750km front and comprised 1,929,406 men, of which 1,183,719 were directly subordinated to Bock. KTB, Army Group Centre. BA-MA RH 19 II/123. On 27 September the *Stavka* rather belatedly directed that the three fronts opposite Army Group Centre were to assume a 'rigid' defence, as they lacked sufficient operational reserves, mobility, and command and control to better resist the expected German onslaught.
6. T-315, R-205 4.Pz.Div.
7. These vehicles were from the recently arrived 150th Tank Brigade (OG Ermakov), which included a dozen T-34s.
8. Burdick and Jacobsen (eds), *The Halder War Diary*, 10.1.41.
9. 141st Tank Brigade (OG Ermakov).
10. Guderian, *Panzer Leader*, 176. In his diary for 1 October, Halder provided statistics on a 120,000-tonne fuel-availability shortfall that meant the Wehrmacht was 'in no position to embark on any large-scale operation'.
11. Although *Ostheer* personnel losses had been high, and replacements unable to keep pace, the Red Army was in considerably worse shape, with its rifle divisions (for example) reduced by upwards of half of their allotted strengths. Klaus Reinhardt, *Die Wende vor Moskau* (Stuttgart: DVA, 1972), 61.
12. 'Kampfgruppe Hochbach' included II./103rd Artillery and I./11th Antiaircraft Regiments, and 34th Motorcycle Battalion.
13. Artur Wollschlaeger, 'The Raid on Orel', *Knights Cross Panzers* (Mechanicsburg, PA: Stackpole Books, 2010), 125.
14. KTB, 4th Panzer Division, 3.10.41. T-315, R-196.

15. 34th Motorcycle Battalion, II./103rd Artillery Regiment, and two guns from I./11th Antiaircraft Regiment were added to 'Kampfgruppe Lauchert'. KTB, 4th Panzer Division, 5.10.41.
16. 'Kampfgruppe Gradl' comprised seven Panzer IIs, six Panzer IIIs, an infantry platoon in four SPWs, and a pair of 20mm antiaircraft guns. Franz Kurowski, *Panzer Aces III* (Mechanicsburg, PA: Stackpole Books, 2010), p. 113. Eremenko returned to his command post at Bryansk only to be forced to flee, as German armour had pushed into the area.
17. Guderian, *Panzer Leader*, 178. Given that Ju-52/3m transports could each carry up to ten 200l barrels of fuel, such an expedient would require 227 sorties (if 100,000 Imperial gallons).
18. The Soviet 4th Tank Brigade reinforced 34th NKVD Regiment.
19. 4. PD, Abt. Ia, 22.10.41.
20. With 29th Motorized Infantry Division having taken Lokot' on 6 October 1941, anti-Soviet sentiment in the region incentivised the Germans to make portions of the surrounding three oblasts (equivalent to provinces) a semi-autonomous zone, in return for helping to maintain rear area security.
21. During the height of Stalin's genocide of Ukraine's population through famine (Holodomor), in 1933 Guderian visited the Ordzhonikidze Tractor Plant in Kharkiv, which was mass-producing tanks at a time when Germany had yet to do so per Treaty of Versailles restrictions.
22. Not to be outdone by the Germans overestimating destruction inflicted on the enemy Soviet sources indicated causing 600 casualties and damaging or destroying 38 panzern. TsAMO, f.47, op.1, d.2, 1.15, 16; TsAMO, f.1650, op.8, d.166, l.1.
23. Based on combat reports across his front line, Katukov believed the main German thrust would be on his left flank between the River Zhizdra and Mtensk axis. To provide an ambush a tank platoon and a company of BT-7 tanks was positioned in the area; many of which were hull down to present just their turrets to the enemy.
24. Kozel'sk possessed one of three Soviet camps where some 4,500 Polish officers captured in 1939 were held as 'internees' prior to the NKVD executing them en masse in the woods near Katyn in 1940. US Congress, House Select Committee to Conduct an Investigation of the Facts, Evidence and Circumstances of the Katyn Forest Massacre. Hearings, Vol. 1, October 11, 1951.
25. Guderian, *Panzer Leader*, 181. Reflective of Bryansk Front's depleted strength, 4th Cavalry Division was little more than a regiment. TsAMO, f.208, i.2583, d.6, l.62.
26. 103. Situation Report from 8.10.41.
27. KTB, 3rd Panzer Division, 9.10.41. T-314, R-1100.
28. 265 attack aircraft and Stukas including 18 (KG3), 19 (KG28), 53 (KG53), 27 (II./KG210), 148 (StG77); 144 single-engine fighters with 100 (JG51), 44 (JG3); 13 reconnaissance having 4 (1.(F)/122), 9 (5.(H)/26). 103. Situation Report from 8.10.41.
29. Between *Barbarossatag* and 10 October 1941, NKVD forces had detained 657,364 soldiers that had become separated from their units. Most were sent back into combat, although 25,878 and 10,201 were respectively arrested and shot. Top Secret Memorandum from Deputy Head, Directorate of Special Sections, NKVD, Solomon Milshtein, to Deputy Head of the NKVD, Lavrentiy Beria, on 31 October 1941.
30. KTB, Second Panzer Army, 10.10.41. T-314, R-1100.
31. The Soviet GKO established the Moscow Defence Zone and ordered another defensive line around Moscow proper to be established.
32. On 20 October 1941, 1st Cavalry Division reported taking 8,132 prisoners and capturing 3 tanks, 39 artillery pieces, 91 motor vehicles, and about 250 wagons between the start of hostilities and 11 October, for the cost of 122 dead, 410 wounded and 8 missing. On a broader scale, between 9 and 14 October, XXXXVII Motorized Army Corps captured

23,000 Soviets (7,000 (northern pocket), 16,000 (southern)). KTB, XXXXVII Pz.Korps, 14.10.41. T-314, R-1100.
33. KTB, 4th Panzer Division, 12.10.41. T-315, R-196.
34. On 19 October 1941 Army Group Centre listed a haul that included 673,098 enemy prisoners, 1,277 armoured vehicles, and 4,378 artillery pieces. Abt. Ic/A.G.
35. KTB Nr 1, 9th Panzer Division, Ib, 11.10.41 to 25.10.41.
36. On 15 October 1941 the State Defence Committee produced a secret decision, No. 801, 'On evacuation of the Soviet capital Moscow to Kuybyshev'; a city along the River Volga, some 850km east of Moscow.
37. On 16 October 1941 large-scale looting broke out in the Soviet capital during what was coined the 'Moscow Panic', with government forces essentially putting the city under siege within three days in an effort to mitigate the chaos. Although his train had been readied to evacuate him from the city, Stalin ultimately opted to remain.
38. Between *Barbarossatag* and 18 October 1941 Army Group Centre captured 1,701,529 Red Army soldiers, 9,266 armoured vehicles, 11,906 artillery guns, 915 antitank guns, 522 antiaircraft guns, and 947 aircraft. High Command of Army Group Centre. Abt. Ic/A.C., 6 October 1942.
39. Guderian, *Panzer Leader*, 184.
40. KTB Nr 3, 3rd Panzer Division, 21.10.41.
41. KTB Nr 3, 3rd Panzer Division, 23.10.41.
42. Veterans of the 3rd Panzer Division, *Armoured Bears Volume One*, 818.
43. Hermann Plocher, *The German Air Force versus Russia, 1941*. USAF #153 (New York: Arno Press, 1965), 234–6.
44. 9. Panzer-Division, Abt. Qu./V, 24.10.41.
45. Soviet directive No. 316 ordered Fiftieth Army (217 RD, 258 RD, 260 RD, 278 RD, 279 RD, 290 RD, 299 RD, 173 RD, and 154 RD, 108 TD and 31 CD, and elements from the former Twenty-Sixth Army) to conduct a fighting withdrawal to Pavshino–Slobodka–Krapivna–Plavsk–Trosna–Novosil'–Verkhov'ye.
46. Guderian, *Panzer Leader*, 186.
47. On 26 October XXIV Motorized Army Corps had 10.4m^3 of diesel stockpiled at Orel. Second Panzer Army's daily report for 25.10 to 26.10.
48. On 29 October 1941, 258th (634 men, with no artillery); 154th (1,930 men); and 217th (1,428 men) Rifle Divisions. TsAMO, f.405, op.9769, d.4, 1.31; TsAMO, f.405, op.9769, d.4, 1.39.
49. 143rd Rifle Division had 13,649 men. TsAMO, f.405, op.9769, d.4, 1.50-70.
50. On 30 October Ermakov created the Tula Defence Zone (154th, 173rd, 217th, and 290th Rifle Divisions) to defend areas outside of the town.
51. 69th NKVD Brigade defended Tula's southern edge and included 156th (NKVD) Rifle, Tula Workers', and 732nd Antiaircraft Artillery Regiments.

Chapter 10

1. On 1 November the defence of northern Tula comprised 258th and 290th Rifle Divisions, while 154th, 217th, and 260th Rifle Divisions protected the city south of the River Upa. TsAMO, f.405, op.9769, d.10, l.1a.
2. As an indication of how weakened Soviet forces were, on 1 November, Third Army possessed just 16 T-34s, 16 T-26s, and 3 BT-7s between 121st and 133rd Tank Brigades, as the two units moved north from the Kursk sector. TsAMO, f.202, op.5, d.40, d.14.
3. Guderian, *Panzer Leader*, 188.
4. Matthew Cooper, *The German Army 1933–1945* (New York: Zebra Books, 1980), 331.

5. On 4.11.1941, 31st Grufl, 6.(H) 13 (Pz), 77th Light Antiaircraft Battalion, and 202nd Assault Gun Battalion were removed from XXXXVII Motorized Army Corps, with the latter unit moved to LIII Army Corps. KTB, XXXXVII Pz.Korps [MAC]/Ia. 23.9.1941–31.12.1941.
6. Depending on terrain a German battalion was typically intended to occupy a 400–1,000m attack frontage, and double that when on the defensive.
7. David I. Norwood (ed.), *Handbook of German Military Forces* (Baton Rouge, LA: Louisiana State University Press, 1995).
8. KTB, Second Panzer Army, 11.11.1941, T-314, R-1100.
9. Guderian, *Panzer Leader*, 188; Burdick and Jacobsen (eds), *The Halder War Diary*, Vol. VII, 162.
10. 'Kampfgruppe Munzel' included the reconnaissance battalion, three ad hoc panzer companies, the SPW company of 3rd Rifle Regiment, and 5th Battery of the divisional artillery. Veterans of the 3rd Panzer Division, *Armoured Bears Volume One*.
11. Ibid., 887.
12. N. Findikyan, M. Duke, and S. Sells, *Stress Reviews: I. Thermal Stress-Cold*, Technical Report No. 8, Institute of Behavioral Research, Texas Christian University, Fort Worth, July 1966.
13. Gerhardt Engel, *At the Heart of the Reich* (New York: Skyhorse, 2016), 20.
14. NARA, T. 314, R. 708: XXIV Panzerkorps. F. 98.
15. To hinder German efforts and at the expense of Russian civilians the *Stavka* issued order 0428 that included, 'All villages situated in the hinterland of the German forces, to a depth of 40 to 60 kilometres from the front line and 20 to 30 kilometres to the left and right of the roads, are to be destroyed and reduced to rubble.'
16. As pointed out by Nigel Askey, the widely touted arrival of 'Siberian' divisions that had been freed from the East was little more than a collective moniker (given the comparatively small number of formations from Siberian District) that implied an elite status to an otherwise normal division springing from the ongoing Red Army mobilization. *Operation Barbarossa: The Complete Organisational and Statistical Analysis, and Military Simulation Vol. IIIB* (NVA Publications, 2020), Section 2, 17.
17. II./180th NKVD Regiment, with 125th Separate Tank Battalion and 239th Rifle Division's tank battalion.
18. NARA, T. 315, Roll 195: 4. Panzer-Division, F. 696–8.
19. Burdick and Jacobsen (eds), *The Halder War Diary*, Vol. VII, 159.
20. Respectively, the Soviet 413th Rifle Division, with 32nd Tank Brigade.
21. The battalion was from 817th Rifle Regiment (239 RD).
22. Burdick and Jacobsen (eds), *The Halder War Diary*, Vol. VII, 179.
23. 'Kampfgruppe Eberbach' comprised 5th Panzer Brigade headquarters; 35th Panzer Regiment; 1./II./103rd Artillery Regiment; 3./49th Panzerjäger Battalion; 3./79th Engineer Battalion; and 1./12th Motorized Infantry Regiment. NARA, T. 315, Roll 195: 4. Panzer-Division, F. 703–4.
24. NARA, T. 315, Roll 195: 4. Panzer-Division, F. 705.
25. NARA, T. 315, Roll 195: 4. Panzer-Division, F. 706.
26. NARA, T. 315, Roll 195: 4. Panzer-Division, F. 692–3.
27. NARA, T. 315, Roll 195: 4. Panzer-Division, F. 706–8.
28. Guderian, *Panzer Leader*, 193.
29. NARA, T. 315, Roll 195: 4. Panzer-Division, F. 708–9.
30. Memoirs of the Executive Secretary of the Party Bureau of the 817th Rifle Regiment of the 239th Rifle Division, battalion Commissar F.S. Karpenko.
31. Burdick and Jacobsen (eds), *The Halder War Diary*, Vol. VII, 192.

32. For as bad off as the *Ostheer* was by late November 1941, the Soviets were in far worse shape, having suffered by one estimate 4.5 million casualties over the same period. G.F. Krivosheev, *Soviet Casualties and Combat Losses in the Twentieth Century* (London: Greenhill, 1997), 85–97. While the Germans modestly increased their tank strength on the Eastern Front between September and December 1941, the Soviet tank force was majorly impacted due to the relocation of production facilities, such as at Kharkiv and Leningrad, to the country's interior.
33. Lemelsen (in the division history) and Lieutenant Colonel Nitsche. Vasily Timofeevich Kortukov, a 15-year-old from a hamlet, 5km north of Dudkino.
34. NARA, T. 315, Roll 195: 4. Panzer-Division, F. 710–11.
35. Erhard Raus, *Panzer Operations: The Eastern Front Memoir of General Raus, 1941–1945* (Cambridge: Da Capo Press, 2003).
36. On 1 December 1941 the Soviets amassed some 576,500 soldiers, 5,000 artillery pieces, and 574 tanks to contest Army Group Centre. TsAMO, f.208, op.2511, d.222; TsAMO, f.213, op.2002, d.28; TsAMO, f.202, op.2231, d.11.
37. Operations of the 2nd Panzer Army, RH 21-2 /910.
38. 29. Infanterie-Division (.mot) ktb, 2 Dec 41.
39. KTB 2. Pz Armee, RH 21-2/244.
40. Note: Gef.-Stärke der 3. PD = insgesamt etwa 14 Sch.-Komp zu je 50 – 60 Mann; 20 Pak; 22 Pz. mit 1 V.S. für 30 km. Korpsartl. des 24. PzK = 12 Gesch. (KTB 24. PzK).

Appendix A

1. Officially subordinated to Fourth Army, in practice Second Panzer Army operated independently.
2. Luftwaffe-attached assets to Second Panzer Group.
3. Thomas L. Jentz (ed.), *Panzertruppen: The Complete Guide to the Creation & Combat Employment of Germany's Tank Force* (Atglen, PA: Schiffer Pub, 1996).
4. Allocated during the planning period.
5. For XXXXVII MAC during the River Bug crossing.
6. From Großdeutschland.
7. From 29 MID.
8. From 167 ID.
9. From 18 PD.
10. From XII AC.
11. For XII AC use during the River Bug crossing.
12. For XXIV MAC use during the River Bug crossing.
13. From XXXXVII MAC.
14. From 10 MID.
15. From SS-MD 'Reich .
16. From XXIV MAC.
17. From 267 ID.
18. Nigel Askey, *Operation Barbarossa* (Morrisville, NC: Lulu Publishing, 2014), Vol. IIB, 214.

Select Bibliography

Primary Sources
Bundesarchiv/Militärarchiv, Freiburg im Breisgau
N 910/6, 'Joachim von Lemelsen's diary 10 October 1941–24 April 1942'.
RH/2-2670, 'Oberkommando des Heeres Generalstab des Heeres O.Qu.IV-Abt.Fr.H.Ost (II)'.
RH 19-I/73, 'Heeresgruppe Süd Kriegstagebuch II.Teil Band 4, 16–Sept.-5 Okt. 1941'.
RH 19-II/386, 'Kriegstagebuch Nr. I (Band August 1941) des Oberkommandos der Heeresgruppe Mitte'.
RH 19-II/411, 'Kriegstagebuch Nr. I (Band Oktober 1941) des Oberkommandos der Heeresgruppe Mitte'.
RH 19II/128, 'Tagesmeldungen der Heeresgruppe Mitte vom 22.6.41 bis 15.7.41'.
RH 19II/129, 'Tagesmeldungen der Heeresgruppe Mitte vom 16.7.41 bis 5.8.41'.
RH 21-2/244, 'Kriegstagebuch Nr. 1 2.Panzerarmee Bd.III vom 1.11.1941 bis 26.12.41'.
RH 21-2/819, 'Kriegstagebuch der O.Qu.-Abt. Pz. A.O.K.2 vom 21.6.41 bis 31.3.42'.
RH 21-2/928, 'Kriegstagebuch Nr.1 Panzergruppe 2 Bd.II vom 22.7.41 bis 20.8.41'.
RH 21-2/931, 'Kriegstagebuch Nr.1 Panzergruppe 2 Bd.II vom 21.8.41 bis 31.10.41'.
RH 24-47/258, 'Kriegstagebuch Nr.2 XXXXVII.Pz.Korps. Ia 23.9.41 bis 31.12.41'.
RH 24-48/30, 'Kriegstagebuch XXXXVIII.Pz.Kps. Abt.Ia Oktober 1941'.
RH 26-10/9, 'Kriegstagebuch der 10.Inf.Div. (mot) 11.6.1941-29.12.1941'.
RH 27-3/14, ' Kriegstagebuch 3.Panzer-Division vom 16.8.40 bis 18.9.41'.
RH 27-3/15, ' Kriegstagebuch 3.Panzer-Division vom 19.9.41 bis 6.2.42'.
RH 27-3/218, 'Kriegstagebuch 3.Panzer-Division. Ib 19.5.41 bis 6.2.42'.
RH 27-4/10, 'Kriegstagebuch 4.Panzer-Division Führungsabtl. 26.5.41 bis 31.3.42'.
RH 27-9/4, '9.Pz.Div. Kriegstagebuch Ia vom 19.5.1941 bis 21.1.42'.
RH 27-18/22, '18.Panzer Division, Abt.Ia Kriegstagebuch Teil III vom 30.9.41 bis 19.10.41'.
RH 27-18/69, '18.Panzer Division, Abt.Ia Kriegstagebuch vom 20/10.41 bis 13.12.41'.
RH 21-2/757, 'Verlustmeldungen 5.7.41 bis 25.3.42'.
Oberkommando der Wehrmacht. Die Wehrmachtberichte Band 1: 1939–1941. Munich: Deutscher Taschenbuch Verlag, 1985.
H.Dv. 470/7 Ausbildungsvorschrift für die Panzertruppe (A.V.Pz.) Heft Die mittlere Panzerkompanie, 1.5.41.
Soviet Documents on the Use of War Experience, Volume III: Military Operations 1941–1945, trans. H.S. Orenstein. London: Frank Cass, 1993.
Bird, Lorrin and Robert Livingston. *World War II Ballistics: Armor and Gunnery.* Albany, NY: Overmatch Press, 2001.
Schramm, P.E. (general ed.). *Kriegstagebuch des Oberkommando der Wehrmacht (Wehrmachtführungsstab) 1940–1945,* vols 1–4. Frankfurt am Main: Bernard & Graefe, 1961–5.

Secondary Sources
Books
Absolon, Rudolf. *Die Wehrmacht im Dritten Reich, Vol. 5: 1. September 1939 bis 18. Dezember 1941.* Boppard am Rhein: Boldt, 1988.

Aliev, Rostislav. *The Siege of Brest 1941: A Legend of Red Army Resistance on the Eastern Front.* Barnsley: Pen & Sword Military, 2013.

Bartov, Omer. *The Eastern Front, 1941–45: German Troops and the Barbarisation of Warfare.* London: Palgrave, 2001.

Burdick, Charles and Hans-Adolf Jacobsen (eds). *The Halder War Diary, 1939–1942*, 8 vols. Novato, CA: Presidio, 1988.

Bergström, Christer. *Barbarossa: The Air Battle, July–December 1941.* London: Chevron/Ian Allen, 2007.

—— and Andrey Mikhailov. *Black Cross/Red Star: The Air War over the Eastern Front, Vol. 1: Operation Barbarossa, 1941.* Pacifica, CA: Pacifica Military History, 2000.

Dallin, Alexander. *German Rule in Russia, 1941–1945.* New York: St Martin's Press, 1957.

Detweiler, Donald E. (ed.). *World War II German Military Studies*, 23 vols. New York: Garlan, 1979.

Drig, Yevgeniy. *Mechanized Corps of the Red Army in Battle: The History of the Armored Forces of the Red Army 1940–1941.* Moscow: ACT, Transkniga, 2006.

Eimannsberger, Ludwig Ritter von. *Der Kampfwagenkrieg.* Munich: J.F. Lehmann, 1934.

Engel, Gerhard and Hildegard von Kotze. *Heeresadjutant Bei Hitler, 1938–1943.* Stuttgart: Deutsche Verlags-Anstalt, 1974.

Gerbet, Klaus. *Generalfeldmarschall Fedor von Bock: The War Diary, 1939–1945.* Atglen, PA: Schiffer, 1996.

Geshöpf, Dr Rudolf. *Mein Weg mit der 45. Infanterie-Division.* Linz an der Donau: Oberösterreichischer Landesverlag, 1955.

Glantz, David M. *Operation Barbarossa: Hitler's Invasion of Russia, 1941*, new edn. Stroud: History Press, 2011.

—— *Barbarossa Derailed. The Battle for Smolensk, 10 July–10 September 1941, Vol. 1.* Warwick: Helion, 2010.

—— *Red Army Ground Forces in June 1941.* Self-published, 1997.

—— *Stumbling Colossus: The Red Army on the Eve of World War.* Lawrence, KS: University Press of Kansas, 1998.

—— *Forgotten Battles of the German-Soviet War (1941–45). Vol. I: The Summer-Fall Campaign (22 June–4 December 1941).* Self-published, 1999.

—— (ed.). *The Initial Period of War on the Eastern Front, 22 June–August 1941: Proceedings of the Fourth Art of War Symposium, Garmisch, October 1987.* London: F. Cass, 1993.

—— and Jonathan M. House. *When Titans Clashed: How the Red Army Stopped Hitler*, rev. and expanded edn. Lawrence: University Press of Kansas, 2015.

Götte, Franz (ed.). *Die 29. Falke-Division: 1936–1945 ; 29. I.D.29. I.D. (Mot.)–29. Pz.-Gren.-Div.; eine Dokumentation in Bildern.* Eggolsheim: Ed. Dörfler im Nebel-Verl, 2004.

Guderian, Heinz. *Panzer Leader.* Boston, MA: Da Capo Press, 2002.

Haape, Heinrich. *Moscow Tram Stop: A Doctor's Experiences with the German Spearhead in Russia.* Mechanicsburg, PA: Stackpole Books, 2020.

Hartmann, Christian. *Wehrmacht im Ostkrieg: Front und militärisches Hinterland 1941/42.* Berlin: De Gruyter Oldenbourg, 2010.

Heer, Hannes and Klaus Naumann (eds). *War of Extermination: The German Military in World War II, 1941–1944* repr. New York: Berghahn, 2009.

Jentz, Thomas L. (ed.). *Panzertruppen: The Complete Guide to the Creation & Combat Employment of Germany's Tank Force.* Atglen, PA: Schiffer Pub, 1996.

Lemelsen, Joachim. *29. Division.* Bad Nauheim: Podzun-Pallas-Verlag, 1960.

Lopukhovskiĭ, Lev and Stuart Britton. *The Viaz'ma Catastrophe, 1941: The Red Army's Disastrous Stand against Operation Typhoon.* Warwick: Helion, 2013.

Lucke, Fritz et al. *Panzer Wedge: The German 3rd Panzer Division and the Summer of Victory in the East*, Vol. 1. Mechanicsburg, PA: Stackpole Books, 2012.

Luther, Craig W.H. *Barbarossa Unleashed: The German Blitzkrieg Through Central Russia to the Gates of Moscow June–December 1941.* Atglen, PA: Schiffer, 2013.

Megargee, Geoffrey P. *Inside Hitler's High Command.* Lawrence, KS: University Press of Kansas, 2000.

Mehner, Kurt, *Die Geheimen Tagesberichte der deutschen Wehrmachtsfuehrung im Zweiten Weltkrieg: 1939–1945.* Vols 3 and 4 (1.3.1941–31.5.1942). Osnabrück: Biblio-Verl., 1992.

Michulec, Robert. *4.Panzer Division on the Eastern Front (1) 1941–1943.* Hong Kong: Concord, 1999.

Overmans, Rüdiger. *Deutsche Militärische Verluste Im Zweiten Weltkrieg.* Berlin: De Gruyter Oldenbourg, 1999.

Pabst, Helmut. *The Outermost Frontier: A German Soldier in the Russian Campaign.* London: William Kimber, 1986.

Paterson, Lawrence. *Hitler's Brandenburgers: The Third Reich's Elite Special Forces.* Greenhill Books: Naval Institute Press, 2018.

Rosen, Richard Freiherr von. *Panzer Ace: The Memoirs of an Iron Cross Panzer Commander: From Barbarossa to Normandy.* London: Greenhill Books, 2018.

Rutherford, Jeffrey. *Combat and genocide on the eastern front: the German infantry's war, 1941–1944.* Cambridge University Press, 2014.

Schick, Albert. *Die Geschichte der 10. Panzer-Division 1939–1943.* Winnipeg: J.J. Fedorowicz, 2013.

Schmidt, August. *Geschichte der 10. Division-Division (.mot), 10. Panzergrenadier-Division 1935–1945.* Bad Nauheim: Podzun-Verlag, 1963.

Schüler, Klaus. *Logistik im Russlandfeldzug: die Rolle der Eisenbahn bei Planung, Vorbereitung und Durchführung des deutschen Angriffs auf die Sowjetunion bis zur Krise vor Moskau im Winter 1941/42.* New York: P. Lang, 1987.

Stahel, David. *Operation Barbarossa and Germany's Defeat in the East*, repr. Cambridge University Press, 2012.

Steiger, Rudolf. *Armour Tactics in the Second World War: Panzer Army Campaigns of 1939–41 in German War Diaries.* New York: Berg Publishers, 1992.

Thies, Klaus Jürgen. *Der Ostfeldzug: Ein Lageatlas Der Operationsabteilung Des Generalstabs Des Heeres ; Neu Gezeichnet Nach Den Unterlagen Im Bundesarchiv/Militärarchiv.* Osnabrück: Biblio Verlag, 2001.

Tooze, J. Adam. *The Wages of Destruction: The Making and Breaking of the Nazi Economy*, 1st American edn. New York: Viking, 2007.

Urbanke, Axel and Hermann Türk. *Als Sanitätsoffizier Im Rußlandfeldzug: Mit Der 3. Panzer-Division Bis Vor Moskaus Tore.* Bad Zwischenahn: Luftfahrtverlag Start, 2016.

Weidinger, Otto. *Das Reich III, 1941–1943.* Winnipeg: J.J. Fedorowicz, 2002.

Historical Studies

Deichmann, Gen. (dFl) Paul. *German Air Force Operations in Support of the Army.* USAF #163. 1962.

Guderian, GenOb. Heinz and GenOb. Kurt Zeitzler. *Comments on P-041a-P-041hh.* U.S. Army MS# P-04111, trans. J.B. Robinson. Washington DC: OCMH, 1953.

Halder, GenOb. Franz. *Control of the German Army General Staff.* U.S. Army MS# P-041d, trans. H.F. Baerwaldt. Washington DC: OMH, 1952.

Neumann, Joachim. *Die 4. Panzer-Division 1938-1943, Bericht und Betrachtung zu zwei Blitzfeldzügen und zwei Jahren Krieg in Rußland*, Vol. 1. Bonn: Selbstverlag, 1989.

Plocher, GenLt Hermann. *The German Air Force Versus Russia, 1941.* USAF #153 New York: Arno Press, 1965.

USAF Historical Studies: No. 153 that was published by 'Arno Press' out of New York in 1965

Schwabedissen, GenLt Walter. *The Russian Air Force in the Eyes of German Commanders.* USAF #175. 1960.

Suchenwirth, Richard. *Command and Leadership in the German Air Force.* USAF #174. 1969.

Uebe, GenMaj. Klaus. *Russian Reactions to German Airpower in World War II.* USAF #176. 1964.

Foreign Military Studies, National Archive, Washington DC

T-7 *(1953).* Max Bork. *'Comments on Russian Railroads and Highways.'*

T-8 *(1951).* Alfred Toppe. *'Problems of Supply in Far Reaching Operations.'*

Periodicals

Davie, H.G.W. 'The Influence of Railways on Military Operations in the Russo-German War 1941-1945', *Journal of Slavic Military Studies*, Vol. 30, 2017.

Khorkov, A.G. 'Fortified Areas on the Western Borders of the USSR', *Military History Journal*, No. 12, 1987.

Semiddet, W.A. 'The Origins of the Defeat in Belarus (Western Special Military District by June 22, 1941)', *Military History Journal*, No. 4, 1989.

Center of Military History Publications

104-1-1: Military Improvisations During the Russian Campaign.
104-2: Combat in Russian Forests and Swamps.
104-3: Night Combat.
104-5: Terrain Factors in the Russian Campaign.
104-6: Effects of Climate on Combat in European Russia.
104-14-1: German Defensive Tactics Against Russian Breakthroughs.
104-17: German Armored Traffic Control During the Russian Campaign.
104-22-1 Small Unit Actions During the German Campaign in Russia.

Index

Audörsch, Lieutenant Colonel Oskar (394 MRR (3 PD)), 20, 41, 126, 133

Bacher, Colonel Hermann (515 MER Staff (XXIV MAC)), 90
Bayerlein, Lieutenant Colonel Fritz (Ia SPG), 23
Beigel, Major Fritz (39 MEB), 58, 59, 60
Belorussian SSR
    Alenovichi, 112
    Amkhovaya, 119, 123, 126, 129, 131, 135
    Antopol, 58
    Arkadja, 32, 41
    Baranowicze, 58, 59, 61, 62, 65, 67, 68, 70, 72, 73, 75, 76, 80, 81, 83, 85, 86, 93, 96
    Bel', 118
    Belynichi, 106, 110
    Bereza Kartuska, 52, 53, 55–8, 60, 70, 78
    Bialystok, 51, 54, 65, 66, 70, 111, 133, 178
    Bobr, 107, 110
    Bobruysk, 73, 76, 81–3, 87, 88, 90, 91, 94, 96, 98, 102, 109, 113, 119, 121, 124
    Bogushevsk, 108
    Borisov, 87, 92, 96, 100, 101, 105, 107, 114, 119, 141, 146, 158, 205
    Borkolabovo, 115
    Borok, 109
    Boroviki, 111
    Borovka, 122, 125, 127
    Bratylowo, 45
    Brest, 20, 24, 27, 28, 31, 32, 35, 38–45, 47, 48, 50, 51, 53, 55, 58, 59, 61, 65, 83, 93, 114, 128, 142, 219
    Brodets, 105
    Brodziatyn, 41, 45
    Bronna Gora, 59
    Buchowicze, 56, 57
    Bulkowo, 45, 48, 56, 57
    Bykhov, 98, 103–6, 110, 111, 115, 119–21, 123, 126, 127
    Byten, 58–60, 88
    Chashiki, 108
    Chausy, 122, 123, 126, 127, 129, 137
    Chechersk, 148, 154, 156
    Chechevichi, 90, 94, 98, 115
    Chereya, 107
    Cherikov, 127, 137, 153
    Chernyavka, 106, 110
    Cherven, 93, 99, 106
    Chigirinka, 98
    Chuch'ya, 94
    Chwedkowicze, 56
    Citva, 84
    Czarnawczyce, 65
    Czelejewo, 28, 39, 42
    Czemioly, 70
    Denisovichi, 110
    Dereczyn, 79, 85
    Domaczewo, 36, 47
    Dovsk, 121, 126
    Drachkovo, 92
    Drohiczyn, 55, 58, 59
    Dubrovno, 129
    Dukora, 84
    Durycze, 39
    Dywin, 58
    Dzerzhinsk, 85, 96
    Dzyagovichi, 130
    Faustynow, 38
    Filippovichi, 68, 73
    Franopol', 38, 45
    Gierszony, 32, 41
    Glusk, 88, 98, 132
    Glybokovichi, 90, 94, 98
    Golovichi, 120
    Gomel', 109, 111, 114, 115, 119, 121, 124, 126, 134, 141, 148, 154–6, 160, 163
    Gora Majakowa, 35, 37, 38
    Gorodok, 82
    Gorodshchina, 110, 118
    Grozovo, 88
    Gulevichi, 66, 98
    Hancewicze, 87
    Holynka, 79, 85
    Hoszczewo, 67
    Huznie, 38, 41, 45
    Imienin, 57
    Isakova Buda, 122
    Iwacewicze, 62, 67, 70, 76

Janow, 87
Jeziernica, 68, 70, 79
Kalita, 75, 81
Khodosovichi, 102–4
Kholkholitsa, 106
Khotimsk, 155
Kleck, 72, 75, 76
Klimovichi, 130, 137, 151, 153
Knyazhitsy, 113
Kobryn, 29, 41, 42, 45, 48, 50, 53, 56–9, 62–4, 67, 78
Kokhanovo, 112
Kolbovo, 94, 98, 102
Kolodno, 39, 43
Konstantinovka, 139
Kopys, 110, 111, 117, 120
Korbangvo, 153
Korbanovo, 154
Kosow, 67, 70
Kostary, 26, 40
Kostyukovichi, 153–6
Koszelewo, 45
Kozlovichi, 75
Kozlowicze, 31
Krasnaya Sloboda, 108
Krasnoye, 126
Krasnoye Selo, 107
Krasnyy, 120, 124, 129
Krichev, 127–32, 135, 137, 139–41, 143–5, 148, 150, 153, 166
Krucha, 110
Krugloye, 110, 206
Kublik, 55
Lachowicze, 85
Lesna, 76
Leytichi, 94, 115
Lezhnevka, 117
Linowo, 67
Liskovskaya, 88, 94
Lobanovka, 127
Lobkovichi, 128–30, 132
Lohiszyn, 71
Loshnitsa, 98, 101
Luchin, 103, 104
Luka, 63, 177
Lukowo, 78
Lyadno, 66, 68, 72, 82
Lyady, 129
Lykovo, 115
Lyskow, 66
Madora, 104
Malewo, 75
Maloryta, 37, 39, 41, 45, 50, 57, 64, 77, 78, 85

Malyshevichi, 68
Marynowo, 62
Miedna, 35, 36, 38, 39, 50, 57, 64
Milowidy, 62, 73, 76, 84
Minicze, 63, 70
Minki, 57
Minsk, 39, 45, 47, 48, 51, 54, 55, 57, 61, 62, 65, 66, 70–2, 76, 77, 79–81, 84, 85, 87, 89, 91–3, 95, 96, 99–101, 105, 106, 110, 111, 114, 119, 124, 125, 133, 142, 178
Mogilev, 71, 90, 93, 94, 102, 105, 106, 108–11, 113–15, 117–24, 126–8, 130, 131, 134, 137, 139–41, 211
Mokrany, 50, 78
Molyatichi, 123, 126, 128–30
Moshkovo, 108
Motykaly Wielkie, 39, 40
Mstislavl', 122, 123, 125, 131, 139, 141
Muchowloki, 53
Nacha, 108
Navahrudak, 96
Nepli, 26, 28, 39
Niedzwiedzica, 62, 64
Nieswiez, 72, 75, 76, 81, 83, 85
Nizhnyaya, 104
Novoselki, 108
Novyy Bykhov, 101–4, 109, 113, 115, 131, 139, 140, 143
Nowogrodek, 84
Nowosiolki, 26, 39, 40
Nowy Dwor, 66, 82
Obol'tsy, 107
Ogrodniki, 27
Oltusz, 37, 50
Omgovichi, 81
Omukhovichi, 75, 81
Oranczyce, 59, 85
Oreshkovichi, 106
Orlanka, 41
Orsha, 71, 93, 105–8, 110–14, 117, 118, 120, 121, 124, 186, 204, 246
Osinovka, 107
Osipovichi, 73, 89, 90
Parichi, 111, 124, 131, 134
Pastovichi, 88
Pechery, 122
Pekalin, 92
Peliszcze, 42, 43, 51
Petrovichi, 92
Pinsk, 58, 62, 64, 71, 78, 87
Piszcza, 37, 64
Pobolovo, 102, 103, 109
Poddubno, 42, 44, 54

Podgay, 87
Podores'ye, 75, 81
Pogost, 106, 110
Polatsk, 71
Polonevichi, 85
Polonka, 87
Polotsk, 77
Prusino, 153
Pruzana, 39, 42, 51–5, 59, 66
Przyborowo, 37, 47
Pukhovichi, 93
Put'ki, 126
Pyrashevo, 88
Radwanicze, 48
Rechitsa, 111, 121
Rogozno, 36, 64
Rozana, 60, 61, 68, 82
Rubiezewicze, 100
Rudawiec, 39, 42
Rusinowicze, 64
Ryasna, 107
Rzeczyca, 31, 32, 40
Samary, 78
Selishche, 106, 109
Semezhevo, 68
Senno, 107, 108, 110, 113
Shamovo, 120
Shchitomirichi, 87
Shepelevka, 120
Shklov, 110, 111, 113, 117, 118, 122
Sidorovichi, 119, 120, 122
Sielec, 53, 60
Siniawka, 68, 76
Skephya, 111
Slaveni, 107
Slavgorod, 102, 115, 122, 123, 127, 133, 135, 137, 139
Slonim, 54, 58, 60, 61, 65, 66, 68, 69, 70, 76, 79, 84, 85, 87
Slutsk, 58, 59, 62, 66, 70, 72, 73, 75–7, 80, 81, 84, 87, 88, 124
Smolevichi, 92, 101
Smolicze, 63
Smolyany, 117
Solomenka, 90
Sorogi, 75, 81
Staroset'ye, 143
Staryy Rechki, 99
Staryye Dorogi, 88
Staryye Rechki, 105
Stolpce, 76, 83, 85, 101
Stradecz, 35, 38, 41, 44
Stryhowo, 57
Studenka, 93, 106

Suliczewo, 59
Sushchi, 123
Svisloch', 88–90, 102
Szypowicze, 52, 53
Tartak, 73, 76, 84
Telechany, 70
Tewle, 67
Timkovichi, 75
Titovka, 88, 90, 91, 105
Tolochin, 101, 107, 117
Tolpino, 108
Tomaszowka, 44, 50, 64
Tursk, 104, 113
Tverdovo, 108
Ukhavla, 110
Urech'ye, 75, 77, 80, 81, 98
Usakino, 109
Ust'ye, 117
Usza, 87
Varvarovka, 155
Vil'cha, 81, 88
Vitebsk, 71, 106, 107, 110, 112, 113, 205
Volka, 100
Volkovichi, 120, 123
Voloshevo, 75
Widomla, 42, 43, 52, 65, 66
Wieliczkowicze, 22, 25–7, 39, 40
Wielka Wola, 69, 79, 85
Wielkoryta, 50
Wistycze, 40
Wolczyn, 40
Wolka, 32
Wolkowysk, 68, 87
Yakshitsy, 99, 105, 112
Yartsevo, 124, 131–3, 142
Yasenovka, 98, 102
Yashchitsy, 111
Yelizovo, 88
Zaber, 59
Zabinka, 42, 48, 53, 56
Zablchany, 93
Zabrod'ye, 111
Zakhody, 119
Zakrosnica, 56
Zamostoch'ye, 109
Zaozer'ye, 71
Zaprudy, 52, 53
Zbarov, 104, 109
Zbunin, 35, 36, 41, 47
Zelwa, 68, 79, 80
Zhlobin, 94, 98, 103, 104, 106, 109–11, 115, 119, 120, 131, 134, 154
Zhodino, 92
Zhuravichi, 98

Zubova, 118
Blumentritt, Colonel Günther (CoS Fourth Army), 131, 132
Bock, Field Marshal Fedor von (AGC), 25, 38, 44, 55, 66, 69, 70, 77, 81, 87, 89, 94, 96, 106, 107, 112–14, 121, 125, 131, 132, 137, 138, 141, 142, 146–9, 151, 154, 156–8, 163, 166–70, 172–4, 176, 178, 179, 181, 183, 184, 186, 192, 193, 195, 196, 201, 205, 208, 209, 218
Boltenstern, Brigadier Walter von (29 MID), 27, 56, 65, 68, 79, 87, 112, 117, 120, 124, 151, 193, 213
Bormann, Reichsminister Martin, 127, 219
Brauchitsch, Field Marshal Walther von (Army CinC), 106, 112, 138, 157, 168, 172, 183, 205, 219
Breith, Brigadier Hermann (3 PD), 189, 197, 198, 208
Brest fortress, 24–6, 29–33, 35, 38, 40, 41, 43, 44, 51, 58, 61, 83
Brücker, Lieutenant Colonel Otto-Hermann (Ia XXIV MAC), 23, 103

Corvin-Wiersbitzki, Major Lothar von (3 MclB (3 PD)), 20, 33, 83

Dnepr–Bug Canal, 55, 56, 59, 87

Eberbach, Colonel Heinrich (35 PR (4 PD)), 45, 50, 80, 94, 102, 122, 143, 146, 153, 187, 188, 190, 197–200, 202, 204, 205, 207–10, 213
Engel, Major Gerhard (Führer Adj), 157
Ermakov, Major General Arkadii, 184

Feldt, Brigadier Kurt (1 CD), 36, 98, 113, 117, 118, 168, 169, 173, 194
Fiebig, Brigadier Martin (*Nahkampfgruppe* (II Air Corps)), 180
Fischer, Brigadier Wolfgang (10 PD), 144
Forster, Colonel Kurt (143 Arko), 103
Frank, Major Heinz-Werner (521 PjB), 174, 175, 177
Fremerey, Brigadier Max (18 RB (18 PD)), 160

Gerlach, Colonel Karl von (*Koluft* (SPG)), 69
Goebbels, Minister for Public Enlightenment and Propaganda, Joseph, 37, 77, 156
government general
  Biala Podlaska, 43
  Bohukaly, 43, 46
  Deblin, 32, 83

Dolhobrody, 37
Koch, 32
Koden, 19, 20, 28, 33, 35, 38, 84, 115
Kostomloty, 20, 44
Legi, 22, 27, 40, 66, 68, 82
Miedzyrzec, 25
Neple, 22, 30
Okczyn, 34, 35, 38
Pratulin, 22
Siedlce, 27, 66
Terespol, 20, 25, 29, 31, 32, 56
Wlodawa, 25, 35, 37, 78
Gradl, Major Hans (I./39 PR (17 PD)), 192, 193
Grolig, Colonel Oswin (33 MRR (4 PD)), 143, 207
Guderian, General (Generaloberst) Heinz (SPG), 20, 22, 25, 29, 33, 36, 39–41, 43, 46–8, 50–2, 54–6, 60–2, 65, 66, 68–70, 76–80, 82–5, 87–9, 91, 93–6, 98–101, 103, 105, 106, 108–15, 117–22, 124, 125, 127–9, 131–5, 137–48, 150, 151, 153, 154, 156, 158–60, 162–4, 166–81, 183, 184, 186–97, 199–202, 204, 205, 207, 209–18
Gusovius, Major Manfred (1MRB (3 PD)), 84

Halder, General Franz (Army CoS), 78, 89, 100, 112, 121, 137, 138, 145, 146, 148, 151, 154, 156–8, 163, 166, 168, 170, 172, 183, 207, 216, 218, 219
Hausser, Major General (SS-Gruf.) Paul (SS MD 'Reich'), 51, 105, 109, 113
Hausser, Major General (SS-Gruf.) Paul (SS-MD 'Reich'), 135, 141, 169, 175
Heinemann, Major General Erich (302 Harko), 24
Heinrici, Lieutenant General (*General der Infantrie*) Gotthard (XXXXIII AC), 216
Helmdach, Major Erich (Ic Fourth Army), 25
Hitler, Adolf (German Chancellor, Führer), 17, 20, 25, 29, 34, 65, 82, 89, 96, 100, 107, 111, 112, 117, 121, 122, 127, 129, 132, 137, 141–3, 146, 147, 153, 157, 158, 166–8, 170, 172, 178, 180–2, 190, 192, 195, 205, 206, 214, 216–19
Hoth, General Hermann (TPG), 65, 66, 69, 71, 77–81, 84, 87, 89, 93, 101, 106, 107, 110, 112, 113, 119, 121, 124, 125, 128, 129, 131–3, 135, 141, 142, 146, 147, 156, 167, 181, 183, 197, 209

Jodl, Lieutenant General (*General der Artillerie*) Alfred (OKW Operations Staff Chief), 157

Kahlden, Lieutenant Colonel Wolf von (Hoth's General Staff liaison), 209
Kalmukoff, Brigadier Kurt (31 ID), 40
Keitel, Field Marshal Wilhelm (OKW Chief), 139, 178, 182
Kempf, Lieutenant General (*General der Panzertruppe*) Werner (XXXXVIII MAC), 181, 186
Kesselring, Field Marshal Albert (Second AF), 38, 39, 169
Kleemann, Colonel Ulrich (3 MRR (3 PD)), 20, 60, 75, 90, 98, 104, 122, 123, 128–30, 161, 174, 176, 196
Kluge, Field Marshal Günter 'Hans' von (Fourth Army), 29, 44, 46, 65, 78–80, 82, 87, 89, 96, 99, 101, 105, 106, 111–13, 121, 132–5, 138, 142, 155, 158, 166, 168, 172, 183, 214
Kumm, Major (SS-Stbf) Otto (SS-IR 'Der Führer'), 131

Langermann, Brigadier Willibald Baron (Freiherr) von (4 PD), 35, 39, 50, 66, 80, 105, 119, 122, 123, 132, 133, 137, 143, 151, 153, 169, 171, 187–9, 195, 196, 208, 210, 211, 215
Lauchert, Major Meinrad von (I./35 PR (4 PD)), 190, 191
Lemelsen, Lieutenant General (*General der Panzertruppe*) Joachim (XXXXVII MAC), 22, 25, 27, 42, 44, 52, 53, 54, 58, 61, 65, 70, 76, 84, 85, 87, 91, 96, 101, 102, 106–8, 110, 112, 117, 120, 122, 124, 128, 131, 134, 141, 160, 163, 169, 175, 184, 190, 196, 202, 205, 206, 215, 217
Lewinski, Lieutenant Colonel Werner von (6 PR (3 PD)), 62, 132, 135, 158–62, 164, 169, 177
Licht, Colonel Rudolf-Eduard (40 MRR (17 PD)), 107, 129, 133, 157, 209, 211, 213
Liebenstein, Lieutenant Colonel Kurt Baron von (CoS SPG), 141, 164, 178, 179, 217
Linnarz, Colonel Viktor (5 PBe (3 PD)), 20, 38, 48, 61–3, 73, 75, 77, 82
Löper, Major General Friedrich-Wilhelm von (10 MID), 60, 167, 169, 171, 177, 179, 180, 211

Martinek Brigadier Robert (7 Arko), 148
Materna, Lieutenant General (*General der Infanterie*) Friedrich (XX AC), 154
Meier-Rabingen, Brigadier Hermann (197 ID), 148
Model, Major General Walter (3 PD), 20, 33–5, 38, 39, 41, 44, 45, 48, 50, 56–8, 62–4, 66–8, 72, 73, 75–7, 80–3, 85, 88, 90, 94, 96, 98, 102–4, 109, 113, 115, 117–19, 123, 126, 128–31, 135, 139, 140, 143, 155, 159–64, 167, 169–77, 197, 198
Mölders, Lieutenant Colonel Werner (51 FW), 54, 81–3, 88
Munzel, Lieutenant Colonel Oskar (II./6 PR (3 PD)), 62, 64, 98, 118, 171, 187, 204

Nalibokach Forest, 89
Nehring, Brigadier Walther (18 PD), 22, 27, 28, 39, 40, 42, 43, 52, 54, 56, 65, 66, 76, 81, 85, 87, 92, 96, 98, 101, 108, 112, 124, 129, 139, 162, 194, 205, 207, 208

Oginskiego Canal, 71
OKH, 65, 76, 77, 89, 112, 114, 128, 132, 138, 139, 144, 146, 155, 157, 164, 166, 168, 170, 174, 178, 181, 193, 197, 209, 219
OKW, 85, 96, 132, 147, 170, 182, 195, 196, 214
Organization Todt, 68, 107

Paulus, Major General Friedrich (General Staff Quartermaster I), 164, 166
Pervitin, 99, 100
Pogonia Swamp, 58, 59
Polesie Marshes, 36, 48, 58, 60, 71, 78, 96, 98, 114, 127, 134

Rastenburg, 111, 127, 190, 205
Reichswehr, 20, 34, 51, 84, 144
Reinecke, Major General Hermann (OKW's General Office of the Armed Forces), 173
Richthofen, Lieutenant General (*General der Flieger*) Wolfram von (VIII Air Corps), 129
Ries, Colonel Gottfried (75 MAR (3 PD)), 130, 161
rivers
  Aisne, 30
  Babinets, 155
  Basya, 137
  Bereza, 52, 53, 55–8, 60, 70, 78, 181, 187

Berezina, 78, 80, 82, 83, 87–94, 96, 99, 101, 105–8, 110, 112–14, 119, 121, 124, 132
Besed', 155
Bizh, 179
Bobr, 107
Bug, 19, 20, 22, 24–45, 47, 50, 53, 56, 57, 59, 62, 65, 66, 78, 80, 84, 87, 95, 96, 121, 155, 169, 183
Desna, 121, 122, 128, 131, 142, 156, 157, 159–64, 166–71, 173, 175, 181, 184, 191, 193, 194
Dnepr, 71, 76, 78, 82, 87, 89, 93–6, 98, 100–6, 108–15, 117–22, 124–9, 131–5, 137–40, 142, 143, 145, 149, 153, 154, 160, 163, 168, 169, 173, 176, 178, 181, 183, 187, 192, 219
Dobysna, 94, 98, 102, 103, 115
Don, 211, 217
Drut', 90, 94, 98, 102, 105, 106, 108, 110, 118
Dubna, 155
Hrywda, 59, 63
Iput', 148, 153, 155, 166
Issa, 61
Ivotka, 164
Jasiolda, 51–5, 57–60, 66, 67, 121
Khmara, 129
Kleven', 188
Krasivaya Mecha, 204
Krupnya, 153, 154
Lakhva, 115
Lan, 75
Lesna, 22, 31, 39, 40, 42, 67, 73, 84
Lobzhanka, 135
Loire, 30
Losha, 88
Mecha, 205, 209, 210
Mereya, 129
Moroch', 72
Muchawiec, 26, 32, 38, 42, 45, 48, 52, 53
Myszanka, 62, 87
Nacha, 106
Natopa, 129
Neman, 69, 85
Oka, 190, 193, 196, 199, 205, 209–14
Ola, 94, 98, 115
Optukha, 190
Os'ma, 131
Osetr, 211
Oster, 130, 132, 143–5, 148
Pripet, 153
Pronya, 120, 123, 126, 127, 211

Psel, 188
Ptich', 81, 82, 121
Revna, 193
Romain, 174, 175
Rozhok, 161, 164
Sev, 188
Seym, 170–6, 179–81, 188
Shat, 210, 211, 217
Shevnya, 53
Shostka, 160, 162, 164, 176
Sinitskaya, 85
Sluch', 62, 75, 77, 80, 81
Smyach, 161
Somme, 132
Sozh, 115, 122, 123, 127–30, 132, 135, 137, 139, 143, 153, 154, 166
Stryana, 172
Sudost', 157, 160–2, 164, 169, 173, 193
Sula, 175, 177
Svapa, 195
Svisloch', 89, 93
Szczara, 54, 59–64, 66–8, 70, 75, 76, 82, 85, 121
Ubed', 171
Udoga, 127
Upa, 199, 204, 205, 211, 217
Usha, 92
Ustrom, 172
Uzha, 139
Vikhra, 120, 125
Volga, 112, 138, 201
Volma, 91, 92
Zelwianka, 68, 69, 79
Zhizdra, 193
Zusha, 195, 197, 198
Rommel, Major General Erwin (Africa Corps), 77
Rundstedt, Field Marshal Gerd von (AGS), 36, 112, 134, 156, 163, 167–9, 171, 176, 192, 214
Russian SFSR, 138, 201
Akulichi, 157
Alekseyevka, 205
Aleksin, 205
Andreyevka, 208
Arkhangel'sk, 112
Arsen'yevo, 199
Astrakhan, 112
Belev, 198, 199
Berdychiv, 205
Bityakovka, 139
Bogoroditsk, 204
Bogucharovo, 208

Bolkhov, 194
Bolokhovo, 207, 208
Borodenki, 198
Bryansk, 109, 141, 148, 153, 155, 156, 159, 163, 165, 167, 169, 170, 172, 180, 183–5, 189, 190, 192–6, 201, 203, 205, 207, 210
Bykovo, 208
Dan'kovo, 131
Darovaya, 214
Dedilovo, 207, 208
Dem'yanki, 160
Dmitriyev-L'govskiy, 195, 196
Dmitrovsk-Orlovskiy, 188, 189, 190, 192, 194
Dorogobuzh, 131, 133, 135, 139, 142
Dubrovskiy, 196
Dudkino, 211, 213
Fatezh, 195–7
Glinka, 138, 139
Gorki, 118, 120, 204
Gryaznovo, 215
Il'kovo, 190
Ivanovskaya, 190
Kalinin, 201
Kaluga, 196, 197
Kambovka, 164, 167
Karachev, 190, 192–4
Kashira, 211–13
Kazaki, 145, 148
Khanino, 199
Khislavichi, 127, 130, 141, 150
Klemyatino, 138
Kletnya, 153, 157, 160, 162
Klintsy, 159
Kokurenkova, 197
Kolomna, 212
Kosovskiye, 160
Kozel'sk, 193
Krapivna, 209
Kromy, 189, 204
Kukhtinka, 211
Kursk, 197, 202
Leningrad, 112, 132, 146, 157, 158, 170, 192
Lobanovo, 190, 198
Lokot, 194
Lyubets, 164
Maikop, 192
Mal'tsevo, 138, 144
Maloarkhangel'sk, 202
Maslovo, 204
Mglin, 151, 155, 157, 162

Mikhaylov, 211
Mikulichi, 144
Mishkova, 160
Molod'kovo, 155
Monastyrshchina, 139, 141
Morkovshchino, 207
Moscow, 32, 37, 39, 65, 69, 78, 82, 87, 89, 105, 107, 108, 112, 113, 121, 122, 125, 131, 132, 134, 138, 141, 142, 146–51, 156–8, 160, 161, 163, 168–70, 172, 174, 178, 179, 181, 183, 184, 186, 187, 192, 195–7, 199–201, 204–6, 209–12, 214, 216, 218–20
Mtsensk, 190, 191, 193, 195–8, 209
Nadeykovichi, 130
Navlya, 193
Nikitskoye, 206
Novoselk, 144
Novo-Yakovlevka, 202
Novozybkov, 158–60
Odoyevo, 199
Orel, 109, 180, 183, 184, 187, 189, 190, 193, 194, 197–9, 201, 204, 205, 210, 216, 217
Ozerki, 212
P'yanyy Rog, 164
Panikovka, 164
Parovichi, 164
Pavlovskiye, 145
Plavsk, 202, 204, 209
Pochep, 157–9, 161, 162, 164, 168, 169, 176, 181, 187
Podkhozheye, 211
Pogar, 160, 167, 181, 188
Pskov, 205
Ptan, 212
Rakita, 155
Romanovka, 167
Roslavl', 32, 82, 122, 128, 130–2, 135, 139, 140, 142–8, 150, 151, 153, 157, 159, 160, 166, 170
Rostov-on-Don, 192, 214
Rozhenets, 197
Rudnya, 139, 145
Ryazan, 211, 212, 216
Rybalki, 205
Ryl'sk, 192
Ryukhovo, 159
Rzhev, 118
Sazonov-Pochinok, 135, 144
Semtsy, 161, 164
Serebryanyye Prudy, 206, 214
Sergeyevka, 139

Serpukhov, 199, 201, 215, 216
Seshcha, 158
Sevsk, 187, 188, 191, 194, 195, 202
Shumyachi, 130
Skopin, 214
Smolensk, 71, 77, 82, 89, 93, 96, 106, 111–14, 119–22, 124, 125, 128, 131, 133–5, 140–5, 147, 148, 150, 151, 156, 167, 178, 181, 183, 186
Snigirevka, 130
Solov'yevo, 142, 143, 147
Spas-Demensk, 135
Stalingrad, 138, 192
Stalinogorsk, 199–201, 204, 207, 209–12, 215
Starodub, 155, 158, 160, 166, 175
Stomyatka, 139
Strigino, 129
Surazh, 155
Suzemka, 193
Svoboda, 211
Sytenki, 194
Talashkino, 138
Teploe, 204, 209
Trubchevsk, 160, 164, 167, 168, 173, 193–6
Trud, 140
Trukhanovo, 155
Tula, 187, 190, 192, 193, 195–205, 208–12, 214–17
Turdey, 204
Unecha, 155, 157, 162
Uzlovaya, 206–10
Venev, 209, 210, 212, 215
Volokhovo, 200
Volokolamsk, 201
Volovo, 204
Votchinka, 210
Vyaz'ma, 87, 151, 181, 192, 195, 196, 201, 207
Yasnaya Polyana, 204, 215
Yefremov, 205, 207–12
Yel'nya, 82, 125, 128, 129, 131–5, 138–41, 144, 145, 147, 148, 150, 151, 154, 156, 158, 161, 166, 172, 181, 186, 214
Yepifan', 199, 207, 209
Yershichi, 153
Zaraysk, 206, 211
Zhitnya, 157
Zhukova, 157
Zimonino, 139

Saucken, Colonel Dietrich von (4 MBde (4 PD)), 208, 212, 213
Schaal, Major General Ferdinand (10 PD), 59, 60, 66, 82, 105, 118, 139, 144
Schlieper Brigadier Fritz (45 ID), 44
Schmidt-Ott, Major Gustav-Albrecht, 57, 164, 196
Schmundt, Colonel Rudolf (Führer and Wehrmacht CinC Army Chief Adjutant), 142, 146, 205
Schneider, Colonel (Graduate Engineer) Erich (103 MAR (4 PD)), 151
Schönhärl, Major General Hans (167 ID), 44
Schroth, Lieutenant General (General der Infanterie)) Walther (XII AC), 127, 224
Schweppenburg, Lieutenant General (*General der Panzertruppe*) Leo *Reichsfreiherr* Geyr von (XXIV MAC), 50, 56, 58, 59, 62, 63, 66, 76, 81, 90, 91, 93, 98, 103, 105, 109–11, 113, 114, 121–4, 126–8, 130, 132, 137, 143, 151, 153, 159, 160, 163, 166, 170–2, 175, 177–9, 186, 188, 193, 200–2, 204, 208, 212, 214–16
Stalin, Soviet Premier Joseph, 35, 67, 81, 92, 100, 184, 206
Stauffenberg, Major Claus von (O QIII), 128
Stolzmann, Lieutenant Colonel Hans-Joachim von (III./17 IR (31 ID)), 48, 67, 68, 73
Strachwitz, Major Manfred von (I./18 PR (18 PD)), 27, 39
Streich, Brigadier Johannes (17 PD), 76, 96, 108, 110

Teege, Major Wilhelm 'Willi' (II./18 PR (18 PD)), 92, 93
Thoma, Brigadier Wilhelm *Ritter* von (17 PD), 129, 138, 144, 157, 160–2, 178
Timoshenko, Marshal Semyon (WF), 111, 120, 121, 124, 126, 168
Traut, Colonel Hans (41 MIR (10 MID)), 171, 179, 180

Ukrainian SSR
  Avdiyivka, 160, 171
  Bakhmach, 176
  Baturyn, 171, 174
  Beyeve, 179
  Bochechky, 179
  Bondarivka, 175
  Borzna, 176
  Buryn, 179, 180

Bylka, 169
Chernecha Sloboda, 180
Chornotychi, 171
Dnipro, 163
Dubinka, 179
Esman, 187, 188
Girevka, 174
Hadyach, 179
Hlukhiv, 161, 181, 184, 187
Horodysche, 172
Ivot, 164
Kamin', 172
Karabutove, 174
Kharkiv, 192
Khmeliv, 176
Kholmy, 160, 161
Konotop, 159, 167, 169, 170, 173, 174, 175, 177–80
Korop, 164, 167, 169–71
Kostobobriv, 160
Kremenchuk, 176
Krolevets, 161, 170, 171, 175
Krolevets-Slobidka, 161
Kyiv, 134, 143, 146, 157, 160, 163, 168, 170, 173, 174, 177–81, 183, 184, 186, 187, 192, 195
Lokhvytsia, 176–9, 187
Makoshyne, 171, 175
Maksaky, 171
Mamekine, 160
Melnia, 171, 174
Nedryhailiv, 179
Novhorod-Siverskyy, 156, 159–63, 167, 168, 173
Obolonnia, 171
Ostroushky, 161, 169
Pryluki, 179
Putyvl, 176, 178, 179, 186, 192

Pyrohivka, 161, 162, 164, 169
Pyryatin, 179
Romny, 173–81
Semenivka, 168
Sencha, 178
Seredina Buda, 194
Shapovalovka, 175
Shtepivka, 186
Sobych, 169
Sosnytsia, 169–71
Sumy, 180, 188
Svarkove, 188
Terni, 179
Voronizh, 161, 162, 164
Vysoke, 175
Yampil, 168, 188
Usinger, Colonel Christian (622 AR), 118

Vietinghoff, Lieutenant General (*General der Panzertruppe*) Heinrich von (XXXXVII MAC), 59, 66, 84, 88, 119, 120, 122, 128, 134, 135, 138, 140, 144, 179

wars
    First World War, 24, 29, 34, 50, 51, 84, 138, 144, 166
    Spanish Civil War, 20, 138
Weber, Brigadier Karl *Ritter* von (17 RBde (17 PD)), 52, 108, 117, 129
Weichs, General Maximilian von (Second Army), 134, 168, 170, 171, 183, 191, 193
Weikersthal, Lieutenant General (*General der Infanterie*) Walther von (LIII AC)), 217
Weisenberger, Lieutenant General (*General der Infanterie*) Karl (LIII AC), 204, 217

Zimmermann, Major Hermann (II./3 MRR (3 PD)), 98